UNTANGLING FEAR IN LAWYERING

A Four-Step Journey Toward Powerful Advocacy

Heidi K. Brown

The materials contained herein represent the opinions of the authors and/or the editors and should not be construed to be the views or opinions of the law firms or companies with whom such persons are or were in partnership with, associated with, or employed by, nor of the American Bar Association unless adopted pursuant to the bylaws of the Association.

Nothing contained in this book is to be considered as the rendering of legal advice for specific cases or psychological advice and readers are responsible for obtaining such advice from their own legal counsel, medical professionals, or psychological counselors. This book is intended for educational and informational purposes only.

Printed in the United States of America.

23 22 21 20 19   5 4 3 2 1

Library of Congress Cataloging-in-Publication Data

Names: Brown, Heidi K. (Heidi Kristin), 1970–, author.
Title: Untangling fear in lawyering : a four-step journey toward powerful
    advocacy / by Heidi K. Brown.
Description: Chicago : American Bar Association, 2019. | Includes
    bibliographical references and index.
Identifiers: LCCN 2019000996 (print) | LCCN 2019002384 (ebook) |
    ISBN 9781641053532 (ebook) | ISBN 9781641053525 (pbk.)
Subjects: LCSH: Practice of law—United States. | Attorney and client—
    United States. | Lawyers—United States. | Fear—United States.
Classification: LCC KF311 (ebook) | LCC KF311 .B76 2019 (print) |
    DDC 340.023/73—dc23
LC record available at https://lccn.loc.gov/2019000996

Discounts are available for books ordered in bulk. Special consideration is given to state bars, CLE programs, and other bar-related organizations. Inquire at Book Publishing, ABA Publishing, American Bar Association, 321 N. Clark Street, Chicago, Illinois 60654-7598.

www.shopABA.org

Some details and identifying information about individuals, entities, and events discussed herein have been changed to protect the privacy of those involved.

Contents

Write what disturbs you, what you fear, what you have not been willing to speak about. Be willing to be split open.

—Natalie Goldberg, *Writing Down the Bones: Freeing the Writer Within*

Also by Heidi K. Brown

The Introverted Lawyer: A Seven-Step Journey Toward Authentically Empowered Advocacy

The Mindful Legal Writer: Mastering Predictive and Persuasive Writing

The Mindful Legal Writer: Mastering Predictive Writing

The Mindful Legal Writer: Mastering Persuasive Writing

Fundamentals of Federal Litigation

Preface

Today I sit down to start writing this book. Day one. Page one. It's my sixth book. By society's standards, I'm officially a writer, an author. All the stars are aligned. I have a book contract. I mapped out a writing schedule: two hours every morning for the next 60 days to complete the manuscript's first draft. I have a chapter-by-chapter outline and 100 already-typed-up pages of research material. I slept pretty decently, for a change. My usual 3 a.m. insomnia granted me a night off. This morning, I awoke, retrieved my iPhone from the living room, slid back under my weighty Anthropologie blanket, tapped open my Insight Timer meditation app, slipped my headphones into my ears, closed my eyes, and listened as a female voice greeted me with a chirpy, "Hi, beauty!" before she guided a 12-minute meditation on clarity, motivation, and confidence. Afterward, while a pot of Trader Joe's coffee percolated in the kitchen, I wrote three longhand stream-of-consciousness pages (a creativity ritual inspired by Julia Cameron's book *The Artist's Way*) in my journal, a new one I bought a few months ago at a museum next to the Duomo in Milan. It has a brown cover with the Italian word *marrone* stamped in lime green ink. *Brown*, like my last name. My apartment is quiet, except for the occasional Brooklyn honking horn. I've allocated the next two hours to begin to write this book that I've been thinking about for a year and living for, oh, approximately 27 years since the day I stepped onto the grounds of The University of Virginia School of Law as a 1L law student.

The blank page on my laptop taunts me. *I dare you to start.* I divert for a moment to craft an indulgent, philosophical, self-motivational Instagram post for my @introvertedlawyer account about how I'm commencing this new huge writing project and am hereby putting it out into the universe. I attach an empowering new "author photo" captured by my photographer friend Krista. In it, I'm striking a Wonder Woman pose in a Denver alleyway flanked with artsy graffiti: hands on hips, the flaps of my favorite leather jacket resting atop a vintage David Bowie T-shirt. An attempt to exude "fearless writer vibe." Right now, in my apartment, staring at a blinking cursor, I hesitate. *How am I going to do this? What if I don't have enough to say? What if people think it's ridiculous?* On cue, an Instagram meme pops into my feed: "It's better to create something that others criticize than to create nothing and criticize others."[1]

Just write it. Write about fear.

What exactly is fear? Before we embark on this quest to define it for ourselves in the context of the legal profession, let's start with a few official dictionary definitions:

- "An unpleasant emotion caused by the belief that someone or something is dangerous, likely to cause pain, or a threat."[2]
- "An unpleasant or strong emotion caused by anticipation or awareness of danger."[3]
- "A distressing emotion aroused by impending danger, evil, pain, etc., whether the threat is real or imagined."[4]
- "A feeling induced by perceived danger or threat that occurs in certain types of organisms, which causes a change in metabolic and organ functions and ultimately a change in behavior, such as fleeing, hiding, or freezing from perceived traumatic events."[5]
- "Profound reverence and awe."[6]

This last one is interesting. Reverence and awe. Reminds me of a sense of wonder. Quite different from danger and threats.

I was pretty fearful for the bulk of my life. In high school, I was an A student, yet I feared failing. I feared criticism—of my developing interests in and opinions about politics, religion, music, culture—from my devoutly religious parents and grandparents. I feared the feeling of exclusion from the cool kids. Transitioning to college, I feared rejection, abandonment, and loss as I stepped into new relationship territory. Entering law school as a naïve 21-year-old, I feared being cold-called by my intimidating law professors. I feared turning red and breaking out in blotchy hives when I got nervous speaking in class or performing mock oral arguments. After I survived three years of law school, passed the bar exam, and started a prestigious high-paying new job as an associate in a boutique construction litigation firm in the Washington, DC, metropolitan area, I feared making a mistake. I feared looking stupid. I feared not knowing or finding the answer. While I loved legal research and writing, and thrived in those roles, I feared taking depositions, going to court, and fighting with opposing counsel. Yet, I forced myself to do all these things. I absorbed and epitomized the mantras: "Just do it!" "Face your fears!" "Fake it till you make it!" I navigated many of these life and legal experiences successfully (by external standards), but I was anxious, depressed, and profoundly lonely much of the time—for nearly *two decades* of law practice and the prime of my twenties and thirties.

I'm a law professor and a writer now. I live in New York City. I travel the world. I attend a ridiculous number of U2 concerts. I take boxing lessons. I'm not the slightest bit afraid to take the subway home to my Brooklyn apartment in the wee hours of the night. Or jump on a plane to a place I've never been and figure out a foreign city alone. Or put myself in a boxing training ring with an ex-Olympic fighter even though I look like a hyperventilating crimson-faced fool. Yet, I experience heart-pounding fear in anticipation of the expectation to speak my mind about controversial subjects at intense faculty meetings. I still battle an onslaught of nerves every time I do a book talk for *The Introverted Lawyer* or a legal conference presentation about topics that are vitally important to me. I feel nauseated and want to hide whenever a new piece of my writing goes live.

Rationally, this contradiction makes no sense.

Why am I afraid in my legal world? What is the perceived *danger* or *threat* to my well-being in this arena for, and within, which I have been training since I set foot in my first Civil Procedure class in law school? Why am I *not* afraid in the face of more tangible, realistic, concrete hazards to my physical safety posed by late-night subway rides or international airline travel? Why do I *not* fear judgment about my appearance and athletic limitations in a boxing ring, but I get a migraine thinking about turning red in an oral argument? In the legal realm, intellectually, I pretty much know what I'm doing now—substantively, procedurally, and (usually) tactically. I "should" feel and exude genuine and hard-earned confidence, grounded in experience and expertise. In contrast, I have absolutely *no idea* what I'm doing when I'm meandering the streets of Málaga, Dublin, or Buenos Aires. But there, the unknown excites me.

Likewise, I have zero expertise, proficiency, or background in the boxing ring. I "should" be completely self-conscious about my epic blushing and profuse sweating into the skull-and-crossbones SoulCycle bandana wrapped around my head. Yet there, I'm able to let go of insecurity and push myself as hard as I physically and emotionally can. It's exhilarating.

This book aims to untangle the difference. Why do some of us experience acute fear in lawyering when other colleagues don't? Why do some of us encounter fear in our professional lives but emanate wonder, audacity, and sheer awesomeness in other venues? Many of us have forced ourselves for years to personify the mantras: *Face your fears. If your dreams don't scare you, they're not big enough. There's nothing to be afraid of. Just do it.* In my experience, these slogans are unhelpful, dare I say useless, harmful even. Our fears *are* real—to us. They are valid and not to be minimized, tossed aside, or repressed—anymore. Instead, let's untangle our fears. Let's identify and extract their component parts and drivers. Let's distinguish fear from other emotions. Let's parse out situations in which we "shouldn't" (by society's standards) feel fear but do, and scenarios in which we understandably (by society's standards) could be afraid but aren't. By truly understanding fear in the context of lawyering and life, we can distill it to its potentially useful properties, cast off the unconstructive parts, and transform this entity into a wellspring of mighty strength in lawyering.

I invite you to step into this self-discovery process with me. As I commence this new project, I am energized. Finally figuring out fear is important to me, for myself, for the amazing law students stepping into classrooms each year, and for all the lawyers out there who are working doggedly but feel hamstrung by anxiety, doubt, and other stressors that can affect mental health. This journey starts with transparency. So, in the spirit of honesty and openness, the fears I hold right in this precise moment are

- not getting this writing work done (even though I always do);
- running out of ideas (though I have a chapter-by-chapter outline);
- being criticized (so what; it's happened before and I lived).

Skeptics might ask, if this lawyering stuff (or this writing stuff) scares us so much, why do it? Why not just take the easier path and go do something else? My answer is: if one—literally one—person within our profession is touched by an open discussion about the reality of fear in lawyering, and feels supported in figuring out a better, healthier, more fulfilling way to practice law, every moment of self-doubt is supremely worth it. Together, we can figure this out, not by burying our fear, but by yanking it right out into the open.

As noted earlier, I'm a huge fan of the Irish rock band U2. I know that might induce some eye rolls, but please bear with me for a minute. These four musicians have worked together for over 40 years; amassed fame, fans, and fortunes; and checked all the boxes of success in marriage, parenthood, and philanthropy. They seem to have it all. And yet, the reality of fear permeates their music. Consider googling the "fear" lyrics in these songs: "Bullet the Blue Sky," "Red Hill Mining Town," "Every Breaking Wave," "Raised by Wolves," and "Iris"!

As we start this adventure together, you might start taking note of how often you see or hear references to fear throughout your day or week in lyrics, advertisements, or slogans (and write and let me know about them: heidi@ theintrovertedlawyer.com!). The day I started researching this book, a year before I began writing it, I walked past a piece of graffiti on a wall in the Flatiron District in New York City that said, "Sorting out where your fear ends and mine begins."[7] Fear infiltrates many aspects of our daily lives but we rarely take time to talk to one another openly about it. I'm eager to dig into fear with you, what it is, and what it isn't. Let's openly acknowledge the reality of fear in lawyering, in writing, in the art that we create as change makers and advocates. Then together, we can help one another untangle fear in a genuine, transparent, vulnerable, and ultimately healthy way. As Steven Pressfield, author of *The War of Art*, stated, "The counterfeit innovator is wildly self-confident. The real one is scared to death."[8]

In January 2018, the *ABA Journal* ran an article I wrote called "Turning the Fear of Lawyering into the Power of Advocacy."[9] The piece started with a flashback to the 1992 hit movie *A League of Their Own*, in which Tom Hanks's character—a coach of a women's baseball team—admonishes a sobbing right fielder and barks: "There's no crying in baseball!" This catchphrase always reminds me of messages conveyed in the three aggressive litigation firms where I worked (one BigLaw and two boutique litigation shops): "There's no fear in lawyering! Just do it!" Well-meaning mentors in the early years of law practice furthered this ethos, prodding my fellow junior associates and me into stressful deposition scenarios or first-time courtroom experiences with "Fake it till you make it! Show no fear!"

In the *ABA Journal* piece, I briefly chronicled my endeavors to "just do it." I threw myself into trial advocacy seminars in law school. In law practice, I jumped feet-first into antagonistic interactions with gruff law firm partners, hard-charging opposing counsel, and curt judges. Meanwhile, I thought there was something wrong with me because, quite honestly, I constantly was afraid. I worried I was not cut out for the law, or at least the litigation path I had chosen, even though I loved researching and writing, thinking and analyzing, strategizing and problem solving. In pondering exactly what to do about fear, the usual hortatory slogans come to mind: Fight it, Conquer it, Battle it, Overcome it. These verbs imply that fear is a blobby foe that can be knocked out, skirted, or stepped over. In reality though, the worrisome aspects of doing our jobs as lawyers cannot be carted away in a banker's box. Law school is inherently fraught with apprehension about grades, the curve, making law review or moot court teams, passing the bar exam, and landing a job. Law practice likewise ignites panic over deadlines, win-lose dynamics, and partnership tracks. So instead of just "staring down fear"—a message that sounds empowering but really does not work—I suggested in the *ABA Journal* article, and I urge now in this book, that law students and lawyers first must learn how to *distill* fear, or *untangle* it.

The verb "distill" means to "extract the essential meaning or most important aspects of" something, or to "purify a liquid by vaporizing it, then condensing it by cooling the vapor, and collecting the resulting liquid." "Untangling" is defined as "making something complicated or confusing easier to understand or deal with" or "removing the twists or knots in something." My belief is: if we get to know the entity of fear that permeates lawyering and talk about it out loud, we can distinguish its useful and useless components and transform our emotional, mental, and physical relationship with fear into powerful advocacy.

Scientists confirm that fear blocks learning and performance. It can stoke anxiety and depression in a profession already saturated with mental health challenges. If we can turn down the dial of stress and anxiety even *one* notch for even *one* struggling individual in our profession by sparking a dialogue about the reality of fear in lawyering, let's do it. We can remove a thick layer of stress from law students and junior lawyers—good thinkers, writers, and problem solvers—by expressly acknowledging that some lawyering tasks may be more daunting for some individuals than others. We then can provide not only substantive and tactical guidance but also mental, physical, and emotional strategies for untangling fear and optimizing performance.

Part I of this book discusses the reality, causes, manifestations, and consequences of fear in legal education and practice, from the standpoint of law students, junior attorneys, and even clients. Fear in lawyering impacts the mental health and well-being of law students and attorneys. (In fact, the profession has convened a dedicated group, the National Task Force on Lawyer Well-Being, which expressly mentioned fear in its first official report.) In Part I, we identify and acknowledge lawyering scenarios that likely will ignite more distress in some individuals than others. We also look at how courts handling attorney malpractice and disciplinary cases have directly acknowledged the role of fear in how lawyers make and handle mistakes—an inevitable occurrence in our profession that we need to discuss more in law school and in practical training.

Part II analyzes fear from a cognitive, physical, and emotional perspective. Instead of ignoring or pushing through fear, we must take the time to study the basic science of it and untangle it. Then, we can start to distill fear into its fundamental properties, and realize how we can channel its mental, physical, and emotional elements into impactful advocacy. Part II explains how fear—without conscious attention to it—obstructs classroom learning and professional performance. It also can mask itself in other unproductive emotions or reactive responses like anger, resentment, jealousy, anxiety, and depression, causing individuals to shut down and *resist* learning and engaging interpersonally. In this section, we begin to set aside unhelpful messages like "Fear is motivating" or "Just push through it" and instead honor vulnerability, authenticity, and humility in our educational and professional development.

Part III draws guidance from how other industries address fear (and mistake-making) in education and training. This section gathers some examples from the professional fields of medicine, journalism, engineering, entrepreneurship/business, and sports, with the goal of extracting teaching and training insights that might transfer well and be useful in our legal arena.

Finally, Part IV provides a tangible four-step process for law students and lawyers to reframe fear into fortitude:

1. First, we will identify, compare, and analyze scenarios in our personal and professional lives that *might be expected to* induce fear but do not, and those that arguably *should not* incite fear, but do.

2. Next, we will reframe and reboot our *mental* approach to fear in lawyering—using vulnerability, authenticity, and humility to tap into personal power.

3. Then, we will cultivate an athlete's mind-set toward the *physicality* of fear.

4. Finally, we will foster a culture of fortitude in tackling individual legal challenges and in helping others within our profession untangle fears.

The book concludes with an appendix summarizing the foregoing steps in a handy checklist, plus two additional appendices providing recommendations for how legal educators and law practice managers can cultivate learning and training environments that address character-in-context, fear, and mistake-making in lawyering. A fourth appendix provides insights on how we can help our clients untangle fears. A final appendix suggests topics for "Untangling Fear" discussion groups, workshops, or courses that could be offered in a law school or law practice environment.

We choose love over fear.
—Bono, Paris, December 7, 2015, at a rescheduled concert after
the November 11, 2015 terrorist attacks in the French capital.

Acknowledgments

I'm so thankful to my colleagues throughout the legal writing academy. Your unconditional support energizes me daily to take risks in teaching, writing, and creating.

Thank you to my fellow devotees to finding a healthier way for law students and lawyers to achieve success: Valerie Fitch, Anne Brafford, Jeena Cho, Randall Kiser, Professor Nathalie Martin, Professor Debra Austin, Professor Katerina Lewinbuk, Professor Chapin Cimino, Professor Abigail Patthoff, Professor Lynn Su, Professor Kathleen Elliott Vinson, Professor Samantha Moppett, Professor Shailini Jandial George, Professor Christopher Corts, Dean David Jaffe, Professor Calvin Pang, Professor Marjorie Silver, Professor Susan Brooks, Michael Grohman, and my fellow board members of the Association of American Law Schools' Section on Balance in Legal Education.

To the team at Trinity Boxing Club, and especially my trainer (and photographer!), Raymond Montalvo, thank you for always making me feel like a champ.

To Professor Loreen Peritz, my assistants Joanne Ferris and Marva Skeene, and my research assistants Will Davidson, Whitney Gulden, and Jenny Henck, thank you for following every bread-crumb trail to track down the zillions of sources I needed for this project. Thank you to the Brooklyn Law School Communications and Public Relations teams (Linda Harvey, Peggy Swisher, Clorinda Valenti, Dasha Tanner, and Elliott Frieder) for helping spread the word about the power of introversion and wellness in the legal profession. To my mentors and colleagues Dean Maryellen Fullerton, Professor Ted Janger, Professor Dana Brakman Reiser, Professor Jodi Balsam, Dean Stacy Caplow, and the legal writing team, thank you for supporting and encouraging my teaching and writing.

To my parents, my brother, Kroehl, and his wife, Gina, I know I give you angst every time I hop on a flight to somewhere, or start putting pen to paper on a new project, but thank you for making me think deeply and for modeling true partnership.

At one of my *Introverted Lawyer* book talks, a law firm partner commented, "You're an introvert, but an extroverted writer." I am profoundly grateful to my hilarious and creative friends who deal with my tendency to go off-grid when I'm in writing mode, and make me feel supported and connected even when I'm hiding in my introvert cave: Kelly Woods Nutty, Lauren Brownstein,

Lucinda Heidsieck Bhavsar, Susan Silver Levy, Melissa Jangl, my U2 gals Renee Torina and Michele Morgan, Todd Flournoy, Tim Erblich, Elisabeth Schiff-bauer, Anna Miller, Jenn Liles, Jenna Adikes (fellow world traveler who tolerated me editing this manuscript on three continents), Krista Bonura, Heidi Gilchrist (fellow writer-in-the-trenches), and Clay Edmonds (introvert/creative soul extraordinaire).

To all the law students I have taught at Chapman University School of Law, New York Law School, and Brooklyn Law School: Thank you for giving me the opportunity to learn about life from *you*.

Finally, to my fellow quiet and anxious law students and lawyers, and all the students and lawyers who have shared their stories with me: Thank you for shining your bright authentic light. You're going to change the profession and the world.

Introduction

For many of us, being a lawyer can be scary at times. Being a law student likewise can be scary. As students, we might fear being cold-called in class and on the receiving end of a confusing and persistent Socratic inquiry. Perhaps we are afraid of not knowing the answers, appearing unintelligent before our peers or professors, messing up our one-shot final exams, falling short of law review grade cutoffs, faltering in oral arguments, not landing a summer job, or failing the bar exam—any one of these concerns making us worry that we are not cut out for the practice of law. Through hard work and pushing through or repressing the fear, we "successfully" run this gauntlet; we pass the bar and are sworn in as counselors-at-law. We transition from academia to law practice. Wearing our new suits, sitting on our ergonomic office chairs, staring at a box of crisp business cards, a familiar feeling percolates: fear.

As legal practitioners, many of us remain afraid . . . of accidentally overlooking a case in our research, misunderstanding a complex procedural rule, making the wrong strategic decision, missing a deadline despite multipronged calendaring efforts, being intimidated by aggressive opposing counsel in a deposition or negotiation, not knowing the answer to a judge's question in oral argument, being embarrassed, blushing, sweating, showing weakness. While such fears in lawyering are very real and palpable, unfortunately we spend a lot of time pretending they don't exist. Well-meaning mentors advise: "Fake it till you make it!" "Just do it!" "Never let them see you sweat!" Non-lawyers in our lives remark, "Well, hey, isn't this the profession you chose? If it causes you so much anxiety, maybe you should go do something else." Lawyers who are lucky enough to never have experienced the foregoing types of fear offer seemingly "quick fix" slogans:

- Face your fears.
- Conquer your fears.
- Get over yourself.
- Do something every day that scares you.
- If your dreams don't scare you, they're not big enough.

The mantras, the mottos, the empowerment jargon might work for some individuals who just need a little push to "snap into action," but they don't work for all, perhaps not even most. They definitely didn't work for *me*. Ignoring fear is a completely ineffective tactic for becoming the best lawyers we can be. Putting it bluntly, author Brandon Webb, a former Navy SEAL, says quips like "get out of your comfort zone" are "basic bullshit."[10] Why? Webb explains:

> The problem with "get out of your comfort zone" is that it's a tactic that doesn't address the nature of the problem. It's a nonsolution, like saying, "Oh, you're afraid to jump? Well, just stop being afraid." Not helpful.[11]

In many facets of our legal arena, acting fearless, tough, even intellectually cocky is often a badge of honor. Yet, for many of us, our internal emotional barometer constantly runs on high alert. We are smart, hardworking, and focused researchers, writers, and analysts, but our irrefutable fears can make us feel as if we don't belong. We *do* belong. We have an important role to play in the legal showground.

As a profession, we need to stop pretending fear does not exist in lawyering. Instead, we must start understanding how fear works, distill it into tangible parts, get to know it deeply, and then flip the message: we are effective counselors and advocates *because* we are human and real.

The myth that good lawyers are fearless and also mistake-free germinates in legal education. In law school, we rarely talk about the actuality of fear. We seldom discuss the reality of day-to-day lawyering mistakes. We might touch on *catastrophic* mistakes or ethical breaches, but those such examples can prompt students to reassure themselves, "Well, I would never do that!" Some teachers and mentors advise, "Just be prepared so you don't make a mistake." That's unrealistic and inadequate guidance. The real practice of law is complicated, multilayered, and nuanced. Litigation involves myriad procedural rules which are not always clear or easy to figure out or calculate. In the early days of my career, deciphering Virginia mechanic's lien procedures or the methods of serving a Federal Rule of Civil Procedure 45 subpoena—somehow always on the eve of a long-awaited, on-the-verge-of-being-postponed-again, vacation— felt like translating hieroglyphics. The "right" strategies and tactics in lawyering often depend on others' behavior, to which we must react without much time for deliberation.

Even a seemingly mundane task like an electronic document review can be fraught. The most careful privilege reviewer might experience a few seconds of weariness and click the wrong document category, sending a potentially privileged (even that determination is not always 100% clear) document into the cyber-pile designated for opposing counsel's view. In depositions, negotiations, or courtroom appearances, lawyers often need to make split-second decisions amid multiple competing stimuli. The "correct" maneuver in the moment might not be readily obvious. Later, tactical errors emerge like holograms.

In transactional drafting, mistakes can happen as well. Opposing counsel may sneakily, or even accidentally, recirculate an earlier version of a negotiated draft of an 80-page agreement. Unless the recipient rechecks every Tracked-Change edit, for perhaps the fifth, sixth, seventh time, the wrong phrase can end up in the final executed contract.

It's natural to be afraid of making a mistake, or to dread having to own up to an error in lawyering. Yet we tend to gloss over the reality of frontiers like these in law school. We do not give students many, or enough, opportunities to confront such in-the-field missteps and talk about how to handle or remedy them in an ethical manner. We rarely delve into the emotional, mental, and physical manifestations of the fear of making or admitting a mistake. As Professor Abigail A. Patthoff notes, legal education instead can *foster* fear-based narratives, illustrating attorney failings through catastrophic "cautionary tales" usually "involv[ing] a lawyer or law student behaving unprofessionally and then suffering consequences."[12] But what about the individual who is *not* cheating, cutting a corner, or flouting the rules? How about the diligent one who is endeavoring to decode the rule, adhere to the deadline, make the right judgment call, but still chooses the "wrong" door?[13]

Law practice also can exacerbate fear. When we reinforce messages to job applicants like, "No associate here has ever failed the bar" or "We hire only people that don't make mistakes and there are plenty of them out there" or "That superstar partner has never lost a case," we pave a pathway of fear. Instead of reinforcing the myth of the infallibility of the "successful lawyer," let's train law students and lawyers to *untangle* the knots of fear and circumstances that could lead to mistakes. We can begin by acknowledging and emphasizing in law school and practice that fear exists and mistakes happen in the practice of law. Next, we can provide education and professional development training on how to process fear and reduce, anticipate, recognize, admit, and resolve mistakes. We can cultivate environments in which law students and lawyers can ask for guidance before making a material or costly error, and develop the resilience to confide in a mentor or supervisor upon discovery of a mistake. We cannot just assume that character will win the day if an attorney errs. There is too much at stake: fear of losing one's job, debt, shame, exclusion, judgment, loss of standing.

Fear in lawyering is real. It is not a character flaw for a law student to fear a professor who verbalizes frustration upon encountering classroom hesitation or for a lawyer to fear a screaming boss who punches a hole in an office wall because the new office couch arrived in the wrong fabric color.[14] ~~It is a flaw in our system when we~~ allow toxicity to ferment in our legal arena. Let's start talking about the reality of fear in lawyering, and arm our future lawyers with the substantive and technical knowledge *and* the fortitude, courage, and character they need to advance justice.

As a quiet law student fresh out of college, intimidated by the Socratic method of classroom teaching and other performance-oriented events like oral arguments and negotiation simulations, I harbored a lot of fear. My earliest memory of being afraid in law school at The University of Virginia was the day I was cold-called in Civil Procedure class. My face flushed a deep cherry-red as I fumbled through a response to a question about diversity jurisdiction. I knew the jurisdictional rule intimately, having devoured the assigned reading. Yellow highlighter ink stained my hands. My flash cards, flowcharts, and outlines contained every possible answer to the professor's queries. In that moment in the "hot seat," the gears in my brain immobilized. My classmates chuckled as my professor pointed out that, no, indeed Portland and Seattle are located in *different* states, not the same state, and therefore diversity jurisdiction *did* exist in the hypothetical fact scenario. That was the beginning of my rampant blushing in law school. Every time a professor called on me, or an upper-level student tried to engage with me, my face and neck flamed.

Fear swirled around me—like the dust cloud following the *Peanuts* comic strip character Pig-Pen—as my 1L classmates and I began to receive our first-semester grades. My roommate reveled in the daily intellectual banter of law school. She used words like "ostensibly" and "empirically" even in casual debriefings of *Law & Order* episodes. Being cold-called was her jam. She was popular, always smiling and laughing, and had an ever-present entourage of pals trailing her down the halls and encircling her in ebullient library study group debates. The school released our very first grade—Criminal Law—before all our other grades; professors taught that course in small sections instead of the large lecture format of 80+ students. My Criminal Law grade was by far the worst mark I had ever received in my life: C+. To this day, I don't know why 1Ls discuss grades among their peers (and I constantly counsel my students to keep their grades to themselves), but I quickly learned that my roommate had received an A+. I went home, hurled myself into bed, and wept for days. It wasn't that I just felt stupid and incompetent. (To be honest, I didn't like the course, I found the instruction incomprehensible, and I had zero interest in practicing criminal law.) I was afraid. I feared a report card littered with poor grades in the rest of my classes. I feared being regarded as unworthy of law school. I feared not getting a paying summer job owing to a low GPA. I feared failing out. I feared not being able to pay back my student loans. I also feared the painful familiar feeling of shame.

Of course, a few weeks later when the school released the rest of our grades, I performed fine overall. But to this day, I vividly recall the insomnia, the anvil weighing down my chest, the sensation of terror every morning, wondering if I was good enough, smart enough, worthy of law school and the legal profession.

A few months later, in the spring of my 1L year, I wrote my first brief for my legal writing course. I immediately loved the task of researching statutes and cases, carefully selecting the right precedent, and crafting a persuasive written argument. I methodically typed my brief, and spent days and nights editing it, choosing words and phrases that would best convey the logic and *pathos* of my hypothetical client's advocacy position. Now, reflecting back on that initial brief-writing experience, I understand that those moments were my first law school experience of being in "flow." Flow is the "theory of optimal experience"[15] developed by Hungarian psychologist Mihaly Csikszentmihalyi (pronounced "chick-sent-me-high-ee").[16] Csikszentmihalyi defines "flow" as "the state in which people are so involved in an activity that nothing else seems to matter."[17] He says that "[t]he best moments usually occur when a person's body or mind is stretched to its limits in a voluntary effort to accomplish something difficult and worthwhile."[18] Researching and writing in law school was a full-contact sport for me, a mental and physical gladiatorial feat of strength in which pushing myself beyond my limits felt extraordinary. It was the opposite of how I felt in class.

A newbie to legal research, I felt a jolt when I stumbled upon a quirky case that I could use to argue a difficult point by analogy. I experienced a rush when the mere act of moving two sentences around suddenly added punch to a paragraph. In the quietude of my bedroom, alone with my weighty textbooks and my beagle puppy (a gift from my long-term boyfriend who was not in law school and lovingly thought potty-training an adorable yet stubborn hound would be a healthy distraction from law school stress) chewing on the corner of my Contracts outline, I found my calling in the law.

Unfortunately, after our briefs were hypothetically "filed," next up on our law school assignment docket loomed oral arguments. The oral argument assignment poked the bear of my fear again. I would have loved for my appellate brief to serve as a quietly triumphant capstone to my 1L year. Nonetheless, law school tradition prevailed. Every 1L student was required to participate in a mock oral argument. At many schools, this rite of passage also serves as the tryout for the school's moot court team, an extracurricular activity in which students write briefs and perform oral arguments in competitions around the country. Akin to my total lack of interest in practicing criminal law, I had zero desire to join the moot court team. Everyone else seemed ecstatic about the opportunity. *Is something wrong with me? Am I not cut out to be a lawyer if I don't want to do this argument or be on the moot court team?* A new fear tornado brewed.

I couldn't walk down the school hallways without overhearing students bandying about the legal issues in our briefs and role-playing questions posed by imaginary judges. If I simply could have delivered an uninterrupted ten-minute presentation on the contentions laid out in my brief, that scenario would have been somewhat nerve-wracking from a public speaking standpoint but manageable. Instead, in an oral argument, the advocate begins speaking, conveys approximately 90 to 120 seconds of material, and then a panel of judges interrupts the discourse, peppering the advocate with questions to test the theories and logic of the arguments. This is not exactly an ideal venue for many of us (i.e., introverts) who naturally prefer time to ponder, vet, and test our ideas and responses internally before sharing them aloud. Many of my classmates delighted in this type of intellectual challenge, the spontaneous verbal volley, the battle of brains. I just wanted to deposit my brief in a dropbox and be done with the whole thing.

My actual oral argument was a certifiable disaster. I knew the statutes, the cases, my client's assertions, and my argument's soft spots inside and out. I prepared for days. I bought a suit from T. J. Maxx. Armed with a binder containing my outline and "case law reminder prompts" in the event my mind went blank about the facts or holding of particular precedent, I entered the classroom. My vision blurred. My eyes could delineate the shapes of two 3L students and one alumnus, all wearing judges' robes and sitting at the makeshift daïs. My ears could hear my opposing counsel clicking his pen while he waited for me to take my place at the podium. My heart banged wildly against my rib cage. The familiar prickles of a blush tingled my neck and cheeks. I forced myself to speak. The judges' questions came at me like rogue waves. To one, I had to answer, "I'm sorry. I don't know." Afterward, one swagger-filled 3L advised me to "work on that hair-pulling tic." Apparently, I had been unconsciously yanking at my long hair in an effort to hide my hives.

Today, 26 years later, when I share that story during presentations at law firms and bar associations about my *Introverted Lawyer* book (in which the mission is to help quiet lawyers amplify their voices *authentically* instead of "faking it till we make it"), a member of the audience sometimes will ask, "Well if law school was so scary for you, why didn't you just quit and go do something else?" That reaction always gives me pause, and frankly makes me a little sad (and annoyed). Do we really want law school to only be about, or available to, superconfident speakers? Or can we instead acknowledge that some law school traditions or rites of passage understandably produce more anxiety for some students than others? And that's okay. And does not mean the anxiety-prone students do not deserve to be there, or are unworthy of our profession. Our scared students might be deeply insightful thinkers, writers, and problem solvers who have a lot to say and just need some guidance and support—and empathy, for that matter—to find their *genuine* lawyer voices. I look back on my unpleasant and, quite honestly damaging, oral argument experience and ponder what might have helped me back then. I realize now that I needed a teacher, an upper-level student, or some sort of open-minded mentor to (a) acknowledge the anxiety that I, and likely other of my classmates, felt and (b) provide tangible guidance on how to mentally and physically—not just substantively or procedurally—prepare for that type of performance-oriented event. That didn't exist (for me at least) when I was in law school. Or I didn't know where to find it.

My exams went better that 1L spring, and in response to a 100-résumé mass mailing to law firms, I landed a plum summer job with a boutique construction litigation firm located just outside Washington, DC. At the ripe age of 22, still somewhat naïve about the many facets of the legal profession, I had not yet delved into the distinction between litigation and transactional work, or which area of practice might best suit my personality. I had law school loans. I needed a paying job. And the firm prided itself on being the highest-paying firm in Virginia, even though it was only 20 years old at the time. I stepped into the hard-hitting world of construction law.

I loved that law firm's environment from the moment I walked through the front doors. The firm invested in a robust summer associate program. We summer associates—from various East Coast law schools—had offices, assistants, and access to an overnight word processing team. We received cool softball jerseys, accompanied partners on fancy client lunch outings, and trained and trained and trained.

When I told my law school friends that the firm specialized in construction law, their responses usually entailed a wrinkled nose and a quip of "That sounds boring." Not even close. The legal work was riveting (no pun intended). We researched complicated contractual issues, learned how to read blueprints and engineering designs, and wrote innumerable memoranda, deposition outlines, and briefs. The lawyers were attractive, physically fit (if we weren't going to client lunches, we did group three-mile runs), snappily dressed, and mostly extroverted and loud. The atmosphere was "work hard, play hard." Our softball jerseys bragged, "Losing is not an option." The hallways buzzed with lawyers brainstorming solutions to conflicts. There was lots of jovial swearing. The F-bomb was an ever-present verb, noun, and adjective.

That summer, and the subsequent one after my 2L year, the firm nurtured and encouraged my legal research and writing. I felt happy in the law firm's library stacks, reading headnotes in the burgundy case books and figuring out the structure of the Federal Acquisition Regulations. I experienced pure joy when completing lengthy writing assignments and receiving comments written in the founding partner's trademark blue felt-tip ink that said "Your writing *stuns* me! Great job!" I survived a few mandatory speaking performances: client lunches and requests by another founding partner to explain challenging aspects of client opinion letters that I had drafted. He chain-smoked cigarettes and nodded along. I blushed and got blotchy in those moments. No one seemed to mind.

I finished my 3L year, married my long-term boyfriend, studied for and passed the bar exam, and began my new job as an associate at the construction law firm right after Labor Day. Sporting a new suit inspired by the *Ally McBeal* show—cornflower blue and an impossibly short skirt—I waltzed into the firm expecting life to be as blissful as it was during my summer associate days. To paraphrase Alex Conklin's directive to CIA operative Jason Bourne in *The Bourne Supremacy* movie, "Training [was] over." The firm's cases were high stakes and fast paced. While my role on many case teams involved a lot of legal research and writing at first, my workload soon included depositions, trial work, and negotiations. Mini-cyclones of fear began to churn again. No longer could I hide in the stacks and shine solely through my writing. I was expected to fight.

One of my first interactive engagements with opposing counsel was an assignment by one of the partners to negotiate a "case management schedule" that our respective parties would jointly submit to the trial judge. We needed to determine, and agree upon, how many months the parties would need to handle pleadings, discovery, experts, pretrial submissions, and trial, and set realistic interim deadlines along the way. The only negotiation advice the partner gave me was: "If opposing counsel wants the trial scheduled in two years, you say we want trial in six months. If those guys want trial in six months, you demand a two-year timeline." Gulp. This seemed like terrible advice—to fight for the sake of fighting—instead of taking a realistic look at the breadth of document review the parties would have to undertake, the number of witnesses scattered around the country to depose, what types of and how many experts were needed, whether we anticipated filing evidentiary motions or cross-motions for summary judgment, how many days or weeks or even months of trial would be reasonably necessary. The partner was accustomed to untailored aggression. I was expected to mirror the custom. I felt fraudulent. I had no poker face. My blush was my "tell," and the turtlenecks and scarves I wore to try to hide my blotchy neck merely exacerbated the feeling of suffocation. Migraines and insomnia entrenched.

For the most part, in the early years of my litigation career, I enjoyed my day-to-day life when I was physically present in the office, researching and writing, and generating memoranda and briefs. The atmosphere was collegial and intellectually collaborative. Our softball team trounced our opponents. Our holiday parties rocked. But out in the real legal world, my internal anxiety tornado wrought havoc. I threw up in hotel rooms and restrooms around the country before every deposition and negotiation. My relationships suffered a toll. My fear felt like a weakness. When I did confide my trepidation toward performance-oriented events, well-meaning but not-so-empathetic folks in my life would convey advice like, "Hey, this is the career you chose! Just get in there and do it! Face your fears! Fake it till you make it! Quit worrying! Grow a thicker skin!" Internalizing that advice, I kept doing it, faking it, pushing through, bungee-jumping into the fray and pretending I wasn't afraid. Inside, I was terrified. Afraid of screwing up, misunderstanding a negotiation ploy, overtrusting opposing counsel's word, missing the timing of a deposition objection, not volleying back quickly enough in response to a judge's question.

As I climbed the associate ranks, I eventually became part of a litigation team assigned to a huge case involving a tough client and managed by a volatile partner. The partner was a brilliant, charismatic, hardworking rainmaker with a wild temper. He had many enablers, and I became one. His assistant, paralegals, my fellow associates, and I jumped when he said "Jump!" even off metaphorical cliffs. We dodged flying pens, binder clips, and once, his set of BMW keys hurtling toward a glass door.

The partner and the client sent me to defend a sequence of expert depositions in our highly contentious case with millions of dollars on the line. The usual role of a defending attorney at a deposition is to object to improper questions posed by the questioning attorney. At times, the defending attorney also can use the vehicle of the objection to gently signal to the deponent (our side's witness or expert) to slow down, listen to the question, and not get too carried away. Ethically, a defending attorney is not allowed to coach the witness or intentionally disrupt the flow of questioning other than to preserve the record with proper objections to the form of the queries. Midway through one deposition, the expert I was defending received news that his father had been moved into hospice care and likely would not live through the following weekend. The expert was understandably distraught, yet wanted to continue and finish the deposition instead of rescheduling. He planned to travel to be at his father's side as soon as the deposition concluded. The expert began to stray a bit during his answers and veer into territory that other experts were covering. I worried that he might contradict opinions rendered by our other experts. I attempted to object to the form of the questions a little more often, my stomach beginning to twist like a pretzel. I was doing the right thing procedurally, but I wasn't sure of the wisest tactical move. Do I stop the deposition? On what grounds? We took a break and I called my boss. Amid a flurry of swear words, he screamed, "Just handle it!" I didn't know what *handling it* meant. I couldn't testify *for* the deponent. I couldn't predict or control the words coming out of his mouth. He was a professional expert witness. He knew the deposition drill. He was well aware of the millions of dollars at stake. And I had reminded him of all of that during the break. But he also was human, and his dad was dying.

We got through the deposition mostly unscathed, other than a few responses that could be framed by a good opposing brief-writer as contradicting another expert's opinion about an issue in the case. My boss went ballistic. As did the client. For days, I walked around the firm in a fog, not eating, wincing every time I heard a thud of a door closing or a book falling off a shelf in the library. And then they just got over it.

Six years into my litigation career, shortly before my thirtieth birthday, the most formative relationship of my life detonated. A 12-year bond fragmented into a million little pieces. Though much of the impetus for the split was my decision, my heart cracked apart. My body recovering from a miscarriage, my brain fried, my soul crushed, I needed time alone to figure out what in the world I was doing to the most important relationship I had ever had, and why I was doing it. Struggling to function under a blanket of shame, I moved to New York City to start over, leaving behind the person I loved the most in the world, my friends, my home, and my job. Only a year or two away from a partnership vote at the firm, I resigned.

Teetering on running out of money as Manhattan kicked me around with a steel-toed boot—the hazing many newcomers undergo in adjusting to New York life—I launched another 100-résumé blitz. I landed a job at a BigLaw firm in Tower Two of the World Trade Center. Every day, I took a long subway ride on the 4/5 train from my gloomy temporary uptown digs to Lower Manhattan, averting my eyes from the divorce lawyer advertisements that coaxed, "When diamonds aren't forever." My slim office windows offered a view of the Statue of Liberty, sailboats circling. Depressed and lonely, I tried to focus on editing drafts of banking contracts, sometimes putting my fingers in my ears to block out the bellowing from my next-door neighbor, another hot-tempered partner. I longed to switch places with the sailboat captains.

That year, I alternated between numbness at work and fear at home, terror that I had made a colossal mistake leaving my relationship. Manhattan kept bopping me around like a hacky sack, testing my mettle. At first, I couldn't figure out why anyone would want to live here. Everything smelled; everyone yelled. Nine months into my New York life, as spring approached, I found a fifth-floor walkup apartment in the West Village to sublet. Moving in, carrying a Hefty bag of clothes under one arm and my overweight beagle under the other, I trudged up the four flights of stairs, quads burning. The place reeked of syrupy candle wax. I opened the windows. Wind billowed sheer white curtains. I heard nothing but birds chirping. I saw trees and flowers. I smelled coffee and baked goods involving cinnamon. *Ok, I might be able to handle this.* I listened to Dido music nonstop, bought a few canvases and tubes of oil paint, and began to paint and write.

That summer, I wrote myself into a decision that I needed some time off from the law—at least temporarily—to figure out what I wanted to do with my life. The prior day, I had noticed myself flinching every time the partner next door wailed about misplaced faxes. I had stayed late the prior evening to transmit a document to a German client and the partner was storming around the office demanding the fax confirmation sheet. He dropped a few F-bombs about a rogue staple that pricked his hand. Ultimately, he directed his ire at me.

"You're always rushing through the halls! You haven't made any effort to assimilate! You never stay late to drink tequila with us! What's wrong with you? You need to make this job your number one priority!"

"It's not my number one priority," I murmured.

"Whaahhhh?!!" Steam seemed to blow from his ears, like a cartoon.

I am.

I filled out the paperwork to take an official leave of absence to get my head on straight. I needed to figure out how to heal the chasm in my soul, to adjust to New York, to write, to get healthy. I had buried oil drums full of fear, grief, and pain that needed excavation and remediation. Instead of constantly wishing I were on one of those sailboats circling Lady Liberty rather than at my desk, I needed to find joy and wonder in my life and work again.

After forging a few new Manhattan friendships late that summer, I booked a last-minute flight to join a couple of girls on a spontaneous trip to Greece at the beginning of September. One morning on the island of Santorini, I sat alone on a hotel balcony as the sun rose, bundled in a blanket, a fierce wind pummeling my face. Staring at the dark Aegean Sea, I felt a shift. I could breathe again and my chest didn't hurt. Things were going to be different now. The depression had started to lift. I was going to be okay again. My friends left Greece that day. I flew back to Athens, toured the Acropolis solo, and having miscommunicated with my hotel about accommodations, decided to spend the night in the Athens airport before boarding an early-morning flight home. Sleeping on the rock-hard airport benches proved challenging, but I was excited to get back to New York and start fresh. I flew from Athens to Frankfurt, and was on a Lufthansa flight home from Frankfurt when the pilot diverted the plane to Gander, Newfoundland. 9/11 happened during my flight.

I spent five days in Gander sleeping on a classroom floor in a school called Gander Academy. Emails and phone calls confirmed that my law firm thankfully did not lose anyone on that awful day, though one of my colleagues suffered eye injuries from the ash and debris when the towers fell. In Gander, I met folks from all over the world as Canadians fed, clothed, and supported thousands of passengers. Owing to border closures and boatloads of confusing directives from multiple authorities, my Lufthansa plane flew us back to Frankfurt on the fifth day. Landing in Germany, a few fellow travelers and I quickly grabbed cheeseburgers and fries from the Frankfurt Airport McDonald's and promptly turned around and boarded the first flight back to the United States.

Seeing the missing persons signs posted on the walls outside St. Vincent's Hospital and smelling the burnt metal of Ground Zero smacked me out of my personal relationship trauma. I was alive and I needed to be grateful and make the most of my existence. My own grief and pain had kept me out of Tower Two and away from my job that day. I was on the right plane instead of the wrong one. It was time to get on with being a contributing member of society again. In the early days after the tragedy, I watched way too many CNN profiles of Osama bin Laden, drank way too much red wine, wrote late into every evening, and slept till noon. One afternoon, while walking along the West Side Highway to clear my head, I decided to write a book summarizing everything I knew about litigation and civil procedure that I wished had been easier to find out or grasp when I was a confused and worried junior associate. I wrote constantly, and my first book formed. The depression—which had lightened as to my relationship's demise but dipped again in the immediate 9/11 aftermath—lifted through the writing work. I guess I also didn't feel entitled to be afraid. I felt a spark of my lawyer mojo reigniting, a sense of purpose.

One morning, an email popped into my inbox with an offer from a lawyer I had worked with in the DC area. He was starting his own firm with a former BigLaw partner and wanted a brief writer he didn't have to train. I could work and write from New York except when he needed me to travel for document reviews, depositions, or negotiations. Suddenly, I was a lawyer again.

My third firm specialized in construction litigation (like the first one). Even though this was a small boutique firm of 12 lawyers—in contrast to the 50 lawyers of my first firm and the BigLaw enormity of my second—the vibe was consistent across all three. Strong personalities, tenacious clients.

My brain hummed with determination again. I crafted complex briefs about jurisdictional issues, contract interpretation, and the enforceability of risk-shifting clauses. Clacking away on my laptop, in my apartment or in the firm's office, I once again felt Mihaly Csikszentmihalyi–style "flow." Sifting through reams of discovery to extract the right support for an argument, scouring Westlaw for the perfect case, reorganizing paragraphs to hit the right persuasive tone, my internal fire returned. As the firm's workload heated up and we landed additional massive construction cases, discovery schedules loomed and we all had to pitch in. I hit the road to take and defend another slew of depositions.

One day, in a BigLaw conference room, I was defending the deposition of a key party witness in an insurance dispute. I genuinely liked our opposing counsel. He and I had interacted on multiple occasions throughout the discovery process. He had integrity and was not a bully like some construction lawyers I had encountered over the years. Our deposition started off uneventfully: his questions, the witness's answers, my occasional objections to preserve the record. The witness, a talker and a vibrant storyteller, liked to elaborate on his answers even after lengthy advice on how to listen to the question and answer just the query posed. Still, he was doing okay so far. Just before lunch, my opposing counsel marked a one-page exhibit and slid it across the table to the deponent, also handing me a copy. I scanned it. I saw the name of our client's former in-house counsel. A lawyer. Which meant that the document was arguably attorney-client privileged (though protection from discovery turns on whether an insurance company's in-house counsel is providing legal advice (privileged) or acting in the ordinary course of claims analysis (not privileged)). *How in the world had opposing counsel gotten a copy?* The Bates number at the bottom of the page indicated the email had come from *our* client's files that we had produced in discovery. My heart rammed against my ribs. I objected, stuttering and turning red. My opposing counsel shot me a smug smile. The document—an internal email—contained some troubling statements. This was not good. I immediately felt responsible. Had I been tasked with that particular privilege review? The case involved millions of pages of discovery, and at least five of us had worked on the privilege review. *How should I respond? Is an objection enough? Should I instruct the witness not to answer any questions about the document? Could we write a motion* in limine *to preclude the document from seeing the light of day at trial?* My fear tornado swirled. My opposing counsel sat there watching me decompensate. Uncharacteristically, he seemed to be enjoying it. He made a few arguments on the record about waiver of any purported privilege and the damaging content of the document.

We took a break. I called the firm. One of the partners—prone to angry outbursts (yes, all three firms where I worked had one of these characters)—railed. Heads were going to roll. Including mine. I promptly got sick in the bathroom and finished the deposition, faking all kinds of bravado about all the motions we would file to exclude the document from trial.

Why did I feel afraid? I hadn't personally written that unfavorable email. With multiple team members reviewing millions of pages of electronic documents, one slip-through-the-cracks or inconsistency in a judgment call about the applicability of privilege was simply a litigation reality, even with numerous backstops in place. Civil procedure mechanisms existed to counter the waiver contention. I had preserved the objection in the deposition transcript record. Opposing counsel had a decent argument that the content and some of the document's recipients negated any privilege anyway. Why was I terrified? I was afraid of the rebuke I knew would come from the emotionally volatile partner and possibly from the client. With that scenario as a starting place, my brain promptly jogged down the slippery slope to visions of disciplinary action, losing my job, financial problems, professional ostracization, and so on.

After a lot of one-sided yelling, we all went on to live another day in that case and many others. We won some; we lost others. I successfully managed to stick to contract drafting and brief-writing for discrete chunks of time; inevitably, however, my performance roles in negotiations, depositions, and mediations always expanded. If I had written the particular transactional or litigation documents, I was the logical team member to deal with them in the client's representation. Fear lay dormant when I wrote, then awoke again when I spoke.

Around the same time (at the 14-year-mark of my litigation career), I was invited to teach my first legal writing course at a law school. I had enjoyed the process of writing and publishing my litigation book to help junior associates navigate civil cases in federal courts, and I had been contemplating a formal teaching role for a while. I dove into course planning and shoved my omnipresent public speaking nerves into a dark corner of my brain as I walked into my first class as a law professor. At least in the classroom—in contrast to the courtroom—most participants shared a common positive goal.

Over that first year, I noticed that my strongest legal writing students—my most diligent researchers, thoughtful analysts, and creative problem solvers—were my quietest students and often the most fearful of mandatory performance-oriented events. They were *me*. Observing this pattern across two subsequent cadres of students, I resolved to start doing something about this educational phenomenon; I didn't want these students to worry they were not cut out for the law, as I had. I began researching introversion, shyness, and social anxiety in the legal context. Through piles of readings and intense study, I finally started to understand myself, and why my natural preference for internal processing and writing instead of immediately speaking had always posed challenges in performance-oriented lawyering scenarios. I began to comprehend why I thrived when working alone, and why it took me longer than my colleagues to jump into the fray in a litigation team meeting. I delved deeply into my social anxiety (and shame) and finally grasped why I flinched before combative depositions and in skirmishes with antagonistic and angry bosses, clients, or opposing counsel.

I wrote two law review articles summarizing this research and proposing methods to help law students understand and tackle anxiety about public speaking. I especially focused on law school rite-of-passage experiences like Socratic classroom exchange, mandatory oral arguments, and client-focused simulations. This work led to my most recent book, *The Introverted Lawyer: A Seven-Step Journey Toward Authentically Empowered Advocacy*, which highlights the gifts that quiet individuals bring to our profession. Because the book also recognizes the obvious reality that all law students and lawyers need to be able to speak about the law with vigor (in various circumstances), it provides practical strategies to help us amplify our advocacy voices in an *authentic* manner.

In the early years of my teaching career, I kept one foot firmly planted in law practice, to earn enough money to finance my New York existence. (Legal writing faculty are notoriously underpaid, but through the work of teams like the Professional Status Committee of the Legal Writing Institute, we're working toward pay equity across the academy.) I continued writing construction-related contracts and briefs and conducted many a negotiation, deposition, and client interface. As research for my introversion book developed and grew, I endeavored to unearth my *authentic* lawyer persona after so many years of faking it and trying to be someone I was not. For years, I had absorbed the punches and blows of verbal aggression that are commonplace and accepted in my niche in the legal industry. Not knowing any other modus operandi, I had strived to mirror that behavior, if not in my actions, through my written words. It was exhausting.

Finally, instead of marching into each interactive scenario faking extroversion and forcing confidence, I began testing out a new approach. I had always been prepared with bullet points, charts, outlines. I began *using* my written preparation as a vehicle to take charge of, or direct, conference calls and negotiation meetings. I distributed handouts of talking points, agendas, and spreadsheets of the opposing parties' positions on contract terms or litigation bargaining chips. People stopped talking *at* me and started reading, listening, communicating, and compromising. Instead of raising my voice to meet their decibel levels, I stuck to my natural measured (and slightly amplified) tone, referring to my talking points if I needed to restate my position repeatedly to be heard. I stopped paying deference to aggression as authentic power. I finally realized it wasn't.

In those scenarios, I knew I was going to turn red every time I asserted myself, so I needed to figure out a way to forge a new relationship with my blushing. It wasn't like the blush was just going to stop coming. In my introversion research, I discovered *Living Fully with Shyness and Social Anxiety*, by Erika Hilliard.[19] Hilliard wrote, "To see a blush is to celebrate life's living . . . fullness, ripeness, color, and flourishing life."[20] She emphasized that a blush is a sign that "life is coursing through you."[21] I laughed out loud the first time I read her words. *I'm alive; yay me!* I had never thought about my blush that way. Hilliard gave me the pivot I needed. I promptly stopped wearing the turtlenecks and scarves that had dominated my performance wardrobe yet had accomplished nothing but jack up my body heat. I decided, I'm going to blush; it's what I do. Instead of fighting it, I'm just going to "be the blush." The more I started doing that, not trying to suppress the blush but instead acknowledging its existence, chuckling to myself each time that, once again, *I'm alive, yay me!*, the redness and heat started to dissipate faster. I also decided that anyone who was going to point out my blush—and some people seem to love to do that and think it's cute and acceptable (it's not)—was a clueless dolt.

Now, this new authentic empowerment strategy didn't always go smoothly. It continued to be a work-in-progress as I wrote my introversion book, taught new groups of legal writing students each semester, coached my nervous students through countless oral arguments, and flew around the country litigating. I tried to practice what my own writing preached. Flip the mental messages: *You deserve to have a voice and say your words in your own way; you do not need to mirror others' behavior.* I adopted new physical strategies for maximizing effective blood, oxygen, and energy flow in performance moments and reducing my anxiety. I ramped up my SoulCycle spinning classes and started taking boxing lessons. Through this process, I spent a ton of time seeking to understand my introversion, unpack my social anxiety, and recognize aspects of both as assets in lawyering. The one thing I hadn't really focused on was fear. I began to wonder: What is fear? Is it an emotion? A feeling? A base instinct? Is it different from anxiety? Is it a strength or a weakness? Is it a tool or a nemesis?

The last major performance opportunity in law practice before I transitioned to full-time teaching was an oral argument on an appellate brief I wrote. The case involved an interesting legal standard relating to property ownership and premises liability. Our firm was hired to do the appeal; we had not represented the client at trial. I spent months perusing the trial record: transcripts, exhibits, motions, and briefs. I researched every angle of the applicable law and crafted a lengthy brief articulating why we believed the trial court had erred. When we filed our brief, we had to indicate on the cover sheet the name of the attorney who would deliver the oral argument. I panicked. I knew every nuance of all the cases cited in the brief and each fact captured in the documentary record. I practically had the 58-page brief and three volumes of exhibits memorized. But I was afraid to do the argument. I feared I would freeze, screw up, totally bomb, look like an idiot, and we would lose because of me. My boss, on the other hand, loved the courtroom. We listed his name as the oral advocate on the cover of the brief. I signed and filed the papers.

The argument day arrived. I met my boss at the appellate court building. Even the sight of the metal detectors roiled my stomach. We sat on an ornately carved wooden bench beneath a stained glass domed ceiling. The solemnity of the inspirational legal quotes stenciled onto the walls caused a mini-migraine to starburst at my right temple. My boss chatted breezily about a Scottsdale tennis trip, his kids, sports. My brain couldn't even process his words. I wasn't the one doing the argument but all I could think about was the judges' questions. *What if they focus on the* Quinn *case? That one is tricky but it's distinguishable!*

The bailiff announced that counsel could enter the courtroom, a stunning structure with more stained glass, sculpted woodwork, Latin quotes. Sweat dribbled down my back. Lawyers swiftly angled for seats, bustling their briefcases and briefs. *I am such a fraud; what am I doing here?* The justices filed in, their robes flowing. Three women, one man. The chief justice called the docket.

Lawyers started arguments; the justices interrupted with questions, some abrasive, others merely inquisitive; the cases tumbled off the docket one-by-one. The chief justice called our case. Opposing counsel stormed down the aisle ahead of my boss and me without even a glance in our direction. He greeted the justices by name. They seemed to know him. The chief justice asked me point-blank why my name was on the signature line of the brief and yet my boss—who had to be admitted pro hac vice for purposes of this one case because he was not licensed in the jurisdiction—was delivering the argument. I mumbled something about teamwork.

Because we represented the appellant, my boss took the podium first. I sat at counsel's table, the justices' bench looming above me. My boss commenced the argument, completely straying from the outline I prepared for him as he often did in his courtroom-comfortable style. The justices lasered in and pummeled him with questions. It didn't sound like they had dissected the briefs. The questions seemed to sidestep the established precedent and the clear four-pronged rule. I feverishly scribbled notes on how to answer each question. But my boss stood too far away for me to even think about positioning the legal pad so he could see my urgent words and exclamation points. I realized in that moment that I could have, and should have, done that argument. We still would not have convinced the judges to overturn the lower court's decision. But I regret not taking that life opportunity. Even in that final year—my twenty-first year—of practicing law, my fear hamstrung me. I needed to learn how to get out of my own way. I needed to finally understand my fear. Neither ignoring it nor letting it run my life had ever been an effective strategy.

Writing my last book taught me so much about introversion as an asset in practicing law and also how those of us with social anxiety can amplify our advocacy voices in an authentic manner. I now realize that fear is something different. It crosses personality type. It's an instinctive emotional and physical reaction to a perceived threat or danger. It exists in many facets of lawyering. And yet we don't talk about it enough, or much at all, in legal education and practice. For years, I tried to push through (by ignoring) my intense fear of public speaking, faking it till I made it in depositions, negotiations, and courtroom appearances, and constantly feeling ill. As I completed the introversion book and started this new project, I finally sat down and got to know my fear. It needed to start with vulnerability, humility, and reflection—concepts we don't often teach, praise, or promote in the practice of law.

In doing this work, vulnerability and authenticity, which can be scary territories in and of themselves, helped me begin to understand and address my fear instead of dismissing it or pushing it further down into a storage tank in my psyche to be dealt with later. For example, teaching an Evidence course for the first time to 135 law students, I had to admit—out loud—I was afraid. I was scared of not knowing the answer to a tough question about a tricky criminal evidentiary rule (my years of practice had focused on the civil rules), of turning bright red, of seeming like a fraud to students paying $50,000 a year in tuition and expecting excellence. Drawing upon the resources of many experts, I started analyzing the mental and physical realities of my fear. First, I transcribed verbatim the negative messages I played on a soundtrack in my head at the onset of a fear-inducing event. Next, I assessed what I was doing with my physical body that blocked energy, oxygen, and blood flow, hindering my peak performance. I realized that the detrimental mantras I had adopted from others as gospel in more than two decades of law practice served no purpose for me; rather, they fueled a shame-based fear of judgment. One day, I decided that my days of faking it, of dismissing the reality of fear, were over. In class, I started verbalizing it: "Wow, tough evidentiary question. I need to think about that for a minute. I know I'm turning red right now, but the blush will go away in a minute, so let's break down this question together." Vulnerability and honesty about my fear (in appropriate circumstances, of course) became powerful stanchions.

Now, because of my role as director of the legal writing program in the law school where I teach, many of the issues raised in faculty meetings touch on the future of the program—curriculum, strategic planning, fund-raising, recruiting new faculty, grading standards, and so on—and I need to weigh in and voice a position regularly. While the dean and vice-dean lead our faculty meetings using an orderly protocol with agendas and "queues" of speakers, debates typically involve strong personalities, confident assertions, and fast-paced verbal volley. Quite honestly, though I know what I'm talking about, care immensely about these issues, and feel respected by my colleagues, faculty meetings can stoke my fear. A few months into my new position, I knew I had to decode *why*. What exactly do I fear? Turning red is a given regardless of how badass I am feeling in the moment. I needed to get over worrying about that. *Be the blush.* The truth is: I worry they will think I'm not intelligent enough for their ranks. That they made a mistake in hiring me for this hybrid teaching/administrative position with so many moving parts in curriculum design, personnel, and long-range planning. That they will question my judgment. I had to flip the sound track in my head: *You've been teaching legal writing for nine years, you love it, you love this job, you have good instincts. Think it through, write it out, project your voice, ignore the blush, speak in your own measured—though slightly amplified—voice, make eye contact around the room, state your piece and don't rethink it.*

I consistently applied these techniques, in nerve-wracking committee meetings, in book presentations, in financial and strategic planning pitches, and in the classroom. Through alternating mental and physical *reflection* with mental and physical *action*, and always prioritizing truth over the mask of fake confidence, I slowly became less fearful, and in many instances, surprisingly fearless. This untangling process works. Pretending didn't.

This book seeks to start a conversation in legal education and law practice about fear. We can acknowledge out loud that studying and practicing law is hard, and it should be. We are a noble profession with a soul, doing critically important work to solve problems for human beings, businesses, and communities. Instead of pretending it's not often scary work, consequently making those who experience fear feel weak or inferior, let's start an inclusive conversation. Instead of downplaying fear, ignoring it, shrugging it off, shelving it, or fighting, facing, conquering, or even glorifying it, let's *untangle* it.

Let's understand fear, break it down, use its helpful aspects, and repurpose or chuck the rest.

The law is always going to present scary scenarios, often involving loss: of liberty, financial stability, security, reputation, equality, power, or control. If we, as law students, lawyers, educators, and mentors, endeavor to untangle the complexities of fear, our profession can evolve. The premise of this book is not "Fear is awesome! Let's embrace it!" It's also not "Fear is a foe we must vanquish!" Instead, the platform of this book is that fear is a recognizable, tangible reality in the study and practice of law. Just because we are apprehensive about aspects of our legal studies or day-to-day law practice does not mean we are not cut out to be amazing, impactful lawyers. It just means that we need to equip ourselves with effective mechanisms to recognize and acknowledge fear; untangle its emotional, mental, and physical properties; extract what we can use from it; employ the powerful components of fear in driving our mission as attorneys and advocates; and try to repurpose the rest (like nose-to-tail chefs), or let the useless parts go. This process is going to require some vulnerability in all of us. This is not the way we have always done things. This is not tradition. This is not status quo.

Our first step as a profession is to cease treating fear as a weakness. We need to refrain from asking nervous or fearful law students, "If you don't like public speaking, why'd you go to law school?" Just the other night, at a presentation at a bar association, I shared a personal anecdote about tackling (most of) my public speaking anxiety. In the Q&A, a judge raised her hand and remarked, "Why on earth did you go into litigation? That was the worst career choice for you!" Sigh. No, it wasn't. I loved the research and writing, and I was good at it. I just needed (and lacked) the right guidance to find my authentic litigation voice and unpack the drivers of my fear toward performance scenarios. In my law practice, it felt impossible to say out loud, "I'm afraid to take my first deposition. I want to do it and I'm substantively and strategically prepared. But I'm scared. I don't know where to sit, what to expect, how to start, how to handle difficult opposing counsel. I don't know what to do if the witness is rude, the defending lawyer challenges me, my face turns red. . . ." In the dynamic of the law firms where I worked (even the collaborative one where I started my career), it did not seem to be an option to reveal, "I'm afraid. I want to do a great job. Can you teach me how to handle the fear?" Instead, we played out the mantras: *Just do it. Fake it. Be tough. Be abrupt if you have to. Be as hard-charging as they are. Mirror their behavior.* So, what happens? Many of us do fake it. We prepare substantively, but mentally, physically, even strategically we often experience self-doubt. And this causes strain and stress. Even if the performance event glows with advocacy success, we experience strain and stress. Unnecessarily.

Being on the quieter side within, or initially hesitant about, spontaneous legal exchanges does not in any way mean a person is not fit to be a transformative advocate. But some of us cannot tap into our authentic advocacy voices because we do not yet understand what is igniting, feeding, and perpetuating our fear. Some suggest that this discomfort is part of being a rookie. But does it really need to be? We are an unhealthy profession and we don't need to be. We are capable of evolving into a vocation that balances both rigor and wellness.

In 2016, the American Bar Association's Commission on Lawyer Assistance Programs, the National Organization of Bar Counsel, and the Association of Professional Responsibility Lawyers established a National Task Force on Lawyer Well-Being. In August 2017, the Task Force issued a report[22] initiating a call to action for members of the profession to commit to "reducing the level of toxicity in our profession."[23] The report acknowledges the role of fear (and shame) in law students' and lawyers' hesitance to seek help for mental health concerns and other issues, referencing

- "fear of adverse reactions by others whose opinions are important"
- the impact of "feeling ashamed"
- "fear of career repercussions"[24]

The report indicates that law students "fear . . . jeopardizing their academic standing or admission to the practice of law, social stigma, and privacy concerns."[25] Legal educators need to make it okay to talk openly about fear in lawyering and to arm students with tools, techniques, and the resilience required to untangle fear *before* entering practice. In the words of one 2L student, "our experiences vary and some of us need more help than others to build up the confidence, technical skills, or mental resiliency to succeed in the ever-challenging legal profession." Law students are telling us exactly what they need to thrive; let's listen to them. Another student shared:

While lawyers do tend to exude confidence, it would be helpful for lawyers and anyone interested in practicing law to know it is okay to make mistakes and that there are many circumstances that can arise throughout a case that are simply impossible to control. I think that having workshops of some kind in law school or speakers in law school could help to reduce fear and anxiety that accompany some lawyering activities. . . . If more people know what to expect about day-to-day legal practice prior to entering the field after law school, I think it would definitely have a profound effect on reducing fears.

Likewise, law practice mentors should not regard fear in junior associates as a weakness. Some of the best, brightest, most thoughtful, and most creative legal writers and advocates feel scared and vulnerable when learning. Instead of shrugging their fear aside, let's discuss it.

Unaddressed fear in lawyering can affect performance, leading to mental health and wellness challenges, burnout, and even ethical breaches. Indeed, some level of fear is a natural and inevitable component of a profession designed to navigate conflicts; it is human nature to be afraid of loss, scarcity, exclusion. But when fear rises to a level at which it detrimentally impacts an individual's ability to function in a healthy and productive manner, it invites a conversation. Let's start talking about fear in lawyering. If we can untangle fear—what it is, what drives it, its necessary and unnecessary components—we can distill and repurpose it into a productive force in lawyering.

Even with more than two decades of legal experience under my belt, I admit I'm often still fearful about making a flawed decision, appearing unintelligent, saying something the "wrong" way, or not knowing the wisest or correct answer. But I know that, if I give myself enough time to research an issue, write it out, think, reflect, and then act (while reinforcing mental and physical techniques to channel thoughts, energy, oxygen, and blood flow in a productive manner), I will do the best job I can. It's time for the legal profession to remove unnecessary drivers of fear, and instead provide substantive, mental, and physical training for our newest generation of lawyers to defuse the unhealthy reagents present in our profession. This will require open-mindedness, civility, and empathy. We need to step away from dualisms: strong v. weak, wheat v. chaff, the "haves" and the "have-nots." Every individual who enrolls in law school and endeavors to contribute to our profession in an ethical way deserves a chance to thrive, with appropriate support, training, and guidance. Untangling fear should be part of this educational and professional journey.

Fears are educated into us, and can, if we wish, be educated out.
—Karl A. Menninger[26]

PART I

FEAR IN LEGAL EDUCATION AND PRACTICE

The next few chapters shine a spotlight on the reality of fear in legal education and practice. These chapters are *not* designed to dwell in negativity or draw an ominous cloud over our chosen profession. On the contrary, these chapters are intended to flip the light switch on and illuminate scenarios and situations in law school and law practice that (quite understandably) invoke hesitation and trepidation in many of us, so that together we can make some long-overdue adjustments.

The hardest aspect of my experience in law school and practice was the feeling that I was the only one who felt sick in anticipation of, or during, a performance-oriented event. I often felt lonely and weak, though I was outpacing my billable-hour milestones, achieving successes for my clients through the written work, and even surpassing physical fitness goals outside of my work. On many occasions, I feared that I was unworthy, that the bar examiners had made a mistake, that I would be exposed as an imposter, a fraud. As the next few chapters hopefully will illustrate, many law students and lawyers (as well as clients) experience fear. We are not alone. We go on to achieve great things, yet the stress can take an unnecessary toll. By talking about the realities of fear in lawyering, we can start an inclusive conversation. We can open up, share our vulnerabilities, and begin to untangle this entity called fear. In doing so, we can enhance our day-to-day lives in the law, perform at our highest peak, serve our clients more powerfully, and enhance the health of our profession.

CHAPTER 1

Fear in Law Students

Although of course many features of law school are exciting, inspiring, and intellectually exhilarating, other facets can induce fear in some students. Students come to law school from diverse life backgrounds and educational experiences. 1Ls typically have achieved marked levels of success in their formative education. Yet law school poses different developmental and assessment challenges that may be unfamiliar to newcomers and not always congruent with the way some of us learn best. Many legal educators strive to cultivate an inclusive, collaborative learning environment in the law school classroom. Nonetheless, the traditional law school teaching model naturally breeds a certain degree of competition, jockeying for position, and resultant performance anxiety in some students. As fellow legal writing professor Abigail A. Patthoff notes, "[a]lthough some fear is productive and can motivate students to achieve, too much fear can be debilitating and distracting."[27] (Chapter 6 here suggests an alternative viewpoint toward the "productive" nature of fear.)

Professor Patthoff reports:

> *A decline in well-being among law students, attributed to stress, has been well documented. Fear is one of the culprits contributing to this distress. The Socratic method is famously intimidating, grades are often exclusively earned via one make-or-break exam at the end of the semester, and the news is replete with reports about dwindling job opportunities for law graduates. Law students are not short on reasons to fear.*[28]

Again, this discussion here is not intended to scare anyone further, or to paint a bleak picture of law school as an educational choice. Instead, this conversation is designed to acknowledge and validate the very real existence of fears and worries that can arise during the law school experience, so that we can do something about them. This situation is changeable. Once we name the environmental contributors, the tasks, and the activities that can stoke fear in law students, we—as individuals and as an educational community—can strive to untangle and better understand the drivers of these fears, and develop strategies for students to step into each of these scenarios with enhanced fortitude.

THE IMPOSTER SYNDROME

Some 1L students arrive at law school fearing that the admissions office made a mistake. They worry that their backgrounds do not measure up to the standard of the stereotypical "go-getter" law student. One law student who went to high school in a rural community and then majored in drama at a prestigious urban university shared:

> *I would not take back my unique journey for anything, but without a solid education to prepare me or a family member to guide me, I feel ill-prepared for law school and lawyering, intimidated by the many political science and economics majors fresh out of undergraduate school who excel at test-taking, the former paralegals who bring context and experience to their legal studies, the children of lawyers who have internalized a lifetime of advice, the hallway conversations where legal terminology and law firm stats get tossed around like everyone knows, or should. It makes me shrink.*

Another student also with a creative background—having attended fashion college before law school—conveyed how he felt on the first day he walked into his law school internship, wearing a long-sleeved dress shirt and a suit jacket to hide his tattoos:

> *The first day of my internship, I arrived at the courthouse in a slim fit suit, dress shoes, and a tie. I sat outside and observed attorneys wearing ill-fitted, antiquated suits and [carrying] large files as they entered the courthouse. I felt withdrawn from the sector of the legal world I was about to enter, a sense of disconnectedness that was a source of fear throughout my first year of school and continued to plague me with a deep sense of detachment as I approached my first legal work placement. . . . Intimidated by my assumption that I did not belong, I felt anxious, withdrawn, and regretful that I agreed to work for a judge.*

Another student described how her feelings of fraudulence throughout her first year of law school affected her *physically*:

> *I don't remember exactly when things started getting bad. All I remember is that I thought they gave me the wrong grades after first semester because it didn't make sense that I passed all my classes. . . . Other than for Legal Writing, I never once asked a question to a professor or went to office hours (still haven't) because I didn't feel like I deserved to go up there and speak with a professor like the other students did. I must just be a good test taker. . . . When it came time for spring exams, I couldn't breathe. And not just for fifteen minutes or an hour a day.*

I couldn't breathe for over a month. The chest pain became intense. I was so dizzy from hyperventilating that I could hardly stand up. . . . My parents took me to the ER after I submitted my [journal competition assignment]. The doctors did a lot of tests and found everything normal on me. I even had maximum oxygen in my blood despite it feeling like I couldn't get any. . . . [This happened] because I was obsessed with avoiding the embarrassment of being compared negatively next to my classmates.

One more law student described the degree of fear and anxiety that she felt when stepping into her first summer externship. When a supervisor handed her a new client file and tasked her with "assessing the complaint, contacting and interviewing the client, writing [a] motion, conducting the investigation, and speaking for the client on the record for subsequent proceedings," the student experienced these worries:

Initially, I found myself trying to pull from my brain some memory of a law school 1L class that would help me. I thought back to Criminal Law. I tried to use my 1L appellate brief for writing inspiration. None of this helped. In doing this, I realized I was trying to find some cushion of support to affirm the actions I would take in this case. I was very stressed about this. I began to think I was not meant to be a lawyer, that I could never represent a client, I was not qualified, the other interns knew so much more, etc. I did not want to miss a motion date or argue on the record. How could I ever represent this client when all I knew was how to IRAC a Constitutional Law issue spotter?

The legal profession needs these creative thinkers, these thoughtful legal analysts. We need to provide guidance on how to unearth the roots of such feeling of unworthiness and replace it with fortitude.

THE SOCRATIC METHOD

Many professors manage law school classroom dialogue through the Socratic method. As I wrote in Chapter 2 of *The Introverted Lawyer*, Socrates developed this technique of intellectual query while roaming market stalls, theaters, and public squares in Athens. He sought to stretch his *own* knowledge through questioning individuals from all walks of life. Socrates's method reportedly was inclusive and encouraging, even though his probes gently revealed logic flaws and false assumptions in the responses of his conversation partners. Socrates's mantra was "Know thyself"—a message inscribed on the Temple of Apollo at Delphi. He readily acknowledged his own intellectual limitations and sought growth through colloquy with other citizens.

Socrates epitomized the notion of "intellectual humility." He did not set out daily to prove he was the smartest guy in the room, or in the public square. Instead, he gained wisdom, and strove to cultivate expansion of knowledge in fellow citizens, through creating a level intellectual playing field, where every person participating in his dialogues—no matter what social status— brought value.

For generations, American law professors have used the Socratic method to spur classroom interaction. The law school version of this inquisitorial practice often can seem more intimidating than Socrates's original mode of collaborative discourse as described. Law professors call on students—either at random ("cold calling"), alphabetically, or by some other system—and pose questions about the statutes, cases, and legal concepts in the day's assigned reading. A student may be impeccably prepared for class, with charts, high-lighted outlines, and flash cards systematizing that day's rules, standards, and public policies. Despite this advance work, being in the "hot seat" as the target of questioning by an imposing law professor, conversing in unfamiliar legal terminology within novel intellectual territory, can ignite a degree of fear.

As author Kevin Davis wrote in a 2015 *ABA Journal* article:

> *Not surprisingly, research suggests that many lawyers' fears develop during law school, where students may seem outwardly confident but may be masking feelings of inadequacy, uncertainty and nervousness. The stresses of carrying a heavy workload, studying theoretical concepts rather than practical law and getting good grades contribute to their fears. One of the biggest fears among law students is being humiliated in front of their classmates.*[29]

In a classroom exchange, some of us worry that our peers and our professor will judge us. What if we flub a response or misunderstand the professor's query? If we get nervous speaking in class, we wonder why other classmates don't. We agonize, "If I'm not skilled at speaking in class right away, like every-body else seems to be, am I really cut out to be a lawyer? Shouldn't I be good at this already?"

For some reason in law school, we feel compelled to compare ourselves to our classmates, even as early as the first week of the first semester. In a research study of law student study groups,[30] students reported that "[f]ear of fellow classmates was palpable . . . from the moment they arrived at orien-tation."[31] Students were afraid "of being marked as 'the person who doesn't know.'"[32] One student indicated that "this fear starts in the classroom where a 'left-field answer' or a 'dumb question' quickly elicits ridicule, scorn, and 'a reputation.'"[33]

Another law student (not in the foregoing study) questioned whether "cold calling actually reveals knowledge about the subject matter." She reported:

Sometimes I get too nervous to get my words out correctly, but I know the facts and holding of the case quite well. The downfall of this type of legal environment is that you potentially do not end up with the best possible lawyers, but just lawyers who can withstand that type of nervousness. It sort of rewards people who do not have anxiety, and punishes those who do.

Class participation clearly is one tangible source of fear in law school. Happily, once we name it, we can do something about it, perhaps harkening back to Socrates and modeling his approach to learning from one another. We'll focus more on solutions in Part IV.

FINAL EXAMS AND GRADES

Other law students fear the impact of final exams worth 100% of the grade for each course. We spend all semester taking copious notes in class, crafting detailed outlines, attending review sessions, and churning through practice exams. But what happens if we hit a speed bump during the actual exam? It feels like so much is on the line in each three-hour test. Can our hard work really shine in the moment that counts?

In college and law school, when I took tests, I broke out in ferocious hives. I kept going and finished every test and exam, but professors would pull me aside and ask, "Are you okay?" They could see the pink and red blotches blooming along my cheeks and neck. No amount of preparation could eliminate my body's instinctive reaction in those high-stress performance moments. I pushed through it every time, but without the self-awareness that would come decades later, the strain wore on me.

Once law school grades start to trickle in, some of us fear the sorting by GPAs and class ranks, or perhaps keeping or earning scholarships. We vow not to talk about grades or listen to the buzz in the hallways about them. But inevitably we measure our own performance against others' successes. We watch as some classmates' true personalities come out once the first set of grades has been posted. In the research study about student study groups mentioned above, a student provided this perspective on law school fears:

People were afraid because they had put families and careers on hold; people were afraid because there was too much to humanly do. That kind of fear brings out the worst in some people, making them do things that in another situation maybe they wouldn't do.[34]

Some of us question who we can trust. Can we confide our fears in our friends, our study group, or our section-mates? Or will we seem weak? To whom can we turn for judgment-free support in the face of worries about grades?

More sorting occurs as the masthead for the law review (at many schools, tied at least in part to grades) is announced. Some students' self-assuredness is buoyed by these academic accolades. For others, the imposter syndrome lurks even if they are selected to serve on the law review editorial board. I worked with a wonderfully kind and conscientious law student whose anxiety wove a consistent thread through her law school experience. We often spoke and strategized about her fears associated with class participation, test taking, and oral arguments. Ultimately, she excelled in her legal writing class (taught by a different professor) and in her other courses. She wrote onto law review. At the end of her 2L year, she reached out to me again. She felt she had the leadership skills and dedication to run for the position of editor in chief of the law review, but her fear was circling again. Even though she had checked the box of every prestigious law school achievement, fear accompanied her into the law review executive board elections. She *won*. She grabbed the reins as editor in chief. In response to such well-earned victories, outside observers often note, "See! There was nothing to be afraid of!" That takeaway unfortunately misses the mark. Her fear is real. It hurts—it causes mental and physical pain. It detracts from the triumph. Just telling someone that fear is unnecessary because everything always works out doesn't make the pain magically disappear. Untangling fear does.

Fear about grades and rankings can fuel a judgment-based mind-set, of ourselves and others. As an educational community, if we can identify the drivers of this kind of fear, we can begin to dial down the levels of student apprehension one, two, even three notches and clear a path for enhanced performance and happiness in learning.

PERFORMANCE-ORIENTED EVENTS

A lawyer working in a law firm in Virginia shared this law school memory:

> The memory of my 1L oral argument is both vivid and hazy. I don't remember much about what I said or the questions I received. I don't even remember if I went first or second. What I remember are the frantic moments just before entering the room—sitting with my head between my knees, trying to breathe. I remember stepping up to the podium and being modestly grateful for its support, as I stood there visibly shaking. Incidentally, I have always been jealous

of women who blush, because I think of it as an endearing response (not to minimize the internal stress behind it). I, on the other hand, have the profoundly unladylike response of sweating. I remember starting to speak—my voice even shakier than my stance, feeling drenched (and mortified I looked that way)—and I remember the irrational panic when I was interrupted by one of the "judges." What I remember most about the experience, however, is the overwhelming sense of failure that I felt at the end. I am not the kind of person who has to be the best at everything, and I am generally content knowing that I have put in the work and done the best I could. The thing about my 1L oral argument is that I was incredibly prepared. I was ready. I knew exactly what I wanted to say, and I anticipated and prepared for any question or counterargument I thought could be thrown at me. The failure was that none of that mattered in the moment. I couldn't do my best, and that was devastating.

Performance-oriented events like oral arguments, client-centered simulations (such as mock client interviews, counseling sessions, or negotiations), and tryouts for moot court, trial, and alternative dispute resolution teams, also can kindle fear. Traditions prod us into these events, and professors (and upper-level students) prepare us substantively, procedurally, and stylistically, but often it can feel like no one is talking about how to realistically minimize associated *anxiety*. The vibe seems to be: *This is a rite of passage. Just do it. This stuff is an integral part of law school; if you're not excited about this type of interactive activity, what are you doing here? Just practice and you'll be fine. Besides, if you're not nervous, it means you don't care. And when in doubt, fake it till you make it!*

Grrr. Not helpful advice.

Nonetheless, we watch as many of our classmates seem to slip seamlessly into role-playing exercises, donning suits and rehearsing with vigor. Meanwhile, our stomachs churn. *Why don't I want to do this, yet? Am I pursuing the wrong profession for me if I'm not excited about this form of public speaking?* Classmates with the gift of gab are complimented on their oral communication skills. Their confidence blooms. Friends and colleagues are invited to join the school's advocacy teams, and some of us make the teams too, because we prepared so doggedly for the performances and they ultimately went better than we anticipated. But fear still spirals.

At two different law schools where I have taught, and while researching my introversion book, I launched a series of anxiety workshops prior to the mandatory spring 1L oral argument assignment. In this capstone project of many 1L legal writing courses, students write trial or appellate briefs and then are paired with another student to argue the opposing sides of the legal issues encapsulated in the briefs before a panel of judges. At the law schools where I have taught, each advocate's argument lasts 10 minutes, including the time spent responding to judges' intermittent questions. During each argument, judges interrupt the speaker with inquiries about the cases, theories, and policies to vet and test each orator's legal contentions. For many students, this represents the first, or at least the most intense, law-related debate of their lives—to date. A straight presentation via an uninterrupted delivery is one thing, but the interjection of questions by judges can derail even the most well prepared advocate.

As I mentioned earlier, I struggled in my 1L oral argument, and each year I sense similar heightened levels of anxiety in many students as they approach this year-end challenge. To help dial down their anxiety levels, I construct a series of five workshops in the weeks leading up to the arguments. In the sessions, we start by identifying our individual *internal* and *outward* manifestations of anxiety in anticipating this particular performance-oriented activity. We look at:

- What unproductive or critical *mental messages* might we be telling ourselves internally about our abilities? We transcribe these messages word-for-word, and then ask:
  - Are these messages outdated and irrelevant to our current legal personas?
    - Is this really the long-ago voice of a well-meaning but perhaps misguided teacher, coach, caregiver, sibling, peer, or authority figure?
  - Can we replace these messages with more realistic and positive truths about our current abilities?
    - For example: *I'm prepared; I know every nuance of my brief; I'm entitled to speak in my own voice and in my own style; I don't need to mirror everyone else; this is a dialogue with three humans, not the Super Bowl half-time show. . . .*

- What instinctive *physical reactions* to stress are our bodies undertaking that are not necessarily helpful? We notice the following:
  - Are we physically hunching down, folding inward, trying to make ourselves small or invisible?
  - Are we subconsciously blocking our energy, oxygen, and blood flow, thus making breathing more labored or making our hearts race?
  - Can we make subtle physical adjustments to expand our bodies and frames taller and more open (instead of hunched or folded inward) so we can breathe, move, and think better?
    - For example: we can adopt an athlete's balanced stance with our weight evenly distributed on both feet (seated or standing), open

up our arms and hands, throw our shoulders back, and send excess
energy into a podium or another physical object . . .

Then, armed with this enhanced self-awareness, perhaps for the first time in
our lives, we adopt *new* mental and physical strategies for approaching the
oral argument in a conscious, deliberate, and thoughtful way. This method of
reflection coupled with considered action is the opposite of *just doing it*. Of
course, we address the substance and procedure of the arguments and how to
handle the unpredictability of judges' questions. We also talk a bit about oral
advocacy style. But the primary focus of the workshops is to craft practical *mental* and *physical* strategies to diminish the intensity of our anxiety, so our brains
can function at peak levels and power us through the experience.

To welcome workshop participants, I post flyers around the law school and
advertise on TV monitors in the lobby. At two different law schools, running
these workshops for five consecutive years, I have been gratified to work with
more than a hundred participants. Few things are more rewarding for me as
a teacher than hearing that students who absolutely wanted nothing to do
with the oral argument were able to navigate the challenge, approached it
authentically in their own advocacy voices and styles, were invited to join the
moot court team, and became excited to further untangle public speaking
anxiety!

One year, I was a bit disheartened to overhear a comment about the workshops. This individual did not attend or observe the oral argument anxiety
workshops. Rather, she suggested that, through the workshops' advertisement and promotion at the law school, they set a tone that the oral argument is something *to be feared* when in reality, "there's totally nothing to be
afraid of." Perhaps for her, yes. But for many law students, the fear is real.
Minimizing it accomplishes nothing. The fear also can be exacerbated by
professors who require students to perform mandatory practice rounds in
front of their classmates, with intense questioning and critique, under the
perhaps well intentioned but misguided premise that "the real performance
will be a walk in the park after this more difficult practice experience." No. It
won't. Simply forcing an individual to "face fear" and perform an activity—
especially before a peer audience—with absolutely no focus on the real fear-
inducing aspects of the task achieves nothing; it only reinforces fear in its
purest form.

Of course, workshops like these are not for everyone and may not even
be the best solution, but they accomplish one important task: acknowledging
the reality of fear. Instead of assuming that every law student can just ignore
fear, push through a performance event, and everything will be fine, a little

empathy for those who need a boost and some tangible collaborative guidance can work wonders.

LIVE-CLIENT INTERACTION AND SUMMER JOBS

Law students can encounter another ramp-up of collective nervous energy when applying for and working in clinics: small groups of students working directly with professors in live-client representation. During the clinic application process, some students have confided their fears: *Wait, I'm going to be working on legal matters for real clients? As a 2L? But I don't know anything yet. What if I make a mistake and someone loses money? What if the client goes to jail? What if she gets deported? What if he loses custody of his child?* Of course, these students desire and aspire to real-life legal experience, but the associated high stakes can be more daunting for some classmates than others.

Additionally, as career planning departments schedule summer job search workshops and on-campus interviewing events, another buzz begins. Classmates banter about internships and externships, and career paths targeted toward criminal law, corporate, social justice, public interest, litigation. For some students, yet another internal dialogue commences: *Why does it seem like everyone but me has their lives figured out? If I have no idea what type of law I want to practice, does that mean I'm behind the 8-ball? Does that mean I'm not cut out for this?* As more and more of our friends accept job offers, some of us begin to worry whether we too will land gainful employment. We have loans to repay, rent to cover. The instinct to compare ourselves to others kicks in. As one law student put it, "Since my commencement of law school, I have seen myself spiral into the most irrational mindsets, crippled with the fear that nothing is going to come to fruition."

In reality, we are all unique individuals with different career paths, timelines, and destinies. It is easy in law school to lose sight of this individuality and succumb to the feeling that we should be doing what everyone else is doing, at the same rocket-fire pace. Through doing the work we'll discuss in Part IV, we'll discover who we are as individuals, focus on our authentic legal personas, and forge our own paths.

MISTAKE-MAKING

Eventually, we manage to run all the foregoing gauntlets. We navigate the Socratic method, final exams, oral arguments, client-based simulations, extracurricular organization tryouts, clinics, and the summer job market. We step into our first, or second, or third legal jobs and a new fear can arise. What if we make a mistake? Who can we ask for guidance or mentorship? Will we appear unqualified if we admit we are not sure what substantive, procedural, or tactical move to make?

What if we don't know how to properly redline a contract using "Track Changes"? Did we learn that in law school? How do we decipher seemingly unintelligible procedural rules about serving a subpoena? When is it appropriate to bother the perpetually harried senior partner to ask for clarification about an assignment? What if we have researched literally all night and we still can't find a single case on point? What if we realize someone else in the office made a mistake? What if we are that person?

As one law student notes:

> *To an intern, one mistake can seem like a momentous, life-changing catastrophe resulting in a lifetime of unemployment and debt. How can an intern not feel nervous? . . . A good presentation to a major partner could mean a six-figure job; a bad presentation can mean a lifetime [of] mediocrity. At least that is how it feels as a law student.*

Another law student described his fear and anxiety during his internship this way:

> *The anxieties live between these two poles of expectations: how much am I expected not to know, and how much do I need to know. If the expectations are not clearly defined and no one is there to guide you, the high-wire act becomes especially difficult, and sometimes perilous.*

Another law student summarized how her fear *physically* presented during her internship:

> *My fear and anxiety manifested itself in feelings of nervousness when interacting with clients and more senior attorneys. My palms felt sweaty, my heart was racing, and [my] voice trembled when I had to speak on substantive issues that I was responsible for researching and handling. I was worried that I would look foolish and inexperienced and that I would say something that betrayed my nervousness and lack of certainty regarding my place in the legal profession.*

One more student similarly reported a physical reaction when he was assigned the task of writing an appellate brief for a demanding supervising attorney: "My anxiety tends to manifest in that I either start to stutter somewhat or start to shake a little. I can also tend to lose focus or avoid focusing on the assignment, because the pressure to complete the assignment can overwhelm me."

Concerns about making a mistake in our first legal job can spark fears that we don't address much, if at all, in law school. Later, in Part IV, we'll talk about strategies for untangling these fears and developing fortitude to know when and how to seek guidance from an appropriate law office mentor, in addition to preventing, handling, and addressing mistakes.

Fear of Not Being Able to Find an Answer to a Research Assignment in an Internship, Externship, or a Summer Job

One law student extern described the fear associated with not being able to find the answer to a research assignment:

> I went into my [managing attorney's] office and he immediately assigned me a research assignment. He briefly spoke about the merits of the case and expected me to return with supporting precedent within the next two hours. To make a long story short, I did not have the answers he was looking for. Those two hours were the epitome of my anxiety taking over my mind, convincing me that I was a failure. I was brought to disappointment and fear, as though that moment was the defining factor for his assessment of my work for the remainder of my externship. . . . I neglected to focus on the fact that this was a learning experience, and I am supposed to "mess up."

Another law student shared a similar experience in struggling to find an answer in a research assignment:

> One of the junior attorneys here sent me an assignment surrounding a civil procedure question. . . . Like any other assignment, I rolled up my sleeves and started researching Westlaw and Google for any potential answers. After days of research, which included parsing through treatises, articles, legislation, and case law, I simply could not find the answer. . . . Sweaty palms, heart racing, and thoughts in disarray—the feelings I knew all too well were creeping to the forefront. How was I going to tell this attorney that I could not find the answer? Was I missing something obvious that he would find in no time?

And one more:

> I was finding nothing, and I kept getting more and more fearful that I was not going to be able to adequately perform my task for our client. . . . I knew that

if I did not find any concrete law or any law that I could reasonably interpret to include our client's type of transaction, my research would be entirely speculative, and this made me even more scared. Not only was I nervous that the client was going to engage in this activity based on my research, but I was also nervous that the founding partner and the associates were going to get angry with me since I could not find the answer to the legal issue.

BAR EXAM

Of course, once we walk across the stage to accept our law school diploma, some of us worry about passing the bar exam even though we treat our bar studies like a job, attend every bar prep workshop, and push ourselves through practice multiple-choice tests and essay drills.

As one 2L law student puts it:

> *The difficulty of the bar exam is not only the substance part of it, but also the fear of possible failure. . . . Although many have told me not to worry about the bar exam as a rising 2L, I nonetheless still lose many nights of sleep and frequently stress about it. For me, the room for error is smaller. Unlike many of our colleagues in school, I have a significant other and a young child who depend on me to succeed.*

Then, we ultimately pass the bar. Some well-meaning family members, friends, and mentors razz us with, "See! You worried for nothing!" Your worries are not nothing. Your worries are valid, and I know that they cause pain and distress along the way, even if the result turns out positively. Together, let's figure out a better way to understand our fears and worries so we can dial them down a notch, or two, or three, or remove them altogether—consciously and with self-awareness.

Testimonial from a Third-Year Law Student

I could probably write a book about the fear I experienced in law school and in legal internships. One specific example stands out: my moot court competition. The competition was in March, but my team practiced three times a week for three hours beginning in January. Before every practice, I would get extremely nervous. We would practice in front of peers and older students, and sometimes even professors. My stomach would be in knots the whole morning leading up to practice and my thoughts would race: What if I say something stupid? What if I stumble on my words?

What if I can't answer a judge's question? What if they think I am an idiot? Before my argument, I went through a routine of breathing exercises and repeating mantras to try and remain calm. I would go to the bathroom and practice the "power pose" I learned about in Professor Amy Cuddy's TED Talk[3] and pump myself up. During the week leading up to the competition, I was even worse. I could barely eat and felt on edge the entire week. On the morning of competition, I went through my pre-game routine of breathing, mantras, and practice. I completed the argument and did better than I expected—our team made it to the semifinals. The success does not diminish the fear.

Allison Cunneen, Brooklyn Law School Moot Court Honor Society, 2018–2019 editor in chief of *Brooklyn Law Review*

When I asked Ali whether she preferred I keep her reflection anonymous, she responded, "Feel free to use my name. Not ashamed of my fear!" More powerful words were never spoken!

My college and law school friends used to refer to me in jest as "A-minus Brown." I would fret about all my academic tasks, events, and scenarios, yet often ended up with an A- (except for that pesky C+ in Crim Law, which still haunts me in my dreams). My pals seemed to think that all the ruminating was pointless because I typically achieved my goal. What they didn't, and many still don't, understand is that when fear is involved, until we untangle it, the knowledge or hard evidence that we did well in the past has no correlation to how we automatically and instinctively feel in the present. For many of us, our past accomplishments are never enough to convince us that we are going to win, excel, or even pass. Each time, a fresh fear response takes over, in an all-consuming way. Each new challenge feels like it will be the time we definitely are going to fail, lose, be judged, exposed, kicked out, rejected, excluded. This is why messages like "Just do it!" and "Fake it till you make it!" don't work in this context. We cannot keep stepping into intimidating performance scenarios expecting to *finally, this time*, be fear-free unless we enhance our awareness and change our approach entirely. And we can do that.

UNTANGLING FEAR IN LAW SCHOOL

Although the foregoing scenarios and student testimonials depict vignettes of real fear in law school, fear is not a topic that we discuss much, if at all, in legal education. Let's change this. Let's analyze it. *Why* do some of us feel intense fear in the law classroom? Or in oral arguments? *What* exactly are we afraid will happen? *Who* are we afraid of judging us, or deeming us unworthy? Do those specific individuals have real authority or power over us? Or can we obtain a great legal education *and* reduce or eliminate our fear?

Attorney Richard Friedling notes how the traditional method of law teaching fails to adequately address the reality of fear—in particular, the fear of mistake-making.[36] He writes:

> *Unfortunately, many law schools' methodology consists of three years of blunt force trauma rather than the skillful wielding of a honed scalpel by the rare great teacher. It would therefore be surprising if a lawyer embarking on a first trial was skilled not only in critical examination of facts and evidence, but wasn't also so utterly lacking in confidence that she or he cannot say anything to a judge, jury, or opponent without endless equivocation for fear of making a "mistake" or just plain appearing foolish.*[37]

Some law professors who luckily never experienced this type or level of fear might naturally or instinctively reinforce the advice to "Get over yourself and do what scares you." In fact, at one of my presentations at a regional law conference, a seasoned law professor commented, "I just tell my students to get over themselves. It's not about you; it's about the client." Unfortunately, that approach diminishes the scared student even further. Instead of just telling students to ignore their fears—and that their own fears aren't actually important in the face of a client's issues (which is not at all true)—we can help students understand and work through the fear drivers.

At another national law conference, a professor noted, "Cold-calling is the only way to make sure students are prepared for class. The fear is good for them. It keeps them on their toes." Again, fear is *not* good for anyone in this arena. Many fearful students are impeccably prepared. Terrifying them derails their hard work. Instead, if we have a little empathy for a diligent but scared student and can facilitate a classroom dynamic in which everyone can thrive, these students will shine. Friedling reinforces this view, stating that "[l]aw schools' conviction that inculcating fear and insecurity [works] to engender critical thinking, is seldom accompanied by its intended intellectual pay-off: *Confidence.*"[38]

As mentioned earlier in the Introduction, Professor Abigail A. Patthoff wrote an illuminating law review article called "This is Your Brain on Law School: The Impact of Fear-Based Narratives on Law Students."[39] In the article, she highlights the risks of law professors' use of fear in teaching. Professor Patthoff describes how some professors use "cautionary tales" of "a lawyer or law student behaving unprofessionally and then suffering consequences."[40]

She defines such tales as "a common type of fear-based message that law professors use to motivate students to engage in a number of positive, professional behaviors: to proofread their work, to be candid with the court, to be attentive to citation form, and to update their authority."[41] She cites examples such as "attorneys who were sanctioned for poor citation form, attorneys who were publicly 'bench-slapped' in a court opinion for writing an incoherent brief, or attorneys who lost a client millions with an errant comma."[42] The consequences are dire in some of the war stories we tell our students: disbarment, court sanctions, significant financial loss.[43] Professor Patthoff cautions that "[t]hese kinds of narratives have great potential to persuade students to adopt such [positive] behaviors; however, they also have potential to backfire."[44] Citing social science research describing "a point at which scare tactics actually have the perverse effect of discouraging listeners to adopt recommended behaviors,"[45] she recommends that law professors be "more thoughtful" toward the stakes of using fear to educate.[46]

I'm glad I read Professor Patthoff's article because, unwittingly, I was one of those law professors using the provocative concept of "bench slaps" to demonstrate to my legal writing students the consequences of not following court rules. Two of my published law review articles focus entirely on "benchslappery" (judges' public admonitions of lawyers who submit poorly written briefs or work product that flouts procedural rules)![47] I realized I needed to find a better way to make the point. Just because we've been doing something a certain way for years and it seems to work "fine" doesn't mean we can't change. In fact, renowned choreographer, dancer, and author Twyla Tharp said, "If you only do what you know and do it very, very well, chances are that you won't fail. You'll just stagnate, and your work will get less and less interesting, and that's failure by erosion."

Legal educators can adjust and cultivate an environment in which law students feel comfortable expressing fears to individuals who will listen and help them untangle their worries in a supportive, practical manner. Law students can lead the way in this charge even if their institutions have not begun to do this formally yet (using techniques suggested in Part IV). The Task Force on Lawyer Well-Being has issued a call to action for members of the profession to commit to "reducing the level of toxicity in our profession."[48] The Task Force's 2017 report points out that "[f]aculty have significant sway over students but generally students are reluctant to approach them with personal problems, especially relating to their mental health."[49] To facilitate collaborative dialogue among faculty, law school administrators, and students about the reality of fear in law school, let's change the way we educate, and empower students to be open about expressing fears. We can let go of traditions or methods that reinforce fear and that ultimately hinder and exclude the fearful from learning. The Task Force report posits that "[h]armful practices should not be defended solely on the ground that law school has always been this way."[50]

As a law school community of students, teachers, and administrators, instead of reinforcing a law school culture in which fear breeds and festers, together we can endeavor to recognize our inadvertent promotion of fear-based narratives and reframe our motivational techniques. We can empower students to identify the presence of fear and ask for help. In turn, we can provide tangible resources, strategies, and techniques—perhaps like those described in later chapters and Appendices A through E—so law students can begin to disassemble these fears and distinguish unproductive components from potentially helpful aspects. Then, we can encourage students to forge ahead with enhanced mental and physical self-awareness as they step into performance-oriented scenarios in the legal arena. As Dr. Phil Nuernberger points out, "[w]hile law schools do an excellent job in training lawyers, they do little to train the individual in how to survive as a human being within the legal system."[51] Part of being a human being is honoring real emotions—in ourselves and others. To be healthy and well-balanced students and practitioners, we need to develop enough self-awareness to recognize our own stressors and then incorporate positive mental and physical strategies to defuse unhealthy toxicity. To be effective advocates, we also need to enhance our sensitivity to others' emotions: those of our colleagues, our clients, and our adversaries. This self-growth process can begin in law school. Through acknowledging and addressing fear as a reality in law school, law students will be better primed to handle the intricacies and challenges of law practice.

Law professors might truly believe fear is an effective teaching tool, but law students are straight up telling us it is not. As one law student put it, "It is clear from my observations of other attorneys and my own personal experiences that fear is not a useful feeling in the legal profession. . . . The profession would benefit from focusing a bit more on developing lawyers' confidence rather than scaring law students and lawyers just beginning to practice. The profession should seek to build lawyers up instead of [seeing] if they are tough." Another student poignantly notes, "While the prevailing culture in the legal profession is to keep your head down, work hard, admit no weakness, we cannot be effective attorneys by making decisions riddled by fear." I wholeheartedly agree.

If you are a law student experiencing fear in your educational journey, the first step toward untangling fear is acknowledging it. We can do that here—together—as we work through the chapters of this book. We don't need to hide it anymore, or pretend it doesn't exist. We will become our most powerful and courageous selves by first surfacing our fears, labeling them, and then getting to know them.

I'm not afraid of storms, for I'm learning how to sail my ship.
—Louisa May Alcott

CHAPTER 2

Fear in Lawyers

Unaddressed fear in law school can follow us like a clingy shadow into practice. Once we have passed the bar exam, landed the job, and begun to pay off our student loans, a new menu of fears surfaces in some of us. What if we don't know what we are doing? What if we don't understand the client's question or our boss's expectations on a project? What if we can't find the answer? Find the wrong answer? Spend too much time figuring out a legal problem? What if we take too long to object to opposing counsel's question in a deposition or at trial? Or need an extra few minutes to answer the judge's query? What if we turn red in a negotiation, or accidentally concede a key negotiating point we could have used as leverage for something else our client wants? Many new attorneys fear looking incompetent or unintelligent. They fear making a mistake, despite dogged efforts to research answers, follow the rules, and make smart decisions on thorny issues. Professor Joshua Rosenberg writes about how "many young lawyers often feel fearful, confused, dissatisfied, and generally unhappy."[52] He points to a common scenario in which a law firm partner assigns a research project to an associate and "describes the issue quickly."[53] The associate is not exactly sure how to proceed; she "fears that if she asks questions, [the partner] will be annoyed and will think her less capable. As a result, [the associate] does not ask any questions."[54]

As lawyers become more experienced, some fear malpractice or disciplinary action, despite striving daily to adhere to intricate procedural rules and meet every deadline. The pressure to win cases can spark fear in some litigators. As attorney William A. Trine notes, "The fear of losing, of embarrassment, of rejection by a jury, can immobilize a trial lawyer."[55] Other attorneys fear they may never get a handle on balancing work, home life, and happiness. As our practice goes on, years pass, and we become more senior at our law offices, our performance fears might transition to issues of client retention or business development, partnership contributions, and keeping the firm afloat. What if we can't make it rain?

ABA Journal author and managing editor Kevin Davis validates the existence of these concerns in our profession:

> [L]awyers often are imprisoned by fear. They're fearful that their cases are out of control. They're fearful of looking foolish. They're fearful of negotiating. They're fearful of appearing weak. Even continuing legal education courses can contribute by making lawyers fear that they are not up to date on current practices or wary of the myriad number of things that can go wrong.[56]

Davis explains that "[f]ear has become part of the legal culture because lawyers, like soldiers, often feel engaged in battle."[57] Unfortunately, instead of just vanquishing our legal foes, sometimes *we* become the casualties of war. Lack of conscious awareness of our feelings and our innately programmed responses to stressful situations can perpetuate the detrimental effects of fear. As author and expert on attorney performance Randall Kiser notes, "lawyers tend to be unaware of the 'wishes, fears, beliefs, and defenses that motivate our actions.'"[58]

In my first law firm, I loved nestling into a law library cubicle to research legal issues and write lengthy opinion letters, memoranda, and briefs related to our construction cases. I felt calm, motivated, and creative. I had a purpose and a mission, and I was successfully fulfilling both. Yet, if a conference call with a surly opposing counsel appeared on my day's schedule, my fear of sounding stupid, inexperienced, or weak would invade and disrupt those productive writing vibes in a nanosecond.

I fretted in anticipation of the unpredictable roller-coaster days involving depositions, negotiations, and court appearances. I ruminated before every client team meeting, worrying that I would be asked to justify each imperfect response a witness or expert gave in that week's testimony. I also feared the wrath of a particularly volatile partner if I exhibited a moment's hesitation over a directive to edit the same letter for the seventh time because I hadn't been able to read his mind or interpret his jot of "fix" in the margin. Though I learned a ton from him about litigation strategy and working every angle of our massive federal cases, I feared his erratic temper, his control over most daylight hours of my life, and the imminent yet inevitable demise of my most important relationship because I prioritized my boss and billable hours over the person I cared about the most. My life was a train wreck happening in slow motion. I ran three miles a day during lunch to fight the migraines, feign a healthy lifestyle, and fit into my chic power suits. Inside, I was a tangled emotional and mental mess.

Unresolved trauma?

In my second law firm—the BigLaw one in New York—I juggled new fears about never recovering from the grief of my relationship implosion with worries about my ability to function at a high intellectual level again. My work in that law firm was not as inspiring or interesting as my cases at the first firm. Having yet another explosive partner hurling books around the office next door did not do wonders for my psyche. I chugged along, alternatingly numb and flinching.

In my third firm—the small boutique one—my primary role as a brief-writer remotivated me. My fears persisted with respect to the performance scenarios though: the combative depositions with aggressive opposing counsel, negotiations of multimillion-dollar construction contracts with cocky lawyers disinclined to compromise, and even seemingly innocuous internal team meetings with yet *another* partner who had rage issues.

"Why did you stay in it so long if it was so awful?" people ask. Well, I kept telling myself that the stress was outweighed by the opportunity to get paid primarily to write for a living. I convinced myself that the anxiety was offset by the intermittent moments of case triumphs based on the briefs I crafted or the performance scenarios I successfully piloted. I enjoyed the creative challenge of figuring out each client's problem. On the flip side, I also still perceived my fear as a personal weakness that I just needed to deal with on my own. After all, I consciously had chosen this profession and a litigation-focused career path. I had invested years of hard work and efforts toward achieving sufficient personal growth to "deal with" my demons. I had sacrificed my most important relationship. In my mind, I had earned the right to make a decent salary, and *this* was my best option. Indeed, some mentors and other people close to me implied I was lucky to be paid so well and, thus, I just needed to absorb the negative stuff. It just went with the territory, right? No job is perfect, right?

Through the difficult yet revelatory personal work I did in writing *The Introverted Lawyer*, and now in shaping *this* book, I realize how damaging those environments (and the messages to "suck it up and deal" reinforced by key influencers in my life) were. It was harmful for my law firms to normalize the bad behavior that junior associates endured from some bullying partners and adverse counsel. It was toxic to label those of us who resisted the combative approach as weak. *Just grow a thicker skin* is not acceptable professional development advice. Our profession is, or should be, better than this.

In those three different law firm experiences spanning more than two decades, not once do I recall anyone talking about the reality of fear or anyone's mental, physical, or emotional well-being. Conversely, it was a badge of honor among my peers to run ourselves ragged and pretend we wanted more, more, more. *Work hard, play hard, and never admit weakness. Never let them see you sweat.* The National Task Force on Lawyer Well-Being's 2017 report sheds some light on this historical aversion to talking about wellness (or lack thereof) in our profession:

> *Many in the legal profession have behaved, at best, as if their colleagues' well-being is none of their business. At worst, some appear to believe that supporting well-being will harm professional success. Many also appear to believe that lawyers' health problems are solely attributable to their own personal failings for which they are solely responsible.*[59]

In a profession often reflecting this "head in the sand" mind-set, lawyering becomes a survival of the fittest: who can weather the stress, the competition, the relationship fissures, the case wins and losses, the pressure to land new clients, and come out on top, outwardly unscathed and invincible. For many of us, even if we accomplish all the external manifestations of achievement, we hide the reality of fear inside. Its savage undercurrent takes a toll.

Now, lest this all sound too doomy-and-gloomy, I believe it is possible to stop the vicious cycle. By first acknowledging the existence of fear within our profession and pinpointing its unhealthy drivers, we can identify its detrimental consequences and begin to change our professional culture. Fear is not just an issue of personal well-being and job satisfaction affecting a small cadre of individuals in our law office environments. It has ripple effects on our relationships with one another and our clients, and on our ability to perform to our greatest potential. Through increased awareness of these broader influences and repercussions, we can start to untangle fear and make much-needed adjustments to the way we approach the practice of law and our interaction with one another and the people who need us most.

Let's first consider the tangible effects of fear in lawyering.

FEAR DIRECTLY AFFECTS ATTORNEYS' RELATIONSHIPS WITH CLIENTS

An attorney's obliviousness to, or unwillingness to honor, the reality of fear can interfere in the lawyer-client relationship. Professor Stephen Ellman and the four coauthors of *Lawyers and Clients: Critical Issues in Interviewing and Counseling*[60] underscore how certain emotions can obstruct the flow of communications between attorney and client. These authors urge attorneys experiencing road blocks in a relationship with a client to self-evaluate:

> *You as the attorney must be willing to engage in rigorous self-examination. You may and will have clients that you experience as "difficult," but you must always*

engage in reflection upon yourself, your skills and attitudes as a professional first, before you start a reflection upon and critique of your client.[61]

Professor Emeritus John Lande points out that "[m]any lawyers seem afraid of emotions."[62] This is not surprising; the detachment of emotions from lawyering arguably starts in law school. Law professors have acknowledged how "the traditional law school curriculum . . . asks students to apply rules and use reasoning detached from emotion."[63] Indeed, historically, law school has taught "students to compartmentalize rather than integrate their emotional and rational selves."[64]

Professor Lande urges, however, that "[e]motions provide a lot of valuable information, such as what is particularly important. Lawyers should particularly focus on their own fears, which typically permeate legal practice."[65] The authors of *Lawyers and Clients* identify fear as the number one emotion for "hindering"[66] a successful attorney-client relationship. They assert that fear "is often the foundational emotion for other hindering categories."[67] These authors validate the reality of fear in lawyering, stating, "[t]here are any number of situations that can and should cause fear and anxiety in a lawyer. For example—You are a new attorney. Or an old *civil* attorney doing *criminal* law."[68] However, this commentary takes it one step further and reinforces the message—one that unfortunately does not work for many of us—that fear is a *necessary* aspect of being a good lawyer:

If you have no fear or anxiety then you probably do not care enough about what you are doing, about yourself as a professional and person and/or about your client's life, liberty, property, or dignity. And then it is time to leave lawyering.[69]

Hmmm. We should either be afraid or leave lawyering? I've heard this from other academics too (and students repeating this notion), but I respectfully disagree. In my experience, the message that "fear is necessary and shows we care" is not encouraging, motivating, or problem solving for those of us who are truly struggling. Destructive fear in our personal or professional lives is not healthy or essential in any measure or volume. Instead, by acknowledging and analyzing the reality of fear in our profession, we can untangle the toxic drivers of unnecessary mental and physical strain from the potentially healthy motivational catalysts, reframe our relationship with fear, and enhance our ability to perform at heightened levels of happiness, satisfaction, and excellence. We should not have to leave the profession to live a life without noxious fear. Thus, a huge first step is taking a step back to observe ourselves, and asking: Am I afraid of some aspect of this client relationship? *It's okay if I am.* And then we figure out why, and consider what we can do about it.

FEAR CAN LIMIT LAWYERS' CREATIVITY

Good lawyers are creative: in research, in problem solving, in argument development, in drafting. Sometimes the best solution to a legal dilemma is not immediately obvious from the contract, the statute, the regulation, the case law. In those circumstances, we must be flexible and imaginative. Unfortunately, fear can obstruct our ingenuity. Attorney William Trine states, "Trial lawyers are often prevented, by fear, from being creative."[70] Professor Kaci Bishop notes how "fear of failure might stifle attorneys' creativity in advocacy or willingness to take cases that might be more challenging but also more impactful."[71] Professor Bishop explains that "fear of failure can make someone more likely to overlook creative ways to advocate for his client and more reluctant to take a meritorious case just because he might lose it."[72]

I believe we can switch this "fear → creativity blockage" linkage around and, working backward, use creativity to unlock ourselves from fear's grip. The poet Sylvia Plath said, "The worst enemy to creativity is self-doubt." The artist Henri Matisse echoed this sentiment, stating, "Creativity takes courage." Turning this around and looking at it in reverse, creativity can be a salve or a foil to fear. In many lawyering activities in my construction practice, when my fear tornado began to orbit, I afforded myself a reprieve to think creatively about a problem. If the flow of a brief wasn't working and yet the deadline loomed, I tried to think of sometimes off-the-wall analogies that could apply even when the governing case law wasn't helping. When the partners were asking me to write yet another strident demand letter to opposing counsel, matching our opponent's combative tone, I brainstormed a different tack: What if we acknowledge in the letter that this nonstop bluster wasn't getting us anywhere, and use our imagination to try to address the human component of the conflict? This approach didn't always work (and I certainly encountered resistance), but it allowed me to step out of the fear cyclone and kick-start my brain. Regarding myself as an artist—even for just moments at a time—gave me a different perspective toward the client's legal problem and tempered my fear.

> Fear → Creativity Block
>
> Creativity → Can Unlock Us from Fear

As author Meera Lee Patel writes in her masterful book *My Friend Fear: Finding Magic in the Unknown*,[73] "[W]e are all artists ourselves. Living is art. Taking chances is art. Being present for ourselves and others is art."[74] Similarly, renowned dancer, choreographer, and author Twyla Tharp says,

"Creativity is an act of *defiance*. You're challenging the status quo. You're questioning accepted truths and principles."[75] As lawyers and legal writers, we can use creativity to rock the proverbial boat. If "business as usual" isn't working to solve a legal problem, let's get a little bit creatively *defiant*. Steven Pressfield, author of the helpful creative process books *The War of Art* and *Do the Work*, confirms that "[f]ear saps passion."[76] For artists (including lawyer-artists), fear manifests in resistance to our *work*.[77] But suppose we move past resistance by stepping into a creative process even momentarily. As Pressfield describes:

> A work-in-progress generates its own energy field. You, the artist or entrepreneur, are pouring love into the work; you are suffusing it with passion and intention and hope. This is serious juju. The universe responds to this. It has no choice.[78]

Thus, while unchecked fear can block creativity in our lawyering work, imagination and authentic artistry can toss fear upside down. (Part IV offers steps for constructing a creative process to help us untangle fear.)

FEAR CAN DETRIMENTALLY INFLUENCE LAWYERS' PERFORMANCE

Legal experts and commentators acknowledge that fear can undercut a smart, hardworking lawyer's ability to perform at peak levels. Professor Lande notes, "While fear often serves an important adaptive function, it is problematic when it is out of proportion to actual threats, is expressed inappropriately, or is chronically unaddressed effectively."[79] He confirms that "some lawyers' fears unnecessarily prevent them from performing well, producing good results for clients, earning more income, and experiencing greater satisfaction in their work."[80] A law student who had the opportunity to listen to numerous oral arguments each day in a judicial internship shared his observations of lawyers' fears affecting performance:

> Typically, there is an audience of approximately 100 people in the gallery. I have seen lawyers freeze under questioning, stuttering into dead air and unable to proceed. . . . [An] attorney who was allotted 6 minutes spent approximately half their time simply calming their own nerves, as the judge attempted to guide and coax them to words. On the one hand, one feels sympathy for those anxious lawyers; they remind you that everyone is human. On the other hand, the lawyer's client is paying them a substantial amount of money to represent them and ultimately succeed on that issue.

Further, *trauma* can beget fear, which in turn can decrease a lawyer's ability to connect and engage with clients, colleagues, and other key players in the legal arena. As we will explore in Chapter 13, which discusses fear in the context of sports performance, some of us experience trauma in the form of an abusive coach (or boss), a humiliating loss or failure, or an embarrassing mistake.[81] Indeed, some lawyers who handle cases for *traumatized clients* exhibit such symptoms of "vicarious trauma" as "a decreased sense of energy, no time for one's self, increased disconnection from loved ones, social withdrawal, and an increased sensitivity to violence, threat, or fear."[82] Lawyers with vicarious trauma also might experience "intrusive imagery, nightmares, increased fears for the safety of oneself and loved ones, avoidance of violent stimuli in the media, difficulty listening to clients' accounts of events, irritability, and emotional numbing and disassociation."[83] Chapter 7 will delve more deeply into the science of how and why fear blocks our performance as lawyers.

UNADDRESSED FEAR CAN LEAD TO MENTAL HEALTH ISSUES IN LAWYERS

Unchecked fear also can manifest in mental health challenges within the legal profession. In a 2015 *ABA Journal* article, "Lawyers Shackled by Fear, Fear Not," Kevin Davis reported that "[w]hile it's normal to feel anxiety before and during a trial, some attorneys may find their fears all-encompassing."[84] He explained that fear in lawyering "can be a problem when fear is out of proportion to the actual threats and remains unaddressed. It can lead to obsessive-compulsive disorder, panic attacks, phobias, and post-traumatic stress disorder."[85] Likewise, Professor Lande reiterates how unattended fear in lawyers "can lead to serious problems including mental health and substance abuse problems."[86]

Dr. Phil Nuernberger, author of the article "From Gunfighter to Samurai: Bringing Life Quality to the Practice of Law," advises corporate executives on stress management. He warns that "[t]he practice of law has become a dangerous occupation. While law practice can be intensely rewarding, its demands can create subtle traps. Even financial success doesn't prevent the increasing toll in poor health, alcohol and drug problems, fractured family life, and loneliness."[87] Dr. Nuernberger, a well-known psychologist, notes that "[f]ears of letting a client down, of losing a case, of losing income—all these fears prevent concentration, and interfere with every function of your mind."[88]

We can stop this phenomenon. It starts with acknowledging the reality of fear in lawyering and no longer letting it go untended.

A GIANT FIRST STEP: LAWYERS OPENING UP ABOUT THEIR EXPERIENCES WITH FEAR

Since January 2018 when my *ABA Journal* piece about fear in lawyering ran,[89] I have been receiving emails from lawyers across the country (and one from Australia), sharing their experiences with, and perspectives on, the reality and role of fear in their legal careers. These emails reflect voices of lawyers from a wide range of experience levels in law practice and wildly different geographical locations and substantive areas of focus. Their words echo a common theme: Fear in lawyering is real. Here are a few excerpts.

You don't know me and I don't know you. But your article about fear has changed my approach to the practice of law. In my short three years of practice, I haven't yet read an article or heard another lawyer spell out the way I've felt quite like your article articulated. I want to express appreciation to you for sharing those thoughts. I've resolved to be an advocate of the truth, which includes how I really feel (sometimes very fearful), and I'm confident that will make me a better lawyer.

—Danny C. Leavitt, fourth-year associate, Nebraska

I'm a young lawyer, still at my initial job out of law school, which is nonpartisan counsel to the Nevada Legislature. We are regularly called on to distill complex legal questions on the spot in legislative hearings, on the record, to be forever recorded in legislative history, and potentially used in future court battles over controversial laws. Not many understand what type of pressure this puts on attorneys who strive to provide thoughtful and complete analysis, let alone an attorney who is also introverted in nature. Add in the partisan politics of the individual that makes up our client—the Legislature as a whole—and you have the recipe for disaster for a quiet attorney. I'll be sharing your insights with others in my office. Your words are gold here.

—Michael K. Morton, Senior Deputy Legislative Counsel, Legal Division, Legislative Counsel Bureau, Nevada

My path as a bankruptcy attorney contained many of the same hurdles mentioned in your article: late nights, fear of failure, and well-meaning mentors who told me to "google imposter syndrome" and "don't f-ck it up," and admonished me when I hesitated to go up against adversaries with better legal arguments (and twice my experience). The worst part: being civil was deemed "dovish" in my department. Despite being a firm poster-child (high billable hours, full time status, bar association speaker, writer, and a mother) for seven years, I was regularly belittled for being civil. The sad part was, junior attorneys were slowly losing their civility.

I retrained in a new practice area and joined an in-house legal department. I still work on difficult assignments, go up against tough adversaries, and work long hours. I also have a half dozen individuals around the globe who report to me, am responsible for a department budget, and still put out lots of fires. However, I am no longer harassed or belittled. As department lead, I not only set the tone but have the power to enforce it. It has been a life changer. Do I regret working 3000+ hours a year during the economic downturn, almost getting divorced, and almost missing the first 5 years of my child's life? No. It was great training and my salary kept my family housed, fed, and clothed. But, to the point of your article, does the benefit really outweigh the cost? It depends on the day.

—Senior counsel at a tech company, New Jersey

I joined an insurance company immediately after graduating from Wake Forest Law—many years ago. Something like '79 rings a bell. . . . [W]hen the Wake placement office called me one day about a lead [for a job at an insurance company], I said please send [them] my résumé. No worries that I hadn't taken the insurance elective or that Contracts was not my best subject in law school. I needed a job. Long story short, I grew from being petrified every time my phone would ring at work into being the chief legal officer of a publicly held insurance group. One of my mentors at my first job told me "Mike, don't be afraid of telling someone you don't know the answer." That was really great advice. I still stand by that today when a question comes my way that I need to research. There's still some "faking" going on out there today, but your article was spot on, and should be required reading for all 1Ls.

—Mike Colliflower, in-house counsel for a major insurance company

[The reality of fear is] very true for so many lawyers. One of my dearest friends became a permanent law clerk because she would get physically ill before every argument and would cringe any time her phone rang.

—BigLaw partner, New Orleans

I have had fantastic legal mentors over the years providing great technical mentoring. But I have received very little mentoring on coping with the normal fears of being a lawyer or coaching emotional legal intelligence, if there is such a thing. . . . I continue to work at my fears, particularly in those spontaneous moments when faced with an aggressive opponent where I do not have the luxury of time to reflect. Even recently, I have been told by my partners that I could have been more aggressive in certain situations. To what end, I ask myself? My client would not have gained anything had I done so. Perhaps it is purely the optics of those moments as seen by others and what the business world demands. In any event, I am comfortable with my style, reputation, and brand as a more soft-spoken lawyer and advocate.

—Financial Services partner, Kansas City

Thank you for putting into words what so many of us are hesitant to express. My former boss who is a truly amazing mentor taught me that preparation can diminish fear. He also taught me to do my best to differentiate between fear and nerves. He told me that nerves are okay because they show that I care about my work, but fear can paralyze. . . . Thank you for saying it's okay and for encouraging mentors to confront the issue.

—Third-year associate, New York

I felt like you elegantly called out an enormous issue that faces the legal industry. You perfectly described so many experiences I've had as well as experiences of my colleagues. Thank you for bringing attention to it and allowing it to be ok to speak of it. I'm quite confident your words had an impact—they certainly did for me.

—Christopher E. Erblich, partner, Husch Blackwell LLP, Phoenix

We need a new and empowering discourse in the law, and one that acknowledges that the law often attracts introverts (such as myself) who have to adapt or perish in order to practice our craft. The skills of legal analysis, research, and structuring an argument often favor introverts whilst the Darwinian culture of the law firm does not without some adaptation. Your article really resonated with my own journey.

—BigLaw partner, Sydney, Australia

I have no question that your conclusions and suggestions just have to be right. I am equally certain that your article will have a life and career enhancing effect on many readers who have experienced the feelings, anxiety, frustrations, etc. that you describe. . . . [In starting this discussion,] [y]ou are doing a great service to law students and to the profession.

—David Schoen, solo practitioner, New York

Additionally, I recently recorded a webinar about the power of introversion in the legal profession (based on the concepts in *The Introverted Lawyer*). As usual, I opened up about some of the fears I experienced throughout my law practice. Afterward, I received this touching note from a participant:

I participated in your webinar yesterday because I am an introvert and an attorney. I have been feeling incredible career pressure lately to "just do it," and have been finding it so difficult to stop the self-perpetuating, negative inner dialogue. The more I try to "be like the other attorneys," the more anxiety I feel and the worse I perform . . . which just makes the cycle worse because every blunder lends support to the inner monologue that someone like me should never have become an attorney in the first place. I was honestly in tears listening to your presentation. The sense of relief I felt was overwhelming. Not to minimize the value of your incredible advice, but what reduced me to tears of relief was the realization that I am not the only attorney who feels this way.

—Counsel, law firm, Virginia

The foregoing reflections attest to the reality of fear in lawyering and the willingness of lawyers in various career stages and subject matter areas of practice to start talking about it more openly. Notably, blog posts reacting to the 2018 death of a partner at the Los Angeles office of the law firm Sidley Austin specifically reference fear. Reflecting on her time as a law firm associate, senior columnist for *The American Lawyer*, Vivia Chen, wrote in a blog, "You live in constant fear that the client or rainmaking partner who's giving you work might cut you off any moment. . . . The cult of perfectionism is indeed pervasive in law firms—the notion that you should feel deep shame about an inconsequential typo or experience terror for not properly reading the unstated wishes of some client or senior partner."[90]

We are not alone in experiencing fear in lawyering. Together, we can acknowledge the existence of fear in our day-to-day life as advocates, and begin to untangle its knots, so that we can become the ever-more authentically powerful advocates we are meant to be.

Courage is the power to let go of the familiar.

—Raymond Lindquist

CHAPTER 3

Fear in Clients

Clients who come to us seeking legal advice experience fear, as well, about potential loss of freedom, property, financial security, reputation, social status, shelter, relationships, and other areas of possible forfeiture.[91] Former *ABA Journal* editor Steven Keeva notes, "[W]hether clients come to discuss a business dispute, a will or a contract, they almost invariably bring confusion, fear, and anger"[92] into the law office. Professional counselor R. Hal Ritter Jr. and Professor Patricia Wilson reinforce this reality: "People fear they will lose a job, their family, money, physical abilities, a marriage, or any other important concern in their life. . . . There is real pain in these words, and it is important that we respect the pain of a client's real or potential loss."[93]

The legal arena can be uncharted territory for nonlawyers, fraught with foreign terminology, lack of control, and confusion. This can be true whether the legal matter involves litigation, a transaction, or another life scenario (positive or negative) necessitating a lawyer's involvement. As attorney Gerald M. Welt points out:

> Whether the catalyst for the lawyer/client relationship is a new home, an invention, a contract, or litigation, suspicion and fear are frequently the client's companions. Anxiety inspired by media horror stories and movie caricatures of lawyers make each contact a delicate exchange.[94]

Indeed, lawyers on television and in movies are not always portrayed as readily empathetic toward clients, or as possessing high levels of the emotional intelligence necessary to sense, let alone reduce, fear in their clients. Authors Myron Kove and James M. Kosakow report that "the public has an ever-present and underlying fear of attorneys. It is neither important nor relevant whether that fear is justified. The reality is that the feeling exists, and if counsel does not take the time to discuss the fear with clients (particularly those with whom there has been a long-term relationship), it could have detrimental side-effects."[95]

Lawyer and legal marketing expert, Henry Dahut, points out that some law firms may be exacerbating potential clients' fears by the way in which they promote legal service offerings. He posits that advertising "[c]ampaigns focusing on fear disempower clients."[96] For instance, advertisements that prey upon business clients' "greed and ego" are really tapping into emotions "rooted in fear."[97] He cites as examples ads that boast about saving clients from business losses and such other benefits as promises of big payouts, or exclusivity or elitism in what types of clients the firm represents.[98] Echoing this concern, certified financial planner and tax counselor, Larry M. Elkin, CPA, wrote a blog article pointing out that "[l]awyers, especially those who specialize in class action suits, have long used television spots to solicit clients. And fear is a particularly potent advertising tactic."[99] To illustrate, he references lawyer advertisements that stoke fear about potential side effects of medication, reporting that ads like those can persuade viewers to stop taking medications without consulting their physicians *or* the law firm.[100]

Clinical law professor Philip M. Genty emphasizes the need for lawyers to have "an empathy of fear, i.e., an understanding of the client's deep fear and mistrust of the very legal system upon which the client must rely for a solution to his or her legal problem."[101] He indicates that this fear might initially have deterred clients from seeking legal assistance in the first place.[102] Similarly, professor and clinical supervisor Marla Lyn Mitchell-Cichon notes, "Sometimes clients' fears are misplaced; sometimes they are legitimate. It is important for the lawyer to probe the client's fears gently and deeply before proceeding with the case."[103]

Some lawyers who handle cases of the same types over and over might forget that a new client never has encountered any of the players, issues, or procedures comprising a given legal situation. Unless we put ourselves—at least temporarily—in the shoes of the client, we might fail to provide enough context. Inadvertently, we might presume that the client understands our references, our shortcuts, our abbreviations; worse, we might assume that the client doesn't need to know *all* the ins and outs of the substance and procedure of the representation. Depriving the client of sufficient context heightens fears, worries, and other destructive emotions.

In *Lawyers and Clients: Critical Issues in Interviewing and Counseling*, Stephen Ellman and his coauthors place fear at the top of the list of clients' emotions, stating that it is "likely to be the foundational emotion for all others that get expressed."[104] The drivers of each client's fear "and how they will show it will vary and be unique to each individual and case."[105] Lawyers—especially those who may not have fully tapped into their own fears—must understand that a client's "fear, stress and concern can be expressed in a range of ways that may not seem logical or appropriate in light of the way [the attorney] may be comfortable in seeing fear, stress and concern expressed."[106] This discomfort in the *attorney* can become a real barrier to effective attorney-client communication.

As attorney J. Mark Weiss describes, in addition to the legal dilemmas that bring clients to our office, those who seek legal advice "may also be dealing with severe grief, fear, anger, depression, denial, shame, contempt, guilt, blame, and other strong emotions. Many lawyers are uncomfortable being around strong emotions."[107] A lawyer's resistance to or minimization of a client's emotions—like fear—can have the deleterious effect of heightening the client's stress.

Weiss reinforces the pivotal role of emotion in a client's ultimate decision to seek legal advice by observing that "[m]ost clients seek legal help only when they are at a point of distress and fear, and are often susceptible to having their fears magnified even when not intended by the professional."[108] Herein lies the conflict: Agonizing emotions that may have prompted the client to seek advice might also hinder the client from communicating openly with the lawyer. The client very well could be enveloped by a heavy cloak of embarrassment, guilt, and shame.[109] Professor Roy M. Sobelson notes that "the fear of being judged may affect a client's forthrightness as much as the fear of disclosure."[110] These feelings can be emotionally and even physically painful.[111]

Professors Stefan H. Krieger and Richard K. Neumann Jr., authors of *Essential Lawyering Skills*, emphasize that the circumstances that prompt clients "to seek legal assistance may be one of the most distressing things that has ever happened to them."[112] Some clients may have experienced emotional or physical *trauma*. As clinical law professor Sara E. Gold writes, "Due to physiological changes in the brain, including the increased release of stress hormones and alterations in systems that detect danger and safety, people experiencing trauma can feel intense fear, helplessness, horror, emotional numbing, or detachment."[113] Clients may attempt to hide their emotions, triggering a tension that impedes effective and open communication with the lawyer.[114] Others may be more demonstrative and may even cry. Drawing an analogy to medical counseling, Professor Linda F. Smith explains that a patient's crying "is not an emotion but a symptom of one of various emotions from fear to anger to despair."[115] Ritter and Wilson emphasize that "[a]nger may also manifest itself as a client's being verbally aggressive, pushy, and demanding. These [expressions] may be loud and tense and often related to loss or the fear of loss."[116]

Clients may be fearful toward specific legal tasks or venues, such as the initial client interview, a deposition, or a court appearance. I have heard some lawyers remark that a degree of fear is good for a client or witness because it underscores the gravity of the performance scenario and motivates the individual to take the experience seriously. However, as attorney Henry Dahut cautions, "It's rare that clients are benefited by having their fears and worries reinforced or amplified."[117]

CLIENT FEARS WITH RESPECT TO INITIAL FACT-GATHERING INTERVIEWS

Even the initial meet-and-greet between a lawyer and client can be daunting. Professor Sobelson notes that "[n]ew clients often approach legal interviews with fear, anxiety, and nervousness. These feelings and the need to discuss embarrassing or damaging information may dramatically affect the communication between attorney and client."[118] In considering the attorney's potential role in exacerbating rather than allaying client fears in initial interviews, J. Mark Weiss reflected on his own techniques in questioning clients to gather preliminary information:

> *I found that the initial interview style I used in my litigation practice tended to magnify fears such as fears of the other party. Magnifying fears was not helpful for people as it tends to create a sense of either anger or helplessness (or both) for the client.*[119]

In writing about his realization, Weiss modeled openness to change: "I needed to unlearn ingrained habits."[120]

Many clients' fears about intake interviews can be fueled by the failure of the attorney to provide enough information about the logistics and purpose of the questions and answers. Regarding initial client interviews, Professor Laurie Shanks notes that "[r]arely does the lawyer explain to the bewildered or apprehensive client why the questions are important or how the answer will be used."[121] In Appendix D to this book, we will explore ways to untangle client fears in lawyering activities like these.

CLIENT FEARS ABOUT DEPOSITIONS

Two other lawyers, Kyle A. Lansberry and J. Robert Turnipseed, highlight how "[m]any witnesses are typically, and understandably, nervous, worried, or apprehensive about their depositions."[122] Depositions involve one (or more) opposing counsel questioning the deponent. The witness responds to questions under oath and penalty of perjury while a court reporter transcribes the entire exchange. Meanwhile, the witness's defending attorney interjects objections to the form of the deposing attorney's questions. Depositions are sometimes antagonistic. Even the most collaborative exchanges can be mentally, emotionally, and physically draining over several hours or a full day of questioning. Deponents who do not understand the questioner's logic or tactics may be afraid of saying the wrong thing. The presence of the court reporter and sometimes even a videographer lends an official air to the proceedings that can intimidate a layperson. Lansberry and Turnipseed caution lawyers against glossing over a deponent's fear:

> *Although young lawyers, and many seasoned veterans, are themselves nervous about the prospects of engaging in a deposition, the prudent practitioner should not overlook his client's fears of the deposition process. Indeed, a client's fear or anxiety toward his deposition can greatly diminish the value and quality of his deposition testimony.*[123]

Conversely, providing thorough context with respect to the logistics and dynamics of a deposition can help dial down a deponent's fear within this type of lawyering event.

CLIENT FEARS RELATING TO THE COURTROOM

The courtroom can ignite a certain level of fear in even the most composed client.[124] Lawyers and authors Lisa Blue and Robert Hirschhorn encourage attorneys to understand that "[y]our client is probably much more nervous about going to court than you are. She may be experiencing just general nerves, or she may have some specific fears that are overwhelming her."[125] Walking into a courthouse, navigating metal detectors, finding the proper courtroom, and being around hordes of other agitated, nervous people can cause a client (especially an introverted one) to feel overstimulated, overwhelmed, and out of control. Inside the courtroom, the docket might move quickly, and the client might feel dizzy as the players in the room maneuver and banter, using language the client does not understand. Even the nicest bailiffs, clerks, and judges might seem abrupt as they move cases forward. Whereas many litigators enjoy and thrive within the courtroom's heightened energy field, a client can feel lost and bewildered. A client may even feel misplaced shame simply being in the courthouse and the subject of a legal problem. These scenarios might be everyday occurrences for lawyers, but they can spark fear in clients because of their unpredictable nature: "Most clients are fearful of unknown challenges."[126]

WHEN LAWYERS OVERLOOK CLIENTS' FEARS

Two potential roadblocks exist with regard to an attorney's handling of client fears or other emotions. In one, the lawyer fails to perceive the emotion in the first place. In the other, the lawyer perceives the emotion but fails to address it at all, or doesn't display appropriate consideration. Professor Serena Stier describes one example of poor lawyering: "The lawyer is aware of the client's emotions—he notes that she looks scared—but he expresses no empathy with her fear."[127] Professor Stier quotes legal ethics scholar Charles Wolfram as follows:

> *The failure of lawyers to appreciate that they deal here with emotions, human values, beliefs, secret hopes and fears, prejudices, all of the aspects of humanity, is probably the single most important reason for client dissatisfaction with legal services.*[128]

Wolfram emphasizes that "the psychological needs of the person being provided the service may be the most compelling reason why the professional's services were sought."[129] Avoiding the client's fear—or implying that the client should just toughen up—is not the answer. Professor Stier advocates for addressing the client's fear directly.[130] How do we do this?

To be effective advocates, we first need to untangle the concept of fear in lawyering and get to know its drivers, starting with our own fears. Ideally, the process should start in law school, and then continue into practice. As Professor Shanks candidly states, "Law students don't know how to listen to a client's pain, fear, anger or despair."[131] The traditional law school curriculum does not meaningfully and sufficiently address the reality of client fears, or law student fears for that matter. Accordingly, many practicing attorneys do not know how to effectively address their own fears and then those of their clients—encumbrances that can become entwined. Clinical psychologist Dr. Stephanie Sogg and attorney Wilton Sogg illuminate the interrelationship between attorneys' and clients' fears, stating, "[y]our own fear is not only an echo of your client's fear, your fear itself may represent the very reaction your client expects from others."[132] If our clients worry about others' perception or judgment, and we reinforce that unease by our resistance to, or inability to process, emotions that are naturally triggered by the client's legal circumstance, the relationship will falter.

Together, we can fix this gap. Through the concepts explored in Part IV, we can heighten our awareness of our own fears, and understand how to disarm the inhibiting aspects of fear, and enhance our own personal power. In doing so, we will better notice and understand our *clients'* fears and be able to help them move through the cogs of the legal system with the right support.

Some lawyers may resist the notion that our job necessitates a closer look at our feelings and those of our clients, and an effort to attend to emotions that pose barriers to attorney-client communications. As Ritter and Wilson point out:

> *Mention the word "feelings" or emphasize too much of the lawyer's role as counselor and many attorneys are likely to write off such talk as touchy-feely nonsense, which at best will have no impact on the success of a particular matter, and at*

worst will shortchange the success of the case in favor of giving clients the warm fuzzies just before they are carted off to jail or sent home with a take-nothing judgment. For a lawyer to hold such a view, however, is potentially to shortchange the lawyer's own success in representing his or her clients.[133]

Similarly, Professor Melissa L. Nelken emphasizes that the practice of law "inevitably involves the lawyer deeply in the hopes, fears, and conflicts of her clients."[134] Indeed, if we gloss over feelings and simply barrel forward, focusing solely on rules, contract terms, or policy, we risk overlooking an essential component of effective legal representation and intelligent problem solving. Professor Barbara Glesner Fines and attorney Cathy Madsen highlight that "[f]eelings are facts that are relevant to the client's informed decision-making."[135] Fines and Madsen urge:

To ignore fear, anger, anxiety, sadness, denial, or any other psychological states of mind is to leave the client in a condition that makes rational informed decision-making difficult, if not impossible. Extreme stress interferes with the ability to receive information and to store that information in working memory. Simply put, if you are so distracted by fear ringing in your ears, you literally cannot hear much of what someone is saying to you and are unlikely to remember well that which you did hear.[136]

Professor Marjorie Silver affirms that "[w]e serve our clients best if we have emotional intelligence, if we are able to understand their fears, hopes, and dreams."[137]

To help us better understand the reality of client fears in various practice settings, experts in criminal law, immigration matters, domestic violence cases, domestic relations law, medical malpractice, corporate representation, estate planning, elder law, and bankruptcy have provided the following glimpses into client fears across those legal realms.

A GLIMPSE INTO CLIENT FEARS IN CRIMINAL LAW SETTINGS

Clients in criminal settings might fear their *lawyers* from the outset. Professor Roy Sobelson reports that some clients facing criminal charges "may fear that their lawyers are more committed to enforcing criminal laws than representing them as advocates. Clients may thus consciously or unconsciously fail to report critical information or express genuine feelings to their lawyers."[138]

Naturally, some defendants in criminal cases also fear going to jail or prison. Attorney Christopher T. Powell Jr. notes, "Initially, the intake experience is what intimidates clients, and then they fear everyday life behind bars followed by the fear of re-entry into society."[139]Andrew Snyder is a therapist who works with "first-time offenders and their families before, during, and after serving time."[140] He confirms that many "clients are distressed about going to prison and being away from their families."[141] He counsels these individuals about the reality of prison life, family separation issues, danger levels in various institutions, and possible manipulation by other inmates.[142]

An attorney with the New York County Defender Services, Katherine Bajuk, provides a poignant summary of client fears in the criminal justice realm. She reports:

> The greatest fear I see clients express is that of losing their liberty—being removed from their home, loved ones, jobs/school—and being incarcerated. Some of these clients are people who [have] built up their lives and are in terror of losing everything they've attained. Sometimes this is the first apartment they've ever had, or the first "on the books" or steady employment, or period of sobriety or mental stability.[143]

Bajuk further relays how many criminal defense clients "are also afraid of the unknown, and of things being beyond their control," including what evidence the prosecutor might present at trial (if not required to be produced in discovery), what the demographics of the jury might be, or which judge might be assigned to the case.[144] Bajuk indicates that "[s]ome clients express these fears by making desperate decisions."[145] Some leave the state or the country, or avoid returning to court, "hoping everything just goes away."[146] Bajuk shares how some clients communicate fear through "verbalizing anger," at the system, or at their own attorney.[147] Some clients convey fears through crying, especially when they hear news about higher-than-expected bail, no plea offers beyond jail or prison time, or felony rather than misdemeanor charges.[148]

Further, Bajuk emphasizes that "[c]lients who have intellectual deficits, [or] cognitive or mental health issues may have the above fears exacerbated from a lack of being able to understand what is happening, or having their anxiety, PTSD or depression heightened by the stress of the court process itself."[149] She notes visible physical signs of such fears, which include "shaking, fainting, involuntary movements of arms, legs or head (tics), rapid eye shifting, becoming incontinent, or slamming their heads against counsel table."[150]

Bajuk describes how "[s]ome of these clients refuse to discuss the case or engage with me in any way—either refusing to speak with me in court, refusing to be produced for counsel visits and video conferences, or never making eye contact."[151] Bajuk reports that fears in criminal clients can even lead to suicide attempts.[152]

One law student shared an observation of a client's fears during a summer externship in the criminal law field:

> *He was gaunt and much skinnier than the pictures I had seen of him in news articles and official documents. . . . Our client's eyes struggled to focus and his shaking hands made clear the fear that had taken hold of him. . . . It was not uncommon for [him] to cry during our meetings. . . . The agony from this unknown period of waiting caused his voice to tremble and his thoughts to circle to despair.*

A GLIMPSE INTO CLIENT FEARS IN IMMIGRATION CASES

One legal advocate who works in the immigration law arena shared her observations of client fears in immigrants navigating our legal system:

- Fear of never being with family again: spouses, children, grandparents, or unmarried loved ones
- Fear of running out of money for food, housing, and other essentials
- Fear of the ramifications of having to move to more expensive cities to obtain proper immigration documents
- Fear of children missing out on education while immigration status is pending
- Fear of death or conscription of children upon return to a home country
- Fear of being in limbo in perpetuity, unable to work and earn an income
- Fear of feeling useless or hopeless
- Fear of depression, especially in the family breadwinner
- Fear of instability
- Fear of not being believed
- Fear of the inability to protect one's family in unfamiliar surroundings
- Fear of getting sick (possibly due to different food, water, heat/cold, sanitation systems) and not having access to health care

A GLIMPSE INTO CLIENT FEARS IN DOMESTIC VIOLENCE CASES

A domestic violence component to an immigration client's legal matter can add several additional layers of fear. Domestic violence advocate Leslye E. Orloff, attorney Deeana Jang, and Professor Catherine F. Klein highlight that "[s]ome of the obstacles faced by battered immigrant women include a distrustful attitude toward the legal system, language and cultural barriers, and fear of deportation. Some battered immigrant women do not seek legal assistance to free them from an abusive relationship because they fear the legal system. This fear arises from their experiences with legal systems in their native countries."[153] These experts emphasize that "[f]or these clients, an inability to communicate emotionally charged experiences effectively in English, compounded by fears and misconceptions of the legal system, makes it virtually impossible for [them] to obtain an effective protective order without legal assistance."[154] Further, battered immigrant clients may "fear that the batterer will take the children out of the country."[155] In today's political climate, to an immigrant wishing to report or testify about a crime committed by someone else, "a courtroom is more daunting than ever."[156]

Attorney Devi Patel is the manager of pro bono programs at an agency called Legal Information for Families (LIFT), whose mission is "to enhance access to justice for children and families."[157] In helping low-income clients navigate family law issues, which often involve circumstances of domestic violence, Patel shares that some clients come to her harboring *initial* fears of not knowing or trusting the role of the person with whom they are speaking.[158] These clients may have been "shuffled back and forth" among different people within the legal system.[159] They are not certain whether the lawyer doing the initial intake interview is actually a representative of the government or the court, or is "on their side."[160] Cultural barriers can inhibit the client from asking about or understanding confidentiality rules.

Patel indicates that some clients fear "starting the journey" to resolve the legal issue.[161] They may never have confided in anyone about the problem necessitating legal intervention. Finally acknowledging the need for legal intervention can be scary and can conjure accompanying feelings of guilt and shame.[162] Some clients fear that the attorney will judge them for having remained in a violent relationship. They fear not being believed. They fear the consequences of sharing information that may, or will, get their family member in trouble.[163] These fears can manifest in crying, the use of selective words or phrasing in their communication, darting eyes, or avoiding eye contact altogether[164]—until the attorney can establish a trust relationship with such clients and help them understand and believe that the *clients* are in a position of power.

In domestic violence cases, clients experience well-founded fears of personal danger, which can result in physical or psychological harm, or even death. These clients may not be equipped to develop a necessary safety protocol; lawyers must recognize the client's fears and be able to assist with safety guidance.

A GLIMPSE INTO CLIENT FEARS IN DOMESTIC RELATIONS CASES

Attorney Harriet Newman Cohen is a founding partner of Cohen Rabin Stine Schumann LLP, a matrimonial and family law firm, and coauthor of *The Divorce Book for Men and Women: A Step-By-Step Guide to Gaining Your Freedom Without Losing Everything Else.*[165] She shared the following list of fears that her divorcing clients express:

- Starting over
- Revenge by one spouse
  - Divorce may be a time for a fresh start or a quest for revenge. For example, in one case, a couple together had decided to freeze embryos that they had created with the husband's sperm and the wife's inseminated eggs while both partners focused on their careers throughout their 30s. When they decided to divorce in their 40s, the wife wanted to have a right to have the embryos implanted, but the contract with the hospital provided that releasing embryos to either spouse would require the signature of both spouses. The husband refused to consent. The wife was devastated, particularly because the husband could procreate until his 80s while her clock was running out. Coaxing and cajoling the husband and his attorneys were of no avail. He remained adamant, and the law was on his side.
- Transitioning from a life of means to one of austerity
  - This fear may manifest in being cut off from adequate support and assets and even in not being able to socialize with the same group of people. The diminution in the standard of living at the time of divorce is particularly common when parties have signed prenuptial agreements (which are very difficult to set aside in New York City).
- Loss of financial security

- Running out of money
  - This is a serious fear even for a financially secure spouse, who can be asked to pay the counsel fees of the less financially secure spouse to "level the playing field." Divorce can and regularly does deplete hard-earned savings set aside for the education and well-being of children.

- Disruption of the family
  - Some spouses take children (both minor and emancipated) into their confidence and disparage the other parent, to the detriment of the children. Such parents frequently are unable to heed or "hear" the pleas of their lawyers to desist from such inimical conduct due to their deep-set hurt and anger at the other parent, or their inability to be introspective.

- The psychological effect of the divorce on one's children
  - Children may need psychotherapy during these trying times. Children also may be interviewed by a judge, assigned an "attorney for the child," subjected to interviews by a court-appointed forensic psychiatrist or psychologist, and made to feel as though they are being asked to choose, i.e., being placed in the middle of the maelstrom.

- Alienation from one's children
  - Some parties allege what is tantamount to the now discredited "parent alienation syndrome," which had traditionally been used to harass the mother and get the divorcing women to take less support from their husbands. Alienation of children does occur, but there are instances when children are reluctant about their relationship with one of the parents as a result of that parent's poor parenting conduct.

- Loss of respect by one's children
  - Not infrequently, battered spouses' children turn against them and side with the batterer, who may be seen as the more powerful parent and, therefore, the safer parent with whom to side. In such instances, the children also may copy the batterer's disrespectful conduct towards the battered spouse and may join in abusing that beleaguered parent, thereby causing the battered spouse to become the target of a child's abuse as well as the spouse's.

- Social stigma and humiliation
- Blackmail by the angry spouse

- ○ Some vindictive spouses are so fueled by their anger that they will contact bosses, friends, new partners of their ex-spouse, publications, and sources on the Internet. This occurs even though it is predictable that if financial reverses occur as a result of the vindictive conduct, the entire family will suffer the financial consequences.
- The spouse's emotional volatility or lack of humanity
- Losing the family home
  - ○ In some jurisdictions, the court has the power to sell the family home to provide each spouse with a fair share of the marital assets ("equitable distribution").
- Opposing counsel
  - ○ The level of stress during the case is directly related not only to the adversary spouse, but also to the personality profile of opposing counsel. Assuming that adverse counsel has control over his or her client, well-adjusted, dimensional, reasonable matrimonial lawyers who were mentored by talented and respected mentors in the field generally portend that a reasonable negotiation may ensue, or that litigation, if the case cannot be settled, will proceed in a civil and even cordial manner, zealous advocacy notwithstanding. Such an adversary will make every attempt to take his or her client in hand and educate and train the client to stay focused on attainable and fair goals, let go of anger, and work on moving forward in a positive and productive way. If adverse counsel, however, is, himself or herself, a warlike person who revels in toxicity, who may, in addition, have been mentored by an attorney with similar negative traits, that scenario foretells trouble for all—the court, the attorneys, the clients, and the families—as well as limitless financial and emotional costs.
- Embarrassment in admitting to counsel that the spouse handled all the finances
  - ○ Even a highly educated spouse may have allowed an overly controlling spouse to handle the marital finances, often to keep the peace. Sharing this with counsel may be embarrassing, and the resulting lack of financial knowledge will hamper the attorney's ability to advise the client as to what the likely financial scenarios will be. Fortunately, since the advent of "equitable distribution," there are mandatory disclosure and automatic orders that prevent a spouse from diminishing the marital "pot" once a matrimonial action has been commenced.

- Stress-related health issues
  - Fears for the future, whether due to loss of an intimate relationship, loss of relationships with the children or friends, or loss of adequate financial security, are not figments of a divorcing client's imagination. These potential losses strike fear into the heart of the divorcing party. This can wreak havoc upon the health and well-being of one or both parties and on the children.
- Loss of health insurance
  - Under the law, at the time of divorce, a spouse may and is likely to lose entitlement to health insurance coverage provided by the other spouse, and may need to obtain it on his or her own, at significant expense and effort.[166]

Other experts on the impact of divorce on clients highlight the reality of financial, social, and "what next" fears,[167] plus the "[f]ear of not being enough to get through your daily activities because there were two of you getting everything done before."[168] One expert emphasizes tangible fears of loss, the legal divorce process, and "what might happen on the other side."[169]

As noted in the preface to *Bounds of Advocacy*, published by the American Academy of Matrimonial Lawyers in 1992, "[f]ew human problems are as emotional, complicated or seem so important as those problems people bring to matrimonial lawyers."[170] While divorcing clients' feelings and outlooks "are central to problem solving and planning," unfortunately individuals going through this particular life trauma "are unlikely to be equipped to easily address those emotions."[171] Professor Fines and attorney Madsen point out that some "divorc[ing] couples avoid attorneys because they fear the lack of control and the exacerbation of conflict that introducing a lawyer may bring."[172] Further, "[t]he 'stakes' in family disputes may be economic, but the economics are imbued with fundamental psychological layers (whether the dissolution of a marriage, the breakup of a family business, or the challenge to an estate plan)."[173] Clients going through a divorce also might be struggling with "the need to relocate quickly, to find a safe place to store valuable possessions, even . . . escalating depression. All of these concerns are very real and sometimes as threatening as the legal trouble itself."[174]

Clients in child custody battles also fear that a spouse will reveal (or contrive) past troubling or compromising behavior by the client.[175] Other fears harbored by custody clients include "the other parent getting sole custody; not being able to enjoy one's full visitation rights; parental relocation or the child being alienated against their own mom or dad."[176] In some geographical locations, parents further "fear an international abduction" by the spouse.[177]

As one law student poignantly noted about his externship in family court, "The Family Court docket, in its nature, is a breeding ground for fear and anxiety. There are countless people who come to court for Temporary Restraining Orders (TROs) and Final Restraining Orders because they fear for their safety. There are people who fear losing custody of their children or have anxiety about their parental rights being terminated. The involvement of fragile, innocent children raises stakes."

Writing about collaborative family law practice, attorney J. Mark Weiss advises lawyers to "[r]ecognize that divorcing clients often cannot think clearly and may make poor decisions if they cannot distinguish reality from their own fears."[178] He emphasizes that family lawyers need to aid clients "by realizing when they are suffering from such fears and stress, and develop client counseling skills to help them move from fear to problem solving."[179] Indeed, family law practitioners "must be interdisciplinary. They must understand the psychological, social, and cultural influences on their clients' decisions and decision-making."[180] Lawyers must focus on understanding how "[c]lients' emotions, their fear, their anger and vulnerability, distort communication, obstruct prediction and paralyze planning—for divorce and for their clients' future."[181]

A GLIMPSE INTO CLIENT FEARS IN MEDICAL MALPRACTICE CASES

Health care risk management advisor Morris Jensby and attorneys Michelle Putvin and Mark A. Basurto advise that "[t]here can be no doubt that medical providers experience an emotional crisis when they are sued. Surprise, shock, anger, and fear are very common reactions to getting sued for malpractice."[182] These authors caution that "[m]inimizing—or completely ignoring—the emotional implications of a lawsuit for a medical provider can not only leave the medical provider feeling alone and abandoned, it can ultimately have a devastating effect on the defense of your case."[183] These authors report that "[m]ore than 95 percent of doctors experience some form of emotional distress in reaction to a medical malpractice lawsuit."[184] Further, "[w]hile the emotions felt by medical providers can vary in both type and depth, at the core are two base emotions: anger and fear."[185] These authors list various fears that can arise in medical malpractice defendants, including

- responsibility for the outcome to the patient
- an adverse verdict

- damage to reputation
- risk to career
- bankruptcy
- public repercussions
- loss of hope[186]

These authors highlight the following signs that might indicate the presence of fear in a medical malpractice client: excuses to postpone appearances at depositions, blame-casting, tears or quietude (which can signify a struggle with guilt or shame), and avoidance of dealing with the case.[187]

One law student described the palpable fears she observed in a medical malpractice *plaintiff* at a deposition that the student attended during her externship:

> *Our client was suing a hospital for negligence and medical malpractice regarding [his wife's] botched surgery. He was obviously not at fault. First of all, he was not even the victim and he was certainly not the one being sued, so I thought, "Why is he nervous? He's done nothing wrong." . . . [He] expressed his anxiety by talking too much and giving too much detail. . . . He kept interrupting and talking at the same time while the opposing counsel asked questions, which seemed to enrage the court reporter and frustrate both lawyers.*

The student shared her perception of how the deponent's own attorney made matters worse by expressing anger and telling the witness to "stop interrupting" in a harsh tone of voice. The witness "kept saying 'I'm sorry,' sitting further up in his chair, and covering his mouth with his hand while sighing at the same time—clearly nervous." Later, "he rubbed his forehead because he was so nervous." Feeling that the lawyer's behavior toward the deponent was adding to his angst, the student offered the deponent some water, advised him to take a deep breath, and reminded him that "not every answer has to be perfect; you don't have to know everything."

A GLIMPSE INTO CLIENT FEARS IN CORPORATE SETTINGS

Fear in corporate clients might seem to revolve primarily around potential loss of money or market share, but personal fears can loom as well. Bill Alsnauer, an attorney with the law firm of Hall Griffin LLP, specializes in construction defect and mortgage servicing litigation and was formerly senior legal counsel for a private company. He describes an unspoken fear among some corporate clients about having to report litigation surprises up the chain.[188] Corporate clients might not come right out and say, "I'm afraid," but they don't like surprises, and the implied fear is that they will have to "go to the C-level with a litigation surprise" without benefit of preparation for all possible outcomes by outside counsel.[189] Some clients fear the costs of litigation or other financial outlay, and bad results. Others fear media exposure—especially with the heightened and fast-paced role of social media—and loss of reputation.[190] Still others fear testifying at depositions and trial, and having to produce emails or other documents in discovery.

Christopher W. Martin, of the law firm Martin, Disiere, Jefferson & Wisdom, LLP, wrote an interesting article about how "the corporate culture of fear" can prevent in-house counsel and trial lawyers from considering the effective role of an apology in the context of insurance claims and litigation.[191] Martin indicates that "[r]esearch has shown that fear is the greatest impediment to an individual or organization ever being willing to issue an apology"[192] to a claimant. He explains that "[t]his corporate culture of fear in the context of an apology is frequently driven by in-house counsel or outside legal advice, which routinely discourage or even forbid corporate apologies in any context"[193]—to avoid the risk of presumed liability, guilt, or culpability.[194]

In a different vein, a professor of business law and ethics, Todd Haugh, reports that white-collar crime defendants experience fear "at the pre-investigation stage, when the individual is often covering up unethical behavior based on fear of losing a job, money, or reputation. This often leads to the actual crime being committed, such as obstruction of justice."[195] Once white-collar defendants are in the attorney's office, Professor Haugh conveys that "much client decision making is driven by fear of incarceration."[196] He indicates that most defendants in white-collar crime cases have had very little experience with the criminal justice system.[197] They fear "the unknown," jail, and being away from their families.[198] They also experience a mix of fears regarding what the people closest to them will think of them. Their fears toward losing their jobs and professional licenses are not unfounded.[199] They have financial fears as well, and worry about the effects on their family if they can no longer provide monetarily for spouses and children. While white-collar defendants might not express these fears directly, the fears are apparent through the questions they ask. Professor Haugh emphasizes that these are individuals who have achieved high levels of success because they are "adept at handling things" but now they are no longer in control.[200]

A GLIMPSE INTO CLIENT FEARS IN ESTATE PLANNING SETTINGS

Stefanie L. DeMario-Germershausen, an estate planning attorney with the Staten Island law firm of Angiuli & Gentile, LLP, shares how many of her clients express one or more of the following fears:

- "Preparing my estate planning will lead to my immediate demise."
- "If I do not put all my assets in a trust, the 'state' will take all my money."
- "If I leave my children as beneficiaries of my estate, my 'in-laws' will get everything."
- "If I put my assets in an irrevocable trust, it is the equivalent of losing control over everything I own."[201]

DeMario-Germershausen notes additional patterns of fears in estate planning clients:

- fear of naming children as fiduciaries
- fear of hurting one child's feelings by not naming that child as a fiduciary
- fear of doing estate planning too early
- fear of doing estate planning too late
- fear of not doing all the same estate planning documents as neighbors or friends
- fear of the unknown costs of estate planning
- fear of not being able to change any designations made in estate planning documents[202]

DeMario-Germershausen emphasizes that "clients that have never consulted with an attorney about their estate planning sometimes come along with much hesitation and fear."[203] She reports that clients "fear losing their nest egg, the costs of long-term care, and the health issues that are prompting the visit to the lawyer's office in the first place."[204] Ultimately, "it is our goal as practitioners to educate sufficiently so that clients understand they are in control."[205]

Professor and clinical supervisor Marla Lyn Mitchell-Cichon highlights similar fears and concerns in estate planning clients:

- "family pressure and undue influence"
- "failing physical or mental health"
- "loss of self-direction and power"[206]

Elder clients "may be afraid others will make decisions for them or simply 'take over' their lives."[207] Further, "[s]ome clients misunderstand or fear the very documents that can assist them. It is the lawyer's job to address those concerns and fears."[208]

Michael D. Grohman chairs the Private Client Services Practice Group at Duane Morris LLP, and heads the firm's New York office. He practices in the areas of tax and estate planning and administration, with particular emphasis on estate planning for owners of closely held businesses, professional athletes, and entertainers.[209] Grohman reports that some of his tax and estate planning clients fear loss of money, market share, and lifestyle.[210] Others fear what will happen to their businesses through family succession; some even fear "ruining their children" through too large an inheritance. Clients also fear illnesses when they begin to think about estate planning.[211]

A GLIMPSE INTO CLIENT FEARS IN ELDER LAW SETTINGS

Deirdre Lok is assistant director and general counsel at The Harry and Jeanette Weinberg Center for Elder Justice at the Hebrew Home at Riverdale. She shares the following fears that older adult clients exhibit:

- "Their worlds getting smaller and smaller," perhaps through cognitive decline, reductions in their ability to communicate, family members moving away, etc.
- The role of the lawyer, i.e., a new and unfamiliar authority figure in their lives
- Facing their own mortality or that of their life partner
- Facing financial, health care, and property disposition decisions in the first place
- Family dynamics and the influence of adult children or others over their daily lives and autonomy
- Losing their children's love or attention
- Manipulation or duress (emotional or physical)
- Perpetrators of abuse or violence, potentially within their own families
- Not having physical mobility to visit their attorney's office, or being dependent upon another person for mobility and transportation
- An office not having physical accommodations for a person who has difficulty climbing stairs or accessing spaces in a wheelchair

- Not having assistance to frequent the restroom
- General ageism, and the embarrassment or shame that can accompany shakiness (due to Parkinson's disease), declining eyesight, the onset of deafness, or personal hygiene issues (grooming, hair, teeth)
- Judgment of an inability to write or speak articulately
- Falling
- Confusion or "sundowning" (disorientation that can occur in clients with dementia or Alzheimer's disease)
- Losing personal possessions or making the right decisions on transition of possessions
- Being able to trust individuals providing advice, and then trust those persons ultimately designated to carry out one's wishes (including health care proxies)
- Not being able to stay in one's home
- The costs of insurance[212]

Like many clients in other practice areas, some clients in elder law cases are afraid to go to court, fearing the unknown and the judge.[213] Elder immigrant clients, and those with cultural differences or language barriers, experience an added layer of fear. Lok also relays how victims of elder abuse harbor a different set of fears, a reality that requires a lawyer to be "trauma-informed."[214]

A GLIMPSE INTO CLIENT FEARS IN BANKRUPTCY SETTINGS

Michelle Walker, an attorney with the North Carolina law firm of Parry Tyndall White, shared the following fears that she has observed in her bankruptcy clients:

- Fear of the debt collectors' persistent phone calls
- Fear of losing "things," the family home, the children (even if that fear is unfounded), and employment opportunities
- Fear of public shaming if individuals in the debtor's social circles find out about the bankruptcy
- Fear of impact on one's credit score and future ability to obtain credit

Walker indicates that bankruptcy clients can exhibit almost a "survivalistic" mentality. While they might not use the words, "I am afraid," she emphasizes that "the worry is evident."[215]

One law student shared her perception of the fear experienced by pro se bankruptcy debtors—on their own and without a lawyer—trying to "navigate through the technicalities of their bankruptcy cases in front of a large group of people." She described one debtor in particular who, at an initial case management conference, "was visibly nervous." Specifically, "he was unable to make eye contact with the judge and his voice shook as he was giving basic information about the case." Throughout the hearing, his "answers became increasingly unintelligible because he would become increasingly nervous." At a later hearing, the debtor "was clearly distraught; I could see perspiration collecting on his hairline and his voice shook as he explained to the judge that he could not afford to lose his home. I noticed people in the courtroom become uncomfortable as they noticed [the debtor] becoming increasingly anxious."

In Appendix D, we will explore strategies for recognizing, and then addressing, client fears.

> *Our deepest fear is not that we are inadequate. Our deepest fear is that we are powerful beyond measure. It is our light, not our darkness that most frightens us.*
> —Marianne Williamson

CHAPTER 4

The Role of Fear in Mistake-Making

Before we leap into untangling fear in lawyering, let's first touch on the role of fear in attorneys' approach to mistake-making in the practice of law. We'll soon move away from highlighting the challenging aspects of our profession and begin to focus on *solutions*. It's important, however, to recognize the role that fear plays in some lawyers' reluctance to ask for guidance on complex lawyering scenarios. This reticence can lead to errors and, further, subsequent hesitancy to admit a mistake. Unfortunately, missteps of both types can result in disciplinary or malpractice actions. For an attorney who is really struggling with fear in day-to-day practice or the pressure of interacting with fearful clients, these consequences can be traumatic. Yet, they are avoidable and solvable with the right level of self-awareness and an insightful action plan. As the report of the National Task Force on Lawyer Well-Being asserts with regard to serious attorney wellness concerns, "Discipline does not make an ill lawyer well."[216]

In 2006, Professor Michael Hatfield questioned whether there is a potential link between a client's fear and a lawyer's ethical transgressions:

> *Whether or not lawyers are more inclined to ethical lapses when their clients are in dangerous or highly fearful situations—or when the lawyer has an empathetic sense of the client's fear—has apparently not been systematically studied.*[217]

Further, he suggested, "Since clients only seek lawyers when they have some fear of loss (of money, business or freedom), the effect of fear in lawyers' ethics ought to be studied."[218] He also posed the question of "whether or not working in a pervasive context of fear has a significant part in a lawyer's self-reported low quality of life and high risks of alcoholism and depression."[219]

This book endeavors to shed some light on fear within the profession so that we can be happier, more effective, and ethically sound advocates.

EVEN GOOD LAWYERS MAKE MISTAKES

Attorney Jeffrey B. Kahan describes the scene vividly:

> *At one time or another, all attorneys stride confidently into the office, their minds focused on the job, to feel in a single stomach-tightening, knee-weakening moment their carefully built composure crash into oblivion as they recall one law never taught in law school—Murphy's. Like so many lawyers before them, their attention will return, perhaps on seeing their desk, to the oppositions they forgot to file, the court appearances they failed to make, or the winning arguments they failed to include in their last filings. However much a professional may strive for excellence, the human condition remains tragically mired in the imperfections of day-to-day life. Attorneys should therefore anticipate their fallibility and learn to cope with it.*[220]

The first two blunders just described sound like mistakes that ideally could be averted through a good calendaring system and electronic (and human!) reminders. But the third, a prevailing argument that might not have percolated by the time the lawyer drafted the brief under perhaps a quick turnaround deadline? That one is less clear-cut. What about the lawyer practicing for the first time in a new federal jurisdiction, say, the Eastern District of Virginia? She knows the FRCP discovery rules intimately but somehow missed the Local Rule 26(C) requirement that objections to discovery must be served within *fifteen days* after service of the discovery request, rather than the usual *thirty-day* deadline imposed in other federal jurisdictions. And then there is the associate who painstakingly sorted thousands of client files, making sure to scan every document to decide whether the content was privileged, or not privileged and therefore producible in response to opposing counsel's discovery request. He was unaware of a flash drive buried in the bottom of a production box that contained correspondence between counsel and the client. And the flash drive got swept into the production pile.

Mistakes happen in the practice of law, as some courts and lawyers have openly recognized. For example, in resolving a discovery dispute and evaluating a party's request for sanctions, one federal district court acknowledged that "all lawyers and all courts make mistakes."[221] Attorney R. Jeffrey Neer confirms, "Lawyers constantly face procedural requirements, deadlines, and the press of other business, and mistakes are guaranteed to occur."[222] Former attorneys and current law professors, Julie A. Oseid and Stephen D. Easton, concur:

> *Nobody can do anything of consequence in the practice of law without making mistakes. Every day you practice law you make mistakes. In fact, make that every*

hour—or almost every hour. Our profession is so complicated, so much "art"
instead of "science" that we all make mistakes, even though we try our best to
avoid them. I have made some doozies, and so has every single lawyer I respect."[223]

Professors Oseid and Easton reiterate that "mistakes are inevitable for all of
us flawed human beings, including the most caring and skilled of lawyers."[224]

Likewise, attorneys Dolores Dorsainvil, Douglas R. Richmond, and John
C. Bonnie quote the Idaho Supreme Court as stating: "Attorneys are human
beings who make mistakes; it is part of the profession. In some cases, it is what
an attorney does after a mistake that defines him or her, ethically."[225] Former
counsel to the Maryland Bar Glenn M. Grossman similarly advises new lawyers
that "they will make mistakes in the practice of law. How do I know? I tell them
I know because we all make mistakes. There should be no fear of making mistakes; mistakes are a given."[226]

Attorney Gaston Kroub challenges, "Show me a lawyer who has not made
a mistake in their career, and I will show you a lawyer who has never practiced a single day. Mistakes happen. Lawyers are human, and no matter how
well-trained, or how high their billing rate, there will be times when someone
screws up."[227] Nevada attorney Ryan J. Works corroborates this reality: "In this
profession, we all make mistakes. The problem is, not everyone takes responsibility for those mistakes."[228] Referencing a recent cut-and-paste drafting
mistake—which received major press coverage—involving an assistant U.S.
attorney who inadvertently disclosed charges against Wikileaks founder Julian
Assange in an unrelated court filing, a judge indicated, "We're all human. . . .
I make mistakes all the time."[229]

Mistake-making obviously is not unique to American lawyers. Canadian and
British lawyers recognize the reality of errors in the practice of law. Toronto
legal affairs writer Ann Macaulay quoted an unnamed lawyer as saying, "In
our business, we all make mistakes."[230] British legal reporter John Hyde agrees:
"Mistakes are inevitable."[231] In describing a British solicitor who made a mistake but hid it, Hyde urged law firms to "encourage a culture of openness and
make clear that admitting to a mistake will not cost staff their career. . . . When
a solicitor is so fearful to admit his own mistakes he will cough up £5,000 to
hide them, something is seriously wrong. Young solicitors should not be working in fear."[232]

Seasoned lawyers and judges know from experience that mistakes inevitably
happen in lawyering, despite diligence and care. Yet we seem to convey the
opposite message to law students and junior attorneys: the notion that good
lawyers are infallible. This fallacy can breed fear, a reluctance to ask for guidance, and the temptation to hide mistakes.

FEAR OF SHOWING WEAKNESS

Fear is a reality in lawyering, as the foregoing chapters illustrate, yet it is not a word often used in the law classroom or training ground. Benjamin Sells, author of *The Soul of the Law*,[233] describes this problem area in the training of lawyers. He highlights attorneys' internal conflict: we do not want to appear weak, but at the same time, we can find ourselves grappling with issues of integrity when confronted with a confusing legal quandary or a mistake. Sells explains:

> *For a lawyer to admit ignorance is to admit weakness, and to admit weakness is to open oneself to attack. People who are close to lawyers can attest to the depth of this training and often comment how rare it is to hear a lawyer admit to not knowing something. Lawyers are taught to bluff, expected to bluff. Lawyers must always give the impression of knowledge and confidence, must always know.*[234]

Sells notes, "The roots of the imposter syndrome begin in law school where lawyers are taught it is better to bluff than to admit ignorance."[235]

I vividly remember a scene from my evidence class in law school. To illustrate the wide coverage of the hearsay rule, my professor regaled us with a war story of one of her trials in which she admittedly was not paying rapt enough attention during opposing counsel's examination of a witness. At counsel's table, the senior partner sternly elbowed her, indicating she needed to object to the line of questioning. My professor described how she leapt from her chair and shouted, "Objection, hearsay!"—a mere guess at the flaw in the examiner's last question. "Sustained!" responded the judge. The class burst into laughter and applause. The lesson? Bluffing (or winging it with swagger) is cool.

Sells highlights the risks to our profession in promoting a bravado mind-set. He says that "[t]his kind of training creates a cult of individualism that leaves lawyers no way out. Expected to be forever self-sufficient, strong, knowing, aggressive, and confident, the lawyer is expected to be more than human."[236] He cautions that the "individuality taught in law school is false individuality. . . . *From the perspective of soul, individuality has to do with uniqueness and eccentricity, not self-confident isolation.*"[237] Sells notes how the legal profession struggles to "acknowledge weakness, vulnerability, quirkiness, and uncertainty as *essential* to our deepest individuality."[238]

A scholar on legal decision-making and author of *Soft Skills for the Effective Lawyer*, Randall Kiser, reports that the ABA has concerns about our profession's "tendency to overestimate our knowledge and underestimate its limitations."[239] Kiser reiterates that "[k]nowing what we don't know—and being upfront about it with clients—is particularly difficult for attorneys who have succeeded in an educational system that rewards quick answers and treats hesitancy as a scholastic deficiency."[240] Kiser notes the role of *fear* in lawyers' reluctance to pose questions that might showcase a lack of knowledge on a given subject.[241] Kiser explains the very real prevalence of the imposter syndrome in the legal profession and "a sense of intellectual phoniness" that can be reinforced by fear.[242] Of course, lawyers cannot possibly know every nuance of every law, rule, or factual consequence in a given substantive area, even if they have been practicing for years. Lawyers often need time to research, read, think, and analyze before conveying sound legal advice on a new dilemma posed by a client. Yet admitting or asserting the need for this processing time can feel uncomfortable in a profession that praises the quick confident assertion.

To counteract fear and to foster reasoned problem solving, Kiser emphasizes the need for "psychological safety" in learning and professional environments.[243] Professor Amy Edmondson of the Harvard Business School characterizes this concept as "a climate in which people feel free to express relevant thoughts and feelings."[244] More specifically, "[i]n a psychologically safe environment, people trust and respect each other and 'believe that if they make a mistake others will not penalize or think less of them for it. They also believe that others will not resent or humiliate them when they ask for help or information.'"[245]

Kiser describes an initiative by Google called Project Aristotle. As reported by Charles Duhigg, author of *Smarter, Faster, Better*, the company launched Project Aristotle "to study hundreds of Google's teams and figure out why some stumbled while others soared."[246] The positive impact of psychological safety became clear through Project Aristotle: to be an enthusiastic contributor in a healthy work environment, employees need to "know that we can be free enough, sometimes, to share the things that scare us without fear of recriminations."[247]

This idea of psychological safety is not talked about much (or enough) in legal training, especially in the context of the reality of fears relating to certain lawyering tasks and of making mistakes. As intellectual property lawyer, Gaston Kroub, describes:

> As with many other things related to law practice, younger lawyers are often not taught how to deal with the inevitable mistake when one happens. . . . In fact, other than being told not to make mistakes, younger lawyers, whether at Biglaw or smaller firms, often receive no training at all with respect to this issue. Making things worse is the tendency of firms to turn partners into demigods, who must have never made a mistake on the way to their current position. And no firm would ever admit that one of its current partners is capable of error. While definitely not true, this aspect of firm "culture" often serves to inculcate in younger

lawyers an irrational fear that if they make a single mistake—disaster. Bye-bye to their jobs, at least. . . . This is a silly state of affairs.[248]

Kroub recommends a straightforward and collaborative solution: teaching junior lawyers, and refreshing the recollection of seasoned ones, about how to appropriately handle mistakes, from a team-based perspective.[249] Junior lawyers need to know that "[e]ven hard-charging lawyers are able to forgive honest mistakes."[250] We need to change the message from "the best lawyers are infallible" to "mistakes will happen, and we are judged on how we deal with them."[251]

This training should start in law school. Legal education should incorporate more opportunities for law students to spot and diagnose tricky real-life circumstances in which substantive, procedural, and tactical mistakes can occur. Instruction should include acknowledging and discussing how fear of making a mistake or of asking for help can lead to flawed decision-making. Students can be proactive and seek out and learn practical strategies for requesting appropriate guidance from a superior in making a calculated choice or solving a legal dilemma. Through transparency and open dialogue about fear and mistake-making, law students can develop problem-solving competencies to prevent mistakes, own up to errors if they occur, and then remedy legal missteps in an ethical manner.

Glenn M. Grossman, former counsel of the Maryland Bar, acknowledges the role of *character* in teaching new attorneys how to handle lawyering mistakes:

> *It is their response to the mistakes that will often take character, integrity and perhaps, courage. I tell them that taking responsibility is not only a proof of character, but in the case of a lawyer, it's mandatory. So often in disciplinary work we see attorneys who simply will not admit to errors but blame others—the clients, opposing counsel, and failing those excuses, employees. The disciplinary result in such cases generally is not favorable.*[252]

Good attorneys distinguish themselves from bad ones, not in whether they make mistakes in complicated legal scenarios in the first place, but in how they handle legal errors.[253] Obviously, we want to avoid and prevent mistakes, but the real strength in lawyering lies in navigating missteps with integrity when they occur. Attorney Ryan J. Works echoes the same theme: "Almost all errors in life are manageable, easily fixed and thereafter soon forgotten by most. However, if you hide your mistake and someone else discovers it (which is certain to occur), you will have undoubtedly lost the trust of that person and will always be remembered for the attempted cover-up."[254]

It seems obvious to assert that persons with integrity and character will admit their mistakes, and that attorneys are no exception to this standard. But sometimes mistake acknowledgment is easier said than done in the legal context.

In selecting students for admission to our nation's law schools, various institutions' applications pose "character and fitness" questions to elicit information about prior academic or professional disciplinary history and criminal records. Some schools also ask about issues with financial responsibility and discharges from military service. Three years later, a candidate's admission to many state bars is contingent upon passing a character and fitness evaluation and submitting affidavits of good moral character. Bar applications ask questions about military service, academic and professional history, civil and criminal records, and financial history. Our profession seeks information about an applicant's character *before* law school, and then again *after* law school, but what are we doing *during* law school to cultivate character? Can we do more to shape fortitude, courage, and other positive character traits in our students, assets that will help them navigate substantive and tactical challenges in practice, admit when they need additional guidance, and manage mistakes appropriately? This raises the question: Is character a fixed innate state, or is it learnable?

IS "LAWYERING CHARACTER" LEARNABLE?

The Institute for the Advancement of the American Legal System (IAALS) is a "national, independent research center at the University of Denver dedicated to facilitating continuous improvement and advancing excellence in the American legal system."[255] Educating Tomorrow's Lawyers is an IAALS initiative focused on aligning legal education with the needs of the legal profession.[256] In July 2016, IAALS and Educating Tomorrow's Lawyers issued a report summarizing a national, multiyear project called Foundations for Practice. The goals of the study were threefold:

1. to identify the "foundations" that beginner lawyers need to launch successful careers in the legal profession;

2. to create assessable and transferable models of legal education that offer opportunities for law students to develop these foundations; and

3. to take a hard look at whether the requisite foundations dovetail with hiring practices, and if not, incentivize positive change in how employers recruit new attorneys.[257]

The executive summary of the report asserts that "new lawyers need character."[258] The findings gathered from a survey of more than 24,000 attorneys indicate that, in addition to an intelligence quotient and emotional intelligence, lawyers should consider their "character quotient (CQ)."[259]

The report starts by contending that "[t]he current dichotomous debate that places 'law school as trade school' up against 'law school as intellectual endeavor' is missing the sweet spot and the vision of what legal education could be and what type of lawyers it should be producing."[260] The report distinguishes among *characteristics*, *competencies*, and *skills*, defined as follows:[261]

- *characteristics*: "foundations capturing features or qualities" of a person
- *professional competencies*: "skills seen as useful across vocations"
- *legal skills*: proficiencies "traditionally understood to be required for the specific discipline of law"[262]

According to the lawyers surveyed, newly minted attorneys need *characteristics* such as integrity, trustworthiness, conscientiousness, and common sense, in addition to professional *competencies* such as active listening, good oral and written communications, and punctuality.[263] The survey respondents even prioritized the foregoing attributes over *skills* like dispute resolution techniques, trial preparation, or taking depositions.[264] The survey results' bottom line? New lawyers must possess a blend of legal skills and professional competencies, but also must demonstrate character.[265] The report indicated that "attorneys largely see *characteristics* as the most important foundations new lawyers need in the short term."[266]

While the ability to handle or admit mistakes was not an express category included in the survey, the report captured data indicating that "taking individual responsibility for actions and results" and "understanding when to engage [a] supervisor or seek advice in problem solving" rated as "most commonly identified as necessary right out of law school," in the Professional Development criterion.[267] In the Qualities and Talents category, 92.3% of respondents rated "integrity and trustworthiness" as "necessary in the short term."[268] Notably, "assertiveness" only scored 31.9% as necessary in the short term.[269] In fact, in the top 10 categories of foundations identified as "necessary in the short term," the item "integrity and trustworthiness" ranked fourth, after "keeping information confidential," "arriving on time for meetings, appointments, and hearings," and "honoring commitments."[270] "Maintaining core knowledge of the substantive and procedural law in the relevant focus area" scored only 50.7% as "necessary in the short term."[271]

Ultimately, among other recommendations, the report suggested that law schools should use the data to:

1. work with employers and the legal community to develop measurable learning outcomes for legal educators, and create and reward law school programs and courses that develop the requisite *characteristics, competencies,* and legal *skills* in students;

2. build those courses into law school curricula;

3. encourage prospective students and law students to assess their own *foundations* to help them make informed decisions about choosing law as a career path (or certain areas of practice);

4. encourage prospective students and law students to create individual learning plans that help them develop the necessary *foundations* in the courses they choose, and through other opportunities, like work experience and extra-curricular activities; and

5. evaluate the current criteria for admitting students to law school and consider new criteria that paint a picture of each applicant's *characteristics* and *competencies* beyond intelligence.[272]

Again, this call to action raises the question, can character be taught and learned?

According to Paul Tough, author of *How Children Succeed: Grit, Curiosity, and the Hidden Power of Character,*[273] the prefrontal cortex of the brain, which governs decision-making, planning, cognitive processing, management of social behavior, and impulse control, *is* malleable. It is "more responsive to intervention than other parts of the brain, and it stays flexible well into adolescence and early adulthood."[274] Tough states that, in contrast, "[p]ure IQ is stubbornly resistant to improvement after about age eight. But executive functions and the ability to handle stress and manage strong emotions can be improved, sometimes dramatically, well into adolescence and even adulthood."[275]

Dr. Martin Seligman is one of the pioneers and leading scholars of the positive psychology movement. With the late Dr. Christopher Peterson, he coauthored the book *Character Strengths and Virtues: A Handbook and Classification.* These psychologists defined character as "a set of abilities or strengths that are very much changeable—entirely malleable, in fact. They are skills you can learn; they are skills you can practice; and they are skills you can teach."[276] Dr. Thomas Lickona, a developmental psychologist and professor of education, wrote a book entitled *Educating for Character* that offers a "comprehensive approach" to character education, indicating that—according to some experts—character *is* teachable.[277]

In *How Children Succeed*, Tough describes a middle school teacher who experimented with the idea of giving students a CPA—a character point average—in addition to a GPA, as a "useful tool in communicating with students about character."[278] Another teacher noted that the "best way for a young person to build character is for him to attempt something where there is a real and serious possibility of failure."[279] Tough reiterates:

> *If you believe that your school's mission or your job as a teacher is simply to convey information, then it probably doesn't seem necessary to subject your students to . . . rigorous self-analysis. But if you're trying to help them change their character, then conveying information isn't enough.*[280]

Some seasoned legal educators initially might resist the notion of incorporating character building into a traditional law school curriculum. They might ask: Sure, it's fine to focus on character in grade school, but isn't law school too late? How would a law professor teach character? In which course or courses would this even be possible?

We can, and should, teach law students (and junior attorneys) about *character in the context* of lawyering. If courses incorporating character building do not currently exist at a particular institution, students can seek out and create their own educational opportunities to build character-in-context. This can happen through engaging in transparent dialogues with peers, mentors, and practitioners about the reality of fear and mistake-making in lawyering, either in the classroom or in extracurricular workshops or roundtables. Some ideas for how legal educators can help make this happen are found in Appendix B (and Appendix E includes topic suggestions for discussion groups, workshops, and courses). If we ignore these issues and further the myth of the infallibility of the "successful lawyer," we run the risk of perpetuating the existing culture of bravado and unhealthy individuality in our profession (referred to earlier by Benjamin Sells). New lawyers will remain ill equipped to deal with the pressures of fearful lawyering scenarios. They will make mistakes that have ethical consequences.

LAWYERS' FEAR OF ASKING FOR HELP CAN LEAD TO ETHICAL VIOLATIONS

To make these concepts more concrete, it might help to see how courts handling attorney discipline cases have acknowledged references to fear in attorneys' hesitation to seek guidance from more experienced attorneys, in the failure to effectively represent a client, or in outright ethical violations.[281] Obviously, fear does not justify an ethical breach, but increasing our awareness about the reality of fear in our profession might help us avert avoidable mistakes and poor decision-making.

For example, in an attorney grievance matter in Maryland,[282] a junior attorney got into trouble because he cut and pasted opposing counsel's signature into a joint stipulation which differed from the version to which she had agreed, and filed it with the court.[283] The court issued a reprimand sanction rather than a suspension, quoting the lawyer's pleading in the judicial opinion:

> [A] member of the bar for four (4) years, [he] was relatively inexperienced in the practice of law, especially in real property litigation, and was unsure "how to handle the legal difficulties with the case when he was at the . . . firm because he was 'too afraid to ask for help.' "[284]

Three judges dissented from the "slap on the wrist" penalty though, contending that the majority had "trivialized" the lawyer's "serious misconduct."[285]

In a New York case,[286] an attorney was charged with professional misconduct for impersonating another lawyer and intercepting telephone messages left with the answering service of another law firm. He had been contacting potential clients, soliciting retainers from them to perform legal services, and falsely asserting that he had a relationship with that firm. In a subsequent disciplinary proceeding, the lawyer asked "the Court to consider his youth, inexperience as an attorney, and lack of maturity in coping with the 'pressure cooker' atmosphere of . . . the law firm where he worked, which caused him to succumb to his perceived *fear of losing his job* if he failed to bring in business."[287] The court acknowledged the mitigation offered, as well as the lawyer's "previously unblemished record," but disbarred the lawyer on the grounds of serious professional misconduct.[288]

A Kansas case[289] involved disciplinary proceedings against an attorney for failing to timely file an appellate brief on behalf of her client and then not responding to a formal disciplinary complaint. The court directly acknowledged that the lawyer's failures were not caused by "dishonesty or selfishness."[290] Instead, the court realized that the attorney "clearly did not wish to continue to represent the criminal defendant in the Eighth Circuit appeal, but . . . that this was motivated more out of *fear from her relationship with her client* and general disillusionment with the practice of law than out of dishonesty or selfishness."[291] Nonetheless, the court suspended the lawyer from the practice of law indefinitely.[292]

Additionally, in a Rhode Island disciplinary action[293] involving an attorney's neglect in proceeding with his client's case, the court noted that the lawyer also failed to cooperate with the counsel handling the subsequent disciplinary matter. The court acknowledged that the lawyer did not attempt to make excuses, but "attributed this failure to 'embarrassment, fear and . . . inability to deal with the problem.'"[294] Regardless, the court ordered a public censure and required the lawyer to submit a plan under which other attorneys would supervise his future professional work.[295]

Further, in Alaska,[296] an attorney knowingly provided misleading information to a client and bar investigators, and neglected to attentively move client cases forward. In his disciplinary inquiry, the attorney argued that a mitigating factor should include consideration that "every lawyer makes mistakes in his career" and his errors occurred "because he was a human being and he was *afraid for his future* and the future of his family."[297] In this case, the court rejected the "likely effects of a penalty on a lawyer's business, family, and personal reputation as mitigating factors."[298] The court suspended the lawyer from the practice of law for three years.[299]

These cases at least acknowledge the role that fear can play in attorney decision-making. They also show, however, that although fear may explain an attorney's misstep, it likely will not serve to excuse it. Thus, to prevent circumstances in which lawyers' unchecked fear leads to adverse ethical or disciplinary consequences, we should openly talk about the reality of fear in law school and law practice, and arm our future lawyers with tools to untangle it.

COURTS WILL CONSIDER A LAWYER'S ABILITY TO ADMIT A MISTAKE OR WRONGDOING AS A MITIGATING FACTOR IN A DISCIPLINARY DECISION

Of course, some attorneys reveal questionable character when caught in an error. Some disciplinary or malpractice cases involve attorneys who hide a mistake, fail to own up to a blunder or wrongdoing, or show no remorse. But courts acknowledge—as a mitigating factor—the actions of lawyers who *do* readily take responsibility for a mistake.[300] For example, in a Washington case,[301] an attorney violated ethical rules by acting as if he represented a decedent's estate even though he did not have confirmed authorization to do so. The court considered the lawyer's "prompt action to correct his mistake once it came to his attention" and issued a sanction of reprimand.[302]

In an attorney discipline case in Iowa, a lawyer failed to keep a client informed about the status of a matter, failed to comply with reasonable requests for information, and charged unreasonable amounts for expenses.[303] The court considered the attorney's admission of her violations and her "sincere acceptance of responsibility" as a mitigating circumstance, but suspended her license indefinitely.[304]

Further, in a Georgia matter,[305] an attorney entered a guilty plea to two felony counts of filing a false tax return. As a mitigating factor in the related disciplinary matter, the court considered that the lawyer "accepted responsibility for his mistakes" and exhibited "willingness to take full responsibility for his actions and the consequences thereof."[306] The court issued a one-year suspension and a public reprimand.

Willingness to acknowledge mistakes is relevant in cases involving judges as well as attorneys. In a North Carolina judicial discipline proceeding,[307] a judge erroneously had solicited and accepted a plea to a charge that was not a lesser included offense. He promptly corrected his mistake when the error was called to his attention.[308] The court declined to censure the judge.

In contrast, courts have considered a lawyer's failure to admit or take responsibility for, or remedy, a mistake or wrongdoing as an aggravating factor in attorney discipline cases. In a Colorado case,[309] an attorney mishandled funds in his trust account and also billed a client 12 hours for work not performed on that day. The court noted that "[w]hen the [billing] mistake was called to his attention, he failed to correct it."[310] The attorney was disbarred. Further, in a New Hampshire matter,[311] a lawyer prepared faulty incorporation documents for a company. Once he discovered that the secretary of state had rejected the incorporation documents, he exerted no efforts to promptly notify the company or fix his error.[312] The court suspended his bar license for one year.

Of course, it can be scary to admit a lawyering mistake, especially for attorneys who fear losing their jobs. Professor Catherine Gage O'Grady, who is also associate dean for academic affairs at the University of Arizona James E. Rogers College of Law, discusses the difficulty of mistake acknowledgment in real-life practice. In a law review article, "A Behavioral Approach to Lawyer Mistake and Apology,"[313] she notes that, for a junior attorney, admitting a mistake likely will necessitate a tough dialogue with a supervising attorney, and possibly even the client.[314] Professor O'Grady reiterates that "while new attorneys understand that they will probably make mistakes, they fear them and their potential consequences because they know they are expected to be 'competent.'"[315] She urges law firm managers to strive to understand the behavioral principles and institutional dynamics that contribute to mistakes but also make owning up to mistakes challenging.[316] Part of this effort involves acknowledging that "the new attorney does not have a track record of correct decisions that might place the mistake into longitudinal perspective."[317] The new attorney might "fear that a mistake will be career-defining, or even career-ending, in a way that a more mature lawyer would not."[318]

As part of our collective quest to untangle fear, legal educators can strive to provide more opportunities for students to develop a track record of making correct lawyering decisions and avoiding mistakes, but also of making mistakes and recovering from them. Notably, the Elisabeth Haub School of Law at Pace University expressly references mistake-making in its publicly posted Learning Outcomes: "Demonstrating self-awareness and reflective capacity, *including learning from mistakes.*"[319] Appendix B to this book suggests tangible ways for law schools to incorporate a discussion of character-in-context, fear, and mistake-making into the curriculum. Students likewise could, and should, request and seek out these learning scenarios.

Further, Appendix C offers suggestions for how law practice managers can cultivate dialogues about fear and mistake-making in practice and help foster realistic perspective in newer attorneys. Law offices of all sizes might appoint an ethics counsel or a confidential internal advisor to whom junior attorneys can turn privately for guidance.[320] Additionally, law firms should explain to junior associates how malpractice insurance works, so they understand the scope of coverage protection for mistakes.[321] These efforts can help minimize fear as a driver in mistake-making and unethical decision-making.

Fear keeps us focused on the past or worried about the future. If we can acknowledge our fear, we can realize that right now we are okay. Right now, today, we are still alive, and our bodies are working marvelously. Our eyes can still see the beautiful sky.
—Thich Nhat Hanh

PART II

THE TANGLE OF FEAR

As the foregoing chapters demonstrate, fear in lawyering exists, at least for many of us, and for our clients. Now let's do something about it. Instead of barreling brazenly forward trying to bushwhack through the vines of fear entangling our lives and our profession, let's first aim to understand it. This part of the book explores fear from a biological and physiological standpoint, describing what happens in our brains and bodies at the onset of, and during, a scary experience. By becoming more aware of how our minds and bodies innately respond to a perceived threat, we eventually can get better at distinguishing imagined from real hazards, and then can take affirmative steps to maximize our authentic power in performance moments. Many of us have been prodded all our lives to: "Face your fears!" and "Do what scares you!" Well-meaning coaches, mentors, and other authority figures may have lauded fear as the world's greatest motivator. In the subsequent few chapters, we'll examine why such "pro-fear messages" are not helpful or productive for many of us. Rather, fear unequivocally blocks our learning and performance, like a big hulking tank occupying the middle of a serene hiking trail. Fear can be a devious chameleon, too, shape-shifting into other unproductive emotions, like anger, guilt, resentment, jealousy, and shame. In these next few chapters, let's get to know fear intimately. Let's unmask it, peel back its layers, expose it, disassemble it. Let's untangle fear, for perhaps the first time ever, and once and for all.

CHAPTER 5

The Science of Fear

To begin to untangle and understand fear, it helped me to learn a little bit about what happens to our brains and our bodies when we experience this emotion and feeling. I'm not a scientific researcher, neurologist, or psychologist, but acquiring even a rudimentary understanding of how our brains and bodies work in the face of fear enabled me to finally realize why my old methods of "just doing it" and "just pushing through" my fears accomplished a grand total of zilch. This chapter explains the basic science of fear: What happens to our body chemistry when we are fearful toward a person or predicament. Once we understand our minds' and bodies' automatic reactions, responses, and processes in the face of fear, we can begin to take concrete steps to increase our awareness *within* fearful moments, and then direct our mental and physical responses in a more productive manner.

Let's get to know our brains a little bit better, in simple terms we can understand. The "cerebral cortex" (or cerebrum) is the "gray matter" comprising the large outside layer of our brain[322]—the wrinkly stuff. The cerebral cortex manages the higher-level functions of our brain. It is divided into four "lobes":

- The frontal lobe, which governs motor skills, speech, and cognitive function
- The parietal lobe, which processes sensory input from touch and pain
- The occipital lobe, which processes information from the eyes
- The temporal lobe, which processes information from the ears, and is responsible for memory, emotion, hearing, and language

Structures of the limbic system are part of the temporal lobe. The limbic system affects emotional behavior and contains, among other items:

- The amygdala: an almond-shaped nugget that controls our emotions and memory
- The hippocampus: also important for memory

- The hypothalamus: responsible for adrenaline and emotions
- The thalamus: a transmitter of sensory signals to and from the cerebrum[323]

The word *amygdala* comes from the Greek word for almond: *amygdale.*[324] In addition, the olfactory cortex in the temporal lobe manages our sense of smell and the gustatory cortex in the parietal lobe manages our sense of taste. Just to round out the science-y terminology, we also might hear people refer to the *prefrontal cortex* and the *neocortex*. Let's think of those like Russian nesting dolls: the *prefrontal cortex* is positioned at the very front of the neocortex; the *neocortex* is the newest (hence, *neo*) and most evolved part of the *cerebral cortex* and comprises 90% of it.

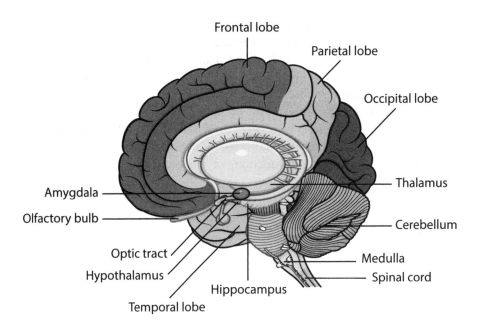

Prefrontal cortex → Neocortex → Cerebral cortex

So how does all this apply to fear? Well, let's start with a stimulus. Imagine that we see, hear, or touch something. The thamalus receives most sensory signals like sight, hearing, and touch; "[s]ensory information regarding smell, however, is sent directly to the olfactory bulb and not to the thalamus."[325] The thalamus passes the sensory information to the amygdala. Neither is *100% sure* yet whether the stimulus poses an actual threat. If the amygdala considers the stimulus a *potential* threat, our almond-shaped pal prepares our body to respond—in a fraction of a second. Professor Patthoff explains:

> [E]volution has ensured that fear has an express lane in our brain circuitry: information from the senses has a direct route to the amygdala, the brain's fear manufacturer. Information moves along this route unfiltered by the neocortex, the area of the brain responsible for higher-order thinking like reasoning and logic. Indeed, before the neocortex receives information from the senses, the amygdala has already made a "quick and dirty" appraisal of the information for potential threats and has begun sending its evaluation to the neocortex.[326]

Professor Patthoff provides a helpful visual image of the imbalance between the number of pathways in our brain that transmit fear messages, versus those fewer conduits that convey rational, calming communiqués ("This is just a test, not an actual threat."):

> The amygdala blasts these messages to the neocortex along profuse pathways— pathways that far outnumber those that travel from the neocortex back to the amygdala. So, while the amygdala is capable of filling the "thinking brain" with fear messages, the ability of the thinking brain to send rational messages to the amygdala is hobbled. This wiring permits fear to easily overtake reason and all but ensures the primacy of fear's power to motivate.[327]

Meanwhile, the thalamus also is sending information about the potential threat stimulus to the cortex—our brain's context provider. While the amygdala is all-systems-go to gear up our bodies to battle or bolt, the cortex's job is to assess the stimulus from a rational perspective, and determine whether it presents a realistic threat. The cortex ultimately sends its dispatch back to the amygdala. If the cortex indeed does deem the stimulus to be an actual threat, our fear response goes full throttle; our heartbeat accelerates, our pupils enlarge, some of us sweat.[328] Authors of *Mind Gym: An Athlete's Guide to Inner Excellence*, Gary Mack and David Casstevens, report that "some people are cardiac responders—their heart rate goes up. Some are skin responders— they begin to perspire. Others begin to breathe rapidly, feel their stomachs churn, or feel their neck and back muscles tensing."[329] Conversely, if the cortex determines that the stimulus does not put us in peril, ideally, we chill out. The prefrontal cortex "mediates sensory overload, and thus provides a calming effect to the fear-generating stimulus."[330]

The disproportionate number of fear signal pathways versus reassurance conduits suggests that our brains are structured to "allow fear to take control," as a self-preservation measure.[331] The amygdala is referred to as the "lizard brain"; it is the "smallest most deeply buried part of our brain. . . . Yet it remains by far the most powerful."[332] As Dr. Joseph Troncale writes, "Many people call it 'The Lizard Brain' because the limbic system is about all a lizard has for brain function. It is in charge of fight, flight, feeding, fear, freezing-up, and fornication."[333] It's the amygdala's job to alert the body to a threat "before the thinking mind can even realize that danger might be present."[334] Indeed, "a fear-evoking stimulus can reach the amygdala in a mere 12 milliseconds, which is evolutionarily advantageous if one's response time means the difference between life and death."[335] The route from the thalamus to the amygdala is short and "imprecise."[336] The "longer, more precise route comes from the medial prefrontal cortex, the area of the brain that is involved in the final phase of fear, in which the brain reacts to danger and chooses a course of action."[337]

Understanding more about the amygdala can help us untangle how our bodies and minds respond to fear.

THE AMYGDALA DOESN'T DISTINGUISH BETWEEN REAL THREATS AND INNOCUOUS EVERYDAY DISTRACTIONS

The amygdala reminds me of a very dramatic beagle I once had named Kirby—the one my boyfriend gave me when I was in law school (and who we shared after we got married), as mentioned earlier in the Introduction. Kirby's primary talents were eating copious amounts of dog food (and the occasional houseguest's sock), disassembling our outdoor grill to lick the grease drip pan while we were at work, and howling. She would howl *bloody murder* at any sound emanating from beyond the front door. It didn't matter if the person lurking on the stoop was the Domino's pizza delivery person or a serial killer, or if the sound was a rogue autumn leaf scratching against the brick steps. Kirby's response was uniform: she'd howl incessantly to warn of danger, a piercing, wailing holler as if someone was chopping off her perpetually wagging tail. If she heard the slightest noise, the world was coming to an end, and she wanted me to know about it. Kirby was the amygdala in beagle form.

As Kristen Ulmer explains in *The Art of Fear: Why Conquering Fear Won't Work and What to Do Instead*, the amygdala "not only is responsible for sending emotional messages but remains on the lookout for anything that might kill you. Which is certainly handy—except it doesn't distinguish between major threats and minor inconveniences. It sees imminent life-ending danger everywhere."[338] Marketing professor Kaylene C. Williams reinforces this notion, noting that our "brain seems to be wired to flinch first and ask questions second."[339] I've officially renamed my amygdala Kirby, the wailing beagle.

During this initial phase of our fear response, while our bodies' fight-or-flee instinct shifts into overdrive, our cognitive functioning oddly downshifts. J. Mark Weiss calls this an "amygdala hijack."[340] He explains, "Biologically, we are all hardwired to ensure that cognitive functioning is impaired, or even shut down, when we are experiencing severe stress. This actually helps our survival as a species yet creates challenges when dealing with conflict."[341] Our hardworking bodies release adrenaline (also called epinephrine, which increases blood circulation and breathing) and cortisol (which affects blood sugar levels and blood pressure).[342] Our hearts pump extra blood to our appendages so we can battle or bolt.[343] Our reflexes quicken.[344] As Russ Harris, author of *The Confidence Gap*, states, "There is a huge amount of energy within our fear. . . . Fear gives us sharpened reflexes, increased muscle tone, heightened awareness, and greater strength."[345] Our brains and bodies focus more on our physical ability to take down or outrun a threat, and less on our cognitive facility to process the danger. In untangling fear, it is important to realize that, in those poignant moments, "fear is more powerful than reason."[346]

WHEN FEAR LINGERS

Ideally, if our prefrontal cortex is working properly and realizes we are not actually encountering a life-threatening stimulus, it sends a signal back to the amygdala to relax. Or, when we navigate a situation involving a real threat and come through the other side, the amygdala is supposed to reset, and then we calm down. For many of us, however, memory of and repeated exposure to anxiety-producing events can cause our fear responses to linger longer than they should, or fire up when they shouldn't. As Dan Gardner, author of *The Science of Fear*, explains, the amygdala's ignition of the body's release of fight-or-flight hormones "is intended to generate a quick reaction to immediate threats but it also contains one element intended to have a lasting effect: The hormones the amygdala triggers temporarily enhance memory function so the awful experience that triggered the response will be vividly encoded and remembered. Such traumatic memories last, and they are potent."[347]

For many of us, if our personal or professional lives expose us to anxiety-producing or stressful situations "over a long period of time, our amygdala is modified and becomes fixed at a high anxiety level. This means that our anxious reactions become ingrained in our sub-conscious mind as a kind of habit."[348] T. Scott Bledsoe and Janice J. Baskin, in "Recognizing Student Fear," describe the effect of repeated fear stimuli on students starting a new course:

> *Normally, the signal diminishes in intensity, returns to the amygdala, and the student, though still fearful, may be able to "pull it together." . . . For some students, however, fear-based responses continue to occur even beyond the normal period of initial adjustment to course dynamics. When this happens, brain functions may shift ominously to accommodate the continuous threats perceived by the student.* [349]

Bledsoe and Baskin explain that, for some individuals, the brain's chain reaction to a fear stimulus skips the hippocampus (associated with memory) and the prefrontal cortex, preventing the brain from distinguishing "between fearful and harmless memories" and transitioning the body back to a relaxed state.[350] Ongoing or repeated fear stimuli can overburden the central nervous system.[351]

So can trauma. A single traumatic experience can exacerbate our instinctive fear response. Professors Sarah Katz and Deeya Haldar write about "trauma-informed lawyering." They caution that "trauma has a distinct physiological effect on the brain, which in turn affects behavior in the short-term and long-term."[352] A profoundly distressing life event "becomes encoded as a traumatic memory and is stored in the brain via a pathway involving high levels of activity in the amygdala, making recall of the traumatic event highly affectively charged."[353] Thus, similar scenarios, stimuli, or environments can automatically reignite the fear or anxiety originally experienced in a traumatic event.[354]

Applied sports psychologists David Grand and Alan Goldberg write about sports trauma, which can include "humiliation from an abusive coach, teammate, or parent," "choking" in a performance that results in a loss, or experiencing or witnessing a serious injury.[355] Since sports trauma can become "frozen" in athletes' bodies, and can stoke fear and block performance,[356] these authors advise that to address and help an athlete work through trauma, it is important to access "the roots of the problem deep in the athlete's *body* and brain."[357] To release trauma that has become ossified in our bodies and minds, lawyers and athletes alike may need to seek professional assistance. The American Bar Association Commission on Lawyer Assistance Programs provides links to resources for professional assistance, including state and local lawyer assistance programs.[358]

So, we might be asking ourselves: If our fear reactions are automatic, instinctive, and physiological, how can we do anything about them?

Increased awareness is the first step.

PUTTING ON OUR "APPRAISAL" HAT

While the body is busy firing off hormones, pumping blood to our extremities, and dilating our pupils, it is not exactly focused on discerning a real threat from a false alarm, or—as psychology professor Mary Pritchard puts it—distinguishing between "the guy in the dark alley and the term paper due in 30 minutes. A stressor is a stressor."[359] But through enhanced self-awareness, *we* can exert a conscious effort to start making these concrete distinctions. As author Meera Lee Patel notes, "Our brain is designed to protect us. It doesn't always know the difference between facing a hungry shark or saying hello to a stranger. It's up to us to teach it the difference."[360] She shares how, in studying her own fear, she began to recognize the power inherent in this intentional discernment: "Fear changes what you see in front of you, but I was learning that how I perceived that change—whether I saw something negative or positive, something that would help or harm—was up to me."[361]

Experts call this "the process of appraisal."[362] A psychologist named Richard Lazarus developed "stress appraisal theory." During the primary appraisal phase, we discern whether a stimulus "poses a threat, will cause harm or loss, or presents a challenge."[363] Experts say that our brains go through the process of distinguishing among a harm or loss that already occurred, a potential harm or loss in the future, and a challenge. A challenge can be positive, such as "events that provide a person an opportunity to gain a sense of mastery and competence by confronting and overcoming a dilemma."[364] After this initial assessment, we move to the next phase: secondary appraisal. Here, we ask ourselves what we can *do about* the pesky stimulus. We realistically evaluate our capability of handling the circumstances or scenario.[365] We consider the depth and breadth of our "personal and social resources available to cope with the event."[366] Pritchard describes secondary appraisal as asking ourselves, "Is there anything I can do to make this fear go away?"[367]

Even though apparently our brains and bodies constantly react to fear stimuli and perform these types of assessments all the time in a mere instant, it helped me to become more conscious and deliberate about this notion of *appraisal.* What if, armed with greater awareness about how our fear works, we train ourselves to (1) recognize the alerts sounded by the amygdala, (2) take a moment to stop any unhelpful automatic chain reactions, (3) consciously determine if a potential menace is genuinely worthy of a fear response, and (4) remind ourselves that we are equipped to manage it?[368] As our fear tornado begins to swirl and we feel the familiar whirl of panic blowing around us, we can practice the firefighter mantra: "Stop, drop, and roll." We can halt the spin cycle—momentarily—and force ourselves to answer these questions: "Is this professor/judge/opposing counsel/supervisor really trying to harm me? Will my heart explode into a million globby pieces and abandon me for dead if I flub this Q&A? Will all the air expel from my body, leaving me oxygen-starved, if I turn red and say the wrong thing?"[369]

Probably no.

Most of the time, hopefully *all* of the time in our lawyering scenarios, the answers to these questions about life-threatening peril will be "No."[370]

No, we likely are not actually at risk of death or bodily harm in those performance moments, though it certainly might feel that way: everything hurts; it does. We don't need to sugarcoat the pain. It physically hurts a lot. Our chests are tight. Our hearts jackhammer against our ribs. Our heads throb. But we absolutely are not going to perish right this instant. And that recognition, that affirmation, is the first step to reducing our mental and physical anguish even just one or two notches, just for the moment, to prevent our "hormones from cascading into alarm."[371] Then, with renewed strength, we can remind ourselves of the multitude of mental, emotional, and physical tools we have within our reach to manage our fear and to navigate the lawyering scenario substantively and procedurally—tools we will identify and build upon in Part IV.

This new, more conscious and proactive approach to wrangling our innate fear response may take time to adopt and launch, but we can train ourselves to "stop, drop, and roll" when the fear tornado begins to swirl. We can take a breath, rationally process the perceived threat, and initiate new personally tailored mental and physical action plans—which we will develop in Part IV. For now, let's take it one step at a time. As Gay Hendricks, author of *The Big Leap*, notes, "[F]ear is always about the unknown."[372] Through this process, together we are going to make the unknown a whole lot more known.

A few months ago, I took a fitness class called, appropriately, The Class, in which the owner and teacher, Taryn Toomey, quietly urged, "Go easy on you." It seemed like she was talking directly and solely to *me*. I sent her an Instagram message to make sure I had heard her correctly. To my starstruck delight, she wrote back, "YES. Go easy on you—you heard it right"! I absolutely needed to hear those words in that particular moment. *Go easy on you*. This doesn't mean we are wimps, snowflakes, or lightweights, or need coddling, or can't take the heat. As Professor Pritchard points out, we've had "30, 40, or 50 years to train [our] body to freak out over every little thing. Give it a break."[373] Let's give ourselves the luxury of time to figure this fear out once and for all.

> *To free our body from fear, what we need is the glorious experience of our soul.*
>
> —Sri Chinmoy

CHAPTER 6

The Ineffectiveness of "Pro-Fear" Messages

Individuals in the legal profession who are fortunate enough to not have to grapple with harmful fear often proffer advice like "Just face your fears . . . If you're not afraid, it means you don't care . . . Conquer your fears . . . Just do it . . . Fake it till you make it . . . Get over yourself . . . Do what scares you . . . If your dreams don't scare you, they're not big enough . . . Fear is the best motivator." Or they might say, "Well, this is the profession you chose. If it's too daunting for you, maybe you should go do something else." The slogans, the mantras, the quick-fix verbiage might work for some individuals who just need a little nudge to "get over it," but they do not work for many of us. As one law student describes:

> Fear . . . is often stigmatized. As children, young adolescents, and adults, society teaches us to suppress our fears and attack the circumstances that lead to anxiety or uneasiness. The personal mantras surrounding the concepts of overcoming fear and anxiety are vast and ubiquitous. As my father often tells me when I'm stressed—"this too shall pass." As others say so often, "feel the fear and do it anyways." For some this is an easy exercise.

For others, these mantras are useless, and to be honest, undermining. Ignoring or even glorifying fear is a completely ineffective approach for becoming the best advocates we can be. Further, if mentors encourage fearful students or attorneys to "solve" the problem by leaving the profession or choosing a less vocal role within it, we will miss out on pivotal voices and perspectives.

Instead of conquering, facing, ignoring, or pushing through fear, let's untangle it, study it, analyze it, get to know it, distill it down to its essence, and begin to break it apart into useful and useless components. We first must honor the fact, however, that this quest is understandably knotty, partly because we are constantly bombarded with pro-fear or "just overcome it" messages. As if "mastering fear" is a piece of cake. A frolic through the park.

Nike offers a running shoe called Fearless. An ad for Intel's autonomous car shows basketball player LeBron James riding in a driverless vehicle; an article about the ad describes how "he seems to accept this new technology with calm and *no fear*, and would even keep the car at the end."[374] Speaking of automobiles, Mercedes aired a TV ad called "Fearless Is Fuel."[375] In 2015, CareFirst Blue Cross and Blue Shield launched a promotional campaign advising its health care customers to "Live Fearless."[376] I have seen the following motivational messages on Instagram over the past few months:

- "If it scares you, it's a sign that you need to do it." *Beyond the Comfort Zone*
- "Maybe the thing you're most scared of is exactly what you should do." *Law of Attraction*
- "I'm doing my best to embrace things that scare me so I can grow." *Debbie Lash*
- "Always go with the choice that scares you the most, because that's the one that is going to help you grow." *GregMartinez7516*, quoting Caroline Myss

Our society sends us conflicting messages about fear. On one side, we are expected to be fearless (or at least pretend that we are chock full of mettle) because being fearful allegedly connotes weakness or lack of openness to growth. On the other, we are goaded to embrace fear as a good thing, a prod, a catalyst, the answer to all our motivational problems. Neither approach has ever worked for me. Instead, what *does* work for me is focusing on *why* we are afraid and unpacking that before jumping into the fire.

THE UNHELPFUL MESSAGE THAT FEAR IS A WEAKNESS, AND WE SHOULD EASILY OVERCOME IT

As Russ Harris, author of *The Confidence Gap*, points out, "In almost every human culture, fear is demonized as a sign of personal weakness, especially in men. And in our society, the brainwashing starts very young."[377] He reiterates, "From a young age we've been educated to believe that fear is bad: that it's a sign of weakness, that it's unnatural, that successful people don't have it, that it holds us back in life, and that we need to reduce it or get rid of it."[378] This notion reminds me of a scene in the National Geographic Channel's provocative and eye-opening series, *Genius: Picasso*. In a flashback relayed by painter Françoise Gilot, her father pushes the frightened little girl off a landing into a body of water to prod her to be fearless—like a boy. Great Parenting 101?

In a 2015 article entitled "The Emotionally Attentive Lawyer,"[379] Randall Kiser included excerpts of attorney interviews. One attorney's comment struck me as, once again, reflecting unfortunate attitudes toward fear in lawyering.[380] The lawyer described the dynamics of settlement negotiations and stated, "Everybody is afraid—plaintiffs and defendants laying out all this money. *You have to manipulate the other side's fear and have none yourself.* Fear equals the perception of risk—not even risk, but the perception of risk."[381] Again, the bravado mind-set.

As an antidote to the message that fear is a weakness, Harris suggests that "fear is like a powerful fuel. Once we know how to handle it, we can use it to our advantage; we can harness its energy to help us get where we want to go. But while we're looking at fear as something bad, we'll waste a lot of precious energy trying to avoid or get rid of it."[382] For me, even regarding fear as fuel is potentially dangerous unless, as Harris suggests, we learn how to process, rein it in, and channel it in a healthy and productive way. I don't want my fear to be a flammable and combustible fuel which I can't control and which can cause irreparable mayhem. I want it to be more like wood chips. Or maybe corn. Or grass clippings. Eco-friendly fear (or perhaps, ego-friendly).

THE EQUALLY UNHELPFUL MESSAGE THAT "FEAR IS GOOD!"

On the flip side of regarding fear as a weakness, other pundits constantly tell us how useful fear is as a motivator. This message can be equally demoralizing for those of us who experience unhealthy or paralyzing fear and do not yet know how to process it. Consider these words of advice we often hear:

- "Fear can be a powerful motivator."[383]

- "Fear can be a constructive emotion."[384]

- "To live completely without fear is to live foolishly and dangerously. We would be emotionally blind and vulnerable to being harmed. But there is another sense in which fear can be a gift. Feeling scared reassures us that we are alive, that we are capable of feeling."[385]

- "Fear is not only an asset and an ally, but one of the greatest experiences you'll have in your lifetime."[386]

- "It is not (only) your inexperience which creates your fear—it's your intelligence. Your fears are *reasonable* and *rational.*"[387]

- "Fear is reasonable; it is rational; it is often what keeps soldiers alive. Conversely, a lack of reasonable fear would be a real reason for concern."[388]

I agree that regarding fear as constructive is infinitely better than regarding it as a flaw or a weakness. But, without further context and guidance about how to separate the toxic agents of fear from its helpful properties, even these messages still leave some of us feeling isolated and adrift when fear causes us internal pain—emotional and physical—and interferes with our performance and happiness. *If fear is so good for me, why do I still feel so awful?*

Other messages focus on the apparent ease with which we are supposed to be able to tackle fear. Writer and leadership trainer Dale Carnegie prompted, "If you want to conquer fear, do not sit home and think about it. Go out and get busy." Ralph Waldo Emerson opined, "He who is not every day conquering some fear has not learned the secret of life." Eleanor Roosevelt urged us to "Do one thing every day that scares you." Hunter S. Thompson challenged, "Anything that gets your blood racing is probably worth doing." My Instagram feed prods me, "You have to want it more than you're afraid of it."[389]

When I read sound bites like these—out of context—I initially think, "Um, no." My fear never has been motivating, constructive, reasonable, a great experience, a gift, or an ally. It has been the opposite: destructive, unhealthy, noxious, depleting, and manipulative. Also, I have shoved myself out of my comfort zone on plentiful occasions to try to slay it. It's not like I sit around eating artisanal chocolates, dabbing a lace handkerchief to my perspiring brow, and bemoaning my fear. I have pushed myself, jumped into the fire, hurled myself into the fray, thinking that if I just do it, face my fears, look them in the eye, stare them down, things will change. Doing that without enhanced self-awareness to tap into the roots of fear accomplishes precisely zilch.

We need to flip this message.

AN ALTERNATIVE APPROACH: UNTANGLING FEAR

In my experience as a scared law student and lawyer, advice like "fear is just a weakness you need to push through and overcome" or "fear is awesome and represents the golden ticket to all future success" felt unhelpful and unconstructive. As Harris notes, telling a scared person to just quit fretting is "one of the most useless bits of advice you could possibly give someone. After all, if it were that easy to stop, they probably would have done so long before we so wisely suggested it."[390] He indicates that this "'fix-it-up, make-it-right, and get-over-it' attitude lacks empathy and compassion. Such an attitude suggests that either you don't understand or don't care how much the other person is hurting."[391]

Responding to the misguided notion that we can conquer fear simply by ignoring it and thundering ahead, Harris emphasizes that "the more we avoid our own fear, the bigger it grows and the more influence it has over our actions."[392] He says, "[T]rying to get rid of your fear will only amplify it."[393] Instead, let's understand fear. Let's learn how to recognize it, disentangle *perceived* threats from reality, and fortify ourselves with mental and physical strategies for handling specific fear-igniting events in the legal arena.

Dr. Phil Nuernberger, author of the previously mentioned article "From Gunfighter to Samurai," has observed that, "[T]aking on an adversarial role without developing mastery of our inner resources leads only to stress. We often don't recognize just how destructive this can be."[394] He further urges:

We mistakenly believe that we need fear to survive, or to motivate us. What we need is self-preservation, not fear. During self-preservation, we focus on the present. Mind and body are coordinated, and our actions and thoughts are clear and decisive. When we anticipate harm, we distort self-preservation and create fear. Our mind struggles with a future fantasy, not a present reality.[395]

Likewise, attorney Richard Friedling suggests that "[t]he difference between the 'newbie' and the experienced litigator isn't 'fear'; it's the ability to compartmentalize and sublimate the inner fear and concentrate on the case."[396] I like the concept of recognizing the reality of fear, and instead of shelving it or boxing it up, taking the time to disentangle the bad parts and channel the energy that fear ignites into healthy, productive functionality.

Friedling distinguishes "constructive" from "destructive" fear in lawyering:

"Constructive" fear is that which leads you to double-check your jury instructions or in limine motions; to review your trial book; to be open and adaptable to the unexpected change right up to the moment of, and during, trial. "Destructive" fear is that which reduces you to the proverbial deer in the headlights—frozen, unsure of where you are, how or why you got there, but definitely wishing it wasn't where you are.[397]

Let's begin the tango of untanglement.

I will not die an unlived life. I will not live in fear of falling or catching fire. I choose to inhabit my days, to allow my living to open me, to make me less afraid, more accessible, to loosen my heart until it becomes a wing, a torch, a promise.

—Dawna Markova

CHAPTER 7

How Fear Blocks Learning and Performance

In the last chapter, we identified societal messages that laud fear as an influential motivator. In reality though, unbridled and unchecked fear blocks learning and performance. It hinders the ability to process stimuli and information, retain knowledge, interact with others, and make prompt decisions. This can affect us deeply as law students and lawyers, even freeze or immobilize us, *and* our clients. Indeed, some level of fear is an instinctive component within an arena fraught with conflict; it is human nature to be afraid of loss, scarcity, exclusion. But when fear detrimentally impacts our ability to function in a healthy and productive manner—in the classroom, the office, the boardroom, or the courtroom—we must take a harder look at the drivers of our fear so we can implement change.

I recently spoke at a legal conference about the reality of fear in the law classroom, aspiring to raise awareness about the destructive impact of fear on law students, and suggesting simple changes we can make to facilitate a more constructive learning environment. As I mentioned in Chapter 1, a professor challenged my remarks, asserting his belief that governing a classroom through unpredictable cold-calling and keeping students under pressure in the "hot seat" was the "only way to ensure students are prepared for class." He dismissed the notion of fear as a block to learning, maintaining that his mode of intimidating students was the *best* way for them to learn the law. Education authors disagree. For example, Rebecca Bright affirms that "fear can seriously disrupt or inhibit learning."[398] Leah Levy likewise acknowledges that the "fight or flight reaction may be useful in some situations, but it is highly detrimental in the classroom."[399] While the body's physiological fear response "may be good for truly life or death situations, this stress response makes learning difficult, as the stimulated senses are not those associated with deep learning."[400] For one thing, "[i]n the short term, acute stress prevents memory storage."[401] Rather than focusing on the course content, fearful students exert mental energy ruminating over their classmates' and professors' potentially negative perception of their in-class performance. In doing so, "they create memories not of the class material but of their own apprehensive feelings, thus inhibiting their understanding of that class material. So, though they prepared before-hand, the students are unable to recall salient elements of the assigned material when classroom discussion occurs, perhaps never having really learned the material at all."[402] Telling these students to snap out of it does not work. That's mission impossible.

Education consultant Bob Sullo confirms that "many teachers still believe that fear—fear of failure . . . , fear of the teacher, fear of ridicule, or fear of an unpleasant consequence—is a prime motivator for students to do high-quality work."[403] He reports that "[t]he intentional creation of fear in the classroom remains one of the most widely used strategies for managing student behavior and encouraging academic achievement."[404] This is a profound educational contradiction because "fear compromises our ability to learn."[405] Fearful students "downshift to survival mode"; "their primary focus is on self-protection."[406] Law professor Kaci Bishop describes how, "in law school, a resistance to failure may become a fear of failure, which can paralyze students and hinder their learning."[407]

In "Strategies for Addressing Student Fear in the Classroom," Bledsoe and Baskin report that some students "develop ongoing or chronic feelings of worry and apprehension, and this constant fear can hinder learners' attempts to understand the information that is required for academic success."[408] According to these authors:

Fear can cause students to experience adverse responses physiologically (e.g., shortness of breath), cognitively (inability to focus or concentrate, obsessive thinking, replaying in their minds problematic incidents that occurred in previous classes), and emotionally (easily agitated, overcome by excessive nervousness, frustration, and other negative feelings).[409]

Fearful students often have trouble processing teachers' questions quickly and then speaking aloud in class; they may experience (and exhibit) physical discomfort through blushing or sweating—which has the added effect of being embarrassing.[410]

Indeed, some "learners consistently experience problematic emotions that hinder their ability to meaningfully connect with the course-related content presented in class."[411] Bledsoe and Baskin note that students "may be afraid, so consumed with anxiety—for a variety of reasons—that their very cognitive processes are short-circuiting, making it virtually impossible to participate, concentrate, read, study, or pass an exam."[412] This is because "[f]ear isn't just a matter of sweaty palms and rapid heart rate. It impacts our cognitive processes—how we perceive our environment, how we remember things, whether we can focus and pay attention, how well we plan and then execute that plan, and how well we problem-solve."[413] Repeated exposure to fear-based environments "overload[s] the central nervous system, resulting in a snow-balling effect of undue stress, and its resultant negative effects on learning."[414]

Bledsoe and Baskin emphasize that it is a teacher's duty to take note of this fear and do something about it: "when [fear] enters a classroom and sits there like an invisible elephant, crushing the breath out of a student's self-efficacy, motivation, and engagement, an educator needs to be prepared to act."[415] The same goes for law practice mentors, practitioners, and even judges. The detrimental effects of fear on performance obviously are not limited to the classroom. They follow law students like a shadow into their roles as advocates. Mediator and arbitrator Robert A. Creo avers that "[a]nxiety and fear affect performance" in lawyering.[416]

In a different niche of our culture in which peak performance is the holy grail, sports psychologists confirm that the "primordial state of fear" can plague an athlete.[417] Drs. Grand and Goldberg explain how fear "dramatically disrupts the athlete's ability to stay loose, calm, and focused, which is a critical prerequisite for expanded performance. What we call choking is actually the fight/flight response acting out of time and place."[418] This is why it doesn't work to tell a scared person—a student, a lawyer, a client, even an elite athlete—to "face your fears and just do it." Untangling the fear *does* work.

You must fight hard to shine the light of words upon [fear].
Because if you don't, if your fear becomes a wordless darkness that
you avoid, perhaps even manage to forget, you open yourself to
further attacks of fear because you never truly fought the opponent
who defeated you.

—Yann Martel, *Life of Pi*

CHAPTER 8

How Fear Hides Behind Other Unproductive Emotions

If we have long absorbed and tried to apply the rote "Face your fears!" mantras referenced in Chapter 6, we may have become pretty successful (on the surface) of pushing through fear. However, suppressed or ignored fear can mask itself in other painful but valid emotions, such as anger, resentment, jealousy, frustration, anxiety, or sadness. As author Meera Lee Patel notes, "[F]ear has become a complicated, winding emotion that now bears paralyzing secondary emotions like guilt, despair, and shame—things most of us experience on a daily basis. . . . Many people feel the effects of fear through guilt, despair, and shame for extended periods of time, often lasting for weeks or even years."[419]

Instead of allowing alternative labels or masks to cover up or camouflage our fear, which does not help us convert it into something useful, let's get curious about fear, peel back its veneer, and begin to take it apart.

The following is a somewhat embarrassing anecdote, but writing it out helped illuminate for me how my fear morphs into and hides behind other emotions.

This morning I jolted awake at 3:10 a.m. in a medieval village an hour and a half by train from Rome—my favorite city in the world. I should be exhilarated that today I get to teach an English legal writing course to 15 Italian PhD students. I've taught the fundamentals of the course basically 20 times now in different iterations (and published three textbooks on the subject matter). It's not like I don't know what I'm doing. I know the materials and content inside and out. Plus, because I'm teaching native Italian speakers in English, I can proceed more slowly than the usual velocity expected in Brooklyn. (I need to be mindful of any limits on the students' understanding of English legal jargon and my American tendency to contract words together and use slang.) I also have no real pressure to impress anyone. I'm doing this for free; no one is paying me. Neither my job, my livelihood, nor any future evaluation for academic tenure depends on my performance today in any way. While obviously I want to do a good job, connect with my students and the Italian faculty, and not embarrass myself as an American in a challenging global political climate, this teaching junket—in essence—serves to broaden my horizons and also legitimize my living in Rome for a full month while I work on this book. I should be ebullient, eager, motivated, relaxed. I'm a bohemian writer living the dream, pursuing my craft as an expat in Europe, sleeping in medieval quarters converted to a modern-esque B&B.

Instead, it's now 3:12 a.m. and frankly . . . I'm scared. Maybe it's the jet lag and lack of sleep that are plucking at my nerves like guitar strings. I arrived in Italy three days ago and have yet to fully adjust to the six-hour time difference. Whatever it is, instead of feeling like a rock star American law professor jetting off to Europe, living and writing and teaching and learning, I feel sick.

What in the world are you afraid of, again?

Knowing that if I don't nip this sleep intrusion in the bud, the whirring in my head will keep me up all night, causing a migraine to starburst inside my temples and then I will feel awful and this whole thing *will be, is already, will be, is already* a disaster. I illuminate the bedside lamp and grab my travel journal and a pen. I try to label exactly what I am feeling so hopefully I can expel it from my brain and go back to sleep. What am I afraid of?

For starters, I'm afraid of my host professor, Luciana, thinking I'm stupid and disorganized. That I completely missed the mark on what she expects me to teach her top students, even though she told me eight thousand times I could teach whatever I wanted, however I wanted, and that her students were starting nearly at ground zero in their knowledge of American legal procedure. I'm afraid she will think I'm just some New World American teacher who isn't intellectual enough to teach Italian PhD students.

Why do I think this? She's been nothing but nice and welcoming to me over countless emails and in-person twice over meals during her visits to New York.

I'm also afraid of the students: What if they are bored? Don't care? Think I am wasting their time?

Why do I think this? I haven't even met any of them yet. Plus, this is the fourth time I have taught in Italy, and the students have never been anything but completely joyous, cheery, engaging, and eager to absorb and converse about comparative law. Legal writing is *my* expertise, not theirs. English is *my* native language, not theirs. They likely won't be resistant; they opted into my class by their own volition. *There is absolutely no risk here.*

It doesn't matter that I tell myself these things. All these rational and evidence-based things. I'm afraid. I'm still awake at 3:45 a.m. and now I'm also scared I won't be able to fall back asleep. I'll be exhausted as usual. I probably will have a raging sleep-deprivation headache all day. I won't understand the students' questions, their profoundly beautiful yet intense accents reverberating off the stone classroom walls. *Stupid medieval echoing wall acoustics!* What if I don't have enough material to fill each two-hour class session? What if the technology doesn't work? *Of course it won't work! First day technical glitches are a given! You know that! Why didn't you print a backup copy of your PowerPoint?!*

What if the students think the hypothetical client scenario I crafted—an effort to balance real-life global legal issues with classroom dynamics potentially involving racial, gender, ethnic, and socioeconomic tensions—is stupid and unrelatable (*or even somehow accidentally offensive!*), though similar fact patterns have worked fine several times with my American students? What if they get annoyed and irritated that they're not getting their money's worth? *Wait. You're not taking money out of anyone's pocket! Stop thinking. Now. Just stop.*

The fear starts to transmute into other emotions. I'm *irritated*. At myself, the suddenly scratchy B&B linens, the lack of arctic air conditioning I blast back at my Airbnb in Rome. Minutes later, I'm *resentful*. Why did the course details and logistics change so many times? First, the class was scheduled for six days over two weeks, then four days, then back to six, now back to four. The first class session was slated from 3 to 5 p.m., but in yesterday's email, my host said we start at noon. Which is it? Originally, we were supposed to have a mixture of university and PhD students, and I was asked to create different assignments appropriately tailored to the students' different educational levels; apparently, now it's all PhD students? Resentment quickly morphs into *anger*, at the uncertainty and at myself. Why do I always say yes to these things? Life experience? Ughhh. Haven't I had enough life experience? I feel unprepared. Why am I doing this now when I could have just come to Italy to write? I'm *annoyed*. *Why can't I ever sleep?*

I do finally fall back asleep. Seven hours later, late-morning, zombie-like, I join my host at our designated meeting spot on the cobblestones outside the B&B. Instead of guiding me directly to the university classroom to set up my PowerPoint, she suggests we first enjoy an authentic village *pranzo*, lunch. I absolutely do *not* want to eat a giant decadent Italian meal (my favorite go-to culinary guilty pleasure) before stepping into a new classroom to teach a sea of unfamiliar faces. I politely decline. She insists. Of course, I oblige. We walk in the scorching summer sun to a trattoria and sit outside by a moss-covered fountain. As she is pescatarian, she orders pasta for me, hand-made tornel-lini with guanciale (the world's best bacon) and shaved black truffles, which are only in season for a few more weeks. I gobble every bite as the searing sun prompts rivulets of sweat to trail down my spine. The meal is delicious. Heavy. An explosion of musky earth. I feel awe and wonder—my favorite travel emotions—and then minutes later, as she nurses an espresso, I feel sick. And suddenly *resentful*, again. Why did we eat a meal, outside in the blistering heat, before teaching? And now, I realize as I glance at my watch, we are running late. I don't do *late* well.

The Italian higher education system holds a tradition in which each class—even if it is scheduled to start on the hour—does not actually start until a quarter past the hour. Right now, it is ten past the hour. We are going to be late to my first class. With my new PhD students. And I don't have one earthly idea if my PowerPoint is going to work. Is there even a screen or projector in the room? My *anxiety* resurfaces. Yes, it was generous of her to feed me. The meal was lovely and rich and packed with life essence on a zillion levels, and she is kind and funny and wildly interesting, but my pre-class ritual usually involves at least a few minutes of prep. I like to get the technology set up, escape to the restroom, and at least take a couple calming breaths alone before entering a classroom of new students unfamiliar with my wacky teaching style. I feel *agitated*.

We amble in the aggressive sunshine to the university. I endeavor not to twist an ankle on the cobblestones. I curse myself for opting for aspirational shoe fashion over practicality. We arrive at the law school, and eventually, the classroom. Now it's a good 20 minutes past the hour. No one seems to care about the late start but me. We encounter a coterie of students sharing ciga-rettes and chatting happily in rapid Italian outside the classroom. They leap up to greet my host—their professor—and seem a little shy as she introduces me. There is confusion over who has possession of the classroom. A bunch of local lawyers in stylish suits occupy the desks and chairs therein, awaiting a different lecturer who is even more tardy than we are. *Normale. Nessun problema.* My host resolves the double-booked classroom problem. She evicts the law-yers and finds another spot for their lecture. My students slide into the empty wooden seats. I try to repress my rising panic, my exhaustion, frustration, and umbrage. I enter the classroom, take a deep breath, smile, sit in the lecturer's chair, and adopt a balanced seated stance—both feet planted on the floor, arms open on the armrests. I attempt to practice what I preach about physical-ity (which we will explore in Chapter 16) to facilitate optimal oxygen, blood, and energy flow. My heart jabs at my sternum. As I breathe, I know deep down that all these sideshow emotions—anger, annoyance, frustration, resentment, irritation—have nothing to do with my kind and generous host or the relaxed Italian approach to timekeeping, schedules, and classroom dynamics. These tangential emotions have everything to do with my raw, knee-jerk, persistent, and counterintuitively self-protective *fear*.

Reflecting on this situation the next evening on the train back to Rome alone, after two successful, interactive, and fun classes, and spirited debriefs with my host over delicious espresso, I discern that I wasn't really afraid of the class not going perfectly or smoothly. The stakes were low. The Italians don't really care about strict syllabi. The class was pass-fail, so no one's educational career hinged on the quality of my instruction. This was simply a great opportunity for me to practice imparting insights about the American legal system with open-minded Italian students and one generous professor, and to exchange cross-cultural experiences. It was also a chance to expand my flexibility as a teacher. In reality, nothing was on the line. Yet, I *created* stakes. I *concocted* lines, of being judged and valued, or devalued. I was afraid of being perceived as stupid or unworthy, and then of being rejected—by the students and my host.

Deep down, it's these experiences, even at the prime of my legal career and halfway (hopefully!) through my life, in which I realize that my greatest fear in life has always been exclusion and rejection. Being discarded, or cast out. Less than. Flawed. Unworthy of acceptance, appreciation, and care, of love, even. The amazing creativity book by Steven Pressfield called *The War of Art*[420] explains how the fear of rejection works, and why it is such a powerful reagent:

> *Evolution has programmed us to feel rejection in our guts. This is how the tribe enforced obedience, by wielding the threat of expulsion. Fear of rejection isn't just psychological; it's biological. It's in our cells.*[421]

He says we are "wired for" tribal *in*clusions.[422] Thus, when *ex*clusion is a possibility, it can be terrifying.

In actuality, I know deep down I'm a good teacher—in Italy *and* America. I can read a room. I usually can tell when students are confused, when their energy is fading, or when they want me to shift gears and spice things up. I work hard to stay on top of ever-changing substantive content, and I strive for appropriate depth based on my students' educational history and level of comprehension. I invest time in developing creative, up-to-date coursework that merges legal theory with practicality. I aspire to craft workable syllabi with realistic pacing—not too much or too little workload for each class. In each class session, I endeavor to reach a variety of learners within the four walls of the classroom. But in rich life opportunity moments like this one in Italy, my knee-jerk instinct is to *distrust* my system. To *doubt* my competence. Even after all this time—so far, 10 years of teaching law students—I still fear being exposed as a fraud, an imposter, a poseur, in a profession populated by intellectuals who rarely show weakness.

Trust—in ourselves first and foremost, and then in others if it is earned—can help us untangle this type of fear. As author Susan Jeffers noted, "Our level of fear slowly starts to drop as it is replaced by a greater sense of trust in [our] ability to handle [our] world."[423]

Over two decades of practicing law, I've observed a different type of fear in individuals who *do* deem themselves worthy of respect or power. These folks clearly possess (and trumpet) the requisite academic and professional credentials to sit at the head of the lawyering table. However, an insidious kernel of fear—masked in aggression, intensity, sarcasm, or disparagement—pervades the way they treat others, especially subordinates, junior associates, staff, and even opposing counsel. Across three firms, I experienced senior partners who yelled profanities about rogue staples, hurled Magic Markers across conference rooms, and punched holes in walls in reaction to typographical errors. Highly successful rainmakers and astute legal minds, they managed us under regimes of "shock and awe." It's possible that these particular guys were just jerks. But in the spirit of aspiring toward empathy, as well as trying to make sense of my own circuitous professional journey, learn from mistakes, and make our profession better, I choose to believe that they defaulted to scaring others to alleviate their own fear. These individuals were financially successful. By all external accounts, they had it all: the nest egg, the big house, the trendy car, the exotic vacations. Yet, I think they operated under a *scarcity* mind-set: Any successes that befell others somehow chipped away at their achievements. If someone else won, they had lost a piece of their pie, or their pie had become less appealing.

This type of firm leader doesn't promote a collaborative, team-building mind-set. Flickers of fun or celebration of an achievement in the office seem to threaten this leader's control. More joy and happiness for us as employees somehow equates to less for the leader. At least, that's the way it seems and feels. I believe this individual's scarcity mind-set fuels his fear. He yearns to regain supremacy. Scaring us through aggression, gaslighting, and volatility takes away our intermittent joy and job satisfaction, which tips the scale back in his favor. When one of his outbursts sends us scurrying back to our offices where we spend the next few days of billable hours with our "heads stapled to our desks," the power dynamic recalibrates. He successfully dumps his fear tanks into ours, for the interim at least. Psychologist Susan Jeffers poignantly described the relationship between fear and scarcity; "People who fear can't genuinely give. They are imbued with a deep-seated sense of scarcity in the world, as if there [isn't] enough to go around. Not enough love, not enough money, not enough praise, not enough attention—simply not enough."[424] When we encounter these types of, well, bullies, we can try, as professional counselor R. Hal Ritter Jr. and Professor Patricia Wilson suggest, to "listen for emotional words"[425] (intimating fear, loss, anger, pain, or hurt)[426] that might give us insights into whether a scarcity mind-set may be in play. Ritter and Wilson indicate that "fear is related to a threat of injury or loss."[427]

I also have observed the scarcity mind-set in legal academia. Some tenured faculty at some schools remain resistant to engendering pay equity and status parity for legal writing (and other) professors. It's often the same refrain; "Good heavens, no, we can't do that." One even joked, "Nice try" when an advocate for equity suggested tenure-track status for legal writing faculty at one institution (though at least 40 schools nationwide reportedly have taken that path). I believe the scarcity mind-set plays a role in this context as well. By including "nontraditional" faculty in the spoils of academia, some traditional tenure and tenure-track faculty perhaps think that their educational territory must somehow shrink, a scary and threatening proposition for them. Decisions about curriculum innovation and strategic planning then evolve from a fear-based and risk-averse mind-set. Then nothing changes, even though our society evolves, our law advances, and the profession progresses around us. In our insular microcosm, academic pie distribution cements. Boundaries stain in darker ink. Fiefdoms entrench. The haves and have-nots stay the same.

None of this is growth. None of this is evolution. Or innovation. None of this is education of our minds, or cultivation of our legal souls. It's exclusion, nonsensical hierarchy, and rejection, for no legitimate reason. How do we disrupt this model? In our roles as law students, legal educators, and lawyers, we must take note, and pause, when we perceive emotions such as anger, frustration, resistance, and irritability in ourselves and others. We must consider whether, at the root of these emotions, fear lurks—fear of scarcity in some individuals, and of rejection or exclusion in others. By recognizing and peeling back these masking emotions, exposing fear in its raw unpretty state, and then untangling it, together we can progress.

As Marie Curie said, "Nothing in life is to be feared. It is only to be understood. Now is the time to understand more, so that we may fear less." When I first read this quote, I instinctively flinched at the notion that "nothing is to be feared," because I genuinely believe we are entitled to be afraid of certain circumstances in our lawyering lives. But I love Madame Curie's urging that we enhance our understanding. Now *is* the time. Our investment in the time to untangle our fears, to enhance our knowledge about their drivers, and to distinguish useful from useless components, will enable us to step away from scarcity and exclusionary mind-sets that perpetuate unhealthy fear.

Undertaking this endeavor to untangle fear in the legal profession might, at first glance, seem like a daunting task. Thus, I thought it might be useful to first take a look at how *other* professions have addressed fear—in education and training. Let's see what we can learn from other great minds, and extract ideas that may transfer over to the practice of law.

Courage is knowing what not to fear.

—Plato

PART III

HOW OTHER INDUSTRIES AND PROFESSIONS UNTANGLE FEAR AND MISTAKE-MAKING

As law students, legal educators, lawyers, and law practice managers, we might benefit from considering how other industries and professions have approached fear (and mistake-making) in their educational and training platforms. This section of the book—while of course not exhaustive—seeks to extract examples and ideas from the fields of medicine, journalism, engineering, business/entrepreneurship, and sports, of how to more overtly and consciously acknowledge the reality of fear and mistake-making in personal and professional development. For example, experts in medical education have shared how some medical schools are openly addressing mistake-making in medical teaching. Some of these educators are directly acknowledging the reality that medical mistakes happen despite the best efforts of well-trained personnel; then they teach medical students what to do when missteps occur, how to communicate with patients and families about medical errors, and how to avoid repeating mistakes. Some medical schools have implemented new curricula specifically designed to address the reality of medical mistakes in a "non-fear-based" learning environment. Likewise, journalists have acknowledged the tangible presence of fear in their industry; some journalism professors have incorporated mindfulness into their curricula to help students build emotional self-awareness; others offer resources designed to help journalists understand and address trauma. Similarly, some engineering professors have incorporated mistake-making into their curricula to expressly address fear of failure. Educators in the business and entrepreneurship arena teach the "fail fast" principle, seeking to approach early mistakes and failure as learning opportunities rather than weaknesses.

In the field of sports, fear is an issue that can dramatically affect athletes at all levels of play—junior, college, amateur, professional, Olympic. Fear of failure, injury, choking, losing, and embarrassing oneself can rattle even the most hardworking and best-trained competitors. Sports psychologists provide a wealth of information about techniques for empowering athletes to unearth the roots of their fears, develop and trust a training *process*, and ultimately rise to the occasion in fear-invoking performance moments.

Legal traditionalists may posit that the legal realm is different, unique, more theoretical, intellectually peculiar—and therefore, the methodologies of other professions and fields are not relevant in our world. I disagree. Part of our job as legal analysts is to draw analogies from other sources when the rules on point are insufficient to solve a legal problem. Our profession has a problem with fear. Our current tools for addressing it seem deficient. Let's get creative in crafting solutions, and learn from others.

CHAPTER 9

A Glimpse into Fear and Mistake-Making in Medical Education and Training

In 1999, the Institute of Medicine issued a report called "To Err is Human: Building a Safer Health System." The report announced that at least 44,000 to 98,000 deaths occurred annually from medical errors committed in American hospitals.[428] This dramatic statistic prompted the medical profession to take a hard look at how medical education and training tackled the reality of medical errors. Interwined in the analysis of medical mistakes is the presence of fear within the medical profession—in medical school and practice.

In 2006, medical education experts noted the informal nature—at the time—of most teaching and training mechanisms regarding medical errors.[429] Scholars acknowledged a "hidden curriculum" in medical education, defined as the "influences of organizational structure and culture on learning."[430] One writer described this hidden curriculum as "a far more influential teacher" than formalized medical curricula, and one that "has been shaping the behavior of young and seasoned physicians alike"[431] for a long time. The hidden curriculum refers to

the messages transmitted implicitly [by teachers] through everyday vocabulary, practices and habits, all of which have powerful effects on individual attitudes and practices. This phenomenon is particularly relevant to medicine, which has long-standing and often rigid traditions about hierarchy that allow the actions—positive and negative—of senior physicians to strongly influence student behavior.[432]

In other words, a medical teacher's tone, language choices, demeanor, body language, and mode of interacting with students can have more impact—beneficial or detrimental—on a medical student's learning and development than the substantive aspects of the curriculum. This powerful educational undercurrent is said to have contributed to a culture of *fear* in which medical students and doctors-in-training are, or were, afraid to speak up about patient safety issues and potential or already-committed medical errors.[433] By calling attention to this hidden curriculum, members of the medical profession have acknowledged *out loud* that being a medical student can be scary, and some teachers are, or were, part of the problem.

American medical schools are not alone in this perceived "culture of intimidation." An anonymous 2002 article in a Canadian newspaper reported how "Canada's top medical educators" know that interns fear that divulging mistakes will jeopardize their careers.[434] University of Toronto medical ethics co-coordinator at the time, Dr. Philip Hébert, reiterated the point that "our hospitals and institutions don't have ways to make it acceptable to discuss these mistakes."[435] Dr. Jerry Tenenbaum, who once served as director of the International Medical Graduate Program for Ontario, affirmed that error-reporting was regarded as a "punitive process."[436] Another Canadian physician, Dr. Brian Goldman, reinforced the notion that "every doctor makes mistakes but medicine's culture of denial keeps doctors from talking about and learning from those mistakes."[437] A 2015 survey of medical students at the University of Sydney and the University of Melbourne in Australia reported that "teaching by humiliation," including a misuse of the Socratic method, has been "part of the culture in medicine."[438] The authors of an article describing the survey urged that "[f]or optimal learning to occur, the environment should be free of fear and unnecessary anxiety."[439]

Some medical educators, doctors, and hospital administrators have called for a "culture shift" that first acknowledges, and then attempts to lessen, the fear of speaking up about uncertainty in medical decision-making and potential or discovered medical errors. Georgia's Emory Hospitals' chief medical and quality officer, Bill Bornstein, states that an important goal within his medical community is to foster a culture in which any team member can raise safety concerns without fear of rebuke.[440] He advocates for a "nonpunitive culture."[441] Dr. Neha Vapiwala, an associate professor of radiation oncology at the Hospital of the University of Pennsylvania, likewise emphasizes the need to develop an educational and training culture that, of course, endeavors to prevent errors but also "makes it OK to admit fault and learn from mistakes."[442] She urges that "[t]his is especially so for medical students and residents, who are both the most vulnerable and the most impressionable members of our workforce."[443] Toronto emergency room physician Brian Goldman also believes that medical schools should forge a much-needed change in the culture of medicine when it comes to mistakes.[444] He recommends that medical schools should teach students that mistakes are going to happen, and teams should cultivate curiosity about mistakes instead of shame.[445]

Gregory Dolin, a physician who also holds a law degree, and law professor Natalie Ram—codirector and associate director of the University of Baltimore's Center for Medicine and Law—note that both medicine and law are "conservative profession[s]."[446] Dr. Dolin and Professor Ram report that "[n]early all American medical schools have followed much the same educational model" since 1910.[447] They describe this traditional educational model as one that "emphasizes teaching students the science of medicine, but [that] is not well equipped for teaching students about the practicalities of medicine or for helping trainees adapt to circumstances that are radically different than those faced by physicians 100 years ago."[448] This echoes a familiar refrain in the context of legal education; learning century-old legal precedent is important as a foundation but not enough to equip young lawyers for the realities of modern legal quandaries.

After a study of "factors that influence how students and residents learn from medical errors"—including "fear and self-doubt"—some doctors believe that "formal curricula should begin early in medical school to counter" the effect of the hidden curriculum.[449] In the past, medical students reported that lectures on patient safety and medical errors were "peppered throughout the curriculum," but medical students were neither taught how to report an error nor encouraged to do so.[450] Now, the emergent trend in medical education seems to be to construct, offer, and formalize coursework and specific training on how medical errors happen, how to develop protocols to prevent them, and how to handle mistakes when they occur.[451] In an article aptly titled, "Letting New Doctors Learn without Fear," writer Katherine Mangan reports that "almost every medical school today has some kind of simulated teaching experience, whether with robots, surgical-skills labs, or actors posing as patients."[452] Some medical schools are integrating new virtual reality technology into their curriculum to supplement lectures. Dr. Kimberly Topp, a professor of physical therapy and anatomy at the School of Medicine at the University of California, San Francisco, "sees the technology assisting more generally in immersion learning, helping learners get used to an environment that is unfamiliar and frightening."[453] Using virtual reality technology to simulate treatment of a trauma patient "allows team members to get used to calming themselves and gaining control over their emotions, thoughts and actions to be useful in the situation."[454]

In 2006, Harvard's teaching hospitals launched a training program in which medical students simulate and rehearse difficult conversations about medical mistakes with actors playing the role of patients.[455] The University of Michigan reports that its groundbreaking model for training its medical professionals to handle medical errors in an open, transparent manner "has become a recruiting tool" for residents.[456] In 2011, the University of Chicago Medical Center designed and launched an innovative "horror room," in which students learn about "potential safety errors in a controlled environment."[457] Doctors at the University of Minnesota Medical Center created a six-part curriculum on diagnostic reasoning and errors that encompasses real-life stories from physicians, malpractice lawyers, and patients' families.[458] The University of Pittsburgh School of Medicine mentions mistake-making in its publicly-posted Learning Objectives for the M.D. Curriculum: "Identify and avoid common sources of medical errors."[459]

David Mayer, who was the academic dean at the University of Illinois College of Medicine at Chicago and is now vice president of quality and safety at MedStar Health, noted the dearth of literature a decade ago on strategies for integrating patient safety into the medical curriculum.[460] Since then, Dr. Mayer and fellow experts have developed roundtables and immersive courses for medical students and residents, emphasizing that "it's about creating a culture in which people feel confident that they can raise their hands when something doesn't feel right."[461] Instead of prompting medical students and new doctors to "Just be brave and speak up," which can remain difficult without training and guidance, these stakeholders in the medical profession seek to cultivate an environment that defuses the fear associated with flagging mistakes. As Dr. Robert L. Trowbridge[462] points out, "[M]any learners low in the educational hierarchy may not appreciate the fallibility of the diagnostic skills of their 'superiors.'"[463] Overall, the foregoing types of courses and programs help remove the "myth of infallibility" of the "good doctor."

Relatedly, members of the nursing profession also have acknowledged the presence of fear in nursing education and training. In 2015, Professor Mark Pijl Zieber of the Health Sciences Department at the University of Lethbridge in Alberta, Canada, and Professor Beverley Williams of the Nursing Department at the University of Alberta, wrote an article calling attention to the "fear and trauma" experienced by nursing students in clinical practice.[464] Their work focuses on the "significant and troubling problem" of how clinical mistakes are handled in nursing practice and nursing education.[465] These professors point out that "[a]lthough educators expect students to uphold the highest ethical and practice standards, they also reinforce a culture of fear and institute policies that make the ethical process of acknowledging mistakes difficult and risk-laden for students."[466] Zieber and Williams urge nursing educators to acknowledge the reality of fear in clinical practice and to stop promoting such unhelpful advice as "Just do not make mistakes."[467] Instead, they posit that nursing schools can better prepare students and practitioners for "the inevitability of the mistake experience" by providing appropriate support and logistical guidance (e.g., simulation training) to foster resilience.[468]

These professors effectively summarize the problem with all fear-based educational and training models: "As long as mistakes are viewed as moral and personal failures, the experience of making mistakes will be traumatic, unproductive, and ultimately concealed."[469] Zieber and Williams indicate that "nursing education has been slow to adopt a *systems-based* approach in the education of students and the management of student mistakes."[470] They describe a three-pronged, systems-based theory of human performance:

- "individuals are rarely solely to blame for mistakes"
- "a non-punitive response that promotes disclosure is the best reaction to mistakes"
- "environmental factors are significant components of any mistake"[471]

Zieber and Williams encourage teachers to realize that "[w]hen mistakes are viewed as learning experiences and part of a risk management process, systems theory indicates that not only should there be fewer mistakes but when mistakes do occur there will be less psychological carnage to the individual involved."[472]

Also studying mistake-making in nursing education, Professor Carey M. Noland of Northeastern University surveyed nursing students enrolled in four-year and five-year programs at universities in the northeastern United States.[473] The survey participants "stated that they were taught to report mistakes and tell someone, but they were not told how to do it."[474] Professor Noland urged nursing professors "to think about how to conceptualize medical mistakes and teach students about mistakes."[475] She underscored the need to teach students "how to communicate about mistakes, how to behave when they made a mistake, and how they could resolve the emotional turmoil they felt."[476] She suggested that educators might openly share their own experiences with nursing errors, "which could be valuable learning tools."[477]

Further, in the pharmacy field, Kraig Schell, a professor of psychology and sociology, wrote an article in 2006 highlighting the need for better training of pharmacists and technicians with regard to medication errors.[478] He relayed how some researchers "have portrayed pharmacy management as a 'culture of punishment.'"[479] Professor Schell posited that "error management training" in the pharmacy arena has been deficient because of the misconception that mistakes "can be completely avoided."[480] He warned that treating errors as "taboo" leads to the perception that "their consequences are always negative and that the person committing them is somehow inadequate."[481]

He indicated that "[t]his mindset is so pervasive in some contexts that errors are not even allowed in training exercises."[482] To fix this problem in pharmacy training, Schell advocated for error management training that intentionally exposes students to "difficult tasks that tend to produce errors."[483] Under this training regimen, students can employ metacognition,[484] defined as "thinking about thinking." They can observe their own thought processes as they undertake tasks, and subsequently learn from mistakes. Rather than fostering a fear-based or punitive learning environment, Schell encouraged pharmacy educators to regard mistake-making as a "teaching tool"[485] to improve and enhance performance.

> *[Fear] has the ability to split us open like a knife does a*
> *pomegranate, spilling seeds of beauty and incredible possibility from*
> *the inside.*
>
> —Meera Lee Patel[486]

CHAPTER 10

A Glimpse into Fear and Mistake-Making in Journalism Education and Training

In 2014, the magazine *Rolling Stone* retracted an article entitled "A Rape on Campus" about an alleged incident at my alma mater, The University of Virginia. The magazine conceded misstatements, discrepancies, and journalistic failures—in essence, a pretty major lapse of professionalism. In a 2015 article in the *Columbia Journalism Review* entitled "Fear of Screwing Up,"[487] columnist Monica Guzman referenced the UVA blunder. She contended that, in addition to ethics and discipline, "maybe what keeps journalists most in line is fear" of making a mistake.[488] To some extent in her article, Guzman promotes the "fear is necessary" message—the one that gives me pause, as discussed in Chapter 6. She says, "To be a journalist, you have to be afraid. Fear makes you triple-check your work. It makes you sharper, faster, more focused."[489] She does, however, acknowledge that fear can be unhealthy. She notes, "In journalism, as in life, some fear is necessary. But too much fear is paralyzing."[490] She queries whether "this is the biggest, deepest challenge facing everyday journalists—how to turn fear into courage."[491]

Journalist Bob Moser notes a familiar bravado mind-set with respect to fear in journalism. He says, "For reporters, it's surely as close to a 'Golden Rule' as journalism affords: Fear nobody and nothing in your quest to unearth hard truths and afflict the powerful."[492] He also acknowledges the reality of financial and other pressures sweeping across a changing journalistic landscape. He explores how "walking a perpetual financial tightrope certainly isn't the sole reason so many American journalists live in a state of fear, or why at least 80 percent experience trauma on the job, or why just 23 percent of journalists even *like* their jobs."[493] He explains:

Journalism has always been an anxiety-fueled profession. . . . But now there seems to be a new source of nightmares: If you're not losing sleep over keeping your job, or figuring out how to make a client pay up, you're fretting about mistakes. The warp speed of the digital news cycle makes errors impossible to avoid. Systems that used to protect embarrassing or career-ending screwups—research, fact-checking, and copyediting departments—have been gutted, and writers are often expected to be their own checks and balances.[494]

Moser quotes freelance reporter Nora Caplan-Bricker as noting that "[s]ocial media makes it a lot worse."[495]

Another writer, Ben Du Plessis, also seems to reinforce the "fearless journalist" aspiration, commenting that "[t]he best journalists . . . smother self-doubt and ignore threats."[496] He contends that "[i]n journalism, fear creates complacency. Complacency means shoddy reporting and lazy copy. Fear is easy. Great journalism is hard; it means thinking deeply."[497] Obviously, though it sounds somewhat cool to couch it that way, I respectfully disagree with the notion that "fear is easy." Du Plessis goes deeper, though, when he notes that "[e]mpathy, honesty, skepticism and rationality are like cardinal virtues in journalism. It takes courage to keep these virtues when confronted by a sea of deadlines."[498] He cites Larry Cornies, who teaches journalism ethics at the University of Western Ontario: "[J]ournalism schools teach students everything they need to be courageous, giving them 'a grasp of the facts, lots of practice questioning people and a sense of fairness with respect to your interview subjects.'"[499] But Cornies also says that "a young reporter's decision to act courageously, to ask the right people the right questions, can't be made for them by a journalism school. Courage is a personal choice."[500] Ultimately Du Plessis notes, "Courage, hard as it is to come by, is the most valuable of journalistic qualities because courageous journalists know how important it is to go further, past the point of comfort, to the real truth."[501] (I wonder, though, if we *can* do more to teach courage in higher education.)

Highlighting the numerous stressors that modern journalists currently juggle, Aidan White, founder of the Ethical Journalism Network, acknowledges that "[i]n the competitive, breakneck pace of the modern newsroom, the pressure on journalists to deliver their stories faster and for different platforms has squeezed the ethical information space."[502] Because "[t]here is less time for editing, additional research, or confident fact-checking and verification,"[503] the risk of mistake-making has been enhanced. This is compounded "as web content and social networks become increasingly important as sources of news and information."[504] White also describes yet another concern in the field of journalism: self-censorship. He explains:

This is when journalism and media are driven not by editorial concerns, but by fear. When a journalist or editor makes an editorial decision over a story and its contents that is motivated by the threat of reprisal—whether from the state, the police, the owner, or the advertiser—it is nothing to do with the principles of good journalism.[505]

Lisa Taylor, an assistant professor at Ryerson University's School of Journalism in Toronto, has acknowledged "debilitating stress" among journalism students. She shared her own personal experience in both journalism and the law:

Prior to becoming a professor, I was a journalist for most of my professional career. But my academic background is in law, and I was in private practice for a short time. It's my observation that the practice of law was a lot like journalism practice in that the mantra of "suck it up"—not to mention "don't eff it up"—was commonplace. And perhaps because of that mentality, and an ethos that seemed to reward people for actively ignoring their emotional well-being, both journalism and law seem to leave a trail of addiction, divorce and substance abuse, and often foster environments where toxic personalities reign.[506]

In response, she and a faculty colleague launched a course to integrate mindfulness into the journalism curriculum.[507] Professor Taylor sheds light on how "the proliferation of new technologies, the intellectual demands of explaining complex subject matter, the fear of getting the story wrong or missing a deadline" can contribute to the development of "a very damaged human being."[508] Melanie Faizer, a journalism professor at the University of Tennessee who wrote about Professor Taylor's course in the online platform Mediashift, describes how new journalism students are quickly sent out into the world to interview strangers, a real-life educational experience that "can create a lot of anxiety among students."[509] The mindfulness course aspires to better prepare students to process this anxiety.

Additionally, Dr. Diana Brecher, a clinical psychologist and scholar-in-residence at Ryerson, along with her colleague Dr. Deena Kara Shaffer, the coordinator of Student Transitions and Retention, developed a semester-long program for all university students (not just journalism students) called Thriving for Action. The program is an "initiative to create student excellence by nurturing the whole person, rather than just focusing on academic skills."[510] Among many other things, they explore mistake-making with students. Dr. Brecher stated, "In an academic community, forgiving oneself for missing the mark or mistakes in judgement [sic], is an essential component of bouncing back after adversity."[511]

Further, as many journalists cover, witness, or experience *trauma* through their work, the Columbia Journalism School offers an online resource center that aims, as part of its multipronged mission, to advocate for "greater awareness by media organizations of the impact of trauma coverage on both news professionals and news consumers."[512] It is called the Dart Center for Journalism and Trauma, with a research center based at the University of Tulsa's Department of Psychology. Dart offers training based on several "values and approaches." These include

- Awareness of the impact of trauma on journalists and newsrooms
- Peer support and management tactics for dealing with trauma exposure, including
  - what to expect in or after a trauma scenario;
  - how to monitor how personnel are holding up;
  - building resilience in the face of undertaking very difficult stories; and
  - how to care for staff and mitigate the impact that traumatic events they cover could have on them directly.[513]

Further, some media companies send personnel who will be stepping into particularly dangerous field environments to specialized training programs, which include lectures, simulations, and interactive exercises.[514]

The opposite of fear is love—love of the challenge, love of the work, the pure joyous passion to take a shot at our dream and see if we can pull it off.[518]

—Steven Pressfield

CHAPTER 11

A Glimpse into Fear and Mistake-Making in Engineering Education and Training

Some engineering schools are modifying traditional curricula to incorporate courses that teach students about the reality of mistake-making in the field. Instead of ignoring the inevitability of mistakes in the profession—which can breed fear and "imposter syndrome" in new engineers—these courses encourage students to experiment with engineering design, make mistakes along the way, and learn how to handle and remedy design errors in a "non-threatening (academic) environment."[515]

Notably, openly discussing failure does not appear to be a new concept in engineering education. In December 1973, the *New York Times* published an article about a course offered at M.I.T. called Failure of Human Systems.[516] The course explored definitions of "success" and "failure," and considered how failure can spark learning, such as "when a scientist's experiment fails, thereby steering him toward a better theory."[517] One of the course leaders noted how, "[i]n a technical environment, error is considered an exciting thing."[518]

In 2003, professors in the Department of Computer Science and Engineering at the University of Washington crafted a new course "with ample opportunities for students to make mistakes—a fodder for reflection—and learn from them."[519] They acknowledged that software engineering obviously requires "hard skills," but it is the "lack of soft skills" that contributes to many project breakdowns.[520] The course originators noted that most engineering school curricula (at least, as of 2003) lacked opportunities for students to build resilience in reacting to mistakes.[521] Their course required students to engage in engineering simulations, make and discover errors, retool their approaches, and try again. The professors emphasized that, "[i]n order to maximize learning, it is important to provide an environment where students feel safe enough to take risks and learn from mistakes."[522]

Similarly, Professor Henry Petroski of Duke University has included the following reference to *failure* in his syllabus for his Introduction to Structural Engineering course: "The course employs failure as a unifying concept for understanding the history and practice of engineering and design."[523] His 2006 book about invention, *Success through Failure: The Paradox of Design,* observes that "time and again, we have built success on the back of failure—not through easy imitation of success."[524]

More recently, David Beach, a professor of mechanical engineering at Stanford University, created a course specifically designed to teach students how to learn from mistakes.[525] Professor Beach commented, "Most Stanford students have always excelled academically. The trickiest thing for us is to convince them that they have to do some bad stuff before they can do good stuff."[526] The course requires students to manufacture an engineered product, a process which inherently involves recovering from errors. With each failed attempt, students learn, revise, and grow in confidence.[527]

To the critic, art is a noun. . . . What artists learn from other artists is not so much history or technique (although we learn tons of that too); what we really gain from the artmaking of others is courage-by-association. Depth of contact grows as fears are shared—and thereby disarmed—and this comes from embracing art as a process, and artists as kindred spirits. To the artist, art is a verb.
—David Bayles and Ted Orland[528]

CHAPTER **12**

A Glimpse into Fear and Mistake-Making in Entrepreneurship and Business Education and Training

Two professors of entrepreneurship at Warwick Business School in the United Kingdom, James Hayton and Gabrielle Cacciotti, describe how "fail fast and often" is the mantra of the "lean startup movement."[529] Lean startup is a business model based, in part, on gathering customer feedback early and often. Even still, these professors indicate that "[f]ear of failure stalks the world of the entrepreneur, from losing key clients to running out of money."[530] They identify numerous sources of fear in entrepreneurs, including financial and funding problems, shortcomings in personal abilities, threats to self-esteem and social esteem, flaws in the fundamental business idea, ultimate ability to execute, and opportunity costs.[531] These professors teach entrepreneurs to reframe the fear of failure.

First, they recommend that entrepreneurs work on enhancing "emotional self-monitoring and control." They describe this a "skill that can be learned" and then applied through (1) "becoming aware of the signs of emotions intruding upon consciousness through feelings and moods," (2) "anticipating" the impact of emotions on thoughts, and (3) "using this awareness" to restrain the effects of emotions on decisions and actions.[532] Second, Hayton and Cacciotti advise entrepreneurs to engage in "problem solving," in other words, "[a]ctively seeking out flaws and weaknesses and doing something about them."[533] They strongly recommend being proactive instead of reactive when it comes to fear and mistake-making, because the former mode is a "powerful means of reducing the fear of failure."[534] Third, they advocate for increased learning opportunities; expanding one's fundamental capabilities and base knowledge can aid in "mitigating one's doubts" about the ability to perform successfully. Fourth, they advise entrepreneurs to garner "support"[535] from others. These professors readily acknowledge and emphasize that fear can "bring higher levels of stress, with potentially negative health consequences. So while fear is a natural state for an entrepreneur, the ability to manage it is a vital skill."[536]

Janet Sernack is an Australia-based CEO and founder of ImagineNation™, a "provocative global innovation education company."[537] In her blog, Sernack echoes the foregoing concept of "fail fast" in entrepreneurship, and advocates that cultivating a "fail fast" culture can "help organizations unfreeze, survive, flow and flourish with the current levels of *fear*, ambiguity, uncertainty, volatility and instability in 21st century organizations."[538] In her business coaching, she emphasizes the importance of making room for open discussion of failures and mistakes. This fosters "permission, vulnerability, safety, courage and trust for the deep learnings that mistakes and failure provide in advancing creativity, invention and innovation."[539] She explains that "in western civil societies and school systems, we learn to see failure as a mistake, as a shortcoming, stupidity or imperfection that we are responsible for and ashamed about."[540] If we demonize failure or mistakes, we bolster risk avoidance, blame-shifting, defensiveness, and stagnation of ideas.[541] Instead, Sernack advises business organizations to nurture an "environment in which making mistakes doesn't strike terror."[542] She recommends a few steps:

- Help individuals enhance their "tolerance to surprises and problems"
- Encourage "people to be, think and act differently"
- Support individuals "to recover, renew and replenish their hearts and minds when they make mistakes and fail"[543]

In a similar vein, Ion Valis, a strategic advisor to entrepreneurs and executives, helps individuals and businesses view errors as "magnificent mistakes." In "Learning from Mistakes: Obsessing about Success Can Prevent Learning from Mistakes,"[544] he advises startups and successful companies on how they can gain knowledge and grow from mistakes.

Computer science legend Ed Catmull cofounded Pixar Animation Studios and retired as president of Pixar Animation and Disney Animation in 2018. In his business book *Creativity, Inc.*, he shares insights about running successful teams. He also describes the approach to business and project development characterized by the slogans "Fail early and fast" and "Be wrong as fast as you can."[545] He emphasizes that the "fail fast" method is vastly different from the notion of "accept[ing] failure with dignity and mov[ing] on."[546] Instead, he explains that "failure is a manifestation of learning and exploration."[547] His philosophy on creative project development is that "[m]istakes aren't a necessary evil. They aren't evil at all. They are an inevitable consequence of doing something new."[548]

At American University, Professor Robert Sicina teaches an undergraduate course called Learn from Failure: The Key to Successful Decision Making, using his book of the same title as a text.[549] He describes the course as follows:

> *This multidisciplinary seminar focuses on how the lessons learned from failure are critically important to improvement in decision making processes. Students develop fresh perspectives on the strengths and weaknesses of standard methodologies applied to this critically important business task. They also learn new methodologies and skills that enable them to analyze actual high profile, failed operational, cultural, tactical and strategic decisions and gain a profound understanding of why those decisions failed.*[550]

In the course, students study how irrationality, complexity, and uncertainty "lead to failure in decision-making."[551] They "learn new skills to strengthen their decision-making capability."[552] Assignments include writing—in Week 1— "a one-page description of one of your major failures and why you think you failed."[553] Six weeks later, students write another paper analyzing their own identified failures using the concepts learned in the course thus far.[554] Professor Sicina reminds students, "We are, after all, the sum of the decisions we make,"[555] and thus he seeks to help them make good decisions in their personal and professional lives.

Can the legal profession learn from our contemporaries in these other fields, in which educators and influencers acknowledge fear and address failure and mistake-making head-on?

> *If I really listened to my fear, I could've clearly assigned value to what moved my spirit: Writing. Painting. Pulling something from nothing.*
>
> —Meera Lee Patel[556]

CHAPTER 13

A Glimpse into Fear and Mistake-Making in Sports Training

From high school or college athletes with scholarships and sports careers on the line, to professional players and Olympic competitors with glory, compensation, or endorsement deals hinging on victory, athletes at all levels wrestle with fear. They worry about mistakes. Sports-themed television and magazine ads promote messages of simply pushing through fear, like Dry Idea deodorant's "No matter what the score, never let them see you sweat," or Nike's "Just do it," or Y&R London's 2018 Olympic ad campaign, "The fearless are here."[557]

I'm more curious about the *reality* of how athletes deal with fear. I'm wondering if we can learn any sports-based techniques for untangling fear and then apply such strategies to performance-oriented activities in the legal arena. Like, when champion diver Greg Louganis hit his head on the diving board at the 1988 Olympic Games, was he afraid—even for a moment—to get back up there? If so, did he take tangible, practical, mental and physical steps to work through the fear? Or was he able to just pretend fear doesn't exist, as many television ads exhort us to do? Are boxers ever afraid to step back into the fight after absorbing a ferocious right hook to the jaw in the prior round? How do skiers or snowboarders mentally recover from scary wipeouts and climb back up the mountain? How do race car drivers slide back into a vehicle after surviving a dangerous crash? What do these athletes tell themselves? Do they put mental and physical rituals into motion to quell the fear? Can we do the same?

In researching this chapter, I stumbled upon a Gatorade ad with the message, "Make *defeat* your fuel."[558] In the ad, Michael Jordan talks about being cut from the varsity team. Peyton Manning mentions his abysmal 3–13 record in his rookie year. Eli Manning references the time he led the league in interceptions. I like this message better than pretending we are invincible. We fall sometimes. And to be great, we pick ourselves up, work hard, and keep going. But exactly how do these athletes address performance fears? Yes, these are exceptional people, but they're not robots. They *must* experience fear at times, not only of injury, pain, or failure, but of judgment or criticism.

I believe, for law students and lawyers to truly be as extraordinary as we are meant to be, we must regard ourselves not only as artists (as we explored in Chapter 2) but as athletes, too. I always liked the term *scholar-athlete*: high school and college players who strive for academic success *and* excel on the field. As law students and lawyers, thinking about ourselves as scholar-athletes can be empowering. As I wrote in *The Introverted Lawyer*, in my serpentine journey toward learning how to conquer extreme anxiety about public speaking, I realized just how deeply intertwined my mental and physical manifestations of stress were. We can't focus on our brains alone; we have to pay attention to our bodies as well. We are scholars *and* athletes.

In researching and writing *The Introverted Lawyer*, I needed to analyze my body's automatic responses to stress in heated performance moments. I discovered that I instinctively cross my limbs, hunch my shoulders, and make myself small. Closing inward is my psychological and physiological attempt to become invisible to a perceived aggressor. Inadvertently but unfortunately, this self-protective origami routine hinders my blood, oxygen, and energy flow. Once I discerned that this was my habitual physical reaction to anxiety-producing stimuli, I needed to train myself to unfold and open back up, each time. When I consciously adopt an athlete's balanced open stance—at the podium or even sitting in a chair—I am able to channel my adrenaline, oxygen, and blood flow much more effectively. In an athlete's stance, I am flexible and ready to counter whatever might come my way. When I am folded inward, I remain restricted and stuck. An easy target. Applying simple structural shifts, I began to notice how subtle changes in physical stance and posture gave my brain a remarkable boost.

To become *more* in touch with my physicality and to build stamina to power through performance moments, I started incorporating a variety of intense physical activities into my exercise routine, like challenging spinning classes and one-on-one boxing training sessions. For the first time in my life, I took myself seriously as an athlete, to make myself a strong scholar-athlete in intellectual bouts. The physical work began to pay sizable dividends in enhanced mental strength in performance moments. I learned how to trust my body to strengthen my mind. I realized that since I hadn't fainted in a 60-minute boxing session at Trinity Boxing Club with my trainer, Ray—even though my face was watermelon red and sweat poured from every pore in my face—I wasn't going to pass out in a stressful law-related presentation. (More on this in Chapter 16.) But now I'm even more curious. What can we learn from athletes, trainers, and sports psychologists about how to untangle fear, from a mental *and* physical perspective? Even for folks who are not yet fans of physical exertion, or who have physical limitations, are there subtle adjustments we can make to our structural frames that can help drive our mental power?

SLOWING OUR ROLL

George Mumford was an aspiring college basketball player, but injuries pointed his life down a different path. Now a mindfulness and sports performance expert, he advises professional athletes on performance issues. In *The Mindful Athlete: Secrets to Pure Performance,*[559] he talks about our instinctive reactions to stressors:

> *Life is all about the stimulus that we experience in the world and the way we interpret that in our minds. We can react to this stimulus in various knee-jerk ways— with anger, agitation, anxiety, fear, craving, doubt, guilt—or we can respond to this stimulus by getting still.*[560]

Echoing some of the concepts we learned back in Chapter 5, Mumford describes how our "fight or flight" response is "hardwired into our DNA and activated by fear, anxiety, and stress."[561] He reiterates that when we encounter an anxiety stimulus, our sympathetic nervous system bombards our body with stress hormones. As these hormones pile up, our "ability to think clearly and respond appropriately" declines.[562] This is where enhanced self-awareness can really help us.

Mumford provides a helpful distinction among "stress, distress," and what Hans Selye, author of *The Stress of Life*, refers to as "eustress."[563] We all experience stress. But "[w]hen stress is persistent, unresolved, and cumulative to the point of being chronic—whether that stress is physical or emotional—it becomes distress."[564] Lingering in protracted distress can lead to mental health issues such as anxiety or depression.[565] Mumford's book introduced me to the notion of "eustress." He says:

> *Eustress, on the other hand, enhances physical and mental functions through such things as strength training and challenging work. This is the "good" kind of stress. Eustress can be described as that space between where we are and where we want to go—or that place between our comfort zones and the fringe of our discomfort zones.*[566]

Mumford explains that when we drive our physical bodies beyond our comfort zones in exercise or sports conditioning, we feel physical manifestations of the exertion: we breathe more heavily, our hearts thump faster, we perspire, we might even sense a few pangs of muscle strain.[567] If we approach the physical conditioning challenge *mindfully*—armed with the knowledge that we actually *can* handle it—our bodies adjust, and we get physically stronger. Mumford says that, "In this way, we set down new neural pathways while increasing our physical skills."[568] Not only are we toning or building muscle, we are changing our brain. We are building self-trust.

Mumford draws parallels between this type of physical growth and mental development:

> *The same is true of our ability to push ourselves mentally. Mentally we can train ourselves to be comfortable with being uncomfortable, to feel calm in the midst of chaos and stay in the eye of the proverbial hurricane.*[569]

Through enhanced self-awareness, we can increase our tolerance for temporary discomfort because we know and trust that it will subside.[570] This reminds me of the advice that Barbara, my wonderful therapist, gave me when I was struggling to stay afloat during my relationship implosion the year I turned 30. "Tolerate the discomfort," she said. "It will get so much better." At the time, everything hurt, brutally. It didn't feel like that pain would ever abate. But I had to trust that I was doing the right thing for my personal growth (really, my survival) and *keep going*. Similarly, Mumford emphasizes how, in learning how to be somewhat uncomfortable yet realize the discomfort will ebb, we learn to trust our minds and bodies and begin to walk through fear. He describes how, "even in the midst of anxiety, we can experience the feeling that everything is going to work out fine; we might even experience the kind of fear that gives us the courage to walk straight ahead, no matter what."[571]

Mumford does not promote the message that fear is the great motivator. Instead, he offers a tangible approach to changing our relationship with fear (and other knee-jerk emotions) so that we can move through stressful performance events successfully. He first notes that, in training, "[o]ur bodies work best when we push them in small increments. If we push ourselves too far, eustress can become distress."[572] To me, this is why all-out "just do it" anarchy, and barreling into lawyering performance scenarios without self-awareness and reflection, does not work to untangle fear. Instead, we must treat the experience of expanding beyond our comfortable boundaries into productive eustress as "a continuous incremental process of romancing your discomfort zone"[573]—in Mumford's words. We have to *slow our roll*.

Athletes (and we as scholar-athletes) "get in our own way."[574] Mumford notes how fear and anger might seem like mighty motivators in the winner-takes-all vibe of mainstream sports.[575] But rather than blindly glorifying fear and anger as performance enhancers, or trying to squash these emotions, Mumford advises that we get to know our fear (and anger). He explains:

> *For example, when anger arises, you [learn to] understand how to let it go without pushing it away or trying to get rid of it, which in any case doesn't work. Instead, with right effort you actually pay more attention to the anger when it arises and take the time to be with it, breathe with it, and let it go without effort.*[576]

Mumford's recommended approach toward fear and other emotions arising during an intense sports scenario is for the athlete to learn how to recognize the emotion and then untangle it without reacting to it.[577] When we are blinded, clouded, or paralyzed by emotion, it "messes with [our] performance."[578] To remove the blindfold or the gauzy haze, Mumford advises us to *slow down* and get to know the messages that "have been in [our] head since childhood"; in doing so, we reveal "established mental patterns, and deep-seated fears."[579] The well-entrenched negative soundtrack will start up again in each performance moment and try to dominate, catapulting us into instinctive thoughtless action. We can stop this negative spin cycle.

In our *training* as scholar-athletes, we can learn to *recognize* the emotions and negative mental messages, a process we will discuss more in Chapter 15. Then, in *performance* moments, we will *notice* when the unhelpful emotions or messages pop into our heads (almost like cartoon dialogue bubbles), pause, ponder them briefly instead of fighting them, address them realistically, and then set them aside and keep going.[580] In this process, we slow down, pay attention, realize, pause, ponder, process, and *then* hit the ball, or throw the punch, or hurl the javelin. Or in the legal arena, we first *notice . . . filter . . . set aside* the unhelpful stuff . . . and *then* ask the tough question, voice the objection, counter the argument. Slowing our roll in *training* helps us master our emotions and internal messages in the *game.*

Applied sports psychologists David Grand and Alan Goldberg explain how traumatic past experiences can become fixed or ossified in athletes' bodies, stoking fear and blocking performance.[581] Like Mumford, they advise that to effectively work through these performance blocks, it is important for an athlete to slow down, get quiet, and focus on "the roots of the problem deep in the athlete's *body* and brain."[582] These experts caution that "unless these wounds are addressed at the core, the athlete can't regain top form."[583] They also emphasize that we are all unique individuals, not one-size-fits-all robots.[584] To address performance issues, we must carve out some time to reflect on our individual past fear (or trauma) experiences, and understand how they have embedded in our bodies and solidified into the negative soundtrack playing in our minds. As former Navy SEAL Brandon Webb points out, "The great majority of the fears most of us experience day to day are nothing but shadowboxing: not a response to a genuine danger but a reaction to the reverberations of events long behind us."[585] Through this work, we uproot these experiences and begin to let them go. This is the opposite of "just do it." This is "just be it."

Yanking Tulips

When I was going through my rough and traumatic relationship split, described earlier, one day I returned to the cute and cozy house I had left behind to retrieve some personal items. As I backed my car out of the driveway for the last time, fighting the urge to cry, or press Rewind and undo all the gut-wrenching decisions I had made, I saw my tulips. I love tulips. I actively dislike roses. And don't even get me started on sunflowers. A few years earlier, I had planted tulips on the rocky hill that flanked my driveway. My guy had ribbed me about the haphazard nature of my bulb arrangement, wanting instead to hire a landscaper. Each spring, my tulips shot out of the ground here and there, no rhyme or reason to their organization. It was fresh, surprising, and imperfectly perfect, and I loved the wildness and unpredictability of it. That day in my driveway, I saw my tulips. I threw the gearshift into park, and leapt from the car. I grabbed and yanked every tulip out of the ground, mulch flying, dirty bulbs swaying. I set my lovely, messy, yanked tulips on the passenger seat and drove away.

Sometimes we need to *yank* those tulips, uproot them in a messy flourish, and gently replant them somewhere else.

COURAGE IS ACHIEVED, NOT BEQUEATHED

Last spring, I attended a fund-raiser gala for a theater company in New York. My host (a good friend and professor colleague) sat me next to a feisty Irishman, envisioning the two of us forging a deep bond over all things Irish once I began to pepper the conversation with references about my favorite band, U2. In an initial fun repartee about grammatical gaffes in the dinner menu, I mentioned a U2 lyric containing a dangling preposition, which admittedly drives me bananas. The Irishman promptly declared his sheer loathing of and disdain for lead singer and humanitarian, my beloved Bono (using much more colorful language). Normally, such a visceral response might have prompted me to case the exits and sneak out when no one was paying attention. But my quest to match this guy's humor supplanted my usual introversion (and knee-jerk judgment of anyone who criticizes my band). I racked my brain for alternative conversation starters. Over appetizers, the Irishman kept leaning behind me to quip about golf strategy with my host's husband, who was seated on my opposite side. Suddenly, it dawned on me who my dinner partner was: a popular golf writer and commentator! By the second course of the meal, I had my new ice breaker.

I ventured, "So, on a more serious note, I'm writing a book about fear, and I want to draw an analogy between lawyering fears and sports fears. Can you recommend any good books or articles written by sports psychologists?"

The Irishman paused, and answered, "Yep, Bob Rotella."

At home later that evening, I googled Bob Rotella. It turns out, Dr. Bob Rotella was the director of sports psychology at UVA—my college and law school! I promptly ordered one of his books, *How Champions Think: In Sports and in Life*.[586]

How Champions Think validates the idea that principles of sports psychology can help performers in other fields. Rotella describes his clients outside the college sports environment as "businessmen or singers or any of a hundred things. But they have performance issues just as athletes do, and the same ideas that help athletes improve can help them."[587] Through his writing and training programs, Dr. Rotella "teach[es] the attitudes and habits of an exceptional life."[588] And luckily, he says the characteristics and approaches he recommends "can be learned."[589] As tennis champion Chris Evert once said, "Competitive toughness is an acquired skill and not an inherited gift."[590]

TRAIN, PREPARE, PERFORM

Rotella teaches his athletes the mantra of "Train it and trust it."[591] He instructs his competitors to "[l]earn the skill thoroughly, so it's ingrained in your subconscious. Then, at the moment of performance, don't think about it. Trust that your subconscious brain will do its job."[592] He cautions, "the trusting won't work if the training hasn't happened."[593] He also advises that this process won't "work if you confuse the subconscious with negative thoughts, fears, or doubts."[594] We need to learn how to greet fear, and then move it aside, so our subconscious can carry us forward unencumbered.

Rotella acknowledges how golfers experience "trembling, wet hands, rapid heartbeat, a sinking feeling in the gut, and sometimes even a feeling that breathing is difficult."[595] Rotella delves into the science of fear: "physical symptoms of nerves are the products of inevitable chemical changes that occur inside the body during moments of high stress, changes like a shot of adrenaline."[596] He advises that these physical manifestations are "outside our conscious control. So it's a waste of time trying to avoid them."[597] Instead, he coaches athletes to develop a "preparation process" and a "performance process"[598] to understand and recognize innate mental and physical responses to stress and then develop routines and strategies for peak performance. We can do the same.

PREPARATION AND PERFORMANCE PROCESSES

Rotella describes how exceptional "performers train themselves to have quieter minds as their bodies get excited."[599] During *preparation* training, athletes condition their minds and bodies to step into each performance phase or activity with a plan . . . a conscious and repeatable regimen. A great athlete (like a great lawyer) would never charge headlong into a match, a game, a competition, an arena, without a strategy.

Then, after preparing through the requisite training, athletes develop a *performance* process, paring down their training into a shorter sequence of thoughts and maneuvers. The purpose of the sequence is to prime the mind and body for the actual performance moment, and defuse any pre-game jitters.[600] It's at this point that the preparation and training transforms into *trust*.

Rotella refers to the pre-performance sequence as a preshot routine. The routine or sequence helps athletes believe in their ability in the performance moment. A preshot routine is a series of brief mental statements and physical movements that lead the athlete right into the "shot." The shot might be a drive, a chip, or a putt in golf. It might be a serve in tennis. It might be a penalty kick in soccer or a field goal in football. Pre-performance routines empower the boxer to step into the ring for a new round, the gymnast to mount the balance beam, the snowboarder to drop into the half-pipe. Rotella explains the preshot routine's effect on the athlete:

> *It calms him. Its mental subtext, if you will, is that this is just another shot, like hundreds of thousands of shots he's hit in practice and in games, using this same preshot routine or performance process.*[601]

The purpose of the preshot routine is to put the athlete's "mind and body into the proper places"[602] in the performance moment and reclaim perspective. Instead of worrying about the stakes, the score, the big picture, statistics, or outcomes, the athlete focuses on simple movement sequences for this sole shot. *I'm inhaling. I'm balancing my physical stance like I've done a thousand times. I'm exhaling. I'm visualizing the angle I need. I'm aligning with this ball, that goalpost, that net, this equipment.* The athlete also runs through a mental check-list for this one discrete shot. *I've prepared for this. I've done the work. My body and mind are strong. I'm going to do the best I can in this moment. Nothing beyond this instant in time matters right now. I'm trusting my process.*

In the moment, we trust our training and preparation. We execute routine physical movements that we know work for us. We remind ourselves to stop overthinking and instead honor the physical and mental work we have already done. *Trust* our system. We don't exaggerate the importance of this one shot. It's just one shot. Then, we move.

Choreographer Twyla Tharp also talks about the importance of ritual. She notes, "Athletes know the power of a triggering ritual. . . . By making the start of the sequence automatic, they replace doubt and fear with comfort and routine."[603] Tharp likewise uses the power of ritual to remind her to trust her own system when starting a creative project. She says rituals and routines reassure the artist (and the athlete), "I've done it before. It was good. I'll do it again."[604]

In an article entitled "How to Manage Stress Like an Olympic Biathlete," Tara Parker-Pope, like Rotella, highlights the importance of an athlete's phys-ical *and* mental preparation process: "Bottom line, it's all about preparation, knowing that you are entering a stressful situation and figuring out ahead of time how you are going to deal with it."[605] She emphasizes the efficacy of trust-ing one's *preparation* process, and then in the moment, putting the *performance* process into action. Parker-Pope quotes Clare Egan, an Olympic biathlete (cross-country skiing and rifle shooting): "I have this task I've done thousands of times that I'm trying to repeat. I know that I'm going to have distractions. The person next to me hit all of the targets. The fans are screaming. The per-son on the loudspeaker says, 'Here's Clare Egan from the U.S.A. Let's see if she can hold it together.'"[606] Egan summarizes how she walks her brain through the sequential steps she developed in preparation: "There's my target, here's my trigger, this is my process, now I'm going to make the shot.'"[607] She describes how her "strategy is to replace goal-oriented thoughts ('I have to hit this last shot') with cue words that help her focus on the things that will get the job done. Words like form, breathing, trigger and follow-through."[608] She empha-sizes the importance of "focusing on your own process and tasks and not being distracted by the potential outcome or how others are performing."[609]

Authors of *Mind Gym: An Athlete's Guide to Inner Excellence,* Gary Mack and David Casstevens, also underscore the importance of conditioning our brains *and* bodies.[610] Why? Because the "athlete's brain or mind can't be separated from his or her body."[611] Mack and Casstevens recount golfer Sam Snead's philosophy: "[P]ractice time is when you put your brain into your muscles."[612]

For athletes, artists, and lawyers alike, "[t]he conscious practice of routines leads to the unconscious habits of success."[613]

SMILE, LET GO, MOVE

Rotella provides another interesting bit of advice: "One tip I've shared with many golfers is a simple one: smile a little bit before each putt."[614] Smile. You've done the work. You've invested the training, the hours, days, months, and years of preparation. Smile and put the preshot routine into action. Let it unfold. As Mumford notes, Olympic snowboard champion Shaun White described his transition into a performance moment in these words: "At that point you're really not thinking, you're just letting it happen. It's a mixture of being completely focused, then slightly not caring."[615] Authors Mack and Casstevens similarly report that Olympic figure skater Scott Hamilton stepped onto the ice before his gold medal performance at the 1984 Sarajevo Games with "refined indifference."[616] These experts emphasize the importance of "get[ting] your head out of the way so your body can perform. Turn off the analytical mind. Switch from the thinking mode to the trusting mode. You can't be thinking and swinging at the same time."[617]

Josh Waitzkin is the author of *The Art of Learning: An Inner Journey to Optimal Performance*. He is also an eight-time national chess champion, the central character in the book and movie *Searching for Bobby Fischer*, and a martial arts champion. Waitzkin advises that in the game of chess, "much of what separates the great from the very good is deep presence, relaxation of the conscious mind, which allows the unconscious to flow unhindered."[618] Overthinking, and even overcaring, are not going to make athletes, or *us*, perform better. We've done the work. In the performance moment, *less* is more. We *trust* our pared-down preshot process, we quiet our minds, we lessen our concern about the outcomes, we smile, and we go.

OUTCOMES, RESULTS, EVALUATIONS

Regarding outcomes, results, and the assessments of others, Rotella advises that "champions rarely let themselves be influenced much by outside evaluations. . . . Faithfully following a rigorous process sets a much higher standard."[619] He explains that successful individuals appraise their performance against their established process standards, not the ultimate outcomes.[620] This doesn't mean they don't care about winning or achievement; rather, they know that such positive results flow directly from sticking to such proven preparation and performance processes.[621] Rotella advises athletes to establish "performance process goals" rather than outcome goals:

Performance process goals involve things like staying in the present moment, accepting whatever happens as it happens, underreacting to everything, being unflappable, and totally trusting in your skills during competition. The exceptional person monitors himself in relation to these goals (though not, of course, in the heat of competition) and uses that evaluation for making course corrections.[622]

The Sport Psych Handbook also differentiates between "task-mastery orientation" and "ego orientation."[623] For athletes grappling with how to balance training/ performance processes and outcomes, it is helpful to understand that "task mastery centers on the process of improvement while ego involvement targets the outcome of competition."[624]

According to Rotella, former University of North Carolina basketball coach Dean Smith once counseled Michael Jordan to spend "no more than ten or twenty minutes to reflect on a bad performance. That would be enough to learn everything that could be learned from it."[625] This advice resonates with me as a writer, too. Instead of worrying about outcomes—manuscript completion, peer reviews, criticism, marketing success or failure—I try to focus on the work. Did I set up a writing *process* (like an athlete's training process)? Yes: two hours every single consecutive day for as long as it takes to get the manuscript done. Did I adhere to that regimen? Yes. That's how the work gets done. That's how I improve and grow. I can't worry about the ultimate outcome. Right now, it's about the words on the page, the work, and "faithfully following a rigorous process,"[626] as Rotella describes. If I'm sticking to my process and doing the daily work, I can feel proud of the achievement. And if I momentarily falter, perhaps because of a bad review or a critical reader response, I follow Coach Smith's advice. I'm allowed to reflect for 10 or 20 minutes, figure out what learnings I can possibly glean, and then I move on.

UNTANGLING ATHLETES' FEARS

Applied sports psychologists Grand and Goldberg discuss how emotional sports trauma from abusive coaching, a humiliating loss, or a scary injury to oneself or another can manifest as fear, and other destructive emotions like shame.[627] During subsequent performance moments, the fear-based fight-or-flight response "act[s] out of time and place,"[628] recalling the past trauma again and again. Grand and Goldberg explain that the automatic "biological stress response dramatically disrupts the athlete's ability to stay loose, calm, and focused, which is a critical prerequisite for expanded performance."[629] They advise that "to heal performance, we must also heal the person."[630] They reiterate that simply striving to avoid fears as an athlete doesn't work because "avoidance sets into motion an escalating cycle of ever-increasing fear."[631]

Instead, athletes must untangle the trauma and fear, in order to expunge these harmful influences.

In addition to working (perhaps with a professional) to reflect and identify stored traumas, Grand and Goldberg recommend flipping our relationship with "negative internal chatter," which can quickly envelop us in a "genuine sense of mortal threat."[632] They suggest taking a fresh look at our fear messages, noting that they really might have a "positive intention"[633] at their root: self-preservation. "Look out! You might hurt yourself again!" "Stop! Are you sure you should be trying that? Seems risky!" "You don't want to make a fool of yourself! Maybe it's better to avoid this altogether!" Have we heard these messages somewhere before?

Instead of bristling and becoming rigid when we hear the familiar and sometimes undermining or "unkind, critical, and demeaning"[634] voices in our heads—messages that perhaps came from past coaches, mentors, family members, teammates, or other competitors—we can refrain from fighting, arguing with, or blocking them.[635] Rather, we can be "curious, relaxed, and accepting."[636] We can recognize a critical message for what it is, perhaps a "misguided" but well-meaning buddy who is just frantically trying to seize our attention.[637] *Mind the gap! Hazard ahead! Too risky! Abort the mission!*

Overall, to start untangling sports fears, Grand and Goldberg recommend

- taking the time to discern what past (emotional or physical) traumas may have occurred in our lives that we may even have forgotten[638]
  - in other words, transcribing a physical and emotional "trauma history"[639]
- working (perhaps with a professional) to unfreeze or unlock any such traumas that are frozen or stuck in the body[640]
- "stretching with awareness"—paying attention to individual muscle groups one-at-a-time—before a performance event to relax the mind and body[641]
- Being "curious, relaxed, and accepting" when negative messages appear, and instead of resisting or trying to knock them out, gently treating them like well-intentioned but "misguided" buddies, ushering them aside, and then moving forward into the performance moment.[642]

As lawyer-athletes, we can learn a lot from these sports psychology techniques:

- Develop a *preparation process* to train our minds and bodies.
  - Experiment with *eustress,* increasing our tolerance for temporary physical and mental discomfort, learning that we can keep going and we will be okay.
- Get still and *slow our roll.*
  - Reflect on past traumas (physical and emotional) and whether (and where) they might have entrenched within us.
  - Get to know our negative messages:
    - What are their roots?
    - Are these past messages in any way relevant to our *current* lives in the law?
    - Or can we reframe our relationship with them? Can we delete or expunge them?
- Learn to *trust* our training.
- Adopt *performance processes* and *preshot routines,* which we will put into action as we step into intense performance moments.
- In the moment:
  - Smile.
  - Breathe.
  - Trust.
  - Let it go.
  - Let the unconscious take over the conscious brain.
  - Flow.
- Focus on processes, not outcomes.
- Celebrate achieving *process* goals.
- Learn from mistakes but don't dwell on them.
- Move on to the next challenge.

There are two basic motivating forces: fear and love. When we are afraid, we pull back from life. When we are in love, we open to all that life has to offer with passion, excitement, and acceptance.

—John Lennon

FOUR STEPS TO FORTITUDE IN LAWYERING

So far, we have reflected on the presence of fear in law school, in law practice, and in our clients. We've examined the role that fear can play in mistake-making by lawyers. We've delved into the science of fear and discussed how this tricky emotion toys with our brains and bodies. We've explored how fear blocks learning and performance, and can mask itself behind other destructive emotions. We've also taken a look at how other professions and industries have approached the reality of fear (and mistake-making) in education and training. Now let's synthesize all those learnings and start doing the work to untangle our fear. This section of the book offers a four-step journey toward fortitude in lawyering:

- Step 1: Untangling fear
- Step 2: Mentally rebooting
- Step 3: Channeling our inner athlete
- Step 4: Cultivating a culture of fortitude

I'm excited to do this work with you.

CHAPTER **14**

Step 1: Untangling Fear

Fortitude is defined as "strength of mind that enables a person to encounter danger or bear pain or adversity with courage."[643] Fortitude in lawyering is our new mission. This chapter explores how—individually and collectively—we can begin to untangle the destructive components of fear from its potentially constructive elements, differentiate fear from other emotions, and understand what is really going on in our minds and bodies in the face of a fear-inducing event.

I will start by sharing four of my personal experiences: two life scenarios that, according to "normal" societal standards, probably *should* make me afraid but somehow do not, and two work-related situations that rationally should *not* make me afraid—based on my years of professional experience—but do. This is an experiment in "comparative fearlessness." In starting to untangle my own fear, it helped immensely to compare and contrast these contradictory scenarios, notice the different automatic mental and physical reactions occurring within each situation, parse out the inconsistencies, and discern what drives the distinctions. Why do some experiences that *should* be scary instead give us "productive and fulfilling" adrenaline rushes, excitement, and a zest for adventure? Why do other situations, which we are absolutely intellectually and professionally qualified to handle, completely freak us out? Our goal through this exercise is to identify the emotional, mental, and physical drivers in scenarios that invoke "good" excitement and adventure, and then bring that swagger into the more intimidating lawyering circumstances in which we feel fear. By doing so, we start to recognize and become more aware of our fear triggers. Then we develop concrete strategies to navigate those experiences with fortitude.

General George S. Patton once said, "Courage is fear holding on a minute longer." Let's hang on together and figure this out.

AN EXERCISE IN COMPARATIVE FEARLESSNESS

I'm Fearless When . . . I Travel

I am *not* afraid to book an airline ticket and hop on a plane to travel alone to a foreign country. Family and acquaintances often gasp, "You're going alone? *There?*! *How* are you going to do that? Won't you be lonely? Afraid? What if you get lost? Or hurt?" This one's also a real encourager: "What are you running away from with all this travel?" And then there's this gem from a few summers ago: "You're not going to find your soul in Rome."

Really? We'll see about that.

I love the ritual of packing my passport, the right electrical converter for the destination country, sunglasses, a pile of books, and my journal. I print my boarding pass, lock the front door to my Brooklyn apartment, and hop in an Uber to JFK airport, ready to leave comfort and predictability behind. I nestle into a window seat on the plane, try unsuccessfully to catch a few hours of sleep, land at an airport with foreign vocabulary directing me toward Passport Control, and slide my documents through the half-moon in the glass partition separating me from the immigration officer. He looks me in the eye. *Yep, it's really me in that photo.* A glint of excitement replaces the sleepiness in my eyes. My heart expands against my ribs, newly blooming after being dormant for a tad too long in my regular life.

I am *not* afraid to figure out the local airport's ATM machine, then reject the sly offers of unsanctioned transportation from men with slick hair and even slicker shoes. A peculiar assertiveness buoys me toward a guy in jeans smoking a stubby brown cigarette and leaning against what looks like a legitimate taxi, its sedan door plastered with currency rates and an official-looking phone number. *"Quanto costa?"* I ask, instinctively in Italian, my brain's go-to foreign language, no matter whether I've just landed in Argentina, Berlin, or the Canary Islands.

I check into the hotel, which I usually book online by cross-checking options on my three favorite travel websites (www.i-escape.com, www.jetsetter.com, and www.mrandmrssmith.com; a small boutique hotel off the beaten path that appears on all three sites is typically a winner). I deposit my luggage in the room or with the front desk if I've arrived too early for check-in. I freshen up my sticky contact lenses, brush my teeth, grab a pair of sunglasses, and go. My heart balloons further as I step out onto the sidewalk, starting a new urban "walkabout."

I'm *not* afraid to meander alone for hours, in search of graffiti street art, which I love, or quirky sights: a wheelbarrow half-full of black spiny sea urchins in Sicily; a broken Vespa lying like a snow angel on a sidewalk in Dublin; a photograph hanging on the wall of a Buenos Aires museum capturing Frida Kahlo coolly smoking a cigarette. I make a note to print a copy of the Frida photo and hang it above the "Bono smoking" photo in my apartment.

I walk for hours. I rarely take cabs. If my legs tire, I'll attempt the local bus, tram, trolley, or subway. I wriggle with self-satisfaction when I am able to negotiate the currency and ticket-buying labyrinths. Even when I'm scolded by ticket collectors for not having the right validation stamp, I shrug my shoulders and smile apologetically. *Oops.* I'm *not* afraid as local public transit drivers careen around serpentine curves, hurtle down impossibly narrow side streets flanked with parked cars, or teeter on precipices completely devoid of Americanized guard rails. In those moments, a familiar rebellious thought prevails: "If this is how I go out, I will die happy."

I'm *not* afraid of the grifters edging closer to me when I sightsee, checking out my level of pickpocketability. I brandish an uncharacteristic "Don't mess with me" vibe. The guys hawking selfie sticks, bottles of cold water, or squealing noisemakers somehow give me a wide berth yet bombard every tourist around me. Instead, I get to marvel. I get to absorb the awe and wonder.

Seeing the name of Marcus Agrippa etched into the portico under the roof of the Pantheon in Rome prompts a spasm in my chest: astonishment. Running my fingers along a chunk of the Berlin Wall caked in graffiti paint launches an eye twitch: curiosity and fascination. Climbing the steps to Barcelona's Olympic Stadium, my fingers gripping my U2 concert ticket tucked into the inside back flap of my crossover satchel, every hair on my body stands at attention: excitement.

I'm oddly *not* unnerved by the presence of stone-faced guards decked out in body armor, holding machine guns, and surveying the hives of tourists. I'm not rattled by dizzying obstacle courses of metal detectors and security checkpoints in some of these international cities. I'm not afraid of getting lost, getting yelled at by a grocery store clerk for not weighing my produce correctly, or ordering the wrong meal (trust me, you only confuse *polpo* [octopus] with *polpetta* [meatball] once!).

I'll admit that two travel scenarios invite a smidge of nervousness, but I can't honestly label them fear-inducing: driving a car, and the first five steps into a restaurant or bar to dine alone.

My birthday a few years ago overlapped with a week-long break from the legal writing course I was teaching at a law school in Trento, Italy. I had taken a six-week hiatus to teach in Trento after I left the law firm world and before I transitioned to full-time teaching in Brooklyn. I booked a flight from Verona to Catania, an airport on the eastern side of Sicily. The day before the trip, I called the 1–800 number for my American car insurance company and engaged in a surprisingly helpful conversation with my insurance agent about the type of rental car insurance I already had, and any additional coverage I needed to purchase. I went online to reserve and pre-pay for a rental car, including what the agent advised was the proper amount and type of insurance coverage for an international rental. The morning of my journey to Sicily, I walked from my faculty apartment near the Adige River to the Trento train station. I figured out the ticket machine and purchased a one-way train ticket to Verona (shooing away the "helpers" lurking by the ticket dispenser). I located the ticket validation machine and stamped my ticket to avoid a stern talking-to and a fine imposed by the ticket collector on the train. I traveled to Verona, gazing out the window at passing vineyards and castles. I found and hopped on a shuttle bus from the Verona train station to the Verona airport. I paid the (unadvertised) excess baggage fee for my flight to Catania, as my duffel bag *allegedly* exceeded the allotted kilogram weight (it didn't). I meandered to the gate for my flight. Attempting to blend in with the relaxed Italians, I sipped an espresso rather than a cappuccino (a social faux pas after noon in Italy—no milk after midday). I observed the families: sexy dads with shocks of thick hair and watchbands that matched their suede shoes, lazily caressing the shoulders of curvy moms with toddlers clinging to their tight-jeans-clad hips. I swallowed a last sip of espresso and boarded my flight. I asked the flight attendant in Italian for a bottle of water, and perused a map of Sicily. So far, so good. *Un'altra avventura.* Another adventure.

Landing, I retrieved my bag, exited the Catania airport, and followed my printed directions to the car rental agency. *Cross the parking lot. Look for a horseshoe-shaped bus stop waiting area. The rental car shuttle will await you.* It didn't. I stood next to a dilapidated crescent-shaped structure that did not look like it had experienced human occupancy in decades. I pulled out my cell phone, reluctant to use it since the "extra data" I had purchased from Verizon kept expiring too quickly every time I used GPS or engaged in one too many hilarious strings of text messages with my friends back home. I dialed the phone number on the car rental agency directions. "*Pronto!*" a voice rasped. I attempted to explain my circumstances in Italian. The phone was passed to another person on the other end who screeched, "Wrong-a number-a!" and hung up.

Dang it.

I scanned the parking lot. Did a gut check. I was surprisingly unworried, unafraid, and unstressed. I had no agenda for the next week. I wasn't going to miss a flight, a train, a bus, a class, a meal, or an appointment. I just needed to figure out where the heck in Sicily my rental car was located. Once retrieved, I would then drive two hours south to Siracusa, or more specifically, the old town of Ortigia, where I had reserved a hotel room near the sea for a few days before exploring other parts of the island. *L'avventura*, I reminded myself.

Suddenly, a taxi zoomed into the parking lot. I sprinted toward it, gesticulating madly. The driver stopped and rolled down his window. I muddled through an Italian explanation of my predicament, and thrust the rental car papers inside the window. The driver nodded. *Allora, andiamo.* I hopped in the back seat. Giant droplets of sweat leapt from my pores. Yet, I didn't feel mentally stressed.

After a 10-minute drive—and €20 later—the driver deposited me at the rental car agency. We both exclaimed, "*Esiste!*" And laughed.

I stood in line behind a blond Norwegian couple, watching the rental car agent use an aging Xerox machine to copy passports and paperwork, then place the materials in plastic sleeves. When my turn came, the agent asked me, "*Italiano o inglese?*" As much as I want to go native whenever possible, I usually feel like I should undertake most financial transactions in English if it's an option. He promptly informed me, "Cars often get stolen in Sicily. You need insurance."

"Yes, I pre-paid for the insurance."

He smirked. "You take-a your chances-a," he said, in his glorious accent.

Sensing a shakedown, I dug in. "Yes. No. I already bought insurance."

"Yessa, but your car likely will be stolen. Better to buy our-a insurance," he responded with a shoulder shrug. "*Va bene.*"

Now I started to feel a smidge of worry. *Stay calm. Trust the universe. You already bought insurance.* I exhaled, which I hoped sounded like an I-can't-believe-you-are-trying-to-scam-me sigh. Then quickly imagined how much a Fiat costs to replace. Who knows. Shrugging off the worry, I stood firm.

"*Capisco.*" I said. "I decline the extra insurance."

"*Va bene.*" His concern for the imminent heist of my car promptly evaporated. He handed me the keys, my passport, and credit card in a plastic sleeve.

I slid on my blue-mirrored Ray-Ban sunglasses in an attempt to act cooler than I felt. They immediately slid off my nose, my flop sweat profuse. I walked to my forest green Fiat and plopped my duffel bag on the passenger seat. I fiddled around a bit with the stick shift and clutch. When I was 16 years old, my father taught me to drive on a beat-up rusty red VW with manual transmission. I felt good about my stick-shift competency, except that as a New Yorker, I hadn't owned a car in years. I checked the mirrors, mumbled a quick prayer to the universe ("Please let me not wreck a car in Sicily."), and gently eased out of the rental car lot and onto the highway access road. After a quick game of what felt like Italian Frogger, I merged onto the autostrada.

Second gear eased into third, third morphed into fourth, and fourth shot into fifth in rocket time. I lingered in the right lane at first, acclimating to the vehicle *and* the velocity. Lego-sized cars whizzed by me, changing lanes without signaling. Trucks carting milk, oil, chickens whooshed by in a blur. I gripped the Fiat's leather-bound steering wheel. *Breathe. Stay in your lane. Stick to your speed.* Incapable of converting kilometers per hour to miles per hour in my head, I hovered at 5 "whatevers" above the posted speed limit and tried to ignore the cars zigzagging around me. *You're fine. You're better than fine. You're awesome!* I kept the radio quiet. For some reason, U2's "Who's Gonna Ride Your Wild Horses" was already playing on repeat in my brain. I didn't need a competing sound track. Each time the autostrada curved, not yet trusting the torque, I downshifted to fourth, then upshifted back to fifth. With each successful twist and turn, I settled further into the seat. Memories of driving my '83 Mazda RX-7 (for which I paid $3,000 in law school), my Toyota Celica GT (my vehicle when I worked at my first law firm), my pre-owned convertible BMW Z3 (the first car purchase I negotiated completely solo) rushed back. The drive became enjoyable. *I'm driving a Fiat on the Italian autostrada. . . .Who's cooler than me? No one!*

Eventually, I had to leave the rhythm of the autostrada and exit in the direction of the town of Siracusa. Having zero faith that my iPhone GPS would function (and also worrying that the dollars-to-data ratio would bankrupt me), I grabbed my printed hotel directions from the passenger seat. I repeated the next three sequential turns aloud. So far, so good.

I eased toward the old town of Ortigia. The hotel website's directions advised that local traffic wardens, called *vigili urbani*, might try to prevent me from crossing a particular bridge but that I should do it anyway. *Geez.* I tried to ramp up my inner scofflaw. I crossed one stone bridge, then another one. So far, no *vigili* encounters. I recited the *next* three turns aloud. The streets became narrower, and one-way. I couldn't find the next left turn. *Pass the ancient fortress and make a left.* I spotted the fortress but not the street. I kept going, circling the island. Ended up back at the same stone bridge. Began the route again. My heart began to pound a tad faster. *Hey. You're not in a hurry. You have all the time in the world. You'll find it.*

I decided maybe I had misunderstood the directions when the road came to a slight fork near a pond with a name involving something about nymphs. This time, I steered the Fiat toward the prong of the fork less traveled. I zoomed through another ancient archway and ended up in a parking lot. A thick chain blocked all traffic toward the other end. I slammed the brakes. My right tire plunked into a deep pothole. I stopped. I realized, in my journey thus far, I had not yet had the need or opportunity to shift the Fiat into reverse. My left foot depressed the clutch. I jerked the stick shift to the left and forward, the maneuver for reverse in every other manual transmission vehicle I had ever driven. The engine roared but nothing happened. I tried it again. *Roar*. No movement. *No panicking. You're not going to be stuck in this parking lot forever. A band of thieves is not going to plunder and loot the vehicle with you in it. Try again, a different angle this time.* I pressed down on the stick shift as hard as I could and tried lurching it to the left again. It worked! Beads of sweat leapt like cliff-divers from my brow.

I reversed out of the parking lot and edged onto the main road again. I passed the fortress anew. Missed whatever turn I was supposed to take. Instead of circling the island again, I screeched to a stop in another parking area next to a sketchy van. A few moments later, I noticed two cyclists in their fifties walking their bicycles toward the van. They must have perceived the confusion oozing from my face as I attempted to find street names on a printed map resembling a crayon drawing that I found in the Fiat's glove compartment. The female cyclist waved. *Make human contact.* Fighting every introverted fiber of my being, I got out of my car and asked the cyclists in Italian if they could help me.

"*Nous ne parlerons pas italien. Français?*" French people!

A hologram of my beloved middle school French teacher, Madame Lasowski, appeared in my psyche. Français! The language I had studied for 16 years! A Sharpie pen materialized, and the kind French couple drew step-by-step directions to my hotel's street onto the back of my rental car contract. I bid them adieu, and nearly wept in relief that I was a mere few turns away. Because the one-way streets prevented me from backtracking, I had to circle the island once more. Passing the fort again, I still didn't see the name of my hotel's street but I took a gamble. Ended up on a street barely inches wider than the Fiat. One way. A chain-link fence fringed the right side of the street, which narrowed ahead to the width of a spaghetti noodle. I peered through the windshield and spotted *Via Antonio Maddeone* painted on a pink wall. The wrong street. But thanks to the French couple's map, I knew the next one down was the correct one. I hurled the Fiat into reverse, praying that I wouldn't shave off its paint job against the chain-link fence. I threaded the needle backward down the alley. I inched the rear end of the car into oncoming traffic on the main road. Miraculously, no one honked, cursed, or hurled Italian idioms at me. I quickly shifted into first gear, spotted Via Santa Teresa painted on the stone wall of the next street, hung a left and jammed both feet on the brakes so as not to bump into a picnic bench jutting into the street. I waved apologetically at a couple and their two children munching on hunks of cheese, and carefully proceeded, scanning the eaves for a sign identifying my hotel, Palazzo del Sale.

A lanky gentleman in a royal blue linen blazer leaned against a whitewashed wooden arch, smoking a cigarillo, and waved as if he knew me. OMG. I *made it.* I parked smack in the middle of Via Santa Teresa, ignoring the cars lining up behind me, opened the door, and raised my fists in the air in triumph. My hotelier laughed, and said, "Benvenuta, Heidi!" He outstretched his hand and gestured at my car keys. I gratefully plopped the keys in his hand. He took my place at the wheel, executed a 14-point-turn parallel-parking maneuver, and wedged the Fiat between two colossal terracotta planter pots flanking the hotel's entrance. I wiped sweat from my forehead, grinned, and vowed not to touch a vehicle for the next four days.

Later that night, once my blood pressure returned to seminormal, I ventured out. I ambled through the streets of Ortigia looking for a restaurant in which I would feel comfortable dining alone. My usual criteria when deciding on a restaurant when I travel include no laminated photos of plates of glistening food, no aggressive badgering by a greeter waving menus at me as I pass, a menu at least partially in the local language rather than all in English, a creative or artsy vibe, and bonus points if the venue claims to be "locally sourced," "healthy," or "farm-to-table." Usually, places like these end up yielding incredible food and learning experiences. I found a trattoria on a side street with outdoor wooden tables. Aquamarine sea glass doubled as paper weights on handwritten menus and cheery yellow-and-blue napkins. I swallowed momentary insecurity and asked, in Italian, for a table for one, outside, and nodded when they queried whether I was really *sola.* Alone. *Yup. Please feed me.*

I ate spaghetti with fresh shrimp and drank Sicilian wine. I reflected on the fact that while the two-and-a-half-hour rental car experience had been blood-pumping, it wasn't actually *fear*-inducing. Adrenaline had definitely surged as I shifted gears and maneuvered the two-ton vehicle through the linguini-thin streets to find my hotel. But I genuinely hadn't been *afraid* of crashing and injuring myself or someone else, or of being lost. Somehow, my rational brain had processed the fact that I was driving sensibly enough that a real crash was probably unlikely, though less-dramatic dings and scrapes could happen, but so what. That's the purpose of insurance. My logical brain also had worked through the realism of the potentiality of being lost: at the time of the ordeal, it was still light out, I had nowhere to be by a certain time, I was on a tiny island with a limited number of street possibilities, and people were refreshingly helpful. I did not fear getting hurt or never finding the hotel. Instead, when it was all over and the hotelier took those keys, I felt jubilant and powerful and brave.

Yet, I Feel Fear When . . . Presenting to Legal Audiences

As part of this "comparative fearlessness" exercise, I have to confide that I routinely feel fear when I know I need to speak at a faculty meeting and when I give presentations at law firms or bar associations about *The Introverted Lawyer*—which is literally my favorite topic in the world to discuss. This automatic rush of panic is reminiscent of the distress I felt in law practice before depositions, negotiations, and court appearances. Full-on paralyzing fear. I know, rationally, this makes zero sense. These are familiar arenas (the opposite of the unknown streets of Sicily), and I possess every qualification entitling me to be there, be present, and be heard.

In my role as director of the legal writing program at the law school where I teach, countless issues raised and voted on at faculty meetings affect our writing program: admissions numbers, class sizes, course scheduling, changes to the grading curve, faculty hiring, strategic planning initiatives, budgets, curriculum reform. You name the institutional issue, it likely touches upon the writing program in some way. As director, it's my job to be forward-thinking and make sure that the faculty considers the legal writing program and curriculum when we make major institutional decisions. This is the third law school where I have taught in my decade-long teaching career. I love my job; it is the absolute perfect role for me and I have found my ideal professional niche. I love teaching, researching, writing, designing, creating, and building. I'm trying to get better at mentoring and managing. I am finally on tenure track (thankfully) and I feel appreciated, respected by my colleagues and students, and intellectually fulfilled. But based on my experience at three schools now, law faculties can be an intimidating bunch. They have fabulous educational pedigrees and strong opinions about most things affecting institutional governance. Many of them also enjoy and are skilled at vigorously asserting and debating these positions at faculty meetings.

At each faculty meeting, I sit in my favorite "introvert spot," the end of a row of chairs with no one on the left side of me. When the agenda includes a topic I'll have to weigh in on, or on which a legal writing voice should be heard, I initiate my physical pre-game regimen (discussed more in Chapter 16). I uncross my legs and plant both feet on the ground. I sit in a balanced seated stance, outstretch both arms on the armrests of the chair, open my hands, unclench my fingers. I focus on slow inhalations, and then even slower exhalations.

I remind myself: no hunching, no crossing of limbs, no allowing any part of my body to block my oxygen, blood, or energy flow. Though my natural instinct is to make myself smaller when I begin to feel afraid, I consciously remind myself that openness—physical and mental—leads to clarity. Even as my heart begins to rattle like a snare drum, I tell myself that these physical rituals will help. "I've done it before. It was good. I'll do it again."[644] Twyla Tharp's confidence-building statement, quoted earlier, bears repeating.

I activate my active listening skills, noting the verbal volley of the extroverts and other confident talkers debating pedagogical or administrative points. When the agenda starts to veer toward the issue that affects my program, I know I'm going to need and want to boldly interject my position, assert a stance, or provide context. My heart bangs against my ribs so stridently, I feel like the colleague next to me can hear it. My legs instinctively cross again. My shoulders cave forward anew. I tug my hair or my shirt collar, an auto-mated attempt to disappear or hide the blush I can feel prickling my neck and cheeks. I consciously realize what I'm doing, chide myself. *Thud, thud*, goes the heart. I compel myself to lift one hand to catch the attention of the vice-dean, who maintains the "queue" of faculty awaiting a turn to speak. He sees me. Now I'm on the list. No turning back.

My cheeks blotch. I write out what I plan to say on my yellow legal pad. Number the points in case my mind goes blank. Edit it a few times. Now my scratches and scribbles make the words unreadable. I tear off the top sheet of paper and start again. Uncross my legs for the third time. Breathe. Remind myself that I know what I'm talking about, I'm smart, I have an opinion and deserve to be heard, I'm not stupid or insignificant. I'm the director of the program, for goodness sake, *just relax! Thud, thud. Blotch, blotch.* The vice-dean works through the queue, name by name. I feel like hyperventilating.

What is wrong with you? It's just a faculty meeting. No one is going to die if you say the wrong thing. You're probably going to say the right thing! You're not going to lose a client a million dollars. It's a faculty meeting . . . in a law school. The stakes are low. Just speak. Just do it. Be a leader, not a wimp. Come on!

Eventually, when the vice-dean gives me the floor, I speak. It doesn't go perfectly. But I convey my message, amping up as much volume as my voice will command. Sometimes I even stand up. I make sure everyone can hear me. I may stumble over a couple of words even though I have them written down. My face is definitely fire-engine red when I'm done. The world does not end.

I analyze. I reflect. What am, or was, I feeling? Genuine fear. Of what, though? And why is this experience different from hurtling a rented Fiat down the autostrada? Zooming through international tunnels and boomeranging around hairpin turns, I'm in unfamiliar territory. I barely speak the language.

My life literally *could* be at stake if a Ducati motorcycle cuts me off and my Fiat flips over. Yet I'm not afraid there. I'm hyped up, but I'm not scared. In contrast, in my professional and intellectual world, I'm often petrified and it makes no sense. Logically, I know that I am qualified and entitled to share a thought, idea, or opinion at a faculty meeting. I have a law degree from The University of Virginia School of Law, am a member of the bar of three jurisdictions, practiced rough-and-tumble construction law for two decades, have been teaching for 10 years, and have written five education-related books, six counting this one. Professionally, I know what I'm doing. But the bottom line is: I'm afraid of what my well educated, tenured colleagues will think of me. I'm afraid they will think—because I turn red and my voice shakes and it takes me a good 43 minutes to warm up to jumping into the fray—that I'm weak or less intelligent than they are. That I'm not worthy of being a law professor. Rationally, I know that's ridiculous. I impact my students, and I care about my vocation very much. But it is my automated, conditioned, innate reflex to feel this type of performance fear: the terror of judgment, rejection, shame, and exclusion.

Likewise, fresh fear surfaces each time I head to a law conference, a law firm, or a bar association to talk about *The Introverted Lawyer*—again, my favorite topic in the world to discuss. I love submitting presentation proposals for law conferences, especially legal writing conferences where my colleagues energetically share collaborative ideas about teaching, writing, and service to the legal profession. I also get excited every time a law firm's director of professional development or a bar association's director of wellness initiatives reaches out to me over LinkedIn or email to invite me to speak about the power of introversion in the legal profession.

Of all the written work I've produced over my lifetime, I am most proud of *The Introverted Lawyer*. I know the content inside and out. I practically have the 227 pages memorized. I love the way the book cover looks, what the cheerful lightbulb image represents, and how the pages inside make me feel when I look at them or touch them for the umpteenth time. Last year, I eagerly accepted numerous invitations for speaking engagements, exhilarated to craft my very own "book tour," hopscotching from Philadelphia to Boston to Boulder to San Francisco to Milwaukee. And yet, every time the morning of the speaking gig arrived, my fear tornado swirled. I barely slept. When I did sleep, I awoke drenched in sweat. I couldn't eat, which is the opposite of my usual jolly appetite. My morning coffee ritual nauseated me. Rationally, it sounds absurd. Someone actually thought highly enough of the topic of my book to invite me to speak to lawyers in hope that I could *help* some of them better enjoy the practice of law. This is my life's mission. My manifesto to the legal profession. My love letter to every anxious or quiet law student or lawyer who feels alone in the world. Yet, each time the event date arrived, I wanted to cry. To escape. To hide. Of course I didn't. I implemented the mental and physical rituals that I'll share in Steps 2 and 3 in the next few chapters. And each event went fine. Some even rocked. I met fabulous people and gained tremendous inspiration from our dialogues. But these successes didn't block the fear tornado from circling the very next gig.

What was I afraid of? That the lawyers would be bored? Disagree with me? That partners would roll their eyes at the touchy-feely-ness of my advice? Surmise that I hadn't been able to hack it as a lawyer? That I was wasting valuable billable time? Why did my brain always take this sharp turn? After all, I literally and unequivocally am an expert on introversion in the legal profession. I mean, I *am* an introvert. I was a law student. I was a lawyer. Why was I afraid? Well, I feared judgment, criticism, rejection, shame, and exclusion. That is the barebones truth about my fear. And thus, I must work hard—every time—to untangle the fear, develop and initiate mental and physical checklists to power me into each performance arena, and forge ahead as unencumbered and unbound as possible. In Chapters 15 and 16, I'll share what mental and physical steps work for me.

But first I'll describe another life situation in which I probably should be afraid, but I'm not.

I'm *Not* Afraid . . . to Climb into the Boxing Ring

I'm *not* afraid to walk into Trinity Boxing Club and box. Well, I admit I was a tad nervous the first day I opened those vintage doors, walked past a boulder-sized tangle of colorful just-washed boxing wraps, and signed in as a "fighter" for the first time. But that initial trepidation had vanished by the end of the first training session.

Trinity is an old-school boxing training club on Duane Street in the Tribeca neighborhood of Lower Manhattan. An imposing red-and-black ring occupies the rear of the space, surrounded by punching bags of different sizes and shapes—cylindrical, teardrop, round—hanging from beams. Vintage boxing gloves and photos of champions line the walls. Banners with inspirational messages like Babe Ruth's "Never let the fear of striking out get in your way" wave in the breeze generated by movement of bodies in multiple directions. At any given time, 5 to 15 boxers of all ages and levels—recreational to professional—punch the bags, engage in one-on-one "mitt work" with trainers, or spar in the ring. It's noisy, hot, sometimes muggy, and chaotic—four adjectives that normally would send me running in the opposite direction. Yet I'm obsessed with it.

Twice a week, I enter the gym, my silver-camouflaged Athleta sports bag slung over one shoulder; it contains yellow Everlast wraps, gold/black gloves, and my super-cool official Nike boxing shoes. I slide two dollars (the charge for a bottle of water) across the desk to Martin, the owner, who greets me with a friendly fist-bump. His freckled, pink-nosed, pit bull puppy, Jack Dempsey, leaps up to see who's there. I grab a water bottle from the fridge and weave through a maze of guys and gals jumping rope, punching the bags, sparring each other, ribbing each other with fight stories. Rap music ricochets off the brick walls. My trainer, former Olympic boxer Raymond Montalvo, waves a well-worn golden mitt from the ring as he finishes a session with another client, often a fierce female, ponytail flying from her headgear, throwing lightning-fast punches. For a second, I wonder how slow I look by comparison. I shelve the negative self-talk, and avoid getting slapped by a razor-sharp jump rope on my way to the women's locker room. (You only make that mistake once).

I knock on the door of the ladies' changing area, an 8 × 8 space containing lockers, a shower, and walls covered with vintage boxing magazine articles. I change into my red and white high-top boxing shoes. I grab my wraps and gloves, a SoulCycle skull-and-crossbones bandana, and the water bottle and head back out. Ray greets me with a smile. He's quiet yet full of presence. Muscular arms covered in sleeve tattoos. A T-shirt bearing a silhouette of Tyson, or Ali, or another boxing champion I've never heard of but will learn about shortly. If the other guys aren't paying attention to the music, Ray will murmur into the Amazon speaker, "Play U2 radio." I grin. Rap fades away and the drums of Larry Mullen Jr. kick in.

Ray hands me a jump rope—the one with the yellow handles. The one that's not too long or too short for me, but is just right for me to jump for three minutes, take a thirty-second break when the bell rings, and then do it again. "You've come so far," he encourages, as I mess up only once or twice and am able to do a rope trick or two. A crossover here, high-knees there. We catch up a bit about the few days since our last session. I try not to gasp for air as I converse while jumping. The bell rings, and chitchat time is over. Ray grabs my yellow wraps and motions for me to extend one hand. He un-Velcros the end of one roll, lets it fall to the floor, and then folds six or seven layers of one end of the stretchy cotton material. He places the folded layers over my knuckles and then wraps my hand, my palm, my wrist. He mimics a fist. I fold my fingers into my hand and he fastens the Velcro end of the wrap around my wrist, then taps my hand. Done. We do the other hand. I love this ritual. No speaking. Just a coach getting his pupil ready. Boxing tradition.

Sometimes, he runs me through some shadowbox moves before we put on the gloves. At the beginning of my training, I felt self-conscious. He watched my every move, my punches, my hip-pivots (or more accurately, my stiff hips), my feet, my eyes. Made quiet corrections. Explained subtle distinctions in movement. In my first session or two, I blushed any time Ray or any of the other coaches—Colin, Butch, John, Martin—spoke to me. I wasted so much time wondering if the other trainers and trainees were annoyed at the presence of an older female in their gym. I quickly learned, they're not. They call me "champ." They fist-bump me. They smile. They include.

Ray doesn't hesitate to put me in the ring. I climb the three metal stairs and am not exactly sure how to fold myself between the ropes in as cool a fashion as the guys and other girls do. He holds one rope down, making space. I climb in. It's not graceful but I don't face-plant. He grabs my gloves and ties them on my wrapped hands one at a time. Another fighter ritual. My hands bound inside bulbous gloves, I'm now incapable of even lifting a water bottle or toweling off my own sweaty face. I have no choice but to be vulnerable, not care what I look like, and trust Ray's system.

A three-minute bell, with a thirty-second break, marks time as Ray calls out instructions, cues, prompts for me to throw particular punches and combinations. I either hit foam "noodles" he holds or punch his monogrammed gold leather mitts: one reflecting his birth year, the other indicating his father's birth year. My face promptly heats up. I warned him during our first session, "My face turns really red when I work out. Like insanely red. But I'm okay. I'm not going to pass out." It's embarrassing how red I get. But it is what it is. He never mentions it so I (try to) ignore it.

I'm slow but I mostly can follow his prompts. The first few sessions, I held my breath. I was nervous about messing up, looking weak, being around the trainers and the other fighters. Ray advised me, "Make sure you breathe. In through the nose, hold it, out through the mouth." At times, he nudged me to speed up my punches; other times, he preferred that I go as slowly as I needed to get it right. "Technique is more important than speed. The fast 'patty-cake' punches are fun and all, but I want you to know technique."

He's a gifted coach. A quiet, thoughtful one. The first few times, I kept forgetting the combos. *Does he think I'm too old for this? Why can't I remember anything? What is wrong with me?* I immediately berated myself. I wouldn't look at him, or any of the trainers. I felt embarrassment. Shame even. He tapped his mitt to my shoulder and said, "Hey, this is hard. It's a new language. Breathe. Let's slow it down."

We did, and I finally connected a complicated combo, or landed a new punch. He pushed me. Hard. The prompts at first were verbal: *Jab. Cross. Hook. Four. Slip. Block. Block to the body. Both sides. Reset. Double-block. Slip my jab. Parry. Chase him down. Three. Your favorite. Under-under.* Occasionally, I could go an entire three-minute round with only one or two mistakes. The bell rang. I laughed. He patted me on a shoulder and grabbed my water bottle and helped me guzzle it, my hands encumbered in my pillow-sized gloves.

After a month of training, Ray's verbal prompts evolved to hand signals. Both mitts extended downward toward me meant four uppercuts and a hook. Mitts flat against his chest, one above the other, signaled my first "favorite" maneuver: two jabs, cross, under, cross, hook, cross. Periodically, I misunderstood him. We adjusted our language, our dialogue. I asked questions. He patiently explained technique and style. Taught me how different fighters do different things. Even talked about MY style. *I have a style!* Taught me to not back away from the fight. Lean toward. Don't be afraid to get hit. Learn what it feels like. "The closer you are to the fight, the safer you are," he said.

I get lazy with my feet. It's exhausting to dance around the ring and punch at the same time. And my hips are stiff and awkward. Ray demonstrates, makes it look easy and cool. I try to imitate his moves, but feel dorky and slow. I seem to always be on the wrong foot. But I look around and no one is laughing at me, pointing at my alarmingly red face, rolling their eyes at me, wishing I would go. I shrug off the unhelpful self-analysis. *Keep moving. Keep going.* Sometimes, everything works: my head bobs at the right time, my feet shift at the right rhythm, a punch connects to Ray's mitt with a smack-crack sound. It's ridiculously fun.

Ray's coaching is creative, and every session has a different twist. Sometimes he has me help him buckle into a big turtle-shell-type body padding. I pull the straps tight. He asks me to hit him. Hard. As hard as I can. I hesitate. "You're not going to hurt me," he says with a smile. It takes me a while to break the barrier of hitting another person (even if you're supposed to). Then I go for it. I try to hit him as hard as I can. Throwing punches like that saps every ounce of my energy. But it's exhilarating. "Thirty more seconds."

"I can do this."

One afternoon, when I arrived at Trinity, Ray said, "I have a little surprise for the end of today's sesh."

Uh oh.

"We're gonna spar." *Yikes.* I had watched many of the guys spar, and several badass girls too. They don head padding and hit each other like a real fight. Or a coach defends while the trainee throws punches.

During the early part of my session that day, I got stuck in my head. Every time I fast-forwarded to the anticipated end-of-session sparring experience, I faltered. I forgot my combos, couldn't remember the sequences.

"Stop thinking."

After 45 minutes of three-minute rounds of mitt-work drills, Ray switched from his baseball hat to the padded headgear.

"Just try to hit me. Throw whatever combos you want."

The bell rang and I tried to chase him down. I couldn't even get close as he danced around the ring. I panicked. Stopped breathing. Forgot everything I learned. Began chastising myself. My face reddened even more deeply. I swung wildly. Nothing connected.

"Sorry. I don't know what's wrong with me."

"Hey. All you need to do is slow down. Not every punch will connect," he said. "Stop. Look. Wait for your shot. The fight will come to *you*."

I tried that. I landed one. Or maybe he let me. I didn't care. I landed one punch and it felt incredible. I couldn't really remember a single maneuver or combo I had been studying for six solid months, so I just focused on trying to connect my glove to his body. One punch at a time. *Just. Hit. The. Fighter.* We did three rounds. I made good contact a few times. At the end, I noticed two of the trainers—Butch and Colin—watching.

"Nice job, champ."

"Haha, thank you," I laughed.

"Remember," they said. "In sparring, there is one rule. Never say you're sorry."

That last rule stuck with me. *Never say you're sorry when sparring.* It makes sense. You have nothing to be sorry about when you're taking the risk of trying something completely hard and new . . . When you're making yourself vulnerable trying to exert focused energy at another human being . . . And you're trying to do exactly what is being asked of you. You have nothing to be sorry about for missing a bunch of shots. Connecting is hella hard. You have nothing to be sorry about for forgetting to breathe and suddenly blanking on all your punches and combos. Putting it all together into real-life motion is a totally different experience from training. You also don't need to be sorry for actually hitting someone when that's exactly what you are supposed to do. *Throw your punch. Don't be sorry.*

I love boxing. I love training with Ray. I love training at Trinity. I love that all the guys, no matter what age or level of fight experience, call everyone "champ," including me. Everyone looks everyone else in the eye. People *see* one another—a rarity in New York—and they *see* me. No one treats me like I don't belong or like I can't do it. I *can* do it. It's hard. I'm beet red and out of breath. I'm not totally fit and ripped like many of the other girls I admire and look up to that train there. People stare at my magenta face on the subway home. But I laugh and am ignited. I feel cool carrying my gloves, sweaty tangled wraps, and boxing shoes home. Sometimes I do feel weak or frustrated or a little embarrassed. But I do *not* feel afraid.

Why am I *not* afraid to get on a plane to a foreign land and figure it out alone? When I travel solo, I could very well accidentally put my physical self in genuine danger: walking down the wrong alley, trusting the wrong person, putting my life in the hands of a hike leader or transit driver not subject to all the safety controls that permeate our American existence. But it doesn't even occur to me to think about that stuff. The spirit of adventure, of wonder, of marvel, of awe, readily supplants any worry. I don't fret about being alone, or looking stupid when I try to speak the language, or ending up on the wrong bus. Adventure fuels courage to try new things, take a risk, trust that I'll be okay.

Why am I *not* afraid to walk into Trinity Boxing Club, lace up my gloves, and get in the ring? Truth be told, the situation is ripe for embarrassment or even shame for someone with my emotional luggage. It's an arena full of outwardly confident men. I'm older than most of them. My face is as red as a pomegranate and I sweat buckets. I look pretty outrageously awful barely 10 minutes into each session. I'm new at this. I don't really know what I'm doing yet. I'm not an athlete. Oh wait, but I actually am. I'm there. I'm training. I'm working. I'm pushing my mind and body into "eustress," as we discussed in Chapter 13. The Trinity guys *include* me—a refreshing experience in our big city culture of "cool and aloof." It's Manhattan. Downtown bankers and lawyers barely look up from their phones, except for the guy in the suit who joked, "Hey, Red," as I walked to the subway overheated after a boxing session. *Lovely.* But the Trinity fighters smile, high-five, encourage, look everyone in the eye, call everyone "champ." That's what cultivating a culture of fortitude looks like.

The gift, the key, the challenge for us in this journey toward untangling fear is to identify specific and concrete scenarios in our lives in which we feel incredibly brave and powerful, even though those environments might, or even probably would, invoke fear in someone else. Then, we can extract exactly what drives our boldness, courage, and strength in those circumstances. For me, in travel, it's the adventure, the wonder, the awe, the newness, the absorption of experience, and the replenishment of creativity sapped by my normal life. In boxing, it's the spirit of inclusion, the feeling of physical power when I hit Ray's mitt and I hear the smack-crack sound, when I can go a three-minute round with barely any mistakes, when I remember a new tricky punch combo and I feel mentally stronger. In both of these venues, I am my most raw, exposed, authentic, vulnerable self. On the road, I'm the novice, the newbie, the outsider, the wide-eyed kid. In the boxing ring, I'm the blotchy, sweaty, rookie girl punching with the boys. In either scenario, arguably I *should* feel nervous about getting it wrong, looking stupid, making a mistake. But I feel the opposite. How are those sensations, feelings, and emotions different from the lawyering scenarios in which I am afraid?

For me, my fear in lawyering scenarios stems from risk of exclusion, rejection, isolation, and shame. I am afraid of being belittled. Criticized as unintelligent. Mocked. Discarded. As former professional extreme skier Kristen Ulmer highlights, we all want "to be seen, heard, loved, understood, and considered."[645] She suggests that "separateness—not the Fear—is the 'problem.'"[646]

It seems strange to me that I fear separateness in circumstances for which I have been training for nearly three decades—since I entered law school—and for which I have earned enough street cred to back up my opinions, assertions, and ideas. Do I feel I have more to lose? Do I fear a harder fall? In boxing or hiking in Patagonia, I *literally* can fall hard or get knocked down. The most difficult part of this self-evaluative journey is being open and vulnerable enough to start identifying these distinctions. Then we get to do something about it.

I invite you to do Step 1 with me. Take a moment, and start by identifying two experiences in your own life:

- one that, according to societal norms, probably *should* make you afraid, but remarkably does *not*, and
- one that, applying "rational" logic, should *not* make you afraid, but *does*.

You may realize that you have more than one scenario to list in each category. Take some time to think about situations in your life in which you feel courageous, brave, invincible. What emotions or sensations do you feel there? Why do you feel that way—mentally and physically—in those scenarios? Do you feel vulnerable but yet powerful at the same time? Does your personal power derive directly *from* the vulnerability or risk?

Next, take some time to really dig deeply into the scenarios in your life— personal or professional—that ignite fear. What is different about those circumstances? What exactly are you afraid of? Are you afraid of particular people? Risk? Loss? Being alone? Exclusion? Embarrassment? Shame? Pain?

This is the first step in untangling fear: getting very specific about the situations that spark fear in us, and also identifying scenarios in which we have unequivocal swagger. Next, we will start to defuse fear by tapping into our mental and physical power.

Fear has a job: to keep you small, stuck and the same.

—Steven Pressfield

Step 1

Exercise: Untangling Fear

- Identify one or two scenarios or situations in your life in which society, your family, or your friends might think or suggest that you *should* feel fear, but you *don't*.
  - What exactly are you doing?
  - Where are you?
  - What is your individual role in this scenario or situation?
  - Who else is present? What are their roles?
  - What emotions or sensations do you feel?
  - Do you experience a rise and fall of emotions, or a steady consistent emotional state?
  - What adjectives would you use to describe yourself when you are in this scenario or situation?
  - How do you feel physically?
  - How do you feel mentally?
  - Why do you think you feel this way in this scenario or situation?
  - Do you feel a sense of achievement at any point in these scenarios? If so, identify what you are achieving.
- Identify one or two law-related scenarios or situations in which you think you *shouldn't* feel fear, but you *do*.
  - What exactly are you doing?
  - Where are you?
  - What is your individual role in this scenario or situation?
  - Who else is present? What are their roles?
  - What emotions or sensations do you feel?
  - Can you pinpoint exactly what you are afraid of? Is it a person? A potential consequence? An emotion? A physical sensation?
  - What adjectives would you use to describe yourself when you are in this scenario or situation?
  - How do you feel physically?
  - How do these physical sensations manifest? In other words, what parts of your body react physically, and how exactly do they respond? Do you sweat, shake, turn red? Does your heart race, your stomach twist, your head throb? Do you make yourself smaller?
  - How do you feel mentally?

- Why do you think you feel this way in this scenario or situation?
- How is this situation *different* (in substance, location, environment, key players, audience, stakes, etc.) from the scenarios above in which society tells us we probably *should* feel fear, but we absolutely *do not?*
- Is any aspect of this situation *similar* (in substance, location, environment, key players, audience, stakes, etc.) to the scenarios above in which society tells us we probably *should* feel fear, but we absolutely *do not?*

Context: Our goal in Step 1 is to begin to untangle fear-igniting scenarios from those in which we feel powerful, identify differences and similarities, and recognize and appreciate our swagger in certain areas of our life. Eventually, we will bring this swagger into *every* scenario, using the mental and physical techniques explored in Steps 2 and 3.

CHAPTER 15

Step 2: Mentally Rebooting

Thus far, we have begun the untangling process by studying our lives and identifying particular experiences in which we probably should feel fear, but *don't*, and other situations in which—by other folks' standards—we logically should *not* feel fear, but we *do*. Now, with this information, we are going to arm ourselves with new-and-improved mental equipment. Instead of storming into performance events determined to blindly push past fear, ignore it, or conquer it, we are going to purposefully approach fear-inducing scenarios from a position of greater mental self-awareness and strength. This takes vulnerability, authenticity, and humility—not fake bravado.

The authors of *Mind Gym: An Athlete's Guide to Inner Excellence* quote a helpful definition of confidence from Phoenix Fire Department Chief Alan Brunacini: "knowing what to do when you don't know what to do."[647] In this chapter, we will develop a *mental* plan to power us through performance moments which normally would rattle us because we "don't know what to do." We will learn how to recognize any unhelpful messages playing on the mental sound track in our minds, press Pause, initiate a mental reboot, and then consciously step into the challenging event, fortified by new personal messages of character, authenticity, and strength.

Let's break our mental approach to fear into two parts: (1) the feelings of fear we experience *in anticipation of* an upcoming event or scenario and (2) the feelings of fear we experience *during* an event or scenario. In the former category, we have the luxury of time to talk or walk ourselves through a new empowering thought process that we can put into motion later in the actual performance moment. At that time, we will adopt an accelerated performance process (like the athlete's preshot routine we learned about in Chapter 13) to untangle the fear more quickly so we can perform at our peak.

Recall in Chapter 5, we explored the science of fear. First, we encounter a stimulus. Let's say, for example, we remember that we have a difficult conference call coming up with a challenging opposing counsel. For some of us, the very glimpse of a notation of the call on our calendars sends a sucker punch to our gut. We might instinctively rush a hand to our temple, our forehead suddenly pounding. Remember, that instant sensation—that uncomfortable poke—is just our amygdala kicking into gear. Imagine Kirby, my beagle, blissfully sleeping in a sunspot on a cushioned window seat, gently snoring, one paw twitching in a dream about bacon. Abruptly, she is barking with profound intensity at a perceived threat on the other side of the front door. It could be the Domino's delivery person, an axe murderer, or a rogue elm leaf. Kirby is howling, her jowls forming a perfect O-shape to amplify the sound. Kirby is effective. It's hard to hear, see, process, absorb anything besides her cacophony. Meanwhile, our brain—accustomed to reacting to the amygdala's alerts—launches its accompanying sound track. Messages about performance "threats" we've been reciting to ourselves for years start to whir. What are your messages? Here are a few of mine:

- OMG, you can't do this.
- Why do you even have to do this?
- Why are they making you do this?
- You don't want to do this.
- Can't you quit and get out of this?
- They're going to think you're incompetent.
- They're going to think you don't know what you're doing.
- They're going to think you're wasting their time.
- They're going to wonder what in the world you're doing here, or how you got in.
- You're going to turn red, and they're going to think you're weird, weak, and ugly.
- You're totally going to make a mistake.
- You're going to get in trouble . . . get yelled at . . . get fired . . . be humiliated . . . be publicly shamed . . . be unemployed . . . be unemployable . . . be broke.
- They're all going to laugh at you.
- I don't even know what to tell you now. You created this situation; you're on your own.

To individuals who do not experience fear or who believe they are deftly able to shrug off fear, these messages probably sound ridiculous. I am not exaggerating the foregoing language. My brain can transform me from a competent, decently functioning contributor to society to an utterly worthless nobody in 30 seconds. It doesn't matter that these thoughts are irrational and make no sense based on years of schooling, decades of practicing law, a decade of teaching, and the monumental amount of work I have invested to improve my mental and physical health and well-being. My brain doesn't care. My brain dispenses these lovely gems . . . every . . . single . . . time I experience fear. *You're not good enough. You're embarrassing. You're hideous. You're stupid. You're not worthy. You should just quit and leave.*

Ugh. Enough.

Let's get off the treadmill to nowhere and focus on tangible and concrete action. So, the amygdala is just doing its (highly annoying) job of ringing the danger alarms. It is now *our* job to notice the lyrics of our mental sound track above the amygdala's racket, recognize the same old boring outdated tune, and then press Pause. Please forgive yet another metaphor, but when you were a kid, do you remember firefighters coming to your school and teaching you and your classmates the "Stop, drop, and roll" refrain? As in, if our clothing catches fire, we are advised to *stop* what we are doing, *drop* to the ground, and *roll* to extinguish the flames? This mantra works for us here in this fear context too. We've got the amygdala going full-tilt, and then we're probably going to hear snippets of our negative sound track no matter how evolved we might feel. (It takes a long time to delete the messages entirely and replace them with pure goodness. I'm still working on erasing all of mine, and instinctively, the bad stuff still shows up first. But, trust me, we get better and faster at recognizing it.) When we hear the taunting voice, "You're gonna suu-uuck," instead of starting to obey and feel sucky, we're going to pause or stop and say, "Oh wait. This is just my nemesis again." *Stop. Drop.* "This is unhelpful. This is not true. Just, NO." Maybe we even name the nemesis.

We stop the sound track. Then we immediately remind ourselves of three to six truths.

Roll. These are the six go-to truths that work for me:

- You worked really hard for this particular event/situation/experience/ opportunity.
- You know what you're talking about and are entitled to have a voice.
- Your fear response is just the amygdala doing its thing; it will chill.
- The negativity is just the voice of the outdated sound track; press Pause (or, even better, Delete).

- You didn't faint in a 60-minute boxing session yesterday; you're tough and strong and powerful.
- Your goal is to reach ONE person with your message. Just ONE. If you reach ONE person, you've made an impact. The rest is unimportant. Now go.

Roll. Somehow this works, for me at least. Some people question positive self-talk or discount it as a bunch of unworkable hoo-ha. In my opinion, these are not just touchy-feely affirmations. Instead, these six statements represent a concrete, repeatable 30-second trigger to ignite the power surge I need to stop my amygdala from catapulting me off the rails. These statements halt the potential onslaught of aggressive internal disparagement and remind me to resume control. In 30 seconds, we can recalibrate and set ourselves onto the right mental path for handling the fear *and* the performance.

Remember we learned in Chapter 5 that the amygdala, the hormones, and the automatic fight-or-flight response don't distinguish between a real and an imaginary threat. They collectively hijack our cognitive processes. Through this 30-second "stop, drop, and roll" maneuver, we take back command and switch on our thinking brain for a moment. We mentally reboot.

In anticipation of a particularly daunting lawyering scenario, I try to craft three to six "reality sound bites" to put the particular event in perspective, in case I need an additional boost beyond my six go-to truths. For example, for a deposition, I might remind myself (1) no one is going to die if I trip over words in a sentence or turn red; (2) bad facts in my client's case are not my fault; (3) I can't control every human being in the room; (4) this is 7 hours of my life and it will end; and (5) I developed a solid substantive plan and I'm going to trust and stick to it. For an oral argument, I might reiterate: (1) this is 10 minutes of my life and it is going to go by in a flash; (2) I wrote every word in the brief and I know what I'm talking about; (3) this is a conversation between me and another human being, not a Super Bowl half-time show; (4) it's okay if I pause to think; and (5) who cares if I get a bit sweaty.

I'll provide one more example before we sit down to do some of our process work. This past year, in spreading the word about *The Introverted Lawyer* through different social media channels—a new and creative experience for me as a writer—folks began reaching out to me for podcasts, webinars, and in-person presentations. As I mentioned in Chapter 14, I built my own mini–book tour. Every time I marked a new speaking gig on my calendar, I got excited about traveling to new spots and connecting with readers and fellow introverts. Then, as each performance day approached, I fell into my pesky pothole of fear. Each time, to climb out of it, I had to work this Step 2 mental process. My amygdala would sound the alarms. The "you're not worthy" non-sense would start to churn. In response, I stopped, dropped, and rolled, and ran through my mental checklist. I modified and shortened the messages to fewer words, so I could run through them faster. This became my new "stop, drop, and roll" refrain:

- YOUR work, YOUR story.
- YOUR voice, no one else's.
- Jump into the ring, and be the ATHLETE you are.
- Only need to reach ONE.
- Be the ARTIST you are.

Warning: Another U2 reference imminent. During U2's 2015 iNNO-CENCE + eXPERIENCE tour, Bono introduced the song "Iris" by reflecting for a few minutes about his mom, Iris Hewson, who passed away when he was 14 years old. Bono credits her for his life's calling and introduces her name-sake song by saying, "She left me an *artist*." Besides making me weep, and also honestly a tad jealous that I did not have a mentor in my youth grip me by the shoulders and insist "You can do it all,"[648] as Iris did for her son, those words fire up my drive to create. I obviously self-identify as a lawyer and a law professor, but more importantly, I'm a writer. And a fighter. And a traveler. And thus, I am an artist. And so are you. We are not only scholar-athletes, but we are artists. Regarding our work as art helps us accept and honor that it *matters*.

Our words and ideas matter. My message (however small it may seem in comparison to those of rock stars and humanitarians and politicians) *matters* when I go give presentations to try to reach anxious law students and lawyers. If our work as law students, lawyers, educators, and mentors helps even *one* person, it matters. That's why it's essential that we untangle our own fear, even if it takes us 100 or 1,000 endeavors to do so. We must disassemble our fear to its core and discard the unhelpful parts that are trying, on the brain's most primitive level, to protect us from perceived threats or from making a fool of ourselves. I finally know I need to be this artist, this jagged misfit soul that talks about stuff that some lawyers don't want to talk about or don't think is important. And if it sounds cheesy or lame to say that my favorite band led me to that realization, so be it. Is there an artist that moves you? Can you channel that artistry into your life and work?

In Step 2, we untangle the mental drivers of fear. We start by reflecting on how our brain works in the face of fear and understanding the protective role of the amygdala. Next, we identify the messages in our mental sound track from folks who might have had our best interests at heart in the past but whose words are holding us back now. Then, we craft a new internal dialogue. This process starts with openness.

LET'S BE OPEN TO LEARNING

"Intellectual humility" plays an important role in this process of learning about ourselves. To be honest, I'm not crazy about the following dictionary definitions of "humility" or the state of being "humble":

- "freedom from pride or arrogance"[649] or
- "the quality of having a modest or low view of one's importance."[650]

I think these definitions are a tad off base because they focus on making or keeping us small. When I use the word *humility*, I'm not implying that we should downplay our accomplishments or in any way devalue our significance or achievements. Instead, I mean that we should take a page from Socrates's playbook and readily acknowledge limitations on our knowledge, so we can expand our wisdom in those particular areas. This type of humility allows us to grow, magnify, and augment, not only ourselves but others.

According to Socrates, we cannot be intellectual without intellectual humility.[651] Acting like we already know all there is to know might make us feel temporarily powerful but it's completely unhelpful in this context. (Reminds me of "fake it till you make it.") A former justice of the Supreme Court of Wisconsin, William A. Bablitch, characterized intellectual humility as "an awareness of what we do not know, and an awareness that what we think we know might well be incorrect. This is particularly important when it comes to the law. The law has a funny way of jumping up and biting you right where it hurts at the most unexpected times."[652] Intellectual humility—or a deep curiosity and openness—about *ourselves* in this context is the key to untangling fear in lawyering.

Professor Christopher Kukk, in *The Compassionate Achiever: How Helping Others Fuels Success*, offers a useful way of looking at intellectual humility. He refers to the concept of "knownauts," or "knowledge astronauts."[653] These are people who are "willing to admit that they don't know something."[654] He says you can spot "knownauts" because they "lean toward you when talking about something that they admit not knowing about."[655] He contrasts these individuals with "knoxers," individuals with a "fixed mindset" who are "afraid to admit that they don't know something," so they fight against new knowledge.[656] Kukk indicates that knoxers "fold their arms close to their chest when learning something new."[657] Applying this to the fear context, if we strive to be knowledge astronauts, or knownauts, we can acknowledge that we don't know everything and thus *want* to get to know the drivers of our fear. How liberating! Then we can literally *physically* (and mentally) open up to the experience—uncrossing our arms and welcoming the flood of learning. Kukk shares how he regards fear "as an opportunity . . . to prove to myself that I could do more than my fears would allow."[658]

Another way of looking at this process is to familiarize ourselves with *metacognition*. Law professor and law school dean Anthony Niedwiecki explains the concept as

> *the internal voice people hear when they are engaged in the learning process— the voice that will tell them what they have to do to accomplish a task*, what they already know, what they do not know, *how to match their previous learning to the new situation, when they do not understand what they are reading or learning, and how to evaluate their learning.*[659]

Metacognition is thinking about thinking, enhancing our conscious awareness of how we process new information and learn. As Dean Niedwiecki points out, real learning involves recognizing what we know and don't know. Acting like we know everything is a barrier to gaining wisdom.

It certainly may sound easier to ignore fear, pretend it doesn't exist, feign bravado to power us through performance moments, and keep chugging forward. However, the process of untangling fear in an honest, vulnerable, and intentional way is so much better for our personal long-term happiness and fulfillment. Author of the book *Grit*, Angela Duckworth, explains how Aristotle distinguished between two methods of seeking happiness.[660] On one hand, we can act in a "hedonic" manner and gallop through life exhibiting behavior "aimed at positive, in-the-moment, inherently self-centered experiences."[661] (This makes me think of an Instagram feed chock full of you-only-live-once [YOLO] and fear-of-missing-out [FOMO] selfies). On the other hand, we can act in an "eudaimonic" manner. *Eu* stands for "good" and *daemon* represents our "inner spirit."[662] Experts have defined eudaimonia as "human flourishing." Duckworth writes that "Aristotle clearly took a side on the issue, deeming the hedonic life primitive and vulgar, and upholding the eudaimonic life as noble and pure."[663] So, emulating Socrates, we can admit what we don't know about fear. Mirroring Aristotle, we can delay instant gratification or the "quick fix" approach and instead really hunker down and figure out our fear drivers. With a two-pronged ethos, we can forge ahead in a way that is truly best for our future inner spirit and also sustainable throughout a hopefully long and fruitful legal career and life.

FIRST, WE MUST STOP REPRESSING FEAR

Last summer I was wandering through the streets of Rome while taking a break from teaching my legal writing course and working on this book manuscript. I like to snap iPhone photos of cool graffiti. I love how urban art contrasts the antiquity of European cities with modern splashes of color, texture, and words. While capturing a picture of male and female torsos sketched in charcoal above a piece of papier-mâché wall art and a page ripped from the T-section of a Spanish dictionary, I noticed these words scribbled in English in black Magic Marker on the dictionary page: "If your Dreams don't scare you, Dream Bigger." *Ugh*, I grumbled. Why is the message always that we need to live in a constant state of terror to become our best selves? Obviously, I understand the concept of pushing ourselves beyond our comfort zones, but in my mind, promoting fear and then telling us to just step on it like a smushed grape on our way to sure-fire invincibility is not a healthy life strategy. Without the right amount of self-awareness, pushing through or side-stepping fear backfires.

Former professional extreme skier Kristen Ulmer, describes "repression of Fear" (which she elevates to a capital F) as "a humanity-wide pathology that is cooking us all alive."[664] Similarly, authors of *Mind Gym*, Gary Mack and David Casstevens, explain that "[w]hen you resist fear you're only keeping it alive. It's like trying to hold a beach ball under water. The more you fight it, the more pressure you're building up."[665]

Ulmer encourages us to stop fighting fear and pretending it doesn't exist in a misplaced effort to charge ahead with false bravado. She cautions, "If you don't work toward having an authentic relationship with [Fear], you can't expect to have such a relationship with yourself, and thus can't possibly have one with anyone else—much less the world."[666] Ulmer writes about the process of "show[ing] a bit of kindness toward Fear" rather than resisting it, which she characterizes as "entirely the wrong effort."[667] She says that it's not actually fear that is our problem; it's our "reaction to Fear."[668]

Author Russ Harris echoes this principle, drawing a distinction between "putting up with fear" or faking our way through it, versus being our authentic selves while "handling fear in effective, life-enhancing ways."[669] He indicates that "[g]enuine confidence is not the *absence* of fear; it is a *transformed relationship* with fear."[670]

NEXT, WE UNTANGLE NEGATIVE THOUGHTS THAT FUEL FEAR

Harris uses the verb "defuse" when discussing how to handle the negative sound track that begins to play on a loop when our brains and bodies engage in the fear dance. He counsels, "Negative thoughts are normal. Don't fight them; defuse them."[671] He suggests a three-step approach:

- "notice we've been hooked,"[672]
- "name what's going on,"[673]
- "neutralize it."[674]

Harris also offers the acronym "NAME": "*notice, acknowledge, make space,* and *expand awareness.*"[675] In other words, once the amygdala alarm bells start ringing and the negative messages begin transmitting, we *notice.* Once we've detected their presence, we stop and simply say, "Oh hey, okay. Fear's here." Name it. Next, instead of pretending we don't hear the blaring sound track, let's directly engage with the negative lyrics (during our *process work*). Let's "expand"[676] our relationship with them or, as Harris urges, "open up and accommodate them"[677] (so that we ultimately can set them aside).

Eventually, we'll have trained ourselves to run through these mental maneuvers quickly in a fear moment, but during this initial *process work*, we have the luxury of time to really get intimate with the words we hear. When "opening up to and accommodating" the negative messages, to "neutralize" their impact, Harris suggests that we "imagine that [our] mind is a radio and [our] thoughts are like a voice coming out through the speakers."[678] By separating the thoughts from ourselves for a moment, we can place those negative messages "into a new context, where [we] can see them clearly for what they are."[679] Harris explains that all the energy that we formerly expended resisting, sparring with, or burying the fear messages, we now can invest in "taking effective action."[680]

Harris perfectly recaps this alternative way of looking at fear:

> *There is another way of responding to fear that is radically different from almost everything our society encourages us to do. We don't "put up with it" or "tolerate it." We don't suppress or deny its existence. We don't distract ourselves from it. We don't try to talk ourselves out of it. We don't try to reduce it or eliminate it with self-hypnosis or other techniques. We don't try to make it go away with medication, herbal remedies, or food or alcohol. We don't try to pretend it's not there (the so-called "fake it till you make it" approach).*[681]

Instead, we "allow it, befriend it, and channel it."[682]

Ulmer espouses a similar methodology. She suggests that we get "curious about what [we]'re feeling in [our] body, and then allow [ourselves] to feel it."[683] She reiterates the impact of getting "curious enough to find the opening."[684] We must stop and really listen to the hand-wringer in our head "fretting in the night" and "ask it lovingly what it needs to say."[685] Instead of the usual mantras we hear around fear—fight, repress, ignore, fake—Ulmer advocates for "consideration, curiosity, respect, and compassion."[686] She emphasizes that this is not about "*accept[ing]* Fear or discomfort."[687] In fact, she contends that "[a]nytime you say, 'It is what it is,' about anything, that's totally passive and a cop-out."[688] Instead, she advises us to let fear offer us "contrast and perspective."[689] In coalescing or fusing with fear instead of shoving it aside,[690] we can generate "awe and celebration of it, and excitement to thrive *because* of it, not in spite of it."[691] This approach refrains from glorifying the motivating force of fear as an entity separate from and superior to us, but instead recognizes its essence as *part* of us—a deep well of wisdom and self-knowledge. Ulmer describes a beautiful, martial arts-esque, respectful greeting of our fear. She says, "Just bow when the Fear shows up," and recite: "The badass in me recognizes the badass in you, and together we are one."[692]

Overall, instead of living a life of resistance, repression, or feigned force, we can flip our relationship with fear upside down. Ulmer encourages, "Have a love affair with Fear and you are powerful."[693] She reassures, "You'll know you got it right when just saying the words 'I feel afraid' makes you fall madly, deeply in love with yourself."[694]

LET'S GET VULNERABLE

In doing the mental pre-work to get us to the point of being able to untangle fear more quickly in the performance moment, we need to be vulnerable, authentic, and humble during the *process* work. This way, eventually during the *performance*, we will be able to proactively move the mental obstacles aside, and use our preparation and genuineness to shine brightly. Doing the *process* work, again I recommend that we begin to think of ourselves, not just as law students or lawyers or law professors, but as artists and athletes. When I think of artists I admire, I think of gritty painters or writers living the bohemian life in Rome or Paris decades or generations ago, covered in paint, seeing poetry in puddles, stringing words together like twinkle lights. I think of them as gritty because they were messy, imperfect, unpolished. They walked around with charcoal on their fingers, ink on their clothes, clay in their hair. They weren't afraid to get dirty in pursuit of their craft and calling. They exposed the very core of themselves to tap into their creativity. Athletes do the same: they sweat; they bruise; they get covered in dirt, dust, and grime as they train and condition.

Likewise, this phase of *our* process might get a little bumpy and unpretty. After all, some of us have been stuffing fear inside a tidy linen box wrapped with a perfectly boring satin bow for years. It's time to hack off that ribbon and rip off the lid. We can do this. Angela Duckworth, author of *Grit*, explains that "[g]rit has two components: passion and perseverance."[695] While we get to know the mental drivers of our fear, we can get raw and real with our emotions, and channel this tremendous energy into forging ahead to becoming our stronger selves.

One law student who had a creative focus in college and worried he didn't fit in within the law school arena shared an experience experimenting with vulnerability and authenticity:

As my [judicial] internship progressed throughout the summer, I repeatedly received the message that no one, not even judges, fit into the tiny mold I constructed for myself. . . . I continued to fear that the judges and court attorneys would discover I did not belong, and found myself more quiet than usual. I even texted my friend one day to tell her I thought I should visit a doctor because I was speaking so little. As I ate my lunch outside with the court attorneys and judges each day, I continued to make the conscious choice to leave on my suit jacket in the 85-degree heat, fearing that someone would see my tattoos through my button-down. But one day one of the well-respected attorneys sat down, took off her blazer, and showed off her completely tattooed arm. I started taking off my jacket at lunch after that.

In this process, we might need to be pioneers of vulnerability in our particular legal arena. As authors Jerome M. Organ, David B. Jaffe, and Katherine M. Bender point out in their pivotal article "Helping Law Students Get the Help They Need: An Analysis of Data Regarding Law Students' Reluctance to Seek Help and Policy Recommendations for a Variety of Stakeholders":

[W]hile in law school, students are socialized into a competitive environment in which showing any vulnerability is discouraged. Seeking help is an acknowledgment of vulnerability. The competitive nature of law school reinforces a message that students are better off not seeking help and instead trying to handle problems on their own.[696]

One law student suggested a different root of this reluctance of lawyers to be vulnerable: "The ego I think is then what prevents lawyers from being as vulnerable as might be helpful, because 'great attorney' and 'vulnerable' are not exactly synonymous." The same student recognized that "acknowledging

[fear], speaking about it, and having general awareness that anxiety and fear are normal in this profession are the keys to not letting it affect my work and also life outside of school."

USING VULNERABILITY AS A STRENGTH

The stereotype about vulnerability in the legal arena is that it is a flaw in others to exploit. We are going to do the opposite. We're going to nurture and expand our own vulnerability and that in others to become collectively fierce and wise. Best-selling author, Dr. Brené Brown, warns that society's "perception that vulnerability is a weakness is the most widely accepted myth about vulnerability *and* the most dangerous."[697] She reiterates that "[v]ulnerability is not a weakness."[698] She urges, "*Vulnerability sounds like truth and feels like courage. Truth and courage aren't always comfortable but they're never weakness.*"[699] Indeed, honoring vulnerability in ourselves and others is another key to untangling fear. The opposite approach—resisting or disparaging vulnerability—keeps us all afraid. Dr. Brown reminds us that "the level to which we protect ourselves from being vulnerable is a measure of our fear and disconnection."[700] Rather, she encourages:

> *Vulnerability is the birthplace of love, belonging, joy, courage, empathy, and creativity. It is the source of hope, empathy, accountability, and authenticity. If we want greater clarity in our purpose or deeper and more meaningful spiritual lives, vulnerability is the path.*[701]

How do we get vulnerable in a way that helps us untangle fear? Well, first let's take some time to listen to the words playing on our automatic mental sound track. Let's reflect on where such language might have originally come from, and realize that such messages of restraint, of staying small, of holding ourselves back because it's respectful of authority, or the opposite of pride, or the "proper" thing to do, are *no longer relevant* in our current lives in the law. Kristen Ulmer encourages us to "[s]hine the light on any dark voice and it, too, becomes light."[702]

TRANSCRIBING MY OWN MESSAGES

In writing *The Introverted Lawyer,* I realized I needed to study the roots of my social anxiety—the driver of my hesitance toward performance scenarios in my law firm life that was *separate* from my natural introverted preference for quiet researching, writing, and thinking. This meant being primally honest with myself and deliberately tapping into the drivers of my fears of judgment and exclusion. Relying on the experts I consulted in my research, I began listening to, transcribing, and pinpointing the original sources of my negative mental sound track. I needed to get super-specific about the words, language, and phrasing that continuously looped in my brain and undermined my confidence. My notebooks and journal transcriptions began to yield unpleasant messages: "Who are you to have an opinion?" "Your voice doesn't matter." "Nobody wants to hear from you." "Your feelings, thoughts, and ideas are unimportant." "You're not good enough." Of course, these incantations are not fun to listen to—over and over—but it was a giant step for me to first *hear* the actual words and then try to *attribute* their origin. Only then could I eventually *expunge* them. Once I had those words captured in ink on paper, I tried to reflect back to my earliest memory of feeling censored, either by my*self* or others.

Let me first establish that, as author Ivy Naistadt advises, this message transcription and source-identification process is "not a blame game."[703] We are not going to call up our elementary school teacher or high school basketball coach and lament, "You ruined my life!" Not at all. The purpose of this exercise is to unearth the actual language of these messages that we repeatedly tell ourselves, and then identify the original (perceived) sources thereof, so we can realize that those words are completely irrelevant to our new lawyering personas today. With that monumental realization, we can begin to delete the outdated and unhelpful messages and replace them with *true* statements about our present and future abilities, strengths, and power. It's okay, and essential, to do this step, even if these messages may have come from people we love, individuals who still may be in our lives. Or even if we interpreted or perceived messages in ways that were not intended by the original messenger. As applied sports psychologists Grand and Goldberg explain:

> Very often, the inner voices of doubt and fear that we hear are very old and come from early in life. These voices originate from our interactions with the most important people we grew up with. . . . Frequently, what we hear in our minds reflects what we heard from these important influences, both good and bad. . . . If our families treat us with kindness, compassion, and praise, we "internalize" these voices and treat ourselves this way as we mature. . . . If those early caretakers and individuals were consistently unkind, critical, and demeaning, however, then we learn to treat ourselves in that way. . . . Add this to our subsequent interactions with teachers, coaches, and teammates in childhood and adolescence and we see how our self-talk is reinforced.[704]

During my reflection process, I began to think back to the most formative influencers in my life: caregivers, family members, teachers, coaches, religious authority figures. Who might have made comments (even well-meaning ones) that planted the harmful seedling in my mind that I'm unimportant, insignificant, or unworthy of having a valid feeling, an opinion, or an idea? It's possible such influencers were just trying to inculcate me with a sense of humility (and they were doing the best job they knew how, from a genuine place of love), but there is a difference between humility and devaluation of the self.

I grew up in a religious household. My father was ordained a minister in the Episcopal church when I was six years old. Much of our family life revolved around Sunday services, my parents' Bible studies, their direction of youth choirs and summer beach ministries (of which I have fond memories), and other church events. My grandparents were Baptist and as devout as my parents. Sunday dinners of corn-flake-crusted fried chicken and butter beans involved spirited debate among the adults about politics and religion. Even though they were all on the same ideological side, many a dinner ended in fiery emotional eruption. My brother and I remained quiet observers most of the time.

The first memory I have of developing a political opinion was during the presidential election in which voters were choosing between incumbent Jimmy Carter and Ronald Reagan. The parents of our church friends who drove my school carpool were Democrats. I somehow gleaned the idea that Ronald Reagan was going to launch a nuclear war. That sounded kinda bad. One day, I came home from school, advised my parents and grandparents of this eventuality, and urged them to vote for Carter. I remember getting a stern talking-to about how I shouldn't use politics to rebel against my family. I was 10 years old. I don't recall us discussing any nuances about the election, or policies, or the world. Instead, it seemed there was simply one correct vote to be had. This confused me. I got, and stayed, quiet. Disagreement seemed scary.

From elementary school through high school, I attended an all-girls Episcopal school. My teachers mostly were gifted educators, especially the French and English teachers who taught me to love language and words. They encouraged us to write creative essays about the work of authors like Baudelaire, Stendahl, Camus. In doing the self-reflective social anxiety work when writing *The Introverted Lawyer* and trying to recall educational experiences in which I felt embarrassment or shame, I distinctly remembered one science teacher from my middle school days. I was always a quiet diligent student. I won spelling bees and National French Contests from an early age. I joyfully toted my report cards home to my parents. I stayed mostly silent in class, happily absorbing math equations and history timelines. In one science class, the teacher led us outside to our school's circular driveway to conduct an experiment with a magnifying glass, paper, and sunlight. Uncharacteristically, I exclaimed—out loud—to my best friend, "Oh wow, if you catch the sunlight in the glass and direct it toward the paper, it'll catch fire!" I was ecstatic! The teacher swooped over to me, snatched the magnifying glass from my hand, and declared, "You've just ruined the experiment for everyone!" My face turned fuchsia.

A few months later, during the winter holiday season, our class participated in a Secret Santa exchange. I was giddy to discover that the biggest, shiniest package under the artificial tree had my name on it. I murmured to my best friend, "Oh my goodness, look! The biggest gift under the tree is for me!" That same teacher asserted—loudly enough for all my classmates to hear— "The best things in life come in *small* packages." My face flashed scarlet. I never spoke in her class again.

Seeking perfection, pleasing others, and avoiding conflict became daily aspirations. Because of my dad's job in the church, our family was on display a lot. I smiled on the outside and worried on the inside about saying or doing the wrong thing. When I turned 12, Dad became the chaplain of a boys' boarding school. We moved into a house smack in the middle of campus, wedged between the library and the dining hall. While growing up as a "faculty kid" was fun—jumping on the field house trampolines and playing tag and hide-and-seek all over the campus with school friends—public observation remained part of our daily lives. For five years, I ate breakfasts and dinners in the massive dining hall with my family, plus 300 prep school boys decked out in seersucker blazers and khaki pants. I navigated puberty in that environment, accompanied by freckles, braces, and awkwardness. My mother, ever chic and stylish, wanted my brother and me to dress up for the dining hall meals. "Brush your hair and put some blush on," she urged in my high school years. Meanwhile, my best friend at school ribbed me for wearing makeup, dressing in knockoff Guess jeans, and carrying a Pappagallo purse that my grandmother had sewn herself. Every morning, I donned Cover Girl makeup to please my mother as we trotted over to the boarding school dining hall to eat institutional eggs and chipped beef on toast. On my commute to school, I wiped off any lingering vestige of mascara and eyeliner to avoid my best friend's chiding. After volleyball practice and homework each afternoon while my mom taught piano in the living room, I re-dressed for dinner and the makeup went back on. I had no idea who I was or who I wanted to be. I knew I wanted to be accepted and not left out. I knew I didn't want to be criticized or ridiculed by my friends. Pleasing others, putting on and taking off one mask after another, seemed to be the best tack for accomplishing that.

In high school and college, I started learning about controversial issues such as abortion and the death penalty. My maternal grandmother was the family member with whom I identified, the one I idolized, the most. She was feisty and smart. With jet-black hair and fiery hazel eyes, she drove a sky blue 1966 Mustang to her bridge tournaments and refused to wear a seat belt to avoid creasing her colorful couture. Scrimping pennies from her Army Chaplains' secretarial job to save up for trips to Egypt, Ireland, Israel, and Panama with my grandfather, she lit the travel fire in me. She enrolled in college around the same time I graduated from high school, majoring in philosophy and religious studies. Home on breaks from my University of Virginia semesters, I tried to partake in Sunday dinner discussions about capital punishment or medical ethics issues, testing out new theories I learned in class. I quickly discerned that any perceived divergence from my family members' beliefs about morality matters resulted in withdrawal: of affection, approval, even my usual college sendoff bag of bargain mac-and-cheese and ramen noodles. My grandmother averted eye contact with me for hours if I ventured into intellectual territory that countered the doctrine and dogma my family embraced. The retraction of attention hurt. I lost trust in my teenage and early-adult voice.

Dating had been a near impossibility in high school given my perceived "hands-off" status as the chaplain's daughter. When I matriculated at The University of Virginia and moved into the Echols Scholar dorm, I promptly fell in love with the first boy I met. He was smart, sweet, and kind and my first—perhaps only, now that I think about it—experience with unconditional love. He wrote poems and made Led Zeppelin mixtapes for me. After a year together, we both needed or wanted to explore college a bit more freely. That quest didn't last long. In the fall of my second year of college, I fell even more deeply in love with one of his fraternity brothers, a guy four years older than I. We dated for the next five-and-a-half years, got married the year I graduated from law school, and spent a total of 12 years together. He was by far the most important formative relationship of my life, and the one with the most devastating end, which occurred the year I turned 30.

Doing the difficult self-awareness work so many years later, I needed to reflect and focus on that primary relationship to realize that the endless quest to look or be perfect in his (and my parents' and grandparents' eyes), and be a people-pleaser, took a profound toll. I was completely terrified of losing *him*, and of disappointing *them*. Above all else in my life, I feared withdrawal of love. I feared (and still fear) exclusion, rejection, and being discarded. Trying to be perfect was the only tactic I knew to minimize this risk. It was inauthentic and exhausting, and doomed for failure.

After a 10-day honeymoon in Hawaii and law school graduation, I passed the bar exam and started my prestigious job at the boutique construction litigation firm. My guy and I purchased a cute modern three-bedroom house and built a picket fence that attempted to enclose Kirby and our other adopted beagle, Lacy. We bought a Jeep Cherokee and a Toyota Celica GT sports car. We hosted wine-tasting parties. I attended all his flag football games, sporting cutoff jeans shorts in an effort to look like the Perfect Wife supporting the good-looking quarterback husband. I drove to work wearing cornflower blue Ally McBeal suits with short skirts; I burrowed in my library cubicle to write lengthy briefs. I ran three miles a day to stay thin. Yet I never felt attractive or perfect enough: too curvy, teeth not white enough, skin too freckly. Too stressed out, too anxious, not go-with-the-flow enough. *Quit worrying so much! Just be happy!* I faked extroversion and confidence at the firm. Bosses quipped, "Thick skin! Never let them see you sweat!" I strove to dazzle on the outside. Fear and insecurity gnawed at my insides. I was terrified of losing my guy, and of screwing up at work. Eventually it all came crumbling down.

Twenty-five days before my thirtieth birthday, our marriage detonated.

Barely functioning, I moved out, struggled to stop crying and get out of bed each morning, and fumbled through each day trying to figure out what to do.

A few months later, after I won a case on a summary judgment brief I'd written in a fog of grief, I quit my law firm job to move to New York and start over. In the shelter of my fifth-floor walkup apartment, I played Dido music at all hours of the night and consumed piles of books about codependence and shame. I found a New York therapist, though people in my life reminded me that they didn't "believe in that psychology stuff." I realized I had no idea who I was authentically. I labored to breathe under a mountain of shame and anxiety about leaving everything I knew and loved and had worked for; I sank into an abyss of depression . . . and meanwhile started my new job as an associate in a law firm in Tower Two of the World Trade Center.

As recounted in the Introduction, about a year into my new life in New York, 9/11 happened. I was on a plane at the time, and my Lufthansa flight was diverted to Canada. I spent five days being fed, clothed, and sheltered by compassionate Canadians in Gander, Newfoundland. That tragic event snapped me out of my divorce grief and spurned me to get on with my life, grateful to be alive.

It honestly took me another 10 years—another long-term relationship layered with insecurity and withholding of affection (I re-created familiar patterns), another toxic law firm job, two moves across country and back, and a transition to teaching—for me to finally understand who I am authentically. In writing *The Introverted Lawyer*, and now this book, I realize that my power derives directly from *authentic imperfection*. I know I can be a force with impact because I am real, flawed, and honest about my ups and downs. I finally know how much strength I have in being exactly who and what *I* want to be, not *someone else*'s idea of who or what I should be. I aspire the same for you.

I'm sharing these rather embarrassing and unpleasant memories with you because, in seeking to untangle fear, it's difficult but essential to be raw and genuine. Doing so helps shine a spotlight on the line between reality and imagination, and illuminate any revisionist history. Until I wrote these experiences down in ink on paper, I only saw and repeatedly relived *my* missteps. I believed the story in my mind about how *weak* I was. My guilt, shame, and fear clouded my memory of other influences that contributed to the pain and self-judgment. When I'd written down these memories, certain truths and patterns became more apparent. I finally realized that, hey, it wasn't okay for that middle school science teacher to shame me—simply a young, naïve, excited student—in front of my classmates. It also wasn't ideal that formative influencers discouraged authentic development of individual opinions about important topics like religion and politics (perhaps in a well-intentioned effort to teach me their principles and moral values, but which led to me distrusting my voice throughout law school and practice). It also wasn't unconditionally loving for my guy to constantly nag at my physical and emotional "imperfections." It wasn't right for three different law firm bosses to scream and yell and throw things, "training us" through criticism and terror. Yet I interpreted these barbs as evidence of *my* failings, and dragged each emotional injury with me into every subsequent performance scenario.

Yes, all of that is now in the past, and might not sound like a big deal to some folks (believe me, I have heard "Get over it" all my life). Yet it was essential in *my* personal growth to understand the pattern of perceived negativity and critiques I interpreted as hurtful and that I internalized and reinforced on my own for decades. Only through identifying the sources of the messages I replayed in my mind relentlessly as an adolescent, an adult, and a professional, could I begin to delete or override such noxious words with truths that I now know to be absolutely certain. *I am* worthy of having opinions that differ from others. *I am* entitled to speak or act in my own introverted manner. I do *not* need to fake or force extroversion or bravado. Never again do I need to heap shame upon myself for being different or imperfect in the way I look, speak, think, or act. I realize now that my fear of being rejected, excluded, or discarded is actually fueled by *others'* fear. I now know there is zero risk in striding away from the pointless quest to be included by those who stoke (intentionally or unintentionally) instead of assuage our fears.

LET'S GET REAL ABOUT SHAME

Shame is an interesting entity that some of us also should get to know during this untangling process. Shame differs from guilt. Guilt is an emotion we may feel when we have done something wrong; we committed a *bad act*. We can, if we try to, distinguish ourselves from the act. We made a mistake. We erred. So what; we can correct it. Shame, on the other hand, is the feeling that we are inherently *flawed* as *human beings*. The *Free Dictionary* defines shame as "[a] painful emotion caused by the belief that one is, or is perceived by others to be, inferior or unworthy of affection or respect because of one's actions, thoughts, circumstances, or experiences."[705] Author Brené Brown characterizes shame as "the fear of disconnection."[706] Her definition is similar to the foregoing one: "*Shame is the intensely painful feeling or experience of believing that we are flawed and therefore unworthy of love and belonging.*"[707]

Dr. Brown emphasizes that "[s]hame keeps us small, resentful, and afraid."[708] She provides a helpful link between shame and fear that can assist us in identifying promoters of shame in our lives and understanding how they fuel our fear. She explains that "[s]hame breeds fear. It crushes our tolerance for vulnerability, thereby killing engagement, innovation, creativity, productivity, and trust."[709] She affirms the idea that shame is emotionally and physically painful "because it is inextricably linked to the fear of being unlovable."[710] Indeed, "feeling unlovable is a threat to survival. It's trauma."[711]

So, with the goal of untangling fear, how do we begin to comprehend the existence, role, and agents of shame in our lives? Quoting from Harry Potter, Dr. Brown advises that "[i]n order to be vulnerable, we need to develop resilience to shame."[712] She defines "shame resilience" as

> *the ability to practice authenticity when we experience shame, to move through the experience without sacrificing our values, and to come out the other side of the shame experience with more courage, compassion, and connection than we had going into it. Shame resilience is about moving from shame to empathy—the real antidote to shame.*[713]

The process that worked for me was to take the time to listen to my negative mental sound track (as unpleasant as it was), identify the original sources of the messages, and realize that those past messages were—even if from well-intentioned people—about trying to keep me small. I had to extricate myself from those shackles and restraints. I needed to name the influencers in my life who I felt had shamed me when I expressed independent views or acted differently from their "perfect ideal" of me. I had to realize that their inability to embrace the real me possibly stemmed from their own fear, perhaps of being unable to control me. My forays into being vulnerable, authentic, and unpretty were freaking them out, so they reacted by trying to shame me, and withdrawing connection—which they knew would then make me panic, hang on more tightly, and try to please again, thereby censoring my voice, squashing my persona. To apply Dr. Brown's notion of shame resilience, the real power comes when we can be self-aware enough to notice when this is happening, understand why we feel shame and fear in those moments, and stay with our vulnerability and authenticity even at the risk of the other person's disconnection. Once we figure out who we are authentically, we build enough resilience to stay true to ourselves, keep moving forward through others' attempts to shame or scare us, and come through the other side not only unscathed but even more vibrant and alive.

Bring. It. On.

If the process of transcribing your mental sound track initially feels uncomfortable or awkward, you might consider establishing a short daily ritual of getting your thoughts out of your head and onto paper (or into a document on your computer). I have ridiculously awful insomnia, and my mind immediately launches a spin cycle of drama the instant I wake up. It's as if the physical embodiment of my negative internal voice has been staring at me all night while I sleep, and the millisecond I open one eyelid, she starts chattering at me: "OMG, that new article you wrote goes live today! What if people hate it?! What if they slam you on Twitter or LinkedIn?!" or "OMG, you have to give that huge presentation in midtown today! What if your content is totally irrelevant to the firm's practice?!" *Ugh.* To rein in the Voice, every single day, no matter what time I get out of bed or what looms on my morning schedule, I do four things:

- I grab my iPhone from the living room, jump back in bed, slip earbuds into my ears, and use the Insight Timer app to play a guided meditation on the subject of "creativity" or "motivation" (you can choose different topics in the app) for 5 minutes, or 10 minutes, or 15 minutes, however long I feel like it.
- I get up, make a pot of coffee, and light a candle in my living room.
- I grab my green journal that says "Rethink" on the cover, which is ironic because I'm trying *not* to think. I write three longhand pages of basically gibberish.

These three pages are called Morning Pages, a technique suggested in Julia Cameron's book, *The Artist's Way: A Spiritual Path to Higher Creativity*.[714] (Her book saved my life during my divorce, a sentiment I conveyed to Ms. Cameron when I met her at a book signing in Manhattan. She signed my book, "To Heidi, For your heart."). Three pages, no more no less. No editing, no reread-ing, no worrying about who might read it. (I have instructed my best friend that if anything ever happens to me, he needs to run immediately to my apartment and "burn all the journals.") I dump onto the journal page every thought that pops into my brain for as long as it takes me to fill three pages. If I have *no* thoughts, I simply write, "Keep going keep going keep going" until a thought comes. I complain. I whine. Sometimes I try to list things I'm grateful for, which inevitably reverts back to grumbling, and then I end with something encourag-ing which is usually a string of stuff like "get out of your own way go easy on you trust your system you're doing great keep going you're awesome you're an artist you're an athlete go create be you now go!"

- I shut the journal, grab a stack of "Seeds of Intention" cards (from www.mayyouknowjoy.com) that I received in a gift box for introverts from www.thewallflowerbox.com, choose a card (with messages like "for today I take a risk," or "for today I am open to possibility"), set it on top of the card stack, blow out my candle, and start my day.

This whole thing takes about 20 minutes depending on how long I do the meditation app. And let me assure you, it *works* to get the annoying chatter out of my head and onto paper, and clear my mind for the morning. Also, certain issues that I didn't even know were affecting me suddenly pop up out of nowhere in the Morning Pages. For me, this ritual or daily habit has helped me recognize my negative mental messages, identify their original sources, and begin to overwrite them.

Step 2 of our untangling fear process is about mentally rebooting. The exer-cise offered below can help us:

- Slow our roll
- Open up to vulnerability and curiosity about ourselves
- Carve out time to listen to our mental sound track
- Transcribe our unhelpful fear (or shame) messages
- Identify the original sources of those unhelpful messages

- Realize that those messages—maybe well-intentioned at the time—are all about keeping us small, and it's time to expand and magnify
- Rewrite our internal sound track
- Build resilience and learn how to kick our new mental sound track into gear in a performance moment
- Stay true to our new authentic selves

Replace fear with curiosity.

—Steven Spielberg

Step 2

Exercise: Mentally Rebooting

Pre-Work (our "Preparation Process," as discussed in Chapter 13)

- Give yourself permission to outright reject cliché messages like "Just do it," "Fake it till you make it," "Do what scares you," or "Embrace fear as a great motivator!"
  - ○ These mantras don't help; at least, they didn't help me!
  - ○ Instead, let's get real, grab a twisty mess of fear, and begin untangling it.
- *First, anticipate* a law school or lawyering scenario that sparks fear, OR the next time you actually *step into* a fear-inducing scenario, pay attention to what happens in your mind (and body, which we will focus on in Step 3).
- *Notice* any instinctive responses.
  - ○ Sense any amygdala alarm bells.
  - ○ Notice any "fight-or-flight" feeling.
  - ○ Notice any ignition of a negative mental sound track.
- Resist the urge (or other people's advice) to repress, ignore, or shrug aside the fear response.
  - ○ Let it flow.
- Listen to, and actually hear, the negative mental sound track.
  - ○ What are the exact words that you are telling yourself?
  - ○ Write them down word for word.
- Get curious.
  - ○ Have you heard these words previously?
  - ○ Honoring the fact that this is not a "blame game" but instead a self-discovery mission, do you recognize who might have said these words in your past, perhaps many years ago?
- Be vulnerable.
  - ○ Allow yourself to acknowledge those past messages and potentially their original source (yep, not fun, but necessary!).
  - ○ How did you feel back then?
  - ○ How did you respond back then? Did you get silent? Self-censor? Shrink yourself? Blush with shame?
  - ○ Do you notice any patterns in those messages? Did you hear them from more than one source?

- Be cognizant of shame-based messages.
  - Do any of your messages suggest that you are not just "bad at" something, but you are "bad"?
- Continue writing down, transcribing, those negative messages—to get them out of your head and down on paper.
- Realize that those past messages likely are completely outdated and irrelevant to your new legal persona and thus can be deleted and overwritten.
  - *Past* caregivers, coaches, mentors, teammates, peers, authority figures, or other original sources of those messages likely have no role or part in the law school or lawyering scenario you are stepping into today, in this moment.
- Craft three to six new, tangible, true statements about yourself.
  - Example:
    - "I have a voice and I deserve to be heard."
    - "I have worked really hard on this and I know what I am talking about."
    - "I am entitled to say this in my own authentic voice."
    - "I am strong."
    - "I am unique and I don't need to act like everyone else."
    - "I am a scholar-athlete and an artist."
- Craft three to six new tangible statements about the task at hand.
  - Example:
    - "This is a _____-minute, low-stakes experience, not the Super Bowl Half-Time Show."
    - "The world is not going to come to an end if I need to pause to collect my thoughts."
    - "I'm substantively and procedurally prepared."
    - "The fear response I'm feeling, mentally and physically, is just the amygdala alarm bell ringing."
    - "The fear messages I'm hearing are just the outdated sound track. It's time to reboot and play my new sound track!"

In-the-Moment Mental Reboot (our "Performance Process" discussed in Chapter 13)

- *Step into* the actual performance scenario (armed with your new mental messages).
- *Notice* any instinctive responses.
  - Sense any amygdala alarm bells.
  - Notice any "fight-or-flight" feeling.
  - Listen for any ignition of the negative mental sound track.

- Don't resist, repress, shelve, ignore . . . just *be* and *feel*.
- *Notice* if/when the negative mental sound track kicks in.
- *Acknowledge* . . . okay, fear is here.
- Stop, drop, and roll.
  - *Wait, this is just fear again.*
  - *I'm prepared for this.*
  - *It's cool . . . I'm cool.*
  - *OK, let's go!*
- Hit the ignition switch for the new mental sound track.
  - Run through your new messages (more than once, if necessary).
- Now, remember "Train and trust" (sports psychologist Bob Rotella's advice described in Chapter 13).
  - You *trained* for this, substantively and procedurally.
  - You *trained* for this, mentally and physically.
  - *Trust* your system.
  - Focus only on the tasks immediately ahead, not on the outcomes.
  - No need to overthink or overcare. Remember Olympic gold medalist Scott Hamilton's "refined indifference" (Chapter 13).
  - The only thing that matters is trusting and following through on your performance *process*.
    - Focus on honoring the *process*, not the outcomes.
- Smile.
- Now, let your body take over, and ignite your "preshot routine" (which we will develop in Step 3 in the next chapter).

CHAPTER 16

Step 3: Channeling Our Inner Athlete

Now that we are armed with techniques for a quick *mental* reboot in a fear-inducing performance moment, we next focus on adopting *physical* strategies for channeling our energy, blood, and oxygen flow in a productive manner. As we learned in Chapter 5, our bodies launch an overdrive response to protect us when we are afraid. Some of our automatic physiological machinations actually can hold us back from performing at our peak with clear minds and physical fortitude. By enhancing our perception of how our bodies move and react in the face of fear, we can make subtle yet conscious changes, both in anticipation of and during performance events. A higher level of self-awareness will, in turn, help us retake control and dramatically enhance our breathing and sense of physical and mental power.

In Step 3, we become lawyer-athletes, or scholar-athletes, or thinker-athletes. Before stepping into an athletic event, athletes run through routines and rituals—every time—to engage muscle memory, ignite oxygen and blood flow, and keep nerves at bay. We will do the same.

THE PROCESS WORK

Again, we start with our pre-event *process* work, or *preparation* work. Once more, the first step is reflection. By noticing and considering major and minor physical movements and sensations, we can enhance our consciousness of how our bodies instinctively react when we encounter a fear-based stimulus. Many of us may never have paused to take a look, to observe, to sense what happens to our physical bodies when we feel fear or anxiety. We are so accustomed to going through the motions, just trying to push through the experience, get it done, survive to live another day. It's truly remarkable when we stop to watch what our bodies are doing—it's like slowing down a film and scrutinizing frame by frame how our physical form reacts, how our limbs and appendages respond, how our skeletal structure folds or unfolds.

BLUSHOLOGY

"Blushing is the color of virtue."

—Diogenes

In writing about social anxiety in *The Introverted Lawyer*, I undertook my own *process* work to pay attention to and assess how my physical body reacts in moments of strain in interpersonal interactions. I mentioned a few times that I have a robust blushing response. My face turns fireball red at the most inopportune times. It happens when I'm the center of attention in a meeting, when I'm not 100% sure of the answer to a poignant question after a presentation, and when I disagree with someone and want to assert myself. It also can happen in situations I like to describe as "misplaced shame" or "inartfully timed embarrassment"—in other words, in scenarios where I have no reason whatsoever to feel shame or embarrassment, but my brain suddenly recalls a *memory* of feeling ashamed or embarrassed. For instance, I could be having a perfectly innocuous conversation with a work colleague about the merits of pink Himalayan sea salt on avocado toast, and suddenly my brain will flash to a time a waiter in Rome smiled and conversed with me in Italian when I flubbed a joke about sea salt and I blushed at my foreign language mistake. Four thousand miles away from that waiter and a year later, I blush again while talking with the work colleague about something as innocent as sea salt. The flash of pink in my cheeks ignited by that Italy memory deepens and darkens into a red fury. Its heat pricks at my skin like little darts. I first feel embarrassed. Then I feel a rush of misplaced shame—like, why in the world did I feel entitled to spend a month in Rome working on a new book when I should have had my head stapled to my desk in Brooklyn? *Huh?* All this from a 90-second conversation about sea salt!

My point is: My body reacts in weird and publicly obvious ways to even nonscary stimuli. In the past, I tried to fight it. In my many years as a litigator, I sported turtlenecks and scarves in performance scenarios like depositions, negotiations, and court appearances, laboring to hide my blush, my blazing cheeks, and my blotchy neck. Trying to fight the flush only exacerbated it. I ruminated over the blush, worried that people could sense weakness. Of course, obsessing about it simply lengthened the time each blush lingered. Swathing myself in clothing twisted like ivy vines around my neck only served to suffocate me, not protect me. I was hot, sweaty, and breathless at times that I most needed to be cool, fresh, and infused with oxygen.

In researching social anxiety, I came across Erika Hilliard's tremendous book in which she describes a blush as evidence that "life is coursing through you."[715] *Living Fully with Shyness and Social Anxiety* states that "[b]lushing is a reminder that you are a vibrant human being, complete with a rich array of emotions. It's a package deal. We laugh, we cry, we fume, we flame."[716] Reading those words changed my relationship with my blush almost instantly. First, it made me laugh. *I blush; I'm alive; yay, me!* For years, I had been fighting the blush, mortified by it, bristling at the many people (colleagues, men on dates, random people on the subway) who like to point out my blushing. (Why do they do that?) Finally, here was someone saying, wait, your blush is an amazing sign of the vigorous life force surging through you. This was a huge start for me to get to know (and dare I say, accept and even appreciate) how my body reacts to stress and strain. I resolved to "be the blush," and see what else about my body I could reframe as powerful instead of resisting, rebuking, and repressing as weak.

In conversation with a doctor about skin care, I mentioned my blushing issue. The doctor offered to prescribe a medication that purportedly would diminish the redness in my face. *Sure, why not. It's worth a try*, I thought. At first, it seemed like a miracle drug! Fast-forward to a legal conference at which I had been asked to moderate a breakout session of a workshop for new scholarly writers. No problem; just me, talking about the writing process—one of my favorite subjects—with open-minded and collaborative legal writing professors. Except that I got a tad nervous, as usual. My blush response kicked in as soon as I opened my mouth to speak. So far, the medication had worked great as long as I never blushed. In this instance, however, the nerves of being the conversation leader, and the tiniest sensation of embarrassment, which then somehow led to misplaced shame, prompted my face to flame worse than ever before. That day at the conference, it burned so fiercely, it actually hurt. I had to say to my colleagues out loud, "Sorry, I'm having some sort of allergic reaction to a new medication, but I'm okay." It was *that* obvious something alarming was happening to my face. Yikes. I got through the workshop, tossed out the medication, and resolved to just "be the blush" forevermore.

UNTANGLING FEAR FROM OUR BODIES

Former professional extreme skier Kristen Ulmer describes the detrimental impact to our bodies of fighting and repressing fear. Honoring Fear with a capital F and our Bodies with a capital B, she says, "When energy in motion stops, it does not get destroyed. It has to go somewhere. . . . Thanks to years of repression, Fear is now trapped, unexpressed in the basement."[717] Indeed, "[t]he Body has become the dumping ground and storage area for unfelt, unwelcome Fear."[718] In her own journey to untangle fear, she realized that "smothering Fear was both physically and emotional[ly] abusive to [her] body."[719] Instead of stuffing fear down into the recesses of our bodies and doing mental and physical gymnastics to keep it there, let's figure out how to open up and let it out, so that we can think and move freely.

To recalibrate my physical approach to fear-provoking scenarios, I needed to step outside myself and observe. What physical sensations do I feel at the onset of a fearful moment? What automatic actions, reactions, and movements does my body initiate? These physical manifestations of fear, anxiety, and strain likely will differ for all of us. Some of us might shake. For others, our throats might go dry, or our palms might sweat. For me, my heart feels like it's thudding against my ribs, like a feral animal hurling itself against the bars of a cage. It hurts. My stomach twists like a pretzel. And, of course, my blush starts to creep around my neck, settling into my cheeks, which burn like a blowtorch.

So, first we *notice* these initial responses. What happens next? When I sense my heart thumping like a deejay speaker, my stomach wringing itself out like wet laundry, and the inferno brewing along my cheekbones, my physique joins in. Its immediate response is: "get small." My shoulders hunch. My legs cross. My arms intertwine. My body folds like origami. It's like I'm trying to become invisible—right there in that conference room, classroom, or courtroom. At the same time, all this bending, folding, and crumpling inward unfortunately is *not* making me disappear but *is* beginning to block my energy, blood, and oxygen flow. My instinctive inclination to hide and protect myself is hindering my body's most valuable assets from doing their jobs.

I *need* energy. I *require* blood flow to my brain. I *must have* oxygen. My body performs its contortions because it thinks it is helping keep me safe. It's not. During this process work, when I became aware of what was happening, I realized it was up to me to reboot physically and retake control. I needed to teach myself, or learn from others, how to regard my body as a source of indomitable power, not an alarmist doomsayer who is going to sabotage me.

I hit the gym.

I never was an athlete in high school or college, except for a brief foray on the high school volleyball team. But I have always liked working out. For years since college, my motivation has been primarily aesthetic: attempt to undo the effects of the Spanish red wine and piles of carbs I consume. During the process of trying to understand my physical reactions to fear and anxiety, exercise gained a new principal function: treat myself like an athlete in training and learn how use my physical body to power me through mental performance moments with the most clarity and strength possible. This became a whole new way of looking at fitness.

As a New Yorker, I love taking SoulCycle spinning classes. The motivational messages from the ebullient teachers, the inspirational wall slogans, the grapefruit-smelling candles, and the pumping music energize me. Now, instead of just sweating in the dark to Rihanna tunes for 45 minutes, I have adopted a new mission every time I sign up for a class: building the self-knowledge and self-trust that if I push my body as hard as I can for 45 minutes and don't pass out or fall off the bike, I can power through an intellectual performance moment, applying the same physical techniques. *Notice the reality of your strength and perseverance. Eyes up. Shoulders back. Sit tall. Heart and chest open. Breathe deeply.*

And then I added boxing. Boxing at Trinity Boxing Club is literally the hardest physical activity I have ever done in my life. There are so many layers to the physical and mental exertion of it, I don't even know where to start. The gym is hot and muggy. It's bustling with activity. A bell tracks three minutes of effort, then grants a thirty-second break, and the next three minutes begin immediately—for everyone. There's no lounging around. Once the wraps and gloves are on and you're staring at the heavy bag, or the trainer's mitts are in your face, or you're in the ring, you simply have to punch. You can't just stand there thinking about it. It's exhilarating, and exhausting. But it doesn't kill me. I turn fire-alarm red, yes, and I sweat buckets and probably look like I need CPR, but I don't die. I now know that if I can handle 60 minutes of three-minute rounds of all-out effort at Trinity, I can survive a stressful meeting, negotiation, classroom dynamic, or debate. Physical strength *directly* ties to mental strength.

When I first started boxing, I was self-conscious. I felt cool in my Nike boxing shoes and my black-and-gold gloves, but my body was, and still is, stiff. My hips don't sway naturally with the punches or in the boxer's dance between punch combos. In the early days, I didn't yet know the lingo and I forgot many of the punch sequences. I honestly worried that I was losing my memory and Ray and the other trainers would think I was too foggy-headed to box. Thanks to his patience and perception, we figured out the problem: I was holding my breath. Nervous about messing up or looking foolish, I wasn't breathing—at all. *Of course, you can't think straight or remember anything! Start by breathing.* We worked on awareness. I'd miss a combo, instinctively chide myself, but then catch myself not breathing. I learned to reboot. I'd take some intentional breaths, shake my gloves a few times, bop back and forth on my feet to spark new energy, step back into my boxer's stance, look my trainer in the eye, exhale and go. *I can do this*, I'll say aloud.

I also had to learn to view my training as a series of tiny increments. Thirty seconds here. Three minutes there. Not some colossal all-important lifetime achievement. The goal is simple: Get through the next three minutes. *You can do anything for three minutes.*

The SoulCycle classes and boxing training help me feel strong in many ways. First, I am doing something healthy for my body, and at the same time I'm clearing my mind of clutter. Second, training is extremely challenging and yet I am able to get through it. Third, in boxing I am making myself vulnerable in a social environment that could be incredibly intimidating, scary, and judgmental, but I am able to step into it. I feel good, not wimpy or unworthy. Fourth, I walk out of each spinning class and boxing session standing up taller, shoulders back a little farther, eyes a little fiercer.

I'll add one more quick example of physical *process work* and then we'll get on with how all this applies to fear in lawyering. As I mentioned earlier, last summer I had the opportunity to teach a legal writing course at a university in a small medieval village just outside Rome. I decided to spend a full month in Rome, as a "writer's retreat" to work on this book. I rented an Airbnb in the Olympic Village (Villagio Olimpico) built for the 1960 Games in Rome. There, I didn't have access to a gym, yet I needed some form of exercise to counteract my daily risotto intake and clear my head (I get pretty blurry when I write). I'd invested in a good pair of Adidas running shoes before leaving Brooklyn. I hadn't run outside on pavement in probably a decade. Plus, Rome in June is swamp heat. And buggy. Not exactly ideal conditions to start running again.

I gave myself two days to get over the initial jet lag, taught my first two classes, and then the time came. I was going to run by the Tiber River. I laced up my sneakers and tucked my apartment key into a zippered pocket. I started slowly, jogging through the Olympic Village, passing street names like Via Jugoslavia, Via Finlandia, Via Argentina. I veered toward the river and crossed an ancient bridge called the Ponte Milvio. I passed a few street vendors hawking used books and landscape paintings. I followed a couple of Romans pedaling bicycles while simultaneously smoking and yelling *con spirito* into their cell phones. Trailing them, I found a running and biking path. I began to jog *slowly* along the river, giving myself measurable distance goals: Just make it to that next bridge and see how you feel. *Hey, even though I am a sweaty mess and have gnats stuck to my cheek, I feel okay. Keep going. Make it to that next boathouse and see how you feel.* When I returned that first evening to the Airbnb and checked my mileage, I realized I had run 3.9 miles! It was hard, hot, and mosquito-y, but I did it.

My daily routine in Rome became: Wake up; use the Insight Timer meditation app for 10 to 20 minutes and do some sort of "creativity" meditation; make coffee in the death trap Moka pot; write my Julia Cameron *Artist's Way* Morning Pages in my journal; hunker down and work on the book manuscript for two hours—no more no less—and then lace up my shoes and run that same route. And then I could go do something cultural the rest of the afternoon. My writing and running fell into a parallel rhythm. When I doubted that I could do the writing or running work, or felt discomfort, fatigue, or annoyance, I told myself, "Keep going. You're not going to die. You're not going to fail. All you have to write today is what gets done in these two hours. You did two hours yesterday. You did two hours the day before. All you have to run today is to the boathouse and back. You ran to the boathouse yesterday. You ran to the boathouse the day before. Go slowly. Stick to the plan. One word at a time. One foot in front of the other. Neither one of these endeavors is a sprint." The rhythm worked. The pages added up. The mileage accumulated. But most importantly, I learned to trust that I didn't need to do more than I was doing each day. The system functioned, and it gave me mini-rewards along the way.

One sweltering day near the end of my month in Rome, I decided to run in the evening instead of the afternoon. As I approached the bridge, several Italian couples were lingering in both pedestrian paths—the sole entryways to the bridge—leisurely chatting, holding hands, and admiring the orange sunset. Ponte Milvio is a "love lock" bridge; lovers scribble romantic graffiti messages to each other and fasten padlocks on the bridge's lanterns and chain links. With the pedestrian entrances blocked by the lovers, I decided I could just as easily get onto the bridge if I leapt over a low thick chain linking two stanchions. As I jumped, my Adidas sneaker caught on a love lock. In what felt like slow-motion, I face-planted on the other side of the chain, my wrists and knees catching my fall on the ancient cobblestones, my iPhone bouncing down the bridge. *Dang it. Dang those lovers and love locks.* Mortified, I picked myself up, retrieved my phone, and kept going, realizing my right wrist was banged up and my "Love trumps hate" bracelet (that I had ordered on Etsy) was bent and contorted. My ego and knees smarting, I kept going. I crossed the bridge, annoyed and frustrated with myself, debating whether to just quit and go home.

As I turned down the riverside path, I came upon an excavation that was usually covered by a blue tarp and surrounded by chain-link fencing. Up to this point, I had assumed it was just utility work. This evening, the tarp had been rolled back, its corners secured with stones. I could see inside the excavation. It wasn't utility work at all; it was an archaeological project. The dig was about 5 feet deep, and 15 feet wide. Archaeologists had unearthed curved layers of stone and a stunning cobalt blue floral mosaic floor. Having visited several preserved underground houses during my time in Rome, I surmised the excavated curvatures were possibly a bath or a pool that was once part of a fancy home. I had been running right past this piece of ancient history for weeks! Who had lived in this structure right by the Tiber? How long ago? Why had their home been covered up? Why had it suddenly been rediscovered? I lingered for several minutes. Then, reinspired, I kept going. I ran and ran and ran.

I realized in that moment how essential it is that we keep going. Even when we face-plant in the most embarrassing way possible, and feel bruised and banged up, we get up and *keep going*. Because we have a purpose here and a place in our collective history. And when we keep going, life gives us incremental surprises and rewards.

I completely understand that not everyone enjoys exercise (and that many individuals have limitations in physical movement). Thinking about incorporating a new fitness regimen into our already overprogrammed lives can seem daunting. But I recommend trying to think of physical conditioning—at even the most basic level and in whatever form—as a giant step toward untangling fear. If we can use exercise or physical movement to get to know our bodies better, understand how our frames function, and trust that we can withstand physical discomfort—staying in "eustress," which we learned about in Chapter 13—and come through the other side unscathed, we can start to use our bodies as powerful equipment in performance moments.

DEVELOPING A PHYSICAL PERFORMANCE RITUAL OR A PRESHOT ROUTINE

Athletes, dancers, actors, and performers of many other types engage in pre-performance routines to get into the zone, prepping their minds and bodies with familiar motions. This leads into the "preshot" routine described by sports psychologist Bob Rotella, in Chapter 13. Habitual pre-performance sequences prime the mind and body for action. They remind us to *trust* our training, and remember that we know what we are doing and that we have gone through these motions before, successfully.

In the world of acting, "pre-show rituals are the touchstones that allow an actor to comfortably make the transition from regular life to performance mode."[720] Distinct from superstitions, these rituals or routines prepare the performer's mind and body. Broadway actress Annaleigh Ashford shared her routine on a particular show: "I would walk from stage right to stage left . . . say 'good show' . . . to the crew stage left, double check my pointe shoe ribbons, rub the pointe shoes in rosin and say a prayer. . . ."[721] Lead singer of the band Coldplay, Chris Martin, has said, "For me, there are about 18 things I have to do before I can go out to perform—most of them are too ridiculous to repeat!"[722] In a book called *Recipes for Good Luck: The Superstitions, Rituals, and Practices of Extraordinary People*, author Ellen Weinstein describes singer Beyoncé's preshow warm-up routine:

> *[I]t includes a prayer and stretch with the band, getting her hair and makeup done in a massage chair, and an hour of peace while she listens to her favorite playlist. She follows this routine to ease stress before performing and to help ensure a great performance.*[723]

Singer-songwriter Leonard Cohen followed a routine with his band in which together they performed a Latin chant that begins "*Pauper sum ego, nihil habeo*" ("I am poor, I have nothing"). As Cohen's backup singers, the Webb Sisters, described, "The bass player plays a note, Leonard starts singing and we all follow. The 10 of us then walk to the stage singing it. It's a great focusing ritual. It's a way of reducing the weight of what we feel."[724]

Adam Clayton, bass guitarist for U2, shared with a podcast interviewer that on show days, he hits the gym as it is "nice for my head."[725] Adam notes the importance of "freeing yourself of being in the practical side of the brain" two or three hours before a performance.[726] He also makes sure to get some "physio" before his shows to loosen up; "Holding an instrument for those 2½ hours, I know that my shoulder and back and neck all need work. . . ."[727]

In the world of athletics, pre-game or preshot routines help competitors garner control over their minds and bodies. In explaining why elite athletes employ familiar routines before performances, sports psychologist Jim Taylor explains:

> *There are a lot of things in sport that athletes can't control such as weather conditions and their opponent. Ultimately, the only thing athletes can control is themselves. . . . Those areas athletes can control include their equipment (is your gear in optimal condition?), their body (are you physically and technically warmed up?), and their mind (are you at prime focus and intensity?).*[728]

Golden Gate Warriors star Stephen Curry engages in a 20-minute pre-game routine that incorporates security staffers, fans, media, and the basketball:[729]

- Curry walks from the locker room into the entrance tunnel wearing a hoodie.
- Security official Norm Davis spots him and yells, "Warrior coming out!"

- Curry responds, "Hold them up."
- Security staffers "repeat the call."
- Curry jumps into the air and sprints through the corridor onto the court.
- Curry walks to the team bench and tightens his shoelaces.
- Curry puts a variety of ball-handling drills into action
  - Dribbling from the scorer's table to the opposite end of the court
  - Same thing from the opposite end but walking backward
  - A series of left-handed shots, in sequences of five
  - A series of baseline shots
  - A series of "circus-like shots"
  - Fifteen shots at five different spots on the floor
  - "Isolation action where he attacks as if he's being guarded by someone"
- Then he walks back to the tunnel and, after catching a ball tossed from a specific security official, Curtis Jones, he attempts a 40-foot two-handed shot.
- Fans yell, "Warrior coming out!"
- Curry "races down the hallway and jumps into the wall inside the locker room to stop his momentum."[730]

All this happens in 20 minutes; it "get[s] him loose."[731]

Next time you are watching your favorite athlete prepare to swing a bat, hit or kick a ball, initiate a dive, perform a vault, leap off the starting line of a race, watch closely to notice any pre-movement habits. Do they close their eyes? Touch a sleeve or tug a wristband? Rebalance themselves? Move their appendages? Breathe in a different or deliberate way? We are not talking about superstitions here; instead, we are focusing on specific repeatable movements that get the body and mind ready to go.

Let's break our performance process into two phases: a pre-performance routine we can do *before* we approach and enter the lawyering performance arena, and a "preshot" routine that comprises a series of infinitesimal movements immediately preceding the commencement of the performance activity. As some of us advance toward the physical site of a performance event, our bodies automatically begin to react to the initial sensation of fear or trepidation and launch those annoying self-protective routines. As we walk toward the courtroom, the boardroom, the conference room, or the classroom, the familiar fear tornado starts to churn. As with our mental sequence of stop, drop, and roll discussed in Step 2, we can apply the same concept to our physique.

Social psychologist and professor Amy Cuddy delivered a great TED Talk about the linkage between standing in a "power pose" for two minutes before a performance moment and a subsequent boost of feelings of confidence.[732] The "power poses" she suggests include (1) sitting in a chair with feet crossed on a desk, hands clasped behind the head, (2) placing hands on hips like a proud superhero, and (3) standing up and leaning forward with hands firmly planted on a table or bureau. All these are balanced and open, the opposite of making ourselves small, caved-in, or pretzel-y. Before entering the performance arena, let's consider finding a quiet place to stand or sit in a "power pose." Here, we can channel our inner athlete for a few moments, adopt a balanced, open, empowered stance, and breathe. Even if people lurk around us, we can subtly stand there with hands on hips, outstretched, or even clasped behind our heads, and we can breathe.

Trust me; I do this all the time—standing or sitting like an imaginary superhero ready to take on the world—and no one notices. Before entering an actual performance arena, I stand or sit in an Amy Cuddy "power pose" and try to channel my inner athlete and rock star. I lengthen my spine, shift my shoulders back, and imagine that this is what my favorite rock star would do. He would slide on his sunglasses and smile, and think, "Hey, I'm mighty. I'm doing this because I love it. I've done all the work to get here. I've trained and rehearsed for this. Not everyone needs to like me. I'm ready to go."

Once we enter the performance space, and determine where we need to sit or stand, we can initiate our "preshot" routine. For me, the moment I sense the heart-thud, the stomach-twist, the blush-starburst, the shoulder-hunch, and the appendage-origami, the first step is for me to notice. *Oh, geez, I'm folding up, collapsing again. No, no. Stand (or sit) like the athlete and rock star you are.* I recalibrate my stance with intention, consciously shoving my shoulders back an inch again, distributing my weight evenly on both legs, uncrossing my arms, opening everything up, and then I breathe. Opening up our frame so that our adrenaline, blood, and oxygen can flow in a constructive manner powers our hearts and brains. Gay Hendricks, author of *The Big Leap*, says, "The best advice I can give you is to take big, easy breaths when you feel fear. Feel the fear instead of pretending it's not there."[733]

Next, we remember to *trust*. We trained for this. In these moments, I remind myself (again) that I didn't fall off the bike in my spinning class. I didn't collapse in the boxing ring. Even when I literally did face-plant while leaping over that pesky love-lock chain on the bridge in Rome, I didn't die! I got up, a little scraped and bruised, and I kept running. If a blush fires up or sweat droplets trickle, remember, that physical reaction just validates that we're alive. *Yay, us!*

Next, I look around for potential fans but I'm also scanning for my perceived "foes," or "threats" in human form so I can look them in the eye. If I need a little extra boost, I channel the swagger I felt when I left the spinning class, or the boxing gym, or the running trail after a 3.9-mile run in the Rome swamp heat. Or the buoyancy I felt when I stepped off the plane in Patagonia and hiked a mountain there. (Remember the areas of our personal lives we identified in Step 1 in which we felt indomitable? We bring those feelings into the lawyering arena here.) This exact moment in the law-related performance arena is why it's important to put ourselves in challenging physical scenarios in our training and be proud when we accomplish them. In the performance arena, we can ask ourselves, *Do I really need to be intimidated by a perceived antagonist in this room if, after all, I'm the one who can endure two back-to-back three-minute rounds of jump-rope? Or I'm the one who can stay strong in a 90-second all-out sprint on the bike?* And then we can truly believe the answer. A resounding *No!* Trust our training. We are strong and mighty.

If we need to dial down the nerves another notch or two, we simply continue breathing and opening our stance. I often consciously adopt the balanced, open stance or seated position initially, and then realize a few minutes later that I am folded like a paper airplane again. This happens all the time. In any given meeting, I might have to uncross my legs and heave my shoulders back four or five times. It's okay. It still works.

We can use this preshot routine to open and calm the body, and reignite feelings of comfort and familiarity. We trained for this. We have done these steps before and they worked. Adding to the mental techniques we adopted in Step 2, we are getting out of our own way, letting our physical training take over. We are defusing the amygdala alarms. We are halting the negative mental sound track. Our ritual physical movements and mental checklists are stopping the fight-or-flight cognitive hijack and allowing us to retake control. We are not overthinking or overcaring. We honor our performance process, and we don't obsess about outcomes. We breathe and let oxygen and blood flow in a productive manner, powering our hearts and brains. We stand (or sit) tall, open, and proud.

My boxing trainer Ray once told me that the owner of Trinity Boxing Gym, Martin Snow, distinguishes the act of *protecting* oneself from the act of *defending* oneself. Martin says that protecting oneself from say, a home invasion, is like hiding in a closet curled up and covering one's face and body. Defending oneself is like grabbing a baseball bat and venturing out onto the porch to see who or what is there. The latter image is proactive. It's literally the movement of grabbing our energy and transporting it outward, out onto that porch to gather more information, then act if necessary. The opposite is waiting around for someone to do something to us, hiding our energy in the closet. Let's project our energy outward. Let's go look and see. Let's take on the world.

It seems to me that the less I fight my fear, the less it fights back. If I can relax, fear relaxes, too.

—Elizabeth Gilbert

Step 3

Exercise: Channeling Our Inner Athlete

Pre-Work (our "Preparation Process" as discussed in Chapter 13)

- *First, anticipate* a law school or lawyering scenario that sparks fear.
- *Notice* the body's automatic physical responses.
  - Do you hunch down? Cross your limbs? Instinctively make yourself small?
  - Do you sweat or blush?
  - Does your heart race? Do you shake? Does your stomach or head hurt?
  - Are you short of breath?
  - Does your mouth go dry?
- Construct a plan to become more "body-aware."
  - Do you like to work out? If so, awesome!
    - Start to approach your workouts as training with a new focus: not only are we trying to get or stay fit, we are striving to become physically powerful for the specific purpose of untangling fear.
  - Even if you don't enjoy exercising (yet!), consider adopting a daily *movement plan* to get to know your physical frame better.
    - Tracking your daily steps with an app on your phone is a great place to start.
    - Consider taking the stairs instead of the elevator or escalator.
    - Walk the dog (or borrow a friend's dog!).
    - Try something new: a spinning class (with a nice, welcoming vibe), a group boxing class (even just putting on wraps and gloves for the first time feels empowering), an introductory weight-training class, a stretch class.
    - Try walking or jogging to a landmark and see how you feel; then pick the next landmark!
  - Practice adopting an "athlete's swagger" and balanced stance.
    - Stand or sit as tall as you can.
    - Throw your shoulders back.
    - Eyes up.
    - Spine long.
    - Weight evenly distributed on both legs or feet.
    - Arms open.
    - All of this helps our adrenaline, blood, and oxygen flow in a productive manner instead of banging around inside us like pinballs!

- Watch Professor Amy Cuddy's TED Talk[734] about "power poses" (although, please keep in mind, that although I LOVE this video and I use its principles daily, I respectfully disagree with the "fake it till you make it/become it" approach).
  - Practice a power pose in private, and then do one in public and observe how no one notices!
- Adopt some new *pre-performance* rituals.
  - Think about your favorite performer: a singer, an actor, an athlete, a dancer, a comedian, a speaker.
  - Research whether they have a series of pre-performance rituals. (*Note:* Some rituals might be healthy and some might not! Our goal is just to understand that great performers have pre-performance checklists, and then craft our own.)
  - Construct a performance routine checklist.
    - Example:
      - A reasonable and realistic time before the event, exercise and eat something that will boost your energy.
      - Within a half-hour of the event, do an Amy Cuddy "power pose" in the restroom, your office, or even subtly at your seat outside or inside the performance location.
      - Channel your inner athlete and rock star as you enter the space (remembering how you feel in other awesome life activities that you identified in Step 1, in Chapter 14).
        - You may even want to imagine a "theme song" playing as you enter the space.
        - If you were a boxer, what "theme song" would play as you entered the arena?
      - Breathe.
      - Step into the performance space.
      - *Notice* the arrival of any mental and physical fear responses.
      - While practicing Step 2 for the mental side (see Chapter 15), initiate your "preshot" routine to channel adrenaline, blood, and oxygen flow in the most productive manner.
        - Readopt your athlete's balanced physical stance (standing or seated).
          - Sit or stand up straight, aligning the spine.
          - Uncross your feet or legs and send fiery energy through them into the ground.
          - Shift the shoulders back.
          - Open up the arms.
          - Rest the hands opened upward on the arms of the chair or the edges of the podium.

- Breathe.
- Trust your physical training.
- Let your training take over.
- Don't overthink or overcare.
- Focus on the performance routine, not the outcome.

In-the-Moment Performance Process

- Minutes before the event, do an Amy Cuddy "power pose" in the restroom, your office, or even subtly at your seat or at the podium in the performance location.
- Channel your inner athlete and rock star as you enter the space.
- Breathe.
- Step into the performance space carrying your performer/athlete's swagger we identified in Step 1 (see Chapter 14).
- *Notice* the arrival of any mental and physical fear responses.
- While practicing Step 2 for the mental side (see Chapter 15), initiate your "pre-shot" routine to channel adrenaline, blood, and oxygen flow in the most productive manner.
  - Readopt your athlete's balanced physical stance (standing or seated).
    - Sit or stand up straight, aligning the spine.
    - Uncross your feet or legs and send fiery energy through them into the ground.
    - Shift the shoulders back.
    - Open up the arms.
    - Rest the hands opened upward on the arms of the chair or the edges of the podium.
  - Breathe.
  - Trust your physical training.
  - Let your training take over.
  - (If you need an extra boost, scan the arena for any fans but also perceived "foes" or "human threats," look them in the eye, and remember: you're the one with the fierce left hook, or the flash of speed on the running trail, or the one who hiked that mountain or survived a difficult yoga class last week).
  - Don't overthink or overcare.
  - Focus on the performance routine, not the outcome.
  - Repeat any steps if you notice your legs or arms crossing again, or if you are slumping down or hunching.
  - Be the strong scholar-athlete that you are.

CHAPTER 17

Step 4: Cultivating a Culture of Fortitude

Not everyone we encounter in the legal profession is going to demonstrate self-awareness, vulnerability, authenticity, humility—or even empathy or the type of support we individually need for our efforts to untangle fear. It is up to *us* to slowly shift the well-entrenched mind-set of bravado in lawyering. This starts simply with working on ourselves, and continues when we set a good example for others. As Dr. Brené Brown says, "Vulnerability begets vulnerability; courage is contagious."[735]

So far, we've learned how to use Steps 1 through 3 to (1) identify the areas in our lives where we already are brave and courageous, thus extracting drivers of our natural strength in those scenarios; (2) recognize and overwrite our negative mental sound track, thus activating an individualized in-the-moment mental reboot; and (3) adopt new physical techniques to enhance our energy, blood, and oxygen flow to power us through each performance event. In Step 4, we add practical strategies for addressing external obstacles, or attempts by others (perhaps coming from a well-meaning but misguided place) to hinder our efforts to untangle fear. Step 4 also involves developing fortitude in the areas of (1) asking for advice and guidance about confusing or unclear aspects of the study and practice of law; (2) seeking assistance from an appropriate mentor when a lawyering task invokes a degree of fear; and (3) requesting direction and counsel from an appropriate mentor in the event of discovery of a mistake or error. Through these endeavors, we build *character* in the context of law school and law practice.

HANDLING PEOPLE WHO TELL US "THERE'S NOTHING TO BE AFRAID OF"

Some folks in our lives might not want us to change or find our authentic power. They (understandably) prefer the status quo because, there, *they* feel most powerful and in control. If we upset that balance by setting new boundaries, saying no, or not reacting to others' habitual fear/shame maneuvers, it might bother or scare them. That's okay. We must be prepared to deal with, or step away from, individuals who don't understand, agree with, or relate to this process, at least during our rebuilding phase.

For starters, if you are beginning the quest to untangle your own fear, please do not listen to anyone who tells you straight off the bat, "There's nothing to be afraid of!" As Kristen Ulmer notes in *The Art of Fear*, when we begin to state out loud that we are afraid, "the only appropriate response [from others] is either to ask a clarifying question or offer a simple, genuine 'That's great,'"[736] as encouragement to grow through our untangling experience. Too often, folks who don't want us to change will try to dismiss or discount our fear. Or they might ignore our brave admission altogether. My promise to you: If you are afraid, I'll see you and I'll hear you.

Ulmer offers these replies—to assert, out loud or internally—when folks teeter on the brink of dismissing our fears:

- "Please don't try to talk me out of feeling my Fear. . . ."
- "Please don't try to rush me through my emotions. . . ."
- "Please stop asking me to repress my emotions to make you feel more comfortable. . . ."[737]

When other people tell us "There is nothing to be afraid of" or "Just face your fears," or when they respond with a casual "I'm sure you'll figure it out as you always do," it has the opposite unhelpful effect of encouraging us to once again repress the fear[738] instead of untangling it and transforming our relationship with it.[739] From now on, we can say—out loud or to ourselves— "ignoring or just pushing through fear is no longer part of my process."

Regarding vulnerability, Brené Brown cautions that we may need to be careful about whom we talk to when we are doing this self-investigatory work. She says, "When it comes to vulnerability, connectivity means sharing our stories with people who have *earned the right to hear them*."[740] We might need to temporarily separate ourselves from people in our lives who will respond to our openness about fear with judgment or dismissiveness instead of empathy.[741] The last thing we need is to feel more shame or internal conflict when we are exhibiting the bravery and courage of vulnerability. As Dr. Brown emphasizes, "shaming someone we love around vulnerability is the most serious of all security breaches."[742]

Indeed, Dr. Brown provides sage advice for handling any less-than-helpful folks, naysayers, or underminers we might encounter during this process. She quotes the words of Scott Stratten, author of the book *UnMarketing*: "Don't try to win over the haters; you're not the jackass whisperer."[743] It's also kind of fun to consider novelist Paulo Coelho's notion (quoted by former Navy SEAL Brandon Webb): "Haters are confused admirers."[744] You do *you*. And if you need someone to tell you to keep going, I've got your back. Email me at heidi-brown@brooklaw.edu or heidi@theintrovertedlawyer.com.

Handling Naysayers

In 2018, I wrote a short column for the *ABA Journal* about the movement toward "inclusive legal writing" in some countries and jurisdictions. Advocates of such changes call for replacing outdated gender-biased language in contracts, statutes, and other legal documents (as well as in literature and even some national anthems!). A conversation also has started around adopting the usage of gender-neutral pronouns like the singular "they" or "their," or new pronouns like ze. In the article, I acknowledged a hesitancy within some grammar circles to adopt the singular "they," which feels grammatically awkward and improper to traditionalists. I admitted that, at least personally, I felt it was time for me to question my own reverence for grammar traditions that might be outdated, and that I want to be open to societal changes (such as recognizing nonbinary gender) that affect long-held grammar rules. This proposition in my column struck a nerve with a handful of legal readers. At first, I received a few thoughtful emails from lawyers and individuals in legal academia who acknowledged that discussions about inclusive language are important, while also indicating that they too struggle with the grammatical ungainliness of the singular "they." Then, I received several emails and typewritten letters criticizing the concepts in the article *and* my writing. These correspondents used words like "astonished" and "disdainful." One reader itemized eight phrases I'd used that deeply bothered him. Another questioned my apostrophe usage. At first, each time I received an email or a letter that I perceived as critical, I panicked. My knee-jerk fear messages kicked in: *OMG, I'm a terrible writer. I'm an idiot. I don't even know how to use apostrophes! This is my livelihood and people think I'm horrible at it. I should be so embarrassed, or worse—ashamed—that I wrote that thing. I'm never publishing anything again!* The disapproving feedback on my written work, especially a piece in which I exposed a vulnerability (grappling with the interplay between grammar norms and societal change), hurt, and frankly scared me. I worried that my employer, faculty colleagues, and students would deem me unfit for my job. But then, I caught myself. I noticed that this was just my pesky fear talking. I stopped the negative spin cycle, implemented my mental and physical reboot, and said to myself, *Wait a minute.* These readers are obviously entitled to their opinion, and I always am interested in expanding my knowledge about writing, even if the lesson stings a bit. But I completely stand by my statements (and my apostrophes!) in the column! My entire mission in writing the piece was to spark a conversation about inclusion and potential obstacles to change. And in terms of causing *sparks*: Mission accomplished. Now, I also would say that some of these readers could have been a little nicer and less abrasive, and might have considered their own possible resistance to inclusion in this context. But that's not actually *my* problem. I can't, and shouldn't, control their points of view or their choices of words. Through working my mental and physical reboot—each time I received a letter or email that I perceived as hurtful or critical—I was able to avert an unhealthy response of fear-based self-censorship, working on gaining strength in my writer voice instead of losing it.

BUILDING CHARACTER IN THE LEGAL CONTEXT

Recall that in Chapter 4 we discussed whether character—and the ability to act with character in the face of fear—is learnable, or teachable, or whether it is something we either have or don't have. According to Paul Tough, author of *How Children Succeed: Grit, Curiosity, and the Hidden Power of Character*,[745] "[p]ure IQ is stubbornly resistant to improvement after about age eight. But executive functions and the ability to handle stress and manage strong emotions can be improved, sometimes dramatically, well into adolescence and even adulthood."[746]

As noted earlier, Drs. Martin Seligman and Christopher Peterson are two of the pioneers and main scholars of the positive psychology movement. As coauthors of *Character Strengths and Virtues: A Handbook and Classification*, they define character as "a set of abilities or strengths that are very much changeable—entirely malleable, in fact. They are skills you can learn; they are skills you can practice; and they are skills you can teach."[747] Developmental psychologist and professor of education Dr. Thomas Lickona's book *Educating for Character* offers a "comprehensive approach" to character education, indicating that—according to some experts—character *is* teachable.[748]

Tough's book cites a teacher who believed that the "best way for a young person to build character is for him to attempt something where there is a real and serious possibility of failure."[749] In my view, law schools also can foster opportunities for law students to learn about, and then develop, *character in the context* of lawyering. These opportunities can include situations in which students talk about the presence of fear in lawyering, and also the reality of mistake-making and failure. Then teachers can provide practical guidance in how to deconstruct fear and handle mistakes. But until these subjects become part of the formal curricula (as in some medical schools and other educational settings explored in Part III), it's up to us as students and junior attorneys to *seek out* educational and training opportunities to build character-in-context, untangle our fear, and understand how best to address the reality of mistake-making in the practice of law. How do we do that? We ask for help—from people who are open and willing to have these important conversations. And we insist on learning, and developing our professional personas, in a nonjudg-mental, encouraging environment. We seek guidance on these issues from a standpoint of deep understanding and real growth, not a "just do it" or "fake it till you make it" mind-set. Here are some suggestions on how we can do that in the law school and law practice contexts.

ACKNOWLEDGING FEAR-INVOKING SCENARIOS IN LAW SCHOOL AND ASKING FOR HELP

There are plentiful scenarios in law school that might stoke fear: a particu-larly intimidating use of the Socratic method, a looming writing deadline, a final exam, a mandatory oral argument, a tryout for the trial or alternative dispute resolution (ADR) teams, a moot court competition, a class presenta-tion, a negotiation or client interview simulation, or a client-based situation in a clinic. Or you might be starting an externship or internship, or a summer associate position, feel like you don't know exactly what you're doing, and are worried about making a mistake. In addition to building personal fortitude with Steps 1 through 3 and working individually to untangle your fear, you also could seize this opportunity to be an ambassador for fostering a culture of fortitude in our profession.

The first step consists of acknowledging your concern about the particular performance-oriented scenario and asking for help from a person who will

- listen to you
- not minimize or dismiss your fear or worry
- exhibit a degree of empathy
- help provide (or get you access to someone who can provide) tangible and practical steps for addressing the fear or worry *without* advice to "fake it till you make it" or "just do what scares you."

Individuals exist at your school who will serve in this role for you—as proactive problem solvers—or will point you in the direction of someone who can. If you take the brave step of reaching out to a faculty member or a law school admin-istrator in this context, and the response is something like "fake it till you make it," "there's nothing to be afraid of," or "it's best to just face your fears," OR if that person steers you toward a particular area of law requiring less "performance-oriented" work, I recommend a response like this: "Respectfully, that advice is not helpful to me right now; instead, I truly want to untangle and understand this fear *now* so I can be the best advocate possible." Or, "Thank you, but ignoring my fear is so far not working for me, and I would like to untangle it *now* so that I can be the strongest advocate I can be." You are not being rude or entitled or disrespectful in voicing this truth. You are proactively seeking help, and you absolutely deserve such guidance. We just need to find the right person. Remember, not everyone we encounter along this path has pondered these issues or grappled with the concept of *untangling* fear (rather than just pushing through it) as we may have done. That's okay. You can move on and find the right person to help.

Please note: You actually might be the *first* person at your school ever to approach fear in this particularly direct way. That's also okay, and yes, taking on that role is fierce and brave in and of itself. You're already a much-needed change maker for the profession. There is absolutely nothing wrong or weak or wimpy about saying out loud in law school, "Hey, this situation scares me." It is through this vulnerability and courage—*naming* a law school fear—that we build tremendous character, untangle our fear, and become powerful advocates. So, first, seek out an individual at your law school who meets the criteria above: a Fear Wrangler of sorts. Your Fear Wrangler perhaps could be a professor who you have observed is open to problem solving, the director of academic success, the dean of students, another academic advisor, a director of student life, or the dean. In a first encounter with a Fear Wrangler, the goals are as follows:

- to *name* the particular law school scenario that ignites our fear
- to indicate to the Fear Wrangler that we seek *concrete assistance* to better understand the logistics, purpose, and dynamics of the specific scenario so that we can navigate it successfully and lessen the anxiety around it
- to acknowledge that the Fear Wrangler might not have all the answers right away, or perhaps isn't the ultimate person to help us with the actual untangling
- together, to construct a *strategy* for enhancing our understanding of the fear-inducing scenario so that we (and other students) can decrease our fear and increase performance strength
  - Strategies might include
    - identifying and working one-on-one with a *mentor* in the school who has particular expertise in this law school scenario

- crafting *small-group workshops* for students to focus on this particular educational or lawyering activity (e.g., an "Untangling the Socratic Method" workshop or an "Untangling the Oral Argument Experience" workshop)

- *removing* any "stigma" associated with asking for help regarding this fear-inducing event.

If you are (understandably) nervous about asking a professor or law school administrator for guidance about fear, another option is to identify an upper-level student who also might be a good Fear Wrangler. This could include a representative from the student bar association, a mentor as part of a formalized student mentoring or advising system, a leader of a student organization, an approachable teaching assistant, or simply a student you perceive to be open-minded and empathetic toward peers who are experiencing anxiety. Remember, the *first* student you connect with might not have all the answers but may be able to point you in the right direction. The ultimate goal is to identify the *right* person to help you untangle this particular law school fear. Again, the right person will

- listen to you
- not minimize or dismiss your fear
- exhibit a degree of empathy, and
- help provide (or get you access to someone who can provide) tangible practical steps for addressing the fear or worry *without* advising you to "fake it till you make it" or "just face your fears."

Once more, remember that you might be *the pioneer* at your school for identifying this particular issue—out loud—as deserving of attention and development of a solution to help nervous students navigate the scenario from a position of enhanced strength and self-awareness. That is okay. Change maker! Trail blazer! Ground breaker!

If you absolutely cannot seem to find a professor, administrator, or upper-level student to help you, first, please feel free to contact me *immediately*! Use either of these email addresses: heidi.brown@brooklaw.edu or heidi@theintrovertedlawyer.com. Second, consider starting and leading your own small group of students to talk through fear toward performance-oriented scenarios in law school. Establish your own "Untangling Fear" group and, with others who need such bolstering, work through the practical mental and physical strategies identified in Steps 1 through 3. (Group discussion topics are suggested in Appendix E). This is what it means to foster a culture of fortitude.

No longer do we—as law students—need to repress our fears, pretend they don't exist, or pummel our way through them. Let's become healthier, happier law graduates by untangling our fears, building each other up, and being better prepared for the challenges of the actual practice of law.

ACKNOWLEDGING FEAR-INVOKING SCENARIOS IN LAW PRACTICE AND ASKING FOR HELP

Individuals experiencing fear with respect to particular lawyering scenarios in the law office environment can undertake a similar approach. As discussed in Chapter 2, there are many performance aspects of our jobs as attorneys that can invoke varying degrees of fear. Are you knee-deep in a research problem for which you just cannot seem to find an answer, and a deadline is looming? Are you getting ready for your first deposition? Or your fifteenth deposition but with an antagonistic witness? A conference call with a difficult opposing counsel? A pivotal oral argument? A status conference with an intimidating judge? A contentious contract negotiation? A client's reaction to a negative result? Sometimes seasoned lawyers forget that, whereas summer law clerks, interns, and new lawyers indeed possess substantive and procedural knowledge, there is a whole pile of practical and tactical knowledge that less-experienced advocates simply don't yet have. Understandably, that reality can be scary. We need to cultivate working environments in which junior employees can acknowledge the reality of fear in these scenarios, ask questions, and gain advice about the practical, tangible, and tactical aspects of day-to-day lawyering activities.

If, while working on Steps 1 through 3 of our fortitude plan, you recognize that the emotion you are feeling in anticipation of a certain lawyering activity is fear, consider these additional strategies:

- Identify *one* person in the office (a Fear Wrangler) with whom you can have an open and honest conversation about fear with regard to this particular lawyering activity.
  - *Note:* The person could be an approachable supervisor, an official or unofficial mentor, a professional development director, a human resources advisor, or simply someone who has a few more years of experience in practice than you.
  - The key is to find someone who will (a) listen to you, (b) not minimize or dismiss your fear, (c) exhibit a degree of empathy, and (d) help provide (or get you access to someone else who can provide)

tangible practical steps for addressing the fear or worry *without* advising you to "fake it till you make it" or "just do what scares you."

- Try to *name* and be as *specific* as possible about your worry.
  - *Note:* Instead of going "big picture" ("I'm afraid we'll lose the case," or "I'm afraid it won't go well"), be more specific:
    - "I'm afraid opposing counsel will try to bully me and I'll start sweating."
    - "I'm afraid I won't know where to sit in the courtroom and I'll look foolish."
    - "I'm afraid I'll miss an objection."
    - "I'm afraid I won't answer the judge's question fast enough."
    - "I'm afraid I won't know if I'm being manipulated in the negotiation."
- Try to differentiate substantive and procedural concerns from logistical and tactical concerns (all of which are valid and important), to zero in on what type of advice you need.
- Indicate to the Fear Wrangler that you seek *concrete* assistance to better understand the logistics, purpose, and dynamics of the specific scenario so that you can navigate it successfully and lessen the accompanying anxiety.
- Acknowledge your awareness of the reality of billable-hour pressure and the Fear Wrangler's likely busy schedule, and indicate that you want to be proactive and gather appropriate resources to work on this challenge on your own, as well.
- Acknowledge that the person you are talking to might not have all the answers right away, or may not be the ultimate person who will help you with the actual untangling of the fear.
- Together, construct a strategy for enhancing your understanding of the scenario so that you (and other junior attorneys) can decrease fear and increase performance strength. Strategies might include:
  - Identifying a one-on-one mentor within the law office who can talk through the realities of fear-invoking lawyering scenarios with a mind-set of inclusion, encouragement, and practical solutions
  - Setting up lunchtime workshops for senior and junior attorneys to talk through substantive, procedural, logistical, and tactical nuances of everyday lawyering activities that invoke fear

- Facilitating opportunities for junior advocates to observe lawyering activities (keeping in mind billable-hour pressures) to enhance knowledge and mitigate the fear of the unknown

- Fostering an environment in which senior attorneys speak openly and honestly with junior attorneys about real fears, and providing practical advice for untangling fears instead of pressuring individuals to (or implying that individuals should) ignore or push through them (suggested discussion topics can be found in Appendix E)

Also, as we explored in Chapter 3, your fears in law practice might be intertwined with your perception or recognition of (but limited knowledge or experience in how to appropriately address) *client* fears. Consider setting up small-group discussions or workshops focused on how to accurately and appropriately perceive and address client fears in your area of legal practice (Appendix D offers some tips). Talking openly about client fears can help foster a culture of fortitude in our law office environments.

Remember, you might be *the pioneer* in your law office for identifying these issues—out loud—as deserving of attention and development of a solution to help junior attorneys navigate lawyering scenarios from a position of enhanced strength and self-awareness. That is okay. Be the pathfinder! If you cannot seem to find a supervisor, a mentor, a human resources advisor, or a professional development advisor within your law office to help you, first, please feel free to contact me *immediately*! You can send an email to heidi.brown@ brooklaw.edu or heidi@theintrovertedlawyer.com. Of course keeping in mind issues of confidentiality and attorney-client privilege, I am more than happy to help and find you the appropriate resource. Second, research whether your local bar association or lawyer assistance program has a mentor network to assist with your particular situation. Third, consider starting and leading your own small group of lawyers. Establish your own "Untangling Fear" group in the office or your local bar association, and work through, with others, the practical mental and physical strategies proposed in Steps 1 through 3. (Suggested discussion topics can be found in Appendix E.) This is what it means to foster a culture of fortitude. No longer do we—as lawyers—need to repress our fears, pretend they don't exist, or pummel our way through them. Let's become healthier, happier advocates by untangling our fears, building one another up, and enhancing our individual and collective strength to tackle the challenges of the actual practice of law.

ADDRESSING FEARS ABOUT MISTAKE-MAKING IN SPECIFIC LAWYERING SCENARIOS

Law students and junior lawyers also should seek out guidance and opportunities to discuss the reality of mistake-making—in classroom work, externships, internships, clinic work, summer associate positions, and the full-time practice of law. When I was a summer associate and a junior associate, I often worried that I would look stupid or incompetent because I didn't know how to start a new or unfamiliar assignment. I believed my ignorance somehow was my fault. It took me a while to realize, *Well, no wonder I don't know how to redline a document in Track Changes, or perfect a mechanic's lien, or serve a subpoena. I have never done this before! No one taught me these tasks in law school!*

Let's get one reality on the table: The law is confusing, substantively and procedurally. Yes, we learn a great deal in our classes (and in the early years of practice) about rules, policies, and theories. But putting them into action, especially for the first time, is unavoidably challenging. It is absolutely normal and okay that you don't really know what you're doing when you start each of these tasks for the first time. Instead of perpetuating the mind-set of "faking it until we make it," let's be ambassadors of developing character and a culture of fortitude—professionals who ask for guidance from the right person. Of course, when we are given an assignment, we don't want to look dumb, or annoy our professor or busy supervising attorney. Yet, as we explored in Chapter 4, mistake-making is a reality in the practice of law. We can learn how best to *avoid* mistakes if we ask for, and receive, help from a good mentor.

Just as in seeking guidance for fear-invoking scenarios, we can use the same steps to approach a lawyering task in which we are worried about making a mistake:

- Identify an individual we perceive to be open-minded and geared toward problem solving.

- Indicate that we are *eager* to work on the assignment but are concerned about making a mistake.

- Try to be specific about the types of mistakes we are concerned about making (e.g., miscalculating a deadline, missing a case in our research, misunderstanding the nuances of a proposed contract provision, mishandling objections in a deposition or during trial testimony, faltering in a negotiation, taking the wrong procedural avenue).

- Identify the steps we have taken and the resources we have consulted so far to avoid the mistake.

- Request guidance as to other potential mistakes that could arise in the scenario.

- Request substantive, procedural, logistical, and tactical advice as to how to avoid those particular mistakes.

Caveat: We may, unfortunately, encounter individuals in law school or the law office environment who simply say, "Figure it out," or "Just don't make a mistake." Or someone might inadvertently scare us with war stories of catastrophic repercussions from lawyering mistakes made by others. Many lawyers were trained in a "rite of passage" regime, the "trial by fire," in which they were expected to learn-on-the-job and figure it out. If these lawyers haven't had a reason or an opportunity to think about more effective teaching or mentoring strategies for *new* lawyers, of course they are going to train the same way they were trained—it worked for them. That's fine and understandable, but obviously, these folks are not the ideal mentors for this particular situation. Please do not be discouraged, censored, or deterred. You are taking the proactive step of asking for guidance; that is absolutely essential to learning how to prevent mistakes in lawyering. You might be the *first* person ever in the law office to approach mistake-making this way. Be the *groundbreaker, the earthshaker.*

To be an impactful advocate and to do the best job you can, you are entitled to more information about how to avoid or ultimately handle lawyering mistakes. The best way to acquire this information is to find an open-minded mentor (a Fear *and* Mistake Wrangler!) in the office, your local bar association, or law school alumni network. Forge a relationship with a more senior attorney, a human resources director, a professional development director, a recruiting coordinator, or some other person who has the law office's (and your) best interests in mind. Consider suggesting a one-on-one mentoring session or a small lunchtime workshop with your colleagues. Short workshops, specifically focused on mistake prevention in your particular type of law practice, plus the *reality* of mistakes and how to handle them practically if they occur, can do wonders to reduce fear of the unknown and enhance performance. The topics must be presented in an inclusive, *growth* mindset (rather than a *fixed* mindset—terms explained in Dr. Carol S. Dweck's book, *Mindset: The New Psychology of Success*) manner, not with a tone of further intimidation. Such workshops can identify specific, tangible, and transparent office protocols for handling mistakes. These discussions can cultivate a dialogue among seasoned and less-experienced attorneys (and even law student interns and summer associates), help defuse the perceived taboos associated with this topic in lawyering, and facilitate a dynamic in which novice advocates can ask questions without fear of judgment. Ideally, mistake prevention will occur at a higher frequency, and those lawyering errors that inevitably happen can be addressed in the most ethical and collaborative way, ultimately improving the health and well-being of the members of our profession.

SUGGESTIONS FOR HOW LAW STUDENTS AND LAWYERS CAN ENHANCE UNDERSTANDING ABOUT MISTAKE-MAKING AND MISTAKE PREVENTION IN LAWYERING

In the law school and law office environment, law students and junior attorneys should seek out and request opportunities to talk openly about the relationships among fear and preventing, making, and handling mistakes. Appendix B offers suggestions for how law professors and law school administrators can incorporate discussions about fear and mistake-making into the law school curriculum. Appendix C suggests ways for law practice managers to facilitate these conversations in professional development and mentoring settings. Until such initiatives are launched on a more formalized level (as in some medical schools and other educational settings explored in Part III), law students and junior advocates can take the initiative and create these opportunities for themselves. Here are some suggestions.

Law Student Initiatives

- In your legal writing course, or other courses with open research assignments, suggest or undertake an assignment in which you research the types of mistakes that lawyers make in a particular type of law practice, or a particular area of the law.
  - Research why and how the mistakes of the types you have identified can happen.
  - Research ways that lawyers can avoid making these types of mistakes.
  - Research ways that lawyers can remedy these types of mistakes.
  - Research resources for obtaining advice about such lawyering mistakes if a law office mentor is not readily available (e.g., bar associations; confidential lawyer insurance hotlines; confidential ethics hotlines in your jurisdiction).
  - Share the results of your research with others.
- In clinics and externship seminars, seek out opportunities to ask supervisors and lawyers questions about common (or even uncommon) mistakes in the particular area of practice.

- Ask (and research) why and how such mistakes happen.
- Ask how lawyers (and law students) can avoid making mistakes of these types.
- Ask how lawyers (and law students) can remedy such mistakes.
- Write reflections about whether you think existing advice on how to avoid or remedy such mistakes is helpful.
- If not, reflect on what other guidance or information might help you avoid or remedy mistakes in scenarios of those types.

- Write reflections on mistakes you make, or observe others making, in clinics, externships, internships, or other summer job experiences. (Of course, remain mindful of confidentiality issues.)
  - Write about why or how each mistake happened.
  - Write about any steps individuals can take to avoid repeating the mistake.
  - Write about how you or the person making the mistake handled it.
  - Write about any ways to improve your handling (or the handling of others) of mistakes of these types once they've been made.

- Organize panels of practitioners to visit the law school and speak to student groups about the reality of fear and mistake-making in the practice of law.
  - Be sure to select speakers with a helpful, *growth* mind-set tone (rather than a *fixed* mind-set tone), to encourage students, rather than scare them further.
  - Avoid speakers with a "fake it till you make it" or bravado mind-set.
  - Consider inviting speakers who can introduce students to how malpractice insurance works, both to demystify the role of insurance in lawyering and to distinguish different categories of mistakes.

- Form small "Untangling Fear" groups within the law school, to address fear and mistake-making from an open and genuine mind-set. (Suggested discussion topics can be found in Appendix E.)

Junior Lawyer Initiatives

- Seek out existing continuing legal education (CLE) programs that talk about mistake-making in lawyering from an open and genuine mind-set, not a fear-based or "catastrophic repercussion" mind-set.

- ○ If such a CLE does not yet exist in your jurisdiction, suggest or request one, or construct one yourself.

- ○ Consider constructing a CLE panel consisting of seasoned lawyers, less-experienced lawyers, attorney insurance advisors, ethics advisors, and perhaps even performance psychologists *with encouraging, concrete, and practical approaches, rather than fear messages* about mistake-making.[750]

- Form small "Untangling Fear" groups within your law office or local bar association, to address fear and mistake-making from an open and genuine mind-set, not a "catastrophic repercussion" mind-set. (Suggested discussion topics can be found in Appendix E.)

- Set up workshops for speakers to visit your law office and explain the nuances of how malpractice insurance works, to help differentiate between minor and more grievous mistakes; errors in both categories require clear, transparent protocols.

- Ask an open-minded and helpful mentor in the law office to help establish and designate *a person within the law firm* to whom anyone can go for confidential, nonjudgmental advice about fear and mistake-making.

BUILDING RESILIENCE IN ADMITTING A MISTAKE

I've made mistakes in my life. In relationships. And in my job. In the past, when I discovered I *may* have made a mistake or realized that indeed I *did* err, my instinctive reaction was to feel completely, 100% responsible and ashamed, fast-forwarding to worst-case consequences. I punished myself before I even began to realistically assess the situation. My fear/shame response kicked in. This was not a healthy response or an accurate assessment of almost any given mistake. Even when a perceived or actual mistake occurred as part of a case at the law firm, I immediately assumed it was all my fault, my blunder, my failing, whereas in reality, I usually had exerted significant efforts to take the right steps, make the correct decisions, think through the proper choices before acting. I am not at all suggesting we deflect blame or shirk responsibility; ultimately character requires taking ownership of our role in legal mistakes without blame-shifting or excuse-making. Rather, I hope to encourage a healthier approach to discovering, addressing, and remedying mistakes, and then moving forward. As *Harvard Business Review* contributing editor Amy Gallo writes,

"[M]istakes are not signs of weakness or ineptitude; recovering from them demonstrates resilience and perseverance."[751]

If you're like me and you experience a knee-jerk, self-attacking response to mistake-discovery and immediately begin to beat yourself up and cloak yourself in fear and shame, here is my advice:

- First, realistically assess and honor your work ethic.
  - Do you strive to do the best job you know how?
  - On a daily basis, do you undertake the substantive, procedural, and tactical steps that you believe are correct?
  - Do you continuously strive to enhance your universe of knowledge of the proper substantive, procedural, and tactical steps for your lawyering activities?
  - In this specific circumstance, did you undertake the substantive, procedural, and tactical steps that you believed were correct based on your universe of knowledge and experience?
- Next, remind yourself that you did not intentionally make this mistake.
- Instead of "catastrophizing" and racing ahead to worrying about worst-case repercussions, start with focusing your mental energy on the first step.
- Identify a trusted advisor in your professional environment with whom you feel comfortable conveying your awareness of the issue—this does not need to be the ultimate decision-maker or your supervisor (yet).
- State the perceived mistake in clear terms.
- Avoid becoming defensive or making excuses, but also refrain from heaping misplaced responsibility upon yourself owing to an overactive fear or shame response.
- Practice shame resilience—reminding yourself that a mistake does not mean *you* are a bad person.
- Work with the trusted advisor to construct a plan for bringing the mistake to the attention of the appropriate person in the firm for assessing, addressing, and remedying it.
- Be part of the remedial solution.
- As former University of North Carolina basketball coach Dean Smith counseled Michael Jordan, limit the time you spend ruminating; Coach Smith advised spending "no more than ten or twenty minutes to reflect on a bad performance. That would be enough to learn everything that could be learned from it."[752]

- Hold your head high and move forward, even if others are angry or stoke fear.

- You are building resilience, and compassion for others who also will make mistakes even though they worked diligently based on their universe of knowledge and experience.

- Everything will be okay. It will.

In undertaking Step 4 and being pioneers in addressing fear and mistake-making head-on in our legal education and practice, we are emulating Socrates, seeking knowledge. We are some of Christopher Kukk's "knownauts": "knowledge astronauts."[753] In doing and being so, we can transform our profession.

> *Scared is what you're feeling. Brave is what you're doing.*
> —Emma Donoghue

Step 4

Exercise: Cultivating a Culture of Fortitude

- Give yourself permission to outright reject cliché messages like "just do it," "fake it till you make it," "just do what scares you," or "embrace fear as a great motivator!"
  - Reject such messages *internally*.
  - If you're feeling particularly ambassador-y, reject such messages *externally* with a reply such as, "Respectfully, this fear is real, and it's not going away unless I address it, and I'd prefer to untangle it, and in doing so, become the best advocate I can be."
  - *Keep going.*
- Resolve to build character-in-context in the legal arena by consciously *seeking opportunities* to learn more about lawyering scenarios that ignite fear.
  - Seek out approachable mentors to ask questions—and get substantive, procedural, logistical, and tactical guidance—about *specific* lawyering scenarios that ignite fear or trigger worries about making a mistake.
  - Seek out *general* opportunities to learn more about substantive, procedural, logistical, and tactical challenges that may arise in particular lawyering scenarios or in your specific area of practice.
    - Construct and undertake individual research projects.
    - Participate in workshops and CLEs, and if these opportunities do not exist, create them!
    - Consider examples of what other professions are doing (explored in Part III) and ask for, or build, similar opportunities into your educational or legal training experience: simulations, workshops, open discussions with more experienced practitioners, protocols, and so on.
    - Enhance your substantive, procedural, logistical, and tactical knowledge to reduce fear of the unknown.
    - Expand your knowledge of how to ethically handle tricky lawyering scenarios, exploring creative problem solving and endeavoring to deter avoidable mistakes.
    - Build resilience in handling difficult situations, asking for help, and knowing (and having the strength to undertake) the appropriate protocol if something does go sideways.
- Start an "Untangling Fear" group in your law school, law office, or bar association, to openly discuss issues around fear and mistake-making in the legal arena (suggested discussion topics can be found in Appendix E).
- Seek opportunities to better understand *client* fears (see Appendix D) and help clients (and others) untangle those fears.

Conclusion

When I was a scared law student and lawyer, I thought I was the only one. I thought there was something wrong with me, and that someone was going to shine a bright spotlight on my blushing face and consternated eyes and eject me from the profession. I had law school loans to repay, and my own and other people's expectations to fulfill. I also didn't know what else to do with my life. Everyone around me seemed to have it all together. I tried to project that image too. I had the law degree, the attractive, athletic boyfriend-then-husband, the house with the picket fence, the two beagles, the Jeep Grand Cherokee, the cute business suits, the Mexico vacations. But inside, I was a wreck. I was alone, and terrifyingly lonely. I had flickers and flashes of joy in my job, mostly through brief-writing and travel. Yet the fear of making a mistake—in my relationships and in my work—permeated my life. I didn't feel like I could talk to anyone honestly and openly about it all.

Trying to follow the "be fearless!" mantras like gospel, I buried my fears even deeper down in a dark place. They bided their time. I write this book now, so many years later, because it's important for us to stop this. Experiencing and feeling fear in law school and law practice is REAL. It's okay. It's brave to feel fear and say it out loud. We must. Then we can begin to untangle it together.

I don't want any of you to go through one more day of feeling alone, isolated, or unworthy. You are not alone. You are not the only one. You are not on your own. You are not invisible. You are not weak. You are not unworthy. Our profession needs you.

As I surged into the home stretch of getting the first draft of this book down on paper, two American creative souls—Kate Spade and Anthony Bourdain—left this world. Both losses gave me pause, but the latter rocked me for several weeks. Last year, a New York friend treated me to a *New York Times* TimesTalk featuring Bourdain. My friend and I sat in the front row, starstruck at the ease at which the rakish chef slid his 6 ft, 4 in. frame into an armchair, sipped a beer, and exuded louche and brilliance about, well, everything, it seemed. To gain inspiration for how to maximize my own travel adventures, I had been following Bourdain on Instagram, his life seeming so expressively artistic and romantic. I don't pretend to know why he left this world. I can only ponder at the possibility that someone with such breadth of human connection across the globe still may have felt so lonely. And that again is why this conversation about fear is important. Untangling our fear starts within us, but it also requires vulnerability and empathy for us to reach out to each other, notice each other, share how we feel, and forge connections. I want you to know that I *see you.*

To snap myself out of my own loneliness as I finished the first draft of this book, I bought a ticket to see Patti Smith sing at an outdoor amphitheater a mere seven-minute walk from the Airbnb apartment I was renting in Rome. As seagulls flew above the auditorium and Italians chatted around me, Patti took the stage and belted out a soulful "People Have the Power." This 71-year-old poet, singer, and artist danced around the microphone with completely cool abandon, her wild long silver-gray hair swaying. She unabashedly pulled a pair of reading glasses out of her jacket pocket and relied on a page of written lyrics as she sang a John Lennon song. She spoke to the audience—about the pope, the environment, and freedom—in English and urged a group of young girls to keep dancing as security tried to corral them. Occasionally, she walked to the edge of the stage and turned to watch her musicians (one member of the band is her son), as if she were a spectator, not the headliner. At one point she tapped her guitarist on the elbow, and encouraged, "Pick it up," to hasten the beat. This was not some slick, high-tech, perfectly manipulated show. This was raw, real, natural, and true.

I walked home from the show, smelling the jasmine bushes that flank the streets, and resolved to keep going, in my own art, and as a scholar-athlete to drive the creative process. This work—the work of talking about the challenges of lawyering—matters. *Your* work matters. *Our* work matters. As law students, lawyers, and law professors, we may not think we are making art, but we are. We may not think of ourselves as athletes, but we are. Every day, to do this job right and, more importantly, ultimately to be fulfilled doing it, we must combine the mental and the physical, and we must create. We already are creating. Every day, we identify problems, needs, gaps, or holes. We are resourceful in our research. We write, and to do that well—whether it's the greatest poem or song of all time, or a good contract that can withstand the signatories' messy falling-out, or a brief that convinces a judge to rule in the client's favor—writing is creating. We innovate solutions to problems. We inspire resolutions to conflicts.

The law is not perfect. It's untidy and complicated. We can be much more authentic in the way we approach learning it, teaching it, and practicing it, if we admit what we don't know. We can be much more open to deeper growth, to human connections within our lawyering lives, if we let down the guard of expertise. Instead of pretending we know everything—a huge factor that drives the fear that we will be discovered as imposters—let's mirror Socrates's state of intellectual humility in seeking knowledge. Anthony Bourdain said, "Maybe that's enlightenment enough: to know that there is no final resting place of the mind; no moment of smug clarity. Perhaps wisdom . . . is realizing how small I am, and unwise, and how far I have yet to go."[754] Like Socrates, Bourdain modeled intellectual curiosity and adventure. He tore down cultural barriers of separation and exclusion, and encouraged inclusion and authentic connection. We can do the same in the legal profession.

Through working on my own fears in lawyering and in life, I discovered that my primary fear is not of being alone, but of being excluded or discarded. In the law, sometimes we reinforce instead of defuse fears by fostering a culture of exclusion and hierarchy, separating winners from losers, the entitled from the unentitled. If we, as educators, mentors, law students, and lawyers can come together to untangle the complexities of fear with an *inclusive* mindset, our profession can evolve. Perhaps we can solve some client problems through pie-enlarging conflict resolution rather than winner-takes-all. Maybe we can improve employment retention rates of junior lawyers at law firms and law offices by highlighting the collective strength that comes from honoring our differences, instead of promoting one stereotype mold of the "successful lawyer." Possibly, we can generate space for inclusion of individuals in our profession who have great potential to be impactful advocates but need a gesture of care to overcome hurdles that others luckily did not have to face.

Though I aspire to spark a community here, in the end, indeed we do most of this internal mental and physical work on our own. It's hard. It can be lonely. But it's so worth it. I promise. By working diligently to untangle our fear drivers, rewrite our mental sound tracks, and implement new mental and physical in-the-moment reboot techniques, we can dial down the volume of fear a notch or two and allow our brains and bodies to soar. Give yourself some time to do this work. Please reach out if you need a boost or someone to tell you, "Just keep going." I've got your back. Eventually, by wrangling and then tempering the intensity of our fear, we will start to see the world (and the legal profession) differently.

There is nothing weak, fragile, or unworthy about acknowledging fear in lawyering. In fact, just the opposite. Law students, lawyers, and legal educators who take this giant step to acknowledge the reality of fear in our profession, and individually and collectively work to untangle it in a healthy productive manner, will be the change makers of our profession. I'm excited to make these changes with you.

Things done well and with a care, exempt themselves from fear.
—William Shakespeare

Appendix A
Untangling Fear Checklist

PRE-WORK (ALSO CALLED PROCESS WORK)

Step 1

- Identify one or two scenarios in your life in which society tells you that you probably *should* be afraid, but you're not.
- Identify one or two scenarios in your life in which society tells you that you *should not* be afraid, but you are.
- Try to parse the differences between those categories of scenarios.
  - What gives you *swagger* in the first category?
  - How can we start to bring some of that swagger into the second category?

Step 2

- When you anticipate or step into a fear-invoking performance scenario, what mental messages do you automatically hear playing on your internal sound track?
  - What are the actual words and phrases you hear? Transcribe the language verbatim.
  - Are these messages negative, or fear-stoking? Do they prompt feelings of shame?
  - Who or what are the original sources of these messages?
    - This is not meant to be a "blame game"; rather, it helps to realize that messages that we interpreted, perceived, or absorbed from coaches, teachers, caregivers, or other influencers earlier in our lives are not relevant in our new legal personas.
  - Declare any unhelpful messages to be outdated. It's time to overwrite or delete them.

Step 3

- When you anticipate or step into a fear-invoking performance scenario, what automatic physical responses does your body exhibit?
  - Notice how you might be making your frame smaller, or subconsciously trying to disappear (e.g., by hunching shoulders, folding inward, crossing legs or arms, averting eye contact).
  - Evaluate whether your physical movements might be affecting the flow of your energy, blood, and oxygen.
  - Do you sweat or blush?
  - Do you become short of breath? Does your mouth go dry? Does your heart race? Stomach hurt? Head throb?

Dancing (Like a Boxer!) Back to Step 2 Again!

- Start to fortify your *mind.*
  - Write a new and updated mental sound track: craft three to six *accurate* mental messages that apply to your life and persona *today* (Example: "I have done the work. I am ready. I am entitled to say this in my own authentic voice.")
    - You also could write out three to six mental messages tailored to the particular performance event, focusing on sticking to your performance *process* (rather than outcomes) and keeping a realistic *perspective* about the stakes of the event (Example: "This is one conversation with a human being, not the Super Bowl half-time show!")
  - Understand that the old mental sound track likely will still kick into gear in the performance moment—that's okay, it's had years to run on autopilot.
  - Resolve that when you notice and hear the familiar words of the old mental sound track, you will *stop, drop, and roll* (see below, in *Putting Steps 2 and 3 Together*).

Dancing (Like a Boxer!) Back to Step 3 Again!

- Start to fortify your *machine.*
  - Get to know your body, frame, and automatic physical responses to stress.
  - Adopt a new fitness or "physical movement" regimen and begin to regard yourself as a "scholar-athlete," with the goal of strengthening your fear-untangling *machine.*
  - Consider watching Amy Cuddy's TED Talk on "power poses."

- Practice adopting a balanced athlete's stance, whether seated or standing—flexible, agile, balanced, open, ready for movement.
- Train yourself to open up your frame in performance moments, to get blood, oxygen, and energy flowing in a constructive direction— uncross your legs and arms, open your arms and hands, lengthen the spine, raise your gaze, throw the shoulders back.
  - You may need to uncross your legs and arms multiple times in a single event; that's okay. We are retraining our bodies.

Putting Steps 2 and 3 Together

- Develop a "preshot" routine: a mental and physical checklist or sequence that you will run through the day of, and in the moments leading right up to, the performance moment.
  - A motivating song?
  - A mental reboot: *stop, drop, and roll* plus your three to six mental messages
  - Your favorite power pose
  - A balanced physical stance
  - A reminder to channel your inner athlete, rock star, and artist.

PERFORMANCE PROCESS

- Initiate your game-day performance process.
- Remind yourself of your new mental sound track and physical "preshot" routine.
- Consider doing an Amy Cuddy "power pose."
- Channel your inner athlete, rock star, and artist.
- Step into the performance space.
- Notice any ignition of the old mental sound track and/or the automatic physical responses.
- *Stop, drop, and roll.*
- Remember that the fear response is just the amygdala alarm bells and the voice of the (annoying and outdated) mental sound track.
- Breathe.
- Launch your three to six new mental messages as a *foil* to stop the old sound track.
- Put your physical "preshot" routine into action.

- ○ Adopt your balanced athlete's stance.
- ○ Open up your frame.
- ○ Breathe.
- ○ Let the energy, blood, and oxygen surge through you in a productive manner.
- Keep going.
- Trust your training.
- Don't overthink or overcare.
- Focus on the performance *routine*, not the outcome.
- Repeat your physical "preshot" routine if you notice your legs or arms crossing again, or if you are slumping down or hunching.
- Restate your mental messages if fresh seeds of doubt sprout.
- Keep going.
- Be the strong athlete, the fierce competitor, and the artist that you are.

CULTIVATING A CULTURE OF FORTITUDE

Step 4

- Give yourself permission to outright reject cliché messages such as "just do it," "fake it till you make it," "just do what scares you," or "embrace fear as a great motivator!"
- Instead, remind yourself, "By untangling fear, I am becoming an even more powerful advocate."
- Resolve to build character-in-context in the legal arena by consciously *seeking opportunities* to learn more about lawyering scenarios that ignite fear.
- Start an "Untangling Fear" group in your law school, law office, or bar association, to openly discuss issues around fear and mistake-making in the legal arena.
- Seek opportunities to better understand *client* fears (see Appendix D) and help clients (and others) untangle those fears.

My face doesn't show it, but in my mind, I smile. I know what this is. This is fear. And I'm about to use it.

—Brandon Webb, former Navy SEAL[755]

Appendix B
Practical Strategies
for Legal Educators

As legal educators, we can cultivate an educational environment in which students, faculty, administrators, and mentors openly discuss the reality of fear in lawyering, and then develop and encourage the use of practical strategies for untangling it. Instead of advising law students to "fake it till you make it" or "just do what scares you" (echoing the advice that many of us received), we can say—out loud—that yes, lawyering can be scary, and some interactive scenarios *will be* more intimidating for some individuals than for others. That does not mean that students who are afraid of such situations are not cut out for law school or practice, or don't deserve a seat at the table. Quite the contrary. By first acknowledging fear in lawyering and then deepening our understanding of its roots and drivers, we can construct and adopt concrete strategies to distill fear and transform it into powerful advocacy for others.

As explored in Chapter 1, some law students experience a host of fears, including fear of failure, judgment, and mistake-making. Starting in each student's 1L year, we can foster a learning culture that includes

- encouraging law students to develop their own authentic legal personas and professional identities instead of feeling pressure to mirror others' approaches or behavior

- helping law students develop an aptitude for asking questions about confusing procedure, strategy, and nuances in the law or a client representation—without fear of judgment or criticism that deters risk-taking and undermines learning

- providing practical, judgment-free *tactical* training, expressly focusing on tough or fear-inducing situations in which lawyering mistakes can happen, and

- teaching law students how to approach a supervisor or mentor upon discovery of a potential or actual error and gain supportive advice about how to remedy the situation, thereby building character.

To lay the foundation for this type of training, we must overtly acknowledge that it is natural for some of us to worry about admitting confusion or lack of knowledge. We also should express our understanding of the perceived risks of owning up to a mistake—shame, embarrassment, a reprimand, penalties, perhaps even a worst-case-scenario malpractice suit, or a disciplinary proceeding—that foster fear-based mind-sets. Next, we can endeavor to *minimize* future mistakes by providing practical and tactical training in how to apply the law to real-world conflicts, specifically in how to approach complex and convoluted decision-making. Of course, many law professors already are doing many of these things, but perhaps collectively we can make this type of training more transparent and formalized.

In legal education, we can honor and strive for excellence, but also acknowledge human fallibility and provide students with realistic guidance in how to navigate the inevitable circumstances in which lawyers struggle or falter. In integrating discussions of character-in-context, fear, and mistake-making into the three-year arc of the law school curriculum, we can help students build a "track record"[756] of decision-making, including preventing avoidable errors but also successfully recovering from mistakes. As Professor Kaci Bishop notes in her article "Framing Failure in the Legal Classroom: Techniques for Encouraging Growth and Resilience," "teaching students to engage productively with failure can thus enhance students' experiences while in law school and help them carry these lessons and habits into practice."[757]

LAW SCHOOL ORIENTATION AND PROFESSIONAL IDENTITY DEVELOPMENT

As early as law school orientation, legal educators can encourage students to learn more about themselves and their personality characteristics, traits, and strengths. This awareness may be increased by using such assessments as the Myers-Briggs Type Indicator Assessment,[758] the VARK Learning Style Questionnaire,[759] Emotional Intelligence assessments,[760] the 16 Personalities Assessment,[761] LawFit (which "measures interests, values, and preferences"),[762] CliftonStrengths,[763] and other measures that focus specifically on character.

Regarding character in the lawyering context, a candidate for the master of applied positive psychology degree at the University of Pennsylvania, Patricia Snyder, conducted a study entitled Super Women Lawyers: A Study of

Character Strengths. In her research, she used the Values in Action Inventory of Strengths (VIA-IS). The VIA-IS is a 240-question survey. It asks participants to react to 10 statements affiliated with 24 character strengths[764] identified by positive psychologists Christopher Peterson and Martin E. P. Seligman. The 24 traits "reside within the six virtues of wisdom and knowledge, courage, humanity, justice, temperance and transcendence."[765] There is also a truncated 24-item version of the VIA-IS called the Brief Strengths Test.

Character strengths in the virtue category of courage (which relates to our quest to untangle fear in lawyering) include "bravery, persistence, integrity, and vitality."[766] The Brief Strengths Test defines bravery as follows: "Also described as *courage* and *valor*, this strength suggests undertaking danger for a good end after reasonably assessing risks."[767] The question posed in the test asks: "Think of actual situations in which you experienced fear or threat. How frequently did you show BRAVERY or COURAGE in these situations?"[768]

The Super Women Lawyers study noted that a "cited avenue for bravery was having the courage to admit a mistake made in trial."[769] One lawyer in the study who supervises several junior attorneys "acknowledged that admitting a mistake or mix-up to a client was hard and a bit risky, but in her experience, ultimately strengthened the client relationship."[770] One lawyer noted that not all legal mistakes are obvious or easily avoidable:

The pressure of having others depend on you in very important matters, the ease with which one can make a mistake; there are lots of ways to screw up and ways to screw up that are not necessarily intuitive. So you have to be ever mindful.[771]

Using a character assessment like VIA-IS (and even Snyder's article summarizing her Super Women Lawyers study) in a law school orientation or a 1L program can serve as a starting point for a conversation with students about courage, bravery, realistic fear in the context of lawyering, and making and handling mistakes. Students can learn that it is very normal to experience fear or trepidation when confronted with certain lawyering tasks and that some law-related scenarios will be more stressful for some students than for others. This does not mean that the fearful students are not cut out for the law or a particular type of law practice. Rather, with additional support to untangle their fears and understand their drivers, they will be able to approach the particular lawyering task with enhanced self-awareness and more robust substantive, technical, mental, and physical strategies.

Law schools also might consider borrowing an idea from Smith College and introducing a workshop series on "Failing Well,"[772] which focuses on the imposter syndrome and the reality that we all make mistakes but can learn from them. According to Rachel Simmons, a leadership development specialist at Smith and an inspiring author on resilience, it is important to instill in students the message that "[F]ailure is not a bug of learning; it's the feature."[773]

Further, acknowledging the practical reality that a junior attorney might make a mistake because of lack of preparedness to develop a healthy work-life balance, Professor Katerina Lewinbuk writes in *Connecting Ethics & Practice*, her textbook on professional responsibility:

> *Sending recently licensed attorneys into the profession without the skills to balance their work lives with their personal lives may lead to attorney mistakes or misconduct when practicing as lawyers.*[774]

Orientation programs could focus on providing students with techniques for cultivating a healthy school-life balance, with the express goal of helping law students and future lawyers minimize mistakes stemming from a lack of skills in managing competing pressures.

In orientation programs and workshops, professors should consider opening up to our students about the fears and mistakes we experienced during our legal careers. As author (and professor) Brené Brown has noted, "[V]ery early in our training, [academics] are taught that a cool distance and inaccessibility contribute to prestige, and that if you're too relatable, your credentials come into question."[775] Yet, as Ed Catmull, co-founder of Pixar Animation Studios and longtime president of Pixar Animation and Disney Animation, says, "If we as leaders can talk about our mistakes and our part in them, then we make it safe for others."[776] Letting down our guard and sharing our own vulnerabilities in our legal education and lawyering experiences just might be the key to helping our students untangle fear, build character, and handle mistakes in a healthy and ethical manner.

SYLLABUS LANGUAGE

In my role as a member of our law school's Curriculum Committee, I reviewed a syllabus for a winter session course proposed by Professor Christopher Michaelsen from the University of New South Wales in Australia. I was beyond happy to see this language in his syllabus:

> *It is recognized that some students are more confident or more practiced in speaking in groups than others. Some, too, like to reflect on what others have said before contributing to the discussion. It will not be the most forward or garrulous who achieve the best marks, but those whose quality of contribution is high. Infrequent but*

very good contributions will be more favorably noticed than numerous more poorly informed or ill-considered contributions. . . . Open discussion of doubts, mistakes, or misunderstandings is part of the learning process and will not be penalized.

Further, Professor Michaelsen highlighted these factors, among many others, as important in his assessment of class performance:

- preparedness to listen actively to others
- no domineering
- respect for other students and their ideas
- sensitivity to other students

Professor Calvin Pang, 2018 Chair of the AALS Section on Balance in Legal Education, includes this excerpt in his Family Law syllabus:

My ultimate aim is to engage students with the teacher, students with each other, and students with the subject matter. Some days will be better than others, but I'll always try to stay true to this aim. I will rely on your insights, wisdom, energy, and experience to help drive this class, so please be ready to share. I realize that for several different reasons, some students have a hard time speaking in class. This includes some who might be among the brightest and best prepared. I hope to create a safe space for everyone to participate.

To cultivate an inclusive learning environment in our law school classrooms, we might consider incorporating language into our syllabi that demonstrates to students that we understand the reality of fear in law school. Our syllabi also can acknowledge the benefits of learning from failure and mistakes. Here is one example of such language.

Fear, Anxiety, Failure, and Mistake-Making

I understand that some performance-oriented aspects of law school are going to be more anxiety-producing or even fear-invoking for some of you than others. That is okay. If you are anxious or afraid in my class or about certain performance-oriented activities in law school (such as the Socratic method or oral presentations), that absolutely does NOT mean you are not cut out for law school or practice, or that you do not deserve to be here. It just means you might need a little more guidance in untangling your anxiety or fear, and tapping into your authentic lawyer voice. Class participation is not about frequency, or the "gift of gab," or outward confidence. It is about quality, thoughtfulness, vulnerability, and authenticity.

I understand that it might initially seem scary to volunteer or be on-call in my class. Please let me know if you are nervous about that. I do not wish for any-one to opt out; rather, we can work together to cultivate a classroom environment in which everyone feels comfortable experimenting with their authentic lawyer voices. Talking openly about anxiety and fear is welcome and encouraged. Talking openly about failure and mistake-making is welcome and encouraged, too.

In an article sharing insights about his interesting stand-alone course, Inter-personal Dynamics for Attorneys,[777] Professor Joshua Rosenberg highlights a disservice we do to our students when we avoid providing a forum to talk about "how the student or anyone else feels about being called on, or the 'meaning' she makes of being called on (for example, whether she thinks to herself that the teacher is picking on her, or is embarrassed by the attention she is getting, or fears ridicule if she gives a wrong answer, or is engaged in and challenged by the theoretical discussion, etc.)."[778] Professor Rosenberg recommends set-ting "a time and a place" for law students to "discuss their personal reactions and internal processes,"[779] whether that is in small groups led by faculty or a formal workshop or course.

LEGAL WRITING CURRICULUM DEVELOPMENT

In the 1L curriculum, legal writing professors might consider developing a research and writing assignment that introduces students to the reality of law-yering mistakes and engages students in problem solving to remedy errors. For example, Jodi Balsam, associate professor of clinical law and director of externship programs at Brooklyn Law School, created a writing assignment involving a lawyering mistake. For the Legal Practice course she taught at New York Law School, Professor Balsam developed a fact pattern in which two co-counsel missed a filing deadline owing to confusion over a time extension to file an answer to a complaint. The court entered a default judgment. Pro-fessor Balsam guided her students in researching and analyzing the standard under Connecticut law that governs a motion to set aside a default judgment. Connecticut General Statutes §52-212(a) states that a default judgment may be set aside within four months of its issuance if a moving party can show

1. prejudice; AND
2. reasonable cause, OR
3. that a good cause of action or defense in whole or in part existed at the time the judgment was entered; AND

4. the party was prevented by *mistake*, accident, or other reasonable cause from prosecuting the action or making the defense.

Professor Balsam's students wrote a memorandum analyzing whether their client likely would succeed in showing that the failure to answer the complaint was due to the two lawyers' *mistake*, accident, or other reasonable cause.

Inspired by my friend and colleague Professor Balsam, I developed a legal writing assignment based on a New York rule, N.Y. C.P.L.R. 2005, under which a court has discretion to accept an untimely pleading or vacate a default judgment, based on an excusable "delay or default resulting from *law office failure*." I created a fact pattern in which students represented a party who *prevailed* on a default judgment. The law firm representing the defaulting party sought to have the court vacate the default judgment on the grounds that a failure to respond to a motion for summary judgment was due to "excusable law office failure." The New York case law indicates that a party requesting the court to vacate a default judgment must show (1) a reasonable excuse for the failure to file a timely pleading or brief and (2) the existence of a potentially meritorious defense to the underlying cause of action. Courts also consider factors such as the extent of the delay, prejudice to the opposing party, willfulness, and the strong public policy in favor of resolving cases on the merits. In crafting the assignment, I did not want to send the message that just *any* old excuse for lateness was okay, as I absolutely do not want my own students to get in the habit of making excuses for the untimeliness of their own work. I intentionally designed the assignment so that the students were representing the *prevailing* party and would have a stake in seeking to persuade the court *not* to excuse the defaulting party's "failure." Nonetheless, working through the factors from the case law sparked open discussion about the reality of mistakes in law practice, fairness, the efforts lawyers can make to avoid errors, and also circumstances in which judges and parties can work together to remedy missteps. (If any professors are interested in these teaching materials, I am happy to provide them. I also am grateful to the Association of Legal Writing Directors for the 2018 Teaching Grant that helped fund the development of these materials!)

Being mindful not to unnecessarily scare students in the first month or two of law school with fear-based narratives[780] of catastrophic mistakes, legal writing professors can consider crafting factual scenarios involving lawyering mistakes. Students could then research substantive and procedural ways to remedy those mistakes (perhaps across different jurisdictions), and also talk about how to bring such mistakes to the attention of a supervisor, particularly if that requires a difficult conversation. Such conversations could be simulated with student-actors playing the role of the supervisor or with practicing attorneys visiting class. Professors further can guide class discussion about character-in-context, prompting students to explore ideas for how to handle mistakes appropriately.

Legal writing professors also can explain to students the philosophy of "teaching with mistakes" and adopting a "culture of error" in the classroom when focusing on our students' research, writing, and editing processes. In an article entitled "Why Our Brain Thrives on Mistakes," Barry Boyce emphasizes that "[b]eing curious about our mistakes is the royal road to learning."[781] He mentions how an "inspired educator" named Richard Curwin has developed techniques for "teaching with mistakes," such as "not marking errors on tests and papers without explaining why they are wrong, always giving students chances to re-do their work, and letting students 'brag about their biggest mistakes and what they learned from them.'"[782] In her book, *The Creative Habit: Learn It and Use It for Life,* choreographer Twyla Tharp references a math professor at Williams College who "bases ten percent of his students' grades on failure."[783] She explains:

> *Mathematics is all about trying out new ideas—new formulas, theorems, approaches—and knowing that the vast majority of them will be dead ends. To encourage his students not to be afraid of testing their quirkiest ideas in public, he rewards rather than punishes them for coming up with wrong answers.*[784]

Further, at the 2018 Legal Writing Institute Conference in Milwaukee, I met fellow legal writing professor Jennifer Cooper, who introduced me to the concept of "the culture of error." Professor Cooper advocates for building a culture of error in the law classroom, which means an environment "in which it is safe to struggle and fail."[785] Professor Cooper pointed me to the work of Doug Lemov, author of an ebook called *Culture of Error,* who indicates that "a classroom that respects error, normalizes it, and values learning from it, is one of the characteristics of a high-performing classroom."[786] He suggests four techniques for cultivating a productive culture of error in the classroom:

- "expecting error": transparently pointing out to students that "errors are a normal part of learning and perform their role best when they are out in the open"[787]

- "withholding the answer": "delay[ing] revealing whether an answer is right or wrong until you've discussed it, and perhaps an alternative"; students "spend less energy evaluating their work . . . and more energy thinking about the underlying ideas"[788]

- "managing your tell": being mindful of our "unintentional cues that reveal . . . whether an answer was right or wrong or whether we valued what a student said"[789]

- "praising risk-taking"[790]

Additionally, Professor Kaci Bishop offers an "introduction to failure pedagogy" in her article "Framing Failure in the Legal Classroom: Techniques for Encouraging Growth and Resilience." She encourages colleagues to use multiple techniques:

- Construct a "failure framework" in the classroom, "letting students know explicitly that we have high expectations for them and their work *and* that we expect them to make mistakes."[791]
  - Also, transparently explain "to our students *why* and *how* struggling helps them learn."[792]
  - "Contextualize failure" by pointing out that many "failures are praiseworthy, not blameworthy."[793]
  - Share our own "journeys, missteps, and failures."[794]
- Deliver "feedback in a constructive manner designed to encourage a growth mindset."[795]
  - Adjust the feedback language and terminology we use.
    - Praise "attitude, effort, and improvement over time" instead of results or outcomes.[796]
    - Try using the word *yet*[797]—such as marking up a student paper with comments like "[T]his paragraph identifies the three elements of the rule and has *yet* to narrow the issue to the particular prong of the rule in question" (implying the student's potential and capability of accomplishing that next step).
    - Try substituting *and* for *but* or *or*.[798]
    - Suggest "opportunities for improvement" or "opportunities for arguments from a different perspective."[799]
- Analyze and predict failure by way of
  - conducting "post-mortems" of assignments,[800] with a "focus on 'what' rather than 'who'"[801]
  - adopting "pre-mortems" to empower students to predict potential future failures.[802]

The legal writing classroom presents rich opportunities to explore fear and mistake-making with students, and to cultivate character-in-context and resilience.

ADDRESSING FEAR AND MISTAKE-MAKING IN LECTURE AND SEMINAR COURSES

Again being mindful not to unnecessarily scare students through "fear-based narratives" of catastrophe, professors of large lecture courses and seminars might consider incorporating into the curriculum classroom discussions and short writing assignments about fear and mistake-making. While it may be tempting to use attention-grabbing examples of "catastrophic" attorney mistakes, "fear appeals" are ineffective as a teaching tool if our students are particularly vulnerable and feel "powerless" to avoid the mistake—because of their lack of substantive or procedural knowledge or because their skills are not yet sufficiently developed.[803] If we *do* use scary mistake scenarios as teaching tools, we must be sure to provide "coping efficacy information sufficient to . . . inform [students] about adaptive behavioral responses."[804] In other words, in addition to describing the lawyering error, we should teach the substantive, procedural, and practical steps students can take to avoid such errors in real-life practice.

For example, professors who teach tax, corporate formation, immigration law, employment law, intellectual property, trusts and estates, criminal procedure, or other subjects might facilitate class discussions and/or short writing assignments on common mistakes lawyers make in those areas of practice. Students could research how to avoid such mistakes, and identify available substantive and procedural mechanisms to remedy such errors.

ADDRESSING FEAR AND MISTAKE-MAKING IN CLINICS, EXTERNSHIP/INTERNSHIP SEMINARS, AND SIMULATION COURSES

In clinic and externship settings, students likely understand that they are expected both to have good character *and* to avoid ethical violations. Some students, however, may not know exactly how to achieve both goals when confronted with real-life legal conflicts. We can use class discussions to delve into the *practical* nuances of character-in-context, mistake-making, prevention of errors, and recovery therefrom. We also can discuss with students how fear can lead to ethical dilemmas (perhaps using some of the case examples in

Chapter 4). Through open discussions about fear and mistake-making, students can consider what it means to have character in the context of lawyering, and also focus on *practical* strategies for developing their character when encountering challenging situations.

The book *Learning from Practice: A Text for Experiential Legal Education*,[805] used in many experiential education courses, mentions that fear can "arise from feelings."[806] It discusses how *reflection* can help us process mistakes and work through challenges.[807] It further advises students that they likely will face ethical questions at their internship or externship placements.[808] The book mentions that character is a factor in the 26 Lawyering Effectiveness Factors of Shultz and Zedeck.[809] The authors of *Learning from Practice* query whether good judgment is innate or learnable; as pointed out in Chapter 4 of *this* book, positive psychology pioneers Seligman and Peterson indicate that character *is* learnable. *Learning from Practice* encourages students to strengthen their judgment through practice and reflection over time.[810] The book remarks that characteristics such as courage are "crucial"[811] in the practice of law. These excerpts in *Learning from Practice* could provide a platform for class discussions or short writing assignments expressly focused on character, fear, and mistake-making in experiential education courses.

The word *fear* appears 32 times in the index of a 2017 book, *Transforming Justice, Lawyers, and the Practice of Law*,[812] edited by Marjorie A. Silver. This book also identifies issues that could provide jumping-off points for a series of dialogues about the presence of fear in legal education, and how this emotion permeates our legal system. Authors of various chapters reflect on fear in different ways:

- Professor Silver delves into law students' fears, emphasizing the importance of professors' "acknowledging our students' fears of insufficiency and invoking our need to embrace the challenges those fears present. To do so, we must face our own fears as well. . . . [Our students] must learn that they will graduate to serve clients who are also filled with fears and vulnerability. Our calling is to offer them—acknowledging our own limitations in so doing—the tools to engage with their own and their clients' fears and vulnerabilities."[813]

- Professor Silver further taps into the presence of fear in the classroom, noting how "students have talked about the shadow or shame culture: fear of being judged, or seeming stupid, or silly, or embarrassing themselves, or seeming uncool by participating freely."[814]

- Professor Rhonda V. Magee refers to our "formidable system of laws based on fear."[815]

- Professors Jeanne Anselmo and Victor Goode call attention to the reality of *clients'* fears, highlighting how the goal of a student or lawyer "practicing therapeutic presence" is to listen to a client "without getting overwhelmed and deterred by the client's frustration, anxiety, fear, or grief."[816]

- Attorney Pamela J. P. Denison likewise focuses on clients' fears in discussing collaborative practices in lawyering. "[I]f only lawyers were willing to set aside their own interests in favor of listening to clients' deepest needs and fears," she writes.[817]

- Author and attorney Sylvia Clute discusses clients' and lawyers' fear with respect to telling the truth—specifically, the "fear that a greater injustice will result from telling the truth than the injustice of just telling 'a little white lie.'"[818]

- Finally, Professor Susan L. Brooks highlights societal fears, emphasizing that the "prevalent culture in our society . . . is driven by our emphasis on individualism and self-sufficiency. Though perhaps the *real* drivers, if we look deeply, are shame and fear."[819]

- Professor Brooks further notes, "Law school and legal practice breed scarcity because of the high level of fear and anxiety that are part of the legal culture."[820]

Each one of the foregoing excerpts could serve as a launching pad for a class discussion or a short writing assignment.

Clinic and externship/internship seminar settings provide ripe opportunities for professors to address fear and mistake-making head-on. Professor William Berman writes about the need for students in law school clinics to learn how to "openly examine mistakes in a non-defensive way" and "how to best handle and learn from their mistakes."[821] He acknowledges that concealing mistakes and feigning infallibility "is a natural human impulse."[822] He recommends that clinical professors first emphasize to students that lawyers are not infallible.[823] Next, he suggests that professors can cultivate a learning environment in which they (1) are open and transparent about their own legal errors, (2) create low-stakes opportunities for students to make mistakes, and (3) allow students to learn from mistakes without shame or embarrassment.[824]

Professor Berman refers to lessons learned from the medical field (a topic we explored earlier in Chapter 9) in which past notions of the "deny and defend" and "shame and blame" culture incentivized medical students and doctors to hide mistakes.[825] That mind-set obviously thwarts learning and professional development. To dismantle educational and training barriers of those types, Berman encourages clinical law professors and externship seminar teachers to strive to promote an atmosphere of trust and accountability, teaching students how to own responsibility for mistakes while not demeaning them for having erred.[826] For instance, for one assignment, clinical teachers and students could collaboratively develop and adopt a mistake-handling *protocol*, including tangible steps such as reporting discovery of an error to a mentor, identifying and taking corrective action, apologizing, reflecting (individually and among classmates), and implementing change.[827]

Reflection assignments are a wonderful opportunity for students to write openly about fear and mistake-making in lawyering. Remaining mindful of student privacy and client confidentiality issues, professors and directors of student externships and internships might offer the following reflection prompt related to fear in lawyering:

> *Describe a situation you observed or experienced at your placement in which you noticed, perceived, or sensed that a person felt fear or anxiety in a lawyering scenario, OR in which you personally felt fear or anxiety in a lawyering scenario. For example, you might notice outward manifestations of fear shown by clients, by victims/witnesses/third-parties, by opposing parties, or by lawyers handling the cases. Perhaps individuals have verbally expressed their fears or worries to you. If you have not encountered such a situation, you may ask your Mentor Attorney or another placement colleague if they have observed or experienced fear or anxiety in lawyering.*

> *Within the bounds of confidentiality, please describe the scenario, and how you noticed, perceived, or sensed another person's fear or worry, OR please describe your own fear or anxiety toward the particular scenario: What were you worried might happen?*

> *If writing about a client's, a victim's, a witness's, or a third-party's fear, please describe whether the lawyers within your placement acknowledged or addressed the individual's fear, and if so, how.*

> *Reflect on the presence of fear in lawyering activities and whether (and if so, how) you think the legal profession can help individuals (including law students) who experience fear while interacting within the legal process.*

The foregoing prompt could facilitate an opportunity for professors to talk with students about the reality of *client* fears. Professors then could draw upon the information provided in Chapter 3 regarding the types of fears that clients experience in different legal scenarios, and the advice in Appendix D for perceiving and handling client fears.

Professors and students could discuss and simulate techniques for communicating with clients about fears across a range of contexts. Professors also might invite lawyers from the relevant area of practice to visit class sessions and openly discuss patterns of client fears. Students and practitioners could brainstorm ideas about how to identify and communicate with clients about those fears.

An alternative written reflection prompt could focus on (1) whether students in clinics, internships, externships, or simulation courses have worried about making a particular mistake, or in fact did make a mistake; (2) the feelings associated with making such mistakes; (3) any steps taken to communicate with a supervisor about a mistake, or to remedy the mistake; and (4) how similar mistakes could be prevented in the future. Professors could invite lawyers from the relevant area of practice to visit class sessions and openly discuss common errors in the practice arena, and offer protocols for preventing but also remedying such mistakes.

A COURSE FOCUSED ON CHARACTER-IN-CONTEXT, FEAR, MISTAKE-MAKING, AND LEARNING FROM FAILURE

In addition to incorporating some of the foregoing content into an existing curriculum, law schools could develop a *new* course specifically focused on character-in-context, lawyering fears, mistake-making, and learning from failure—outside of the live client realm. This course could begin with a focus on character, using the Values in Action Inventory of Strengths (VIA-IS) assessment mentioned at the beginning of this appendix. Professors could use this assessment to spark discussion about character in the context of lawyering.

The course could exemplify the model of "teaching with mistakes" and fostering a "culture of error." Resources for doing so include

- Barry Boyce, "Why Our Brain Thrives on Mistakes," https://www.mindful .org/brain-thrives-mistakes/ (May 3, 2017).

- Doug Lemov, "Culture of Error," http://teachlikeachampion.com/ cultureoferror/.

- Kaci Bishop, "Framing Failure in the Legal Classroom: Techniques for Encouraging Growth and Resilience," *Arkansas Law Review* 70, No. 4 (January 2018): 959.

- Rebecca Cox, "'It Was Just That I Was Afraid': Promoting Success by Addressing Students' Fear of Failure," *Community College Review* 37, No. 1 (July 2009): 52.

- The medical, journalism, engineering, and business school courses mentioned in Part III of this book.

Professors then could structure this type of course around a range of real-life scenarios in which a junior lawyer first is unsure about a substantive or procedural aspect of a client matter or fearful about an upcoming performance scenario and must ask for guidance from an intimidating supervisor. Then later, the junior lawyer realizes that a mistake was made and needs to bring it to the attention of the intimidating supervisor. Example scenarios involving fear of asking for help and fear of addressing a mistake follow.

Fear of Asking for Help:

- The junior attorney has read (several times) the procedural rules for how to construct the appendix for an appellate brief for submission to the New York Supreme Court Appellate Division, as well as the timing requirements. She has reviewed five or six legal blogs trying to seek clarity, all of which expressly acknowledge how *unclear* the rules are. She remains confused about how to "perfect the appeal."

- The junior attorney is researching grounds for recusal of a judge based on a perceived conflict of interest but cannot find a single case on point in the pertinent jurisdiction. The deadline for the draft motion for recusal is looming.

- A senior partner assigned the junior attorney the task of negotiating a Federal Rule of Civil Procedure 26(f)(2) Joint Proposed Discovery and Trial Plan with opposing counsel. It is the junior attorney's first time negotiating such a plan. The only advice the supervising attorney gave was: "If opposing counsel wants trial in two years, you want it in six months. If the other side wants trial in six months, you want it in two years." The associate is nervous about how to approach the negotiation.

- A junior attorney is taking her first deposition of a witness in a case involving multiple defendants. Four defense lawyers present at the deposition are being disruptive. The junior attorney is not sure how to handle or rein in the disruption. The only advice received from the senior partner before the deposition was "Just make sure you get everything you need from this witness."

- A junior attorney filed a motion for Federal Rule of Civil Procedure 11 sanctions against opposing counsel (for wrongfully accusing the attorney's trial team of bill-padding a request for attorneys' fees after winning the case on summary judgment). The junior attorney must go to court to deliver the oral argument before a judge who has a reputation for being abrupt with lawyers.

Fear of Addressing a Mistake:

- A junior associate wrote a brief, which the senior partner signed and filed. Later, the associate realized that a case she cited in the brief had been vacated in part, on the very issue for which she had cited the case. She thought she had KeyCited the case during her original research, and Westlaw had shown no adverse action.

- A junior associate tasked with editing and redlining an 80-page draft contract based on negotiations with opposing counsel realized that the final executed version of the contract contains an earlier version of a contract provision that is less favorable to the client. The associate, who thought he had checked all the Tracked Changes in the last version that came back from opposing counsel, later realized that he apparently missed one provision buried in a sea of final changes.

- A California-based junior associate working his first case before the U.S. District Court for the Eastern District of Virginia was unaware that the deadline for serving objections to discovery requests was 15 days earlier than the usual deadline for discovery objections in federal courts (E.D.Va. Local Rule 26(C) differs from the 30-day deadline in FRCP 33(b)(2)). He missed the deadline for serving objections to interrogatories and is afraid he has waived the right to object.

- A junior associate asked her assistant to forward a draft pleading to the client for review. The assistant emailed the document to opposing counsel by accident, as the names sound similar. The document contained attorney-client privileged communications.

- While a junior attorney was defending a deposition, opposing counsel placed in front of the deponent an exhibit that was clearly attorney-client privileged but somehow had been produced by the junior attorney's firm in discovery, as evidenced by the Bates number. The junior attorney was part of the document review team that performed the privilege review and is certain he pulled the document from the production, but there may have been other copies. The associate is worried about how the partner managing the case will react.

In this course, professors and students can talk openly about how circumstances like these can arise very easily, even if the junior attorney is organized, prepared, and working diligently. Professors can collaborate with students in developing a realistic protocol for approaching a more senior attorney in the law office for guidance on how to work through a confusing legal problem or a challenging situation. Students also can develop a realistic protocol for bringing a mistake to a senior attorney's attention, including emotional, mental, and physical strategies (such as the techniques offered in Chapters 15 and 16) for preparing to approach an unpredictable supervisor. To avoid heightening students' fears of making a mistake (which can paralyze them or inhibit them from being creative problem solvers), we can equip them with tools to process these types of real-life scenarios. Such instruction is best provided in a low-stakes, nonstressful learning environment. Classroom discussion also can focus on character-in-context, inviting students to reflect on readings that discuss various character traits,[828] such as honesty and integrity.

Using a simulation model—perhaps even using virtual reality technology[829]—courses like these could incorporate assignments in which students inevitably will make mistakes as part of the lesson. Students can practice working through each protocol for responding to the mistake.

Professors also might consider inviting attorneys from different areas of practice, and representing different levels of seniority, to visit class and share recollections of being afraid to step into a lawyering task or making and recovering from a mistake. Professors should be careful to avoid choosing attorneys who take a "bravado" approach to fear or who might scare students further with "catastrophic" war stories. Instead, professors should endeavor to invite lawyers who are empathetic, open, and honest in sharing their personal hurdles in lawyering. Notably, in 2017, the law firm of Pillsbury Winthrop Shaw Pittman LLP convened its annual First-Year Associate Conference. One of the sessions facilitated small-group discussions among new associates in Litigation and Transactional-Regulatory breakout groups. The topic was "Post-Mortem of a Mistake: What Happened, Lessons Learned, How to Move Forward, and Q&A." This type of forward-thinking programming can be brought right into the law school classroom, so that students begin to explore how to prevent and handle mistakes early in the arc of their legal careers.

Professors also might consider inviting positive, encouraging speakers from attorney malpractice insurance companies to provide more information to students—in a nonintimidating but informative way—on how malpractice insurance works, the types of mistake that are manageable with simple remedial steps, those that are more grievous, and the protocol in different office environments for handling mistakes. Attorney Mark Bassingthwaighte, a risk manager with ALPS, a professional liability insurance carrier for attorneys, has written blog articles about advising lawyers regarding lawyering mistakes. He describes the nature of conversations with such attorneys as follows:

> *Of these, some were driven by a desire to look for the learning, others were about trying to determine if a misstep had even occurred, and every once in a while, they were about a lawyer regretting not having appropriately dealt with the misstep that did occur.*[830]

Students could benefit from learning more about the practicalities of these issues while in law school, and by practicing these often difficult conversations, developing character-in-context. As Bassingthwaighte notes, "[P]eople are not defined by the circumstances in which they find themselves. They are defined by how they choose to respond to their circumstances."[831] Bassingthwaighte acknowledges the role that fear plays in malpractice scenarios; "too often it can lead to poorly thought through decisions and actions."[832] Classroom discussions around fear and mistake-making, and appropriate courses of action to take upon discovery of a mistake, while directly addressing the potential emotions involved, will help better prepare future generations of attorneys to handle the rigors of practice.

This course also could incorporate a unit on how to recognize and properly address *client* fears. Professors can draw on the information provided in Chapter 3 regarding the types of fears that clients experience across different areas of legal practice, and the advice in Appendix D for perceiving and handling client fears. Then, professors and students could discuss techniques for communicating with clients about fears. Professors might invite lawyers from different areas of practice—such as criminal law, immigration, domestic violence, domestic relations law, medical malpractice, corporate representation, estate planning, elder law, and bankruptcy law—to visit class, openly discuss patterns of client fears in those contexts, and recommend ways to identify and communicate with clients about those fears.

Professors could excerpt course readings from the articles, books, and other sources referenced in the bibliography to this book. A proposed list of course topics can be found in Appendix E.

EXTRACURRICULAR RESOURCES TO HELP STUDENTS WHO OPEN UP ABOUT FEAR

Outside the law classroom, as legal educators, we need to be prepared for and open to conversations with courageous students who come forward and confide their fears to us. As author Kristen Ulmer points out, when an individual comes to us and says, "I feel afraid," we must remember that "the only appropriate response is either to ask a clarifying question or offer a simple, genuine 'That's great'"—focusing on the growth opportunity and offering collaboration to find solutions and answers.[833] Even if we have the best intentions in trying to motivate a student to push through or overcome the fear, we need to be careful not to minimize the student's worries with routine advice like "fake it till you make it," "just do what scares you," or "there's nothing to be afraid of." These slogans can have the unintended but undesired opposite consequence of prodding scared individuals to bury their fears once again.[834] We need to make sure we *listen* to and *hear* the student. It is perfectly fine if we personally are not armed with the immediate solution; we can be the one to link the student up with someone who can provide concrete strategies and techniques.

Amy Florian, CEO of a training company called Corgenius (whose tagline is "Adding heart to the brains of business"), shares similar advice when describing how she coaches financial professionals to interact with fearful clients.[835] She emphasizes the importance of not trying to talk a scared client out of fear but instead "acknowledg[ing] it as if it were well founded."[836] She explains:

> *It is a mistake to try to talk your clients out of being afraid, even when you have compelling evidence of their safety. They first need to tell you about their fears until they are sure you have heard and understood. They need you to acknowledge their fears as valid, whether or not you believe they are. They need to work together with you on solutions rather than having you dominate the conversation with defenses and arguments. Only when your clients believe you have listened well enough to comprehend their fears can you work to find strategies to help them feel safe.*[837]

The same principles apply to our law students. As Florian advises, "Rather than dismissing their fears or trying to talk them out of them, [we can] make the time to hear and understand them. [We] take their fears seriously and help develop effective strategies for coping with them."[838] By cultivating not just empathy but also *compassion* for our scared students, we can help them become prominent change makers in our profession.

Christopher L. Kukk, a professor of political science at Western Connecticut State University and founding director of the Center for Compassion, Creativity, and Innovation, defines compassion as "a holistic understanding of a problem or the suffering of another with a commitment to act to solve the problem or alleviate the suffering."[839] He differentiates empathy from compassion, indicating that the latter "involves understanding *and acting*, but empathy is singular in purpose: to emotionally absorb the feeling of another."[840] Being compassionate toward our fearful law students will not decrease the intellectual rigor of the educational experience we are offering. Rather, it will allow *more* students to thrive and excel. Kukk highlights how scientific research on dopamine-processing genes reveals "that the more compassionate a classroom environment becomes, the greater the level of learning that occurs."[841] He champions compassion as a key to enhancing students' academic success.[842] For students who come to us outside the classroom to seek advice regarding law school fears or how to avoid mistakes, we can adopt Kukk's protocol: Listen, Understand, Connect, Act.[843] We must *listen*[844] to and really *hear* the student. We can ask questions to find out more and *understand*.[845] Kukk indicates that impactful "questions of compassion diminish the sense of loneliness that people feel while also helping them to look simultaneously inward and outward for strength and answers."[846] Through listening to and striving to understand our students—even if we have never experienced their particular kind of fears—we can forge deeper *connections* with them, and identify realistic and helpful *solutions* to help them untangle the fear. If we are not the "right" person with tangible and concrete answers for the students, we can take compassionate *action* by linking them with someone who can lead them to useful resources.

We also can support our students by encouraging them to develop small "Untangling Fear" groups, plan their own workshops, and bolster one another in a collaborative educational environment. As one law student put it, "Everyone in the profession would likely benefit from openly talking about their fears with someone [with whom] they have created a trusting relationship."

By adopting some of the foregoing strategies across the law school curriculum, inside and outside the classroom, we can reduce and hopefully eliminate the stigma of fear in law school. By honoring the reality of fear and mistakemaking in lawyering, and providing practical opportunities to untangle fear, we will help our students become better equipped to handle the rigors of practice and lead heathier professional and personal lives.

> *Remember this. Hold on to this. This is the only perfection there is,*
> *the perfection of helping others. This is the only thing we can do*
> *that has any lasting meaning. This is why we're here. To make each*
> *other feel safe.*
>
> —Andre Agassi, *Open*

Appendix C
Practical Strategies for Law
Practice Leaders and Mentors

This appendix provides practical strategies for law practice leaders and mentors to cultivate a professional development environment in which we more openly acknowledge and discuss the reality of fear (and mistake-making) in lawyering. In doing so, we can foster stronger mentor-mentee relationships and professional development platforms, empowering junior attorneys to (1) more readily seek advice on how to approach fear-inducing scenarios and avoid making mistakes driven by fear; (2) ask questions about confusing or unclear aspects of law practice and obtain advice on strategy, without fear of judgment or criticism that deters risk-taking and undermines learning; and (3) develop the fortitude to bring discovery of a potential or actual mistake to the attention of a mentor, and work collaboratively with the mentor to remedy an error, without misplaced fear of catastrophic repercussions.

CHANGING OUR MIND-SET ABOUT EMOTIONS IN LAWYERS

Our profession requires us to handle myriad challenges for our clients. Some involve positive advances: formation of new businesses, mergers, home purchases and sales, construction of new structures, widening of familial or personal relationships, resolution of lingering conflicts. Others involve losses: money, status, security, control, liberty, property, custody, shelter, relationships. Many legal matters involve analysis of complex rules or regulations and interpretation of standards, judicial opinions, or policies. Our jobs can be stressful, and often the "best" strategy or the "right" answer is unclear. For some of us, this lack of clarity can ignite stress and anxiety, and the fear of making a mistake can be palpable. As the earlier chapters of this book highlight, law schools traditionally have not spent enough time preparing junior attorneys for this reality or building resilience in decision-making. Having worked in three law firms—medium-sized, BigLaw, and small—and struggling with the fear of making a mistake in high-stakes multimillion-dollar construction contract disputes, I can attest that the fear is genuine for many of us. I believe the profession can do a better job of preparing new attorneys to untangle fear. This process starts with acknowledging its presence out loud.

Instead of promoting a bravado or "rite of passage" mind-set, we can begin to say to our newest advocates, "We understand that some lawyering activities are going to be more intimidating for some of you than others. That does not mean you are not cut out for this work or that you don't deserve to be here." And then—of course being mindful of obvious economic pressures surrounding billable hours—we can provide substantive, procedural, practical, and tactical guidance to help our new lawyers navigate fear-inducing lawyering scenarios. We can arm them with more robust context and techniques for reducing the mental and physical manifestations of fear.

Some law practice managers who have been practicing law for a long time may resist this concept or think it is unnecessary or a distraction, as our "survival of the fittest" approach to associate training seems to work just fine. I urge our law office leaders and mentors to please be open-minded. It only takes one person to change the entire trajectory of a young lawyer's career by saying to a fearful junior attorney, "It's okay. There are ways to untangle this fear, and you can do this." From a personal growth standpoint, we also might consider whether any such resistance might stem from our own (understandable) reluctance to untangle complicated emotions in the legal arena. As Randall Kiser suggests, "Lawyers lacking in 'soft skills' tend to devalue their importance rather than address their absence."[847] Similarly, sports psychologist Bob Rotella notes, "[T]here are coaches out there who think that developing an athlete means only criticizing him. There's some ego and insecurity attached to this."[848]

Justice Robert R. Thomas of the Supreme Court of Illinois offers a wonderful response to the notion that talking about emotions and vulnerabilities is a bad idea for our profession:

> *Over the years, I have heard many in the profession say that openly acknowledging our vulnerabilities by publishing articles and offering programs like the lawyer assistance programs paints a bad image of the legal profession—that openly acknowledging our vulnerabilities sends the wrong message to the public, or, even worse, confirms the public's worst assumptions about lawyers. I could not disagree more. Openly acknowledging our vulnerabilities is an essential first step to addressing our collective issues, and only by addressing those issues will the legal profession remain*

strong. Pretending that our problems do not exist does not make those problems go away. As the lawyer assistance programs clearly understand, our paramount concern must be with the health of the profession, not with the image of the profession.[849]

One law student has expressed a similar view about openness, stating, "Mental health is difficult to talk about and often seen as taboo, so creating a standard where it is acceptable to openly talk about and recognize weaknesses could help to turn those into strengths."

Conversely, reinforcing messages of "just do it," "fake it till you make it," or "just do what scares you" is detrimental to the future health of our profession. Instead, we should acknowledge the reality of fear and mistake-making in the practice of law. Then we should provide our new advocates with resources for untangling fear and developing fortitude to ask questions, seek guidance, make wise choices, and ultimately take ownership of their decisions.

Traditionally, our profession has shied away from conversations about the raw and genuine emotions and feelings that affect many of us in our everyday law practice. As authors and legal ethics experts Judith Rush and Pat Burns describe, "[T]he legal profession's culture tends to discourage open dialogue about how we feel and what we believe."[850] Indeed, "[a]s law students and lawyers, we wear our dysfunction as a badge."[851]

A better, more brave approach is to address head-on—and as a community—the difficult emotions that affect many of us in our law practice. If we do not, we simply reinforce hierarchy, exclusion, and lack of empathy, compassion, and civility toward our own colleagues. In my career spanning over 20 years working in three different law firms, I witnessed and experienced incivility certainly outside, but even inside the firm. The most harmful instrument of incivility—which I shrugged off for many years because I thought such behavior "came with the territory"—was certain partners' gruff treatment of associates (or staff) whom they deemed "weak" or "not aggressive or decisive enough." Training through fear or intimidation is not the right way to cultivate wise and self-assured decision-making and get the best out of the future leaders of our profession. Of course, many law firms do not suffer this problem and are able to maintain standards of excellence while also fostering healthy and inclusive work environments, forged by great leadership. Nonetheless, as a community, we can all pay more attention to how fear—derived from a variety of sources—affects our new lawyers. Let's dive deeper into helping peel back the layers of any unnecessary obstacles standing in the way of excellent advocacy and healthy advocates.

Benjamin Sells, author of *The Soul of the Law*, warns that "[t]he soul of the law is suffering."[852] He further reports that "[l]awyers in today's world are lonely, painfully lonely."[853] Sells offers an interesting perspective on the "disturbing rise in incivility among lawyers."[854] He says, "*Incivility is a love disorder, not a result of working too many hours.*"[855] Sells explains that the term "civility" derives from words related to "citizenship" and "members of a household."[856] He suggests that "[i]mposed obedience cannot rekindle the capacity to love. Rather, incivility itself might be pointing the way by directing the Law to citizenship and householding, both of which require attention, caring, and interest more than anything else."[857] An open discussion of fear in lawyering presents a tremendous opportunity for us to think about "citizenship and householding"—in our firms, offices, and bar associations. Instead of "imposing obedience" and allegiance by junior attorneys to the traditional markers of how a "good and successful lawyer should act," let's direct more focused attention to the health of our "households."

Even on a more individual basis as one-on-one mentors, we can reframe how we view success. In *The Compassionate Achiever: How Helping Others Fuels Success*, Christopher L. Kukk uses the term "compassionate achievers" to describe "people who achieve success by helping others."[858] He explains how "[s]ome companies consider 'nice' a four-letter word and are encouraging their employees to practice 'radical candor' or 'front-stabbing' and to be as critical as they want."[859] But this "[i]ncivility causes stress."[860]

Likewise, Dana Ardi, author of *The Fall of the Alphas: The New Beta Way to Connect, Collaborate, Influence—and Lead*, distinguishes between alpha leaders, who are "centralized and hierarchical," and beta leaders, who are "decentralized, horizontal, and inclusive."[861] Beta leaders "influence rather than intimidate."[862] Obviously, in the law firm environment, we have certain hierarchies that make sense from an economic and developmental standpoint: junior and senior associates, junior and senior partners, and so on. But in thinking about professional development overall, if we regard certain colleagues as weak or "less than" because they experience emotion or trepidation with respect to a new or unfamiliar lawyering activity, or struggle in a certain area, aren't we just reinforcing an *unhealthy* elitism? Could we eliminate this catalyst of division by offering a hand instead? Ardi urges that "[p]ractically and symbolically, elitism must be eliminated as much as possible for an organization to succeed and thrive."[863] She emphasizes that "Alpha organizations are by their very nature elitist. In fact, the Alpha concept is predicated on the notion that one person, or several individuals, happens to be better than everyone else in the organization."[864]

In one of the law firms where I worked, fear was a daily menu item. What if it hadn't been? How much more work could the associates have accomplished? How many more hours a week or a month might we have *wanted* to linger at our desks, or in the conference room surrounded by deposition exhibits, or in a warehouse full of documents figuring out a client's challenge? How much more creative might we have been in our research, our problem solving, our writing? Ardi asks, "What fosters [creativity]? Collaboration and freedom from distraction. Not surprisingly, happy employees are far more creative than fearful employees."[865]

So how do we do this? It's simple, actually. By openly acknowledging the reality of fear and mistake-making in the practice of law, we get it out on the table. We say to summer associates and junior attorneys, "This is going to be scarier for some of you than for others. That's okay. It doesn't mean you don't deserve to be here. You can do this." And then we provide substantive, tactical, mental, and physical training to unplug the unhealthy agents of fear in our profession.

PROFESSIONAL IDENTITY DEVELOPMENT

As lawyers transition from law school to practice, or make lateral moves within the profession, law practice managers who are committed to employees' professional development might encourage new hires to learn more about themselves and their personality characteristics, traits, and strengths. This could include assessments such as the Myers-Briggs Type Indicator Assessment,[866] the VARK Learning Style Questionnaire,[867] Emotional Intelligence assessments,[868] the 16 Personalities Assessment,[869] CliftonStrengths,[870] and other measures that focus specifically on character, such as the Values in Action Inventory of Strengths (VIA-IS). As mentioned in Appendix B, the VIA-IS is a 240-question survey. It asks participants to react to 10 statements affiliated with 24 character strengths identified by positive psychologists Christopher Peterson and Martin E. P. Seligman. These 24 traits "reside within the six virtues of wisdom and knowledge, courage, humanity, justice, temperance and transcendence."[871] There is also a truncated 24-item rendition of the VIA-IS called the Brief Strengths Test.

Regarding character in the lawyering context, Patricia Snyder, a candidate for the master of applied positive psychology degree at the University of Pennsylvania, used the VIA-IS to conduct a study entitled "Super Women Lawyers: A Study of Character Strengths."[872] The study noted that a "cited avenue for bravery was having the courage to admit a mistake made in trial."[873] As described in more detail in Appendix B, the study provides a useful summary of the relationship between character and lawyering mistakes. Using a character assessment like VIA-IS (and perhaps Snyder's article) in a law office professional development program might serve as a starting point for conversations with junior attorneys about courage, bravery, and realistic fear, as well as preventing, making, and handling mistakes in lawyering.

ENCOURAGING JUNIOR ATTORNEYS TO IDENTIFY AND NAME FEARS ABOUT PARTICULAR LAWYERING SCENARIOS

Some junior attorneys who are stepping into particular lawyering scenarios for the first time—such as negotiations, depositions, client interaction, and courtroom work—are going to be fearful. It is not helpful to tell them to "Just do it!" or "Face your fears!" or "Never let them see you sweat!" or "Fake it till you make it!" Such directives merely prompt fearful individuals to bury and repress the emotion again. The destructive fear doesn't go away. It just bides its time for eruption at a later date, in a more pronounced and damaging way.

If we care about developing and retaining our junior lawyers, helping our law offices thrive at the highest level, or cultivating a healthier profession, we must stop, take a moment, and say, "Oh. Okay. Right, this is new for you. It's completely understandable to be afraid. Good, now let's talk it through." The billable work can wait for five minutes, ten minutes, even a half hour, while we take the time to understand what is really driving this junior attorney's fear. Is it fear of not understanding a confusing substantive or procedural rule? Many times, it is not the substance or the procedure. Rather, it is the fear of the unknown: where to sit or stand in a conference room or courtroom, what to do if opposing counsel behaves badly, how to handle unpredictable tactical maneuvers, how to know if we are being manipulated by seasoned counsel on the other side. We don't expose students to these conundrums (at least not enough) in law school. The unknown can be scary, and can rattle even the most hardworking, intelligent, and substantively prepared individuals. Sometimes, experienced lawyers forget that the jobs of junior attorneys require mastery of a new legal language and unfamiliar rules of engagement. Taking even a few moments to provide more context goes a long way.

Law offices can invite this type of dialogue on a firm-wide basis, perhaps at the very first "new lawyer orientation" each year, or periodically during lunchtime workshops. The message can be: "We understand that some lawyering scenarios are going to be scarier for some of you than for others. That is okay. You deserve to be here. Now let's talk through the tricky parts." Forward-thinking and inclusive law firm leaders will not minimize the fear, but instead will acknowledge it, encourage junior attorneys to *name* exactly what aspects of the lawyering activity they are afraid of, and then provide more context to explain the unknown.

ENCOURAGING JUNIOR ATTORNEYS TO ASK QUESTIONS ABOUT CONFUSING OR UNCLEAR ASPECTS OF LAW PRACTICE

Many junior lawyers are afraid of making mistakes. But they are often more fearful of appearing incompetent or unworthy of their position by asking the very question that could help avoid a costly or even catastrophic mistake. Law office leaders can cultivate a training environment in which they are transparent about the potential for legal errors and also encourage junior attorneys to ask questions about confusing or complex substantive, procedural, strategic, or tactical aspects of the law practice—with the collective goal of avoiding mistakes. This type of interaction can occur in a one-on-one supervisor-mentee dynamic, or on a broader office-wide level. Law office leaders might consider offering workshops to identify mistakes commonly made by attorneys in the particular area of practice, not from a fear-stoking standpoint emphasizing catastrophic errors, but instead explaining practical protocols to avoid missteps. The most important goal is to foster an environment in which new attorneys can ask questions without feeling ignorant. Junior lawyers can build confidence in making decisions based on full and complete information or, if thorough information is not realistically available, making decisions in a more robustly informed manner.

Law office leaders could structure workshops or discussions around a range of real-life scenarios in which a junior lawyer is unsure about a substantive or procedural aspect of a client matter and must ask for guidance from someone in the law office. Here are five example scenarios.

- The junior attorney has read (several times) the procedural rules for how to construct the appendix for an appellate brief for submission to the New York Supreme Court Appellate Division, and the timing requirements. She has reviewed five or six legal blogs trying to seek clarity, all of which expressly acknowledge how *unclear* the rules are. Yet, she is still not exactly sure how to "perfect the appeal."

- The junior attorney is researching grounds for recusal of a judge based on a perceived conflict of interest but cannot find a single case on point in the pertinent jurisdiction. The deadline for the draft motion for recusal is looming.

- A senior partner assigned the junior attorney the task of negotiating a Federal Rule of Civil Procedure 26(f)(2) Joint Proposed Discovery and Trial Plan with opposing counsel. The junior attorney has never negotiated such a plan. The supervising attorney advised simply, "If opposing counsel wants trial in two years, you want it in six months. If the other side wants trial in six months, you want it in two years." The associate is nervous about how to approach the negotiation.

- A junior attorney is taking her first deposition of a witness in a case involving multiple defendants. Four defense lawyers present at the deposition are being disruptive. The junior attorney is not sure how to handle or rein in the disruption. The only advice received from the senior partner before the deposition was "Just make sure you get everything you need from this witness."

- A junior attorney filed a motion for Federal Rule of Civil Procedure 11 sanctions against opposing counsel (for wrongfully accusing the attorney's trial team of bill-padding a request for attorneys' fees after winning the case on summary judgment). The junior attorney must go to court to deliver the oral argument before a judge who has a reputation for being abrupt with lawyers.

In these workshops, senior and junior lawyers can talk openly about how circumstances or quandaries like these often present themselves, even if the junior attorney is organized, prepared, and working diligently. The answer or "right" approach is not always clear. Participants could discuss a realistic protocol for approaching a more senior attorney in the law office for guidance in how to work through a confusing legal problem or a challenging situation.

Law office managers also might consider inviting attorneys from different areas of, and levels of seniority in, practice to attend workshops and share instances when they were afraid to step into a lawyering task. Coordinators of such presentations should be careful to avoid choosing attorneys who take a bravado or "rite of passage" approach to fear, but instead should endeavor to invite lawyers who are empathetic, open, and honest in sharing their personal hurdles in lawyering.

PROVIDING APPROPRIATE GUIDANCE ON HOW TO HANDLE MISTAKES

Although the initial response to the question "What should a junior associate do upon discovery of a mistake?" might be "Own up to it," we need to provide realistic guidance for new attorneys on how exactly to do that. It's obviously scary to report or admit a potential or actual mistake to a supervising attorney. Saying "Just face your fears" isn't enough to help a junior attorney do the "right thing." Instead, we can provide more context (and this should start in law school, as explored in Appendix B). Indeed, during new-attorney orientations or periodic workshops, professional development leaders can overtly acknowledge the concept of mistake-making in lawyering (perhaps using some of the quotes from lawyers and judges in Chapter 4). Notably, as mentioned in Appendix B, in 2017, the law firm of Pillsbury Winthrop Shaw Pittman LLP convened its annual First-Year Associate Conference. One of the creative and forward-thinking sessions involved small-group discussions divided into Litigation and Transactional-Regulatory breakout groups. The theme was "Post-Mortem of a Mistake: What Happened, Lessons Learned, How to Move Forward, and Q&A." Some seasoned lawyers might balk at the idea of talking about mistakes, as if such a discussion might suggest that mistake-making is fine. Obviously, the collective goal is to avoid and avert lawyering mistakes. But we must arm our junior attorneys with appropriate guidance on how to prevent errors and also how to properly handle mistakes when they happen. As discussed in Chapter 4, mistakes occur in our complicated practice of law even after the exercise of the utmost diligence.

Perhaps with the collaboration of good "teachers" from law-related insurance providers, law practice mentors and junior attorneys could jointly develop and adopt a mistake-handling protocol. This could include tangible steps such as

- bringing a perceived error to the attention of an appropriate supervisor, mentor, or designated law office ethics advisor
- identifying the appropriate corrective action (including whether client notification is required or appropriate)
- reflecting (individually and collectively), and
- implementing change to deter similar mistakes in the future[874]

In this regard, it will be helpful to provide junior attorneys with emotional, mental, and physical strategies (such as the techniques offered in Chapters 15 and 16) for approaching an unpredictable supervisor about a perceived mistake. Discussion could start with hypothetical scenarios in which a junior attorney is concerned that a mistake was made and needs to bring it to the attention of an intimidating supervisor. Here are a few example scenarios.

- A junior associate wrote a brief, which the senior partner signed and filed. Later, the associate realized that a case she cited in the brief had been vacated in part, on the very issue for which she cited the case. She thought she had KeyCited the case originally, and Westlaw had shown no adverse action.

- A junior associate tasked with editing and redlining an 80-page draft contract based on negotiations with opposing counsel realized that the final executed version of the contract contains an earlier version of a contract provision that is less favorable to the client. The associate, who thought he had checked all the Tracked Changes in the last version that came back from opposing counsel, later realized that he apparently missed one provision buried in a sea of final changes.

- A California-based junior associate working on his first case before the U.S. District Court for the Eastern District of Virginia was unaware that the deadline for serving objections to discovery requests was 15 days earlier than the usual deadline for discovery objections in federal courts (E.D.Va. Local Rule 26(C) differs from the 30-day deadline in FRCP 33(b)(2)). He missed the deadline for serving objections to interrogatories and is afraid he has waived the right to object.

- A junior associate asked her assistant to forward a draft pleading to the client for review. The assistant emailed the document to opposing counsel by accident, as the names sound similar. The document contained attorney-client privileged communications.

- While a junior attorney was defending a deposition, opposing counsel placed an exhibit in front of the deponent that was clearly attorney-client privileged but somehow had been produced by the junior attorney's firm in discovery, as evidenced by the Bates number. The junior attorney was part of the document review team that performed the privilege review and is certain he pulled the document from the production; however, there may have been other copies. The associate is worried about how the partner managing the case will react.

Professional development leaders might consider inviting positive, encouraging speakers from attorney malpractice insurance companies to provide more information—in a nonintimidating but rather an informative way—on how malpractice insurance works, what types of mistakes are manageable with simple remedial steps, those that are more grievous, and the proper protocol in different office environments for handling attorney errors.

PROVIDING GUIDANCE FOR IDENTIFYING AND ADDRESSING CLIENT FEARS

Forward-thinking law office leaders also can consider providing appropriate training for junior attorneys in how to recognize and address *client* fears in the context of relevant practice areas. Drawing on the information provided in

Chapter 3 regarding the types of fears that clients experience in specific legal scenarios, and the advice in Appendix D on perceiving and handling client fears, law practice leaders could convene training sessions to discuss and simulate techniques for identifying and then communicating with clients about fears within the legal process.

FINDING THE RIGHT RESOURCES TO HELP JUNIOR ATTORNEYS WHO OPEN UP ABOUT FEAR

As law practice leaders, we need to be prepared for and open to conversations with courageous junior associates who come forward and confide their fears to us. As author Kristen Ulmer points out, when an individual comes to us and says "I feel afraid," we must remember that "the only appropriate response is either to ask a clarifying question or offer a simple, genuine 'That's great'"—focusing on the growth opportunity and offering collaboration to find solutions and answers.[875] Even if we have the best intentions in trying to motivate a junior attorney to push through or overcome the fear, we cannot minimize the person's worries with routine advice like, "Fake it till you make it," "Just do what scares you," or "There's nothing to be afraid of"—all of which have the unintended but undesired opposite consequence of prodding scared individuals to bury their fears further.[876] We need to make sure we *listen* to and *hear* the individual opening up to us. It is perfectly fine if we personally are not armed with the immediate solution; we can be the one to link the junior attorney up with someone who can provide concrete strategies and techniques.

Amy Florian, CEO of a training company called Corgenius (whose tagline is "Adding heart to the brains of business") shares similar advice when describing how she coaches financial professionals to interact with fearful clients.[877] She describes the importance of not trying to talk a person out of fear but instead "acknowledg[ing] it as if it were well founded."[878] She explains:

> *It is a mistake to try to talk your clients out of being afraid, even when you have compelling evidence of their safety. They first need to tell you about their fears until they are sure you have heard and understood. They need you to acknowledge their fears as valid, whether or not you believe they are. They need to work together with you on solutions rather than having you dominate the conversation with defenses and arguments. Only when your clients believe you have listened well enough to comprehend their fears can you work to find strategies to help them feel safe.*[879]

The same principles apply to our next generation of attorneys. As Florian advises, "Rather than dismissing their fears or trying to talk them out of them, [we can] make the time to hear and understand them. [We] take their fears seriously and help develop effective strategies for coping with them."[880] By cultivating not just empathy but also *compassion* for our newest cadre of lawyers, we can help them become prominent change makers in our profession.

Author Christopher L. Kukk defines compassion as "a holistic understanding of a problem or the suffering of another with a commitment to act to solve the problem or alleviate the suffering."[881] He differentiates between empathy and compassion, indicating that the latter "involves understanding *and acting*, but empathy is singular in purpose: to emotionally absorb the feeling of another."[882] Being compassionate toward our fearful junior attorneys will not decrease the intellectual rigor of our professional development experience; instead, it will allow *more* junior attorneys to thrive and excel. For junior advocates who come to us seeking advice regarding lawyering fears or how to avoid mistakes, we can adopt Kukk's protocol: Listen, Understand, Connect, Act.[883] We must *listen*[884] to and really *hear* the individual. We can ask questions to find out more and *understand*.[885] Kukk indicates that impactful "questions of compassion diminish the sense of loneliness that people feel while also helping them to look simultaneously inward and outward for strength and answers."[886] Through listening to and striving to understand our junior lawyers—even if we personally never experienced their particular fears—we can forge deeper *connections* with them, and identify realistic and helpful *solutions* to help them untangle the fear. If we are not the "right" person with tangible and concrete answers, we can take *action* by linking them with someone who can lead them to useful resources.

Great law firm leaders nurture, attract, and retain creative problem-solving lawyers. Ed Catmull, co-founder of Pixar Animation Studios and longtime president of Pixar Animation and Disney Animation, warns about the relationship between a fear culture and a lack of creativity. He says, "In a fear-based, failure-averse culture, people will consciously or unconsciously avoid risk. They will seek instead to repeat something safe that's been good enough in the past. Their work will be derivative, not innovative. But if you can foster a positive understanding of failure, the opposite will happen."[887] He suggests that the objective "is to uncouple fear and failure—to create an environment in which making mistakes doesn't strike terror into your employees' hearts."[888] By working to reduce the fears associated with mistake-making and failure in lawyering, law offices can foster creativity and innovative problem-solving.

Finally, we can support our junior lawyers by encouraging them to develop small "Untangling Fear" groups, plan their own professional development workshops, and encourage one another through collaboration.

By adopting some of the foregoing strategies in the law office environment, we can decrease and hopefully eliminate the stigma of fear in lawyering. We can honor the reality of fear and mistake-making in law practice, and help our junior attorneys become better equipped to handle the rigors of practice and lead heathier professional and personal lives.

> *Money follows ideas, not fears.*
> —Dr. Richard Keeling

Appendix D
Practical Strategies for Helping Clients Untangle Fears

As we explored in Chapter 3, clients can experience a gamut of fears with respect to the many twists and turns of our legal system, whether the clients are individuals navigating a divorce, a custody issue, a contract dispute, a criminal charge, a business formation, or a negotiation, or even if they are experienced corporate players with a lot on the line. Because traditional legal education does not always provide sufficient focus on or insights into the emotional aspects of client representation, many of us initially might feel ill equipped to recognize and ultimately handle intense client emotions such as fear. However, with enhanced awareness of how emotions manifest in ourselves and others, we can make impactful changes in the way we interact with clients, and begin to reduce and hopefully eliminate their fears. Through doing so, we will build trust, open deeper channels of communication, and enable more effective representation.

Some legal educators and practitioners might worry about lawyers "playing psychologist." Yet as Professor Jeffrey Lipshaw writes, "I agree . . . that lawyers cannot treat their clients' psychological problems. I do not, however, see that as a reason why lawyers should not try to understand how their own psychology aids or impairs the counseling process, just as some psychoanalysts seem to do. Or why law schools should not provide nascent lawyers some means for doing so."[889] Indeed, as Professor Barbara Glesner Fines and attorney Cathy Madsen note, to do our jobs most effectively, "attorneys must be especially knowledgeable and skilled in dealing with human emotions."[890] This starts with just a few simple steps. We can

- Acknowledge the role that our clients' fears (and our own) may play in hindering open communication.
- Look for emotional and physical signals in the client to discern the presence of fear.

- Take the time to address, and invite a dialogue with the client about, the concept of fear *before* diving into the substantive and procedural nuances of the legal problem.
- Ask questions.
- *Listen* to the answers.
- Provide deeper context about the substance, purpose, and logistics of lawyering scenarios.
- Explain unfamiliar terminology and procedures.
- Be flexible, be creative, and be prepared to provide ideas and insights about potential nonlegal aspects of the resolution of the conflict or the nature of the transaction.

OPENLY ACKNOWLEDGE THE ROLE OF FEAR IN BLOCKING COMMUNICATION

Chapter 3 digs into the reality that fear can hinder the open flow of communication between a client and legal counsel. It's up to us to help untangle, and *name*, such fears so that the client can feel comfortable trusting us. Part II of this book explores the science of fear and how this particular emotion impacts our brains and bodies. Lawyers can prepare to address client fears by knowing what to look for in clients' emotional and physical behavior. Remember from Chapter 5, once the amygdala takes over and the instinctive fear response kicks in—perhaps at the beginning of an initial client meeting—the client may shift to "automatic pilot." The client may be completely unaware that a rush of hormones and the "fight or flight" self-protective response have effectively "hijacked" the thinking brain. Clients, particularly if they are new to the legal system, may experience anxiety, confusion, embarrassment, guilt, shame, and perhaps even "trauma recall," possibly manifesting in fear; all of this "may significantly inhibit the flow of information between attorney and client."[891] As psychologist Stephanie Sogg and attorney Wilton Sogg emphasize, "when people are in emotional distress, their ability to hear and make use of information and directives is often sharply limited."[892]

In an initial client encounter, we can take just a few moments to observe and perceive any possibly self-protective or reactive physical responses. Is the client crossing limbs, turning away, hunching shoulders, protecting the face or eyes (with a hand, hair, a scarf, or a hat), averting eye contact, shaking, or tapping feet? Is the client clicking a pen repeatedly, fiddling with an object, or crinkling paper? Fear might reveal itself through resistance to talking, misplaced anger or annoyance, aggressiveness, defensiveness, or even tears. The first step for us as lawyers is to take a minute to try to recognize whether any of these potential indicators are present, and then be present ourselves. Are we showing emotional and physical *openness*, or are we closed off, resistant, pushy, or domineering?

Taking a few minutes to talk about the presence of fear, rather than barreling into the substance and procedure of the client's representation, can go a long way toward helping the client interrupt the automatic "fight or flight" chain reaction and regain control over the thinking mind. Attorney J. Mark Weiss emphasizes that, "[a]s client counselors, lawyers can even help clients learn how to take steps to pause and modulate their reactivity by re-engaging the rational thinking part of their brains."[893]

Acknowledging the presence of fear, and then pausing to explain "the interviewing process and the roles the participants must play" can help "make the attorney-client relationship open and productive."[894] Indeed, if we do *not* take the time to discern whether fears or other emotions might be blocking our clients' willingness to open up to us, we cannot do our jobs most effectively. As Professor Susan Salmon writes, "We cannot deliver accurate, clear, effective advocacy for a client without listening carefully to our client's version of the facts, or without understanding our client's fears, goals, and desires."[895]

ASK A FEW QUESTIONS

Before stepping into the substance and procedure of the client meeting, we can consider asking a few questions to invite the client to open up about fears, concerns, or worries. We can't assume we know what the client is thinking. We need to ask: "What are [your] concerns and fears? How can I address those concerns and fears in ways that will be helpful to [you]?"[896] The answers need to come from the client, not our assumptions. As professional counselor R. Hal Ritter Jr. and Professor Patricia Wilson advise, it really can be as simple as asking, "'What are your fears about this issue? What concerns do you have?' And then, *listen!*"[897] Our clients might surprise us.

Amy Florian, who advises financial professionals on how to interact with scared clients, suggests using a "fear assessment"[898] following these steps:

- "Introduce the topic" of fear, with a prompt like, "You probably have some fears, too. Let's see if we can get them out on the table. Then we'll deal with them together so they don't cost you sleep at night."[899]
- "Get them talking freely."[900]
- "Take notes as they talk."[901]
- "Allow silence as they think."[902]
- "Read the list back to them so they can clarify any point or add others."[903]

- "Ask them to prioritize" their fears, noting the "most important or disturbing."[904]
- "Help them imagine solutions."[905]
- "Create a two-column table" listing fears on one side and strategies to address them on the other.[906]
- Schedule a "fear and concern check-in" at a follow-up meeting.[907]

LISTEN

Professor Jennifer Murphy Romig of Emory University School of Law launched a helpful blog called *Listen Like a Lawyer*. She underscores this mission:

> *This blog will explore the theory and practice of effective listening, and how lawyers, law students, and just about everyone involved in the practice of law can benefit from working on their listening. Effective listening provides a distinct advantage to anyone whose job involves communication—a description that certainly fits lawyers.*[908]

When our clients speak, we need to really focus on what they are saying, rather than skipping ahead to how we want to respond. Ritter and Wilson indicate that "*[r]apport* means to listen carefully to the client's fears and to allow the client the freedom to talk about those fears."[909] Let's get the client talking. Let's make eye contact, lean in, and pay attention. Note-taking may heighten some clients' anxiety. In an effort to alleviate clients' concerns, we can ask, "Hey, is it okay if I take some notes so I can follow up with some questions?"

As part of the listening process, attorney G. Nicholas Herman and Professor Jean M. Cary recommend using "the communication facilitators of (1) conveying empathetic understanding for your client's difficult situation, (2) engaging in active listening by non-judgmentally accepting and acknowledging her uncomfortable feelings, and (3) encouraging her to communicate by explaining the need for full information and by expressing recognition for her forthright disclosures."[910] Professors Stefan H. Krieger and Richard K. Neumann Jr. provide similar advice:

> *[L]isten, patiently and attentively, to the client's description of the most painful parts of the situation. Listen with care to anything the client says about the emotional aspect. . . . Try to understand, and let your tone and body language imply that you consider the emotional aspect important and are trying to understand. . . . [A]lthough you cannot honestly guarantee to solve the problem, your commitment to do the best you can may introduce hope.*[911]

One law student shared his perception of how lawyers can be more effective during the client intake process:

> Each person is unique with different wants and needs. It's important to try to adapt to the situation and observe a person's body language, tone, and expression. If you are a law student performing a client intake, try to do your best to show empathy. It may seem easier to read off a paper and to follow each step of an intake process in a robotic fashion, but this may only aggravate a client's anxiety. If a client derails, let them speak their mind and use your best judgment to ease them back on track.

This listening phase, which is essentially important, can be accomplished effectively even in a limited amount of time. As Sogg and Sogg note, "After spending a brief time listening to your client's fears and frustrations, you can then shift into the services that you were trained to provide, namely the giving of explicit technical advice about the best ways to solve this particular problem."[912]

RESPOND IN A LANGUAGE THE CLIENT CAN UNDERSTAND

Even though—as lawyers—we become fluent in legal lingo and procedural terminology, sometimes we forget that our clients may not know basic legal language, abbreviations, and acronyms. As one law student noted in reflecting on her judicial internship and how some courtroom lawyers interacted with clients and witnesses:

> *As lawyers, it is our job to use our analytical skills to benefit those that become overwhelmed and confused by how intimidating other attorneys and complicated bodies of law are. A major part of this includes being considerate of those who come from different educational and professional backgrounds. As lawyers surrounded by other lawyers, it can be easy to take a universal understanding of law for granted. It is important to remember that most clients are not fluent in legalese and that breaking down the law and explaining its components can go a long way in making others comfortable.*

It's our duty as legal advisors to monitor the technical words and phrases we use to make sure we are communicating understandably with our clients. Each year when I teach a new group of first-year law students, I catch myself using abbreviations like MSJ (for motion for summary judgment) or "depo" (for deposition). I see perplexed faces and remind myself once again that I need to take a step back and explain the unfamiliar terms, building my students' new legal vocabulary. Also, while teaching a summer legal writing course in Italy—in English—I had to be mindful that, even though the Italian students had a tremendous command of the English language (much better than my Italian), Americans tend to speak quickly, often use slang and contractions, and do not always enunciate clearly. I slowed down and emphasized clear nouns and verbs. I elongated abbreviations. If I saw confused looks on their faces, I offered alternate synonyms for legal terms (e.g., *judgment* means the court's decision, or the result in the case). We should do the same for our clients.

As clinical professor Philip M. Genty notes, "The attorney must accompany the client into a strange region with its own language and cultural customs and must bring the client through the experience safely."[913] Quoting a survey of parents who had endured the legal process of divorce, Fines and Madsen reported that those clients yearned for "information and guidelines about what to expect from the legal process, and wanted their attorneys to serve as 'interpreters' of the system's unfamiliar language and procedures."[914] In addition to our role as counselors of law, we must serve as translators and decoders.

DO NOT MINIMIZE THE CLIENT'S FEAR

As Chapter 6 discusses, our American approach to fear tends to reinforce bravado messages: "Just do it!" or "Face your fears!" or "Just do what scares you!" or "There's nothing to be afraid of!" Unfortunately, these messages are often ineffective, and can further undermine a person experiencing fear. Minimizing fear serves only to prompt a scared person to repress and bury the harmful emotion once again—unaddressed. As attorneys, even if we personally do not really understand the client's fear and feel certain that the client has little to worry about, we cannot simply tell the client that the fears are unfounded. Instead, we can help the client untangle the fear and move through it.

In writing about how to counsel doctors being sued for malpractice, authors Morris L. Jensby, Michelle S. Putvin, and Mark A. Basurto advise that a lawyer "must help the medical provider identify what he or she is angry about, what he or she is afraid of, or both."[915] They point out how "[i]t is easy to say to your client, 'Don't Worry,' but that is typically not effective. Instead you can guide the client to deconstruct the problem. . . ."[916] Asking questions, listening to the answers, and getting the clients' fears out of their heads and possibly even down on paper, is a much more effective strategy for helping the client navigate through fear toward solutions.

ACKNOWLEDGE ANGER

As the late Anthony Bourdain once said, "Frightened people become angry people—as history teaches us again and again."[917] During U2's 2018 eXPERI-ENCE + iNNOCENCE Tour, Bono repeated several times, "Fear and anger: same thing." If we notice anger bubbling up in our clients, instead of getting defensive and instinctively reacting angrily ourselves, let's take a step back and consider whether the ire is really based in fear, or insecurity. As Ritter and Wilson point out, "[W]e have to be in *relationship* with these angry people. It is not a time to be demanding, controlling, or judging. By accepting clients with all of the anger, we help them accept the anger for themselves."[918]

NOTE AND ADDRESS THE REALITY OF SOME CLIENTS' MISTRUST OF THE LEGAL SYSTEM

It's very possible that, based on past experiences, a client harbors a deep mistrust of the legal system. Unfortunately, we may *represent* or *embody* that very system in the client's mind. Genty encourages us to "look at the legal system through the client's eyes" so that we can "prepare the client for, and guide the client through, an encounter with that system."[919] He explains:

> *This is, of course, an exceedingly complicated role, for the lawyer is, at one time, both a part of the mistrusted legal system and the client's only practical means of gaining access to and results from that system. . . . The empathy skills involved in preparing a client for and taking the client through the fearful experience of a legal proceeding are therefore among the most difficult to master.*[920]

Having a candid conversation about a baseline lack of trust can help build a more open relationship and inspire greater client confidence in the attorney *before* they jointly engage with other players in the legal system.

Using representation of battered immigrant women as an example, domestic violence advocate Leslye E. Orloff, attorney Deeana Jang, and Professor Catherine F. Klein write:

> *Discussing these issues with [an immigrant] client, explaining the American legal system, and directly addressing client fears and misconceptions can dramatically affect the quality of the battered immigrant client's testimony in court. When left unaddressed, the client's fears about the court process can cause her testimony, however truthful it may be, to sound tentative and less credible.*[921]

Wary clients need to be reassured that we are their advocates and champions, even though cultivating that faith and trust may take time.

PROVIDE HELPFUL CONTEXT

As attorney and psychologist Lisa Blue and attorney Robert B. Hirschhorn point out, "One way to address [a client's] fears is by educating him."[922] We can do this—in a noncondescending and nonoverwhelming way—by providing information and context about the substance and procedure of each legal matter, and each lawyering step along the timeline of that matter. Family lawyer and mediator Lisa Fiance, of Epiphany Legal, shared some of her learnings:

> In my experience, most family law attorneys simply tell clients, "Don't worry, I've got this" and then don't share much other information. While that may be reassuring to some clients, I personally find that being told not to worry doesn't actually keep me from worrying. As an attorney, I tend to err on the other side, sharing a LOT of information about my legal strategy with my client so they know exactly what to expect. That approach, however, can become emotionally overwhelming for some clients. Balancing how much detail to share with how much you act as a buffer for your client is a difficult tightrope to walk that differs for each case.

Even basic logistical details that we might think are unimportant or too obvious to require explanation can be hugely helpful and reassuring to a client. Using an upcoming deposition as an example, we can explain to a client how a deposition works, how many people will be present, where the players sit, what the objections mean, how long the questioning will take, whether the parties take breaks, and so on. As attorneys Kyle A. Lansberry and J. Robert Turnipseed explain, "[T]he ultimate goal in preparing a client for a deposition is to ease the burdens and anxieties confronting him so that he can focus on the substance of his answers. The client must be calm enough to understand the questions and respond appropriately."[923] Thus, "a primary goal of preparation is the reduction of a client's anxiety so that the client can promote a sense of confidence during his deposition."[924] In addition to the obviously necessary discussion about the facts and strategy of the case, the lawyer can assuage a deponent's fears by walking step by step through what actually happens in the deposition room. Often, it's the client's fear of the unknown that takes over. Lansberry and Turnipseed emphasize that "[t]hese fears often arise because the witness is uncertain or mistaken about what to expect during his deposition. A lawyer should be able to alleviate much of this fear by explaining to the client what the deposition will be like and exactly what is expected of him."[925] Indeed, "[t]he greater a client's awareness of the deposition process and counsel's expectations of the client, the less anxious the client will be during the deposition."[926]

This same approach applies to other lawyering activities like settlement negotiations or trial appearances. According to attorney Robert Aron, "A lawyer must also remember that many clients will be nervous and anxious about the prospect of appearing in court. Recognizing this apprehension will help the lawyer ease the client's fear. Arranging for a courtroom visit in advance of trial may also cut down the trauma."[927]

GAIN SKILLS IN HANDLING TRAUMATIZED CLIENTS

There is a growing body of literature encouraging the development of *trauma-informed* legal practice. Professors Sara E. Gold, Sarah Katz, and Deeya Haldar have written articles on this topic that are useful for lawyers who counsel clients in need of legal assistance *after* experiencing trauma or whose legal scenarios are *accompanied* by ongoing or past trauma. Gold emphasizes, "Because the client affected by trauma may feel confused or overwhelmed by the legal process, it is important that the lawyer be fully transparent with the client about the legal case in order to facilitate trust and minimize feelings of powerlessness."[928] Katz and Haldar indicate that "teaching trauma-informed practice in law school clinics furthers the goals of clinical teaching, and is a critical aspect of preparing law students for legal careers."[929] Dean Stacy Caplow and Interim Dean Maryellen Fullerton at Brooklyn Law School have introduced students to trauma-informed counseling; they invite experts from the Weill Cornell Center for Human Rights to talk to students working in the Safe Harbor Project (a clinic focusing on immigration issues), and students in a Refugee Law course, about treatment of trauma survivors.

Law offices that handle clients affected by trauma also might consider (if they are not already doing so) seeking advice from trauma experts on how to enhance lawyering skills specifically focused on this aspect of practice.

CONTINUE GETTING TO KNOW OURSELVES

In writing about a well-known mediator named Arnie Herz, former *ABA Journal* editor Steven Keeva described Herz as "remarkably skilled at helping clients get past their fear and the other emotions that distort their sense of what they really need. He can do this, he says, because he is ceaselessly engaged in the process of understanding his own mindsets and motivations. The process benefits both his clients and himself."[930] Keeva quoted Herz emphasizing the importance of really *listening* to our clients:

> *You have to identify and acknowledge any fear and/or anger or confusion that clients may be experiencing. When you do that, the relationship is totally transformed. They then know what it means to be heard, because you're seeing their true interests—which they rarely know they have—rather than a mixture of emotions that sets them off balance.*[931]

To be effective in this regard, we must get to know our *own* fears; otherwise, we will remain limited in our ability to recognize fears in others, especially if those fears are masked by other emotions. In undertaking this task, we will enhance our ability to draw out and address client fears, a mission which can be truly transformational in the attorney-client relationship. As attorney Edward D. Shapiro notes, "Each problem that a client brings through the door is an opportunity for both lawyer and client to let go of judgment, anger, bias, and other manifestations of fear that block the path to resolution and healing."[932] Instead of starting off a client relationship by jumping straight into the "typical" resolution of the legal quandary, we can "take our clients through a process that leads them to actually change, for example, that poorly worded hiring policy, or the ambiguous sales contract, the culture of the organization or the fear that exists within it."[933]

By honoring the reality of fear—in ourselves and in our clients—and working together to untangle our fear drivers, we can solve problems more creatively, improve our clients' relationships with us and others, and enhance well-being in our clients and ourselves.

Courage is what it takes to stand up and speak. Courage is also what it takes to sit down and listen.

—Winston Churchill

Appendix E
Suggested Topics for "Untangling Fear" Discussion Groups, Workshops, or Courses

SESSION #1: SOCIETAL MESSAGES/ STEREOTYPES ABOUT FEAR

- What societal messages or stereotypes do we often hear and absorb about fear?
  - Advertisements? Marketing?
  - Instagram memes?
  - T-shirt slogans?
- Do we hear any messages about fear from family members, coaches, other authority figures, classmates, colleagues, friends?
- What stereotypes are perpetuated about fear in lawyering?
- How do we internalize these messages or stereotypes?
- How do these messages or stereotypes affect our lawyer personas?
- Is it hard to be authentic or vulnerable about fear in lawyering?
- Homework Options:
  - Heidi K. Brown, "Turning the Fear of Lawyering into the Power of Advocacy," http://www.abajournal.com/magazine/article/fear_of_ lawyering (January 2018).
  - Preface and Introduction to *Untangling Fear in Lawyering* book.
  - Chapter 6: The Ineffectiveness of "Pro-Fear" Messages.

- ○ Notice and write down any fear messages/stereotypes encountered over the next week (in the news, on social media, on subway advertisements, in TV commercials, etc.).

SESSION #2: FEAR SCENARIOS IN LAWYERING; CHARACTER-IN-CONTEXT

- What lawyering activities spark fear in some of us? Why exactly? What precisely are we afraid of? Fear of failure? Judgment? Making mistakes?
- Do "good" lawyers ever make mistakes?
- Is it hard for us to admit that we are afraid in law school or law practice?
- Is it hard for us to admit that we made a mistake? If so, why? Do we feel fear? Guilt? Shame?
- Is it ever hard to communicate or talk about someone else's mistake? If so, why?
- What does it mean to have "character" as a lawyer?
- Is character in the context of lawyering learnable, or able to be further developed? Or is it something we either have or don't have?
- Homework Options:
  - ○ For law students: Chapter 1: Fear in Law Students
  - ○ For lawyers: Chapter 2: Fear in Lawyers
  - ○ Chapter 4: The Role of Fear in Mistake-Making
  - ○ Free "character strengths test" offered by the VIA Institute on Character, http://www.viacharacter.org/www/Character-Strengths-Survey
  - ○ Patricia Snyder, "Super Women Lawyers: A Study of Character Strengths," Arizona Summit Law Review 8 (Spring 2015): 261–315

SESSION #3: THE SCIENCE OF FEAR

- What happens to our bodies when we are afraid? What physical manifestations of fear do we individually experience (these likely will differ for each of us)? Shaking, sweating, blushing, heart racing, shortness of breath?
- What happens to the brain's ability to process information, or our ability to quickly respond to questions or form coherent sentences, when we are afraid?
- Does fear block our learning and performance? If so, how?

- Does fear sometimes mask itself in other emotions? Which emotions?
- Homework Options:
  - Chapter 5: The Science of Fear
  - Chapter 7: How Fear Blocks Learning and Performance
  - Chapter 8: How Fear Hides behind Other Unproductive Emotions

SESSION #4: DO OUR CLIENTS EXPERIENCE FEAR?

- How can fear (and other emotions) in our clients affect the attorney-client relationship?
- What is a lawyer's duty or responsibility with respect to identifying and addressing clients' emotions?
- Is a lawyer qualified to identify or address clients' emotions?
- Can we improve our skills at recognizing, and then untangling, clients' fears (and other emotions)?
- Homework Options:
  - Chapter 3: Fear in Clients
  - Appendix D: Practical Strategies for Helping Clients Untangle Fears

SESSION #5: CAN WE LEARN FROM HOW OTHER PROFESSIONS ADDRESS FEAR AND MISTAKE-MAKING?

- Is the legal profession "unique," or can we learn from other professions about how to address fear and mistake-making?
- Homework Options:
  - Chapter 9: A Glimpse into Fear and Mistake-Making in Medical Education and Training
  - Chapter 10: A Glimpse into Fear and Mistake-Making in Journalism Education and Training
  - Chapter 11: A Glimpse into Fear and Mistake-Making in Engineering Education and Training
  - Chapter 12: A Glimpse into Fear and Mistake-Making in Entrepreneurship and Business Education and Training

SESSION #6: ATTITUDES ABOUT FAILURE AND MISTAKE-MAKING IN THE LEGAL PROFESSION

- How is failure or mistake-making perceived in the legal profession?
- Do we feel open to talking about fear, failure, and mistake-making in the classroom or law office? Why or why not?
- Is there anything we can learn from being more open about fear, failure, or mistake-making, especially in law school before transitioning to practice?
- Is there a benefit to discussing and debriefing fears, failures, and mistakes in law practice?
- Homework Options:
  - ○ Barry Boyce, "Why Our Brain Thrives on Mistakes," https://www .mindful.org/brain-thrives-mistakes/ (May 3, 2017).
  - ○ Doug Lemov, "Culture of Error," http://teachlikeachampion.com/ cultureoferror/.
  - ○ Kaci Bishop, "Framing Failure in the Legal Classroom: Techniques for Encouraging Growth and Resilience," *Arkansas Law Review* 70, No. 4 (January 2018): 959–1006.
  - ○ Excerpts from:
    - Henry Petroski, *Success through Failure.* Princeton, NJ: Princeton University Press, 2006.
    - Paul J. H. Schoemaker, *Brilliant Mistakes: Finding Success on the Far Side of Failure.* Wharton Digital Press, 2011.
    - Robert Sicina, *Learn from Failure: The Key to Successful Decision Making.* AuthorHouse, 2017.

SESSION #7: COMPARATIVE FEARLESSNESS

- Are there scenarios or situations in our lives in which society, our families, or our friends might think or suggest we *should* feel fear, but we *don't?*
- Are there scenarios or situations in our lawyering lives in which we think we *shouldn't* feel fear, but we *do?*
- What are the differences between these scenarios?
- Can we bring some of the *swagger* we feel in the first scenarios into the second ones?
- Homework Option:
  - ○ Chapter 14: Step 1: Untangling Fear (and end-of-chapter exercise)

SESSION #8: MENTAL REBOOT

- When we anticipate a fear-inducing performance scenario, what negative mental messages about ourselves, or what fear-based mantras or slogans, do we automatically hear?
- Can we rewrite our mental sound track for our new lawyering personas?
- Homework Option:
  - Chapter 15: Step 2: Mentally Rebooting (and end-of-chapter exercise)

SESSION #9: CHANNELING OUR INNER SCHOLAR-ATHLETE

- When we anticipate a fear-inducing performance scenario, what automatic physical responses do our bodies launch? Do we hunch down, cross our limbs, or fold inward, accidentally closing off our flow of oxygen, blood, and energy?
- Can we identify any unhelpful automatic physical fear reactions, and train ourselves to approach a performance event like an athlete—in an open and balanced stance?
- Can we develop a "preshot" routine or a physical performance checklist that will power us through a lawyering activity with a calm mind and body, like an athlete stepping into a competition arena?
- Homework Options:
  - Chapter 13: A Glimpse into Fear and Mistake-Making in Sports Training
  - Chapter 16: Step 3: Channeling Our Inner Athlete (and end-of-chapter exercise)
  - Amy Cuddy, TED Talk, "Your Body Language May Shape Who You Are," https://www.ted.com/talks/amy_cuddy_your_body_language_shapes_who_you_are (TED Global, 2012)

SESSION #10: CULTIVATING A CULTURE OF FORTITUDE

- Can we reject the not-so-helpful cliché messages to "just do it," "fake it till you make it," "just do what scares you," or "embrace fear as a great motivator"?

- Can we build character-in-context in the legal arena by consciously seeking opportunities to learn more about lawyering scenarios that ignite fear?

- Can we develop a realistic protocol for approaching mentors to ask questions—and get substantive, procedural, logistical, and tactical guidance—about *specific* lawyering scenarios that ignite fear or trigger worry about making a mistake?

- Can we seek out *general* opportunities to learn more about substantive, procedural, logistical, and tactical challenges that may arise in particular lawyering scenarios or in our specific area of practice?

- Can we develop protocols for handling difficult situations, asking for help, and knowing (and having the strength to undertake) the proper protocol if something does go wrong?

- Can we seek opportunities to better understand client fears and help clients (and others) untangle those fears?

- Homework Option:
  ○ Chapter 17: Step 4: Cultivating a Culture of Fortitude (and end-of-chapter exercise)

SESSION #11: REDUCING FEAR OF THE UNKNOWN

- This session could involve a panel of lawyers and insurance providers discussing lawyering mistakes of different types (in a nonintimidating tone that fosters a growth mind-set); panelists could explain how ethics hotlines and malpractice insurance protocols work.

- The session could focus on establishing communication channels in law office settings for asking questions about tricky lawyering issues, and identifying what to do upon discovery of a potential or actual mistake.

- Participants could engage in role playing tough situations that entail asking for help or bringing a perceived mistake to the attention of a supervisor or mentor.

- Homework Options:
  ○ Mark Bassingthwaighte, "Fear of the Public Eye Can Be Disastrous," 2005-FEB *West Virginia Lawyer* (January/February 2005): 17–18.
  ○ Mark Bassingthwaighte, "Malpractice and Fear of the Public Eye," ALPS blog, www.blog.alpsnet.com (November 9, 2012).

- Dolores Dorsainvil, Douglas R. Richmond, and John C. Bonnie, "My Bad: Creating a Culture of Owning Up to Lawyer Missteps and Resisting the Temptation to Bury Professional Error," Annual Conference of the Litigation Section of the American Bar Association, New Orleans (April 16, 2015).
- Catherine Gage O'Grady, "A Behavioral Approach to Lawyer Mistake and Apology," *New England Law Review* 51 (2017): 7–51.

SESSION #12: RECOGNIZING TRAUMA-RELATED FEAR IN OURSELVES AND OTHERS

- This session could involve a panel of trauma experts discussing how to recognize signs of trauma-related fear in ourselves and clients.
- Homework Options:
  - Sara E. Gold, "Trauma: What Lurks beneath the Surface," *Clinical Law Review* 24 (Spring 2018): 201–245.
  - Sarah Katz and Deeya Haldar, "The Pedagogy of Trauma-Informed Lawyering," *Clinical Law Review* 22 (Spring 2016): 359–393.

SESSION #13: CONTINUING TO UNTANGLE FEAR TOGETHER

- Can we craft slogans about fear related to lawyering that are better and more helpful than "just do it!" or "face your fears!" or "fake it till you make it!"?
- How can we cultivate a culture of *fortitude* in our own classrooms, school environments, or law offices?
  - Can we reduce or eliminate the *stigma* associated with talking about fear, mistakes, or failure?
  - Can we incorporate principles of vulnerability, authenticity, and "intellectual humility" into discussions about fear, mistakes, or failure in the legal context?
- How can we support others in their own quests to untangle fear?
- How can we become change makers for the legal profession regarding lawyer well-being when it comes to fear?

Bibliography

LAW JOURNAL AND LAW REVIEW ARTICLES ON FEAR IN LAWYERING

Bassingthwaighte, Mark. "Fear of the Public Eye Can Be Disastrous." *West Virginia Lawyer* (January/February 2005): 17–18.

Bassingthwaighte, Mark. "Malpractice and Fear of the Public Eye." ALPS blog, www.blog.alpsnet.com (November 9, 2012).

Brown, Heidi K. "Turning the Fear of Lawyering into the Power of Advocacy." http://www.abajournal.com/magazine/article/fear_of_lawyering (January 2018).

Creo, Robert A. "Managing Fear and Anxiety." *Pennsylvania Lawyer* (March-April 2016): 58–59.

Davis, Kevin. "Lawyers Shackled by Fear, Fear Not." *ABA Journal* (November 2015).

Lande, John. "Escaping from Lawyers' Prison of Fear." *University of Missouri–Kansas City Law Review* 82 (Winter 2014): 485–512.

ARTICLES AND BOOK CHAPTERS ON FEAR IN THE CLASSROOM

Bledsoe, T. Scott, and Baskin, Janice J. "Recognizing Student Fear: The Elephant in the Classroom." *College Teaching* 62 (2014): 35–41.

Bledsoe, T. Scott, and Baskin, Janice J. "Strategies for Addressing Student Fear in the Classroom." www.facultyfocus.com (April 27, 2015).

Bright, Rebecca. "Tackling Classroom Fears." National Education Association, http://www.nea.org/tools/48480.htm (September 30, 2011).

Cox, Rebecca D. "'It Was Just That I Was Afraid': Promoting Success by Addressing Students' Fear of Failure." *Community College Review* 37 (July 2009): 52–80.

Levy, Leah. "How Stress Affects the Brain during Learning." *Edudemic* (October 13, 2014).

Patthoff, Abigail A. "This is Your Brain on Law School: The Impact of Fear-Based Narratives on Law Students." *Utah Law Review* (2015): 391–424.

LAW JOURNAL AND LAW REVIEW ARTICLES ON LAWYERING MISTAKES AND "FAILURE"

Berman, William. "When Will They Ever Learn? Learning and Teaching from Mistakes in the Clinical Context." *Clinical Law Review* 13 (Fall 2006): 115–141.

Bishop, Kaci. "Framing Failure in the Legal Classroom: Techniques for Encouraging Growth and Resilience." *Arkansas Law Review* 70 (January 2018): 959–1005.

Dorsainvil, Dolores; Richmond, Douglas R.; Bonnie, John C. "My Bad: Creating a Culture of Owning Up to Lawyer Missteps and Resisting the Temptation to Bury Professional Error." Annual Conference of the Litigation Section of the American Bar Association, New Orleans (April 16, 2015).

Grossman, Glenn M. "What I Tell Law Students." *Maryland Bar Journal* 47 (April 2014): 61–62.

Hyde, John. "Young Lawyers Should Not Live in Fear of Admitting Mistakes." *The Law Society Gazette* (January 6, 2017).

Kahan, Jeffrey B. "It Is No Mistake to Admit a Mistake." 23 *Los Angeles Lawyer* (March 2000).

Kroub, Gaston. "Beyond Biglaw: The Dean's 4-Step Formula for Dealing with Mistakes." www.abovethelaw.com (February 24, 2015).

Macaulay, Ann. "Lessons Learned: Lawyers' Biggest Career Mistakes and Successes." *The Canadian Bar Association* (July 3, 2007).

Neer, R. Jeffrey. "What to Do When Mistakes Happen." 29 *Los Angeles Lawyer* (April 2006).

O'Grady, Catherine Gage. "A Behavioral Approach to Lawyer Mistake and Apology." *New England Law Review* 51 (2017): 7–51.

Oseid, Julie A., and Easton, Stephen D. "'And Bad Mistakes? I've Made a Few': Sharing Mistakes to Mentor New Lawyers." *Albany Law Review* 77 (2014): 499–538.

Petmecky, Kalia. "Mistakes: Five Things to Do When You Make One." www .Thinkandquestionbiglaw.com (March 12, 2015).

Works, Ryan J. "Five Practical Tips to Live By as a Young Lawyer." *Nevada Lawyer* 44 (May 2011).

BOOKS ON FEAR AND ANXIETY

Brown, Heidi K. *The Introverted Lawyer: A Seven-Step Journey Toward Authentically Empowered Advocacy.* Chicago: ABA Publishing, 2017.

Cho, Jeena, and Gifford, Karen. *The Anxious Lawyer: An 8-Week Guide to a Joyful and Satisfying Law Practice through Mindfulness and Meditation.* Chicago: Ankerwycke Books, 2016.

Gardner, Dan. *The Science of Fear: How the Culture of Fear Manipulates Your Brain.* New York: Penguin Group, 2009.

Harris, Russ. *The Confidence Gap: A Guide to Overcoming Fear and Self-Doubt.* Boulder, CO: Trumpeter, 2011.

Hendricks, Gay. *The Big Leap.* New York: HarperOne, 2009.

Hilliard, Erika B. *Living Fully with Shyness and Social Anxiety.* Philadelphia: Da Capo Press, 2005.

Jeffers, Susan. *Feel the Fear . . . and Do It Anyway.* New York: Ballantine Books, 2007.

Kushner, Harold S. *Conquering Fear.* New York: Anchor Books, 2009.

Naistadt, Ivy. *Speak without Fear.* New York: HarperCollins, 2004.

Patel, Meera Lee. *My Friend Fear: Finding Magic in the Unknown.* New York: Penguin Random House, 2018.

Ulmer, Kristen. *The Art of Fear: Why Conquering Fear Won't Work and What to Do Instead.* New York: Harper Wave, 2017.

Webb, Brandon. *Mastering Fear: A Navy SEAL's Guide.* New York: Portfolio/ Penguin, 2018.

Wilson, Sarah. *First We Make the Beast Beautiful: A New Journey through Anxiety.* New York: HarperCollins, 2018.

BOOKS ON PERSONAL GROWTH

Brown, Brené. *Daring Greatly.* New York: Penguin Random House, 2012.

Csikszentmihalyi, Mihaly. *Flow: The Psychology of Optimal Experience.* New York: Harper Perennial, 1990.

Duckworth, Angela. *Grit.* New York: Scribner, 2015.

BOOKS ON LEARNING FROM FAILURE

Petroski, Henry. *Success through Failure*. Princeton, NJ: Princeton University Press, 2006.

Schoemaker, Paul J. H. *Brilliant Mistakes: Finding Success on the Far Side of Failure*. Wharton Digital Press, 2011.

Sicina, Robert. *Learn from Failure: The Key to Successful Decision Making*. Author-House, 2017.

BOOKS ON CREATIVITY

Bayles, David, and Orland, Ted. *Art & Fear: Observations on the Perils (and Rewards) of Artmaking*. Santa Cruz, CA: The Image Continuum, 1993.

Cameron, Julia. *The Artist's Way*. New York: Jeremy P. Tarcher/Putnam, 2002.

Catmull, Edwin (with Amy Wallace). *Creativity, Inc.: Overcoming the Unseen Forces That Stand in the Way of True Inspiration*. New York: Random House, 2014.

Pressfield, Steven. *Do the Work*. The Domino Project, 2011.

Pressfield, Steven. *The War of Art*. New York: Black Irish Entertainment LLC, 2002.

Sturges, Tom. *Every Idea Is a Good Idea*. New York: Jeremy P. Tarcher/Penguin, 2014.

Tharp, Twyla. *The Creative Habit: Learn It and Use It for Life*. New York: Simon & Schuster, 2003.

BOOKS ON LEADERSHIP

Ardi, Dana. *The Fall of the Alphas: The New Beta Way to Connect, Collaborate, Influence—and Lead*. New York: St. Martin's Press, 2013.

Kukk, Christopher L. *The Compassionate Achiever: How Helping Others Fuels Success*. New York: HarperOne, 2017.

BOOKS ON SPORTS PERFORMANCE

Grand, David, and Goldberg, Alan. *This is Your Brain on Sports: Beating Blocks, Slumps and Performance Anxiety for Good!* Indianapolis, IN: Dog Ear Publishing, 2011.

Mack, Gary, and Casstevens, David. *Mind Gym: An Athlete's Guide to Inner Excellence*. New York: McGraw-Hill, 2001.

Mumford, George. *The Mindful Athlete: Secrets to Pure Performance.* Berkeley: Parallax Press, 2015.

Murphy, Shane (editor). *The Sport Psych Handbook: A Complete Guide to Today's Best Mental Training Techniques.* Champaign, IL: Human Kinetics, 2005.

Rotella, Bob. *How Champions Think: In Sports and in Life.* New York: Simon & Schuster Paperbacks, 2015.

Waitzkin, Josh. *The Art of Learning: An Inner Journey to Optimal Performance.* New York: Free Press, 2007.

REPORTS ON THE LEGAL PROFESSION

Institute for the Advancement of the American Legal System (IAALS) and Educating Tomorrow's Lawyers, "Foundations for Practice," http://iaals .du.edu/sites/default/files/reports/foundations_for_practice_whole_lawyer_ character_quotient.pdf (July 2016).

National Task Force on Lawyer Well-Being. "The Path to Lawyer Well-Being: Practical Recommendations for Positive Change," August 14, 2017.

Organ, Jerome M.; Jaffe, David B.; Bender, Katherine M. "Helping Law Students Get the Help They Need: An Analysis of Data Regarding Law Students' Reluctance to Seek Help and Policy Recommendations for a Variety of Stakeholders." *The Bar Examiner*, 84, 4 (December 2015): 9–17.

Organ, Jerome M.; Jaffe, David B.; Bender, Katherine M. "Suffering in Silence: The Survey of Law Student Well-Being and the Reluctance of Law Students to Seek Help for Substance Use and Mental Health Concerns." *Journal of Legal Education*, 66, 1 (Autumn 2016): 116–156.

Patricia Snyder, "Super Women Lawyers: A Study of Character Strengths," *Arizona Summit Law Review* 8 (Spring 2015): 261–315.

OTHER HELPFUL RESOURCES FOR THE LEGAL PROFESSION

DeStefano, Michele. *Legal Upheaval: A Guide to Creativity, Collaboration, and Innovation in Law.* Chicago: ABA Publishing, 2018.

Kiser, Randall. *Soft Skills for the Effective Lawyer.* Cambridge, UK: Cambridge University Press, 2017.

Listen like a Lawyer (Blog), https://listenlikealawyer.com/.

Martin, Nathalie. *Lawyering from the Inside Out.* Cambridge, UK: Cambridge University Press, 2018.

Owning Your Value—Lawyers' Edition, a webinar series offered by GenLead and BelongLab, whose mission is "strengthening organizations and individuals through leadership, inclusion, and professional development," http://www .genlead.co/owning-your-value.html.

Robbennolt, Jennifer K., and Sternlight, Jean R. *Psychology for Lawyers: Understanding the Human Factors in Negotiation, Litigation, and Decision Making.* Chicago: ABA Publishing, 2013.

Sells, Benjamin. *The Soul of the Law.* Chicago: ABA Publishing, 2014.

Silver, Marjorie A. *Transforming Justice, Lawyers, and the Practice of Law.* Durham, NC: Carolina Academic Press, 2017.

https://www.susannearonowitz.com/ (Career Coach for Lawyers).

Vinson, Kathleen Elliott; Moppett, Samantha Alexis; George, Shailini Jandial. *Mindful Lawyering: The Key to Creative Problem Solving.* Durham, NC: Carolina Academic Press, 2018.

Well-Being Toolkit for Lawyers and Legal Employers, found at https://www.amer icanbar.org/content/dam/aba/administrative/lawyer_assistance/ls_colap_ well-being_toolkit_for_lawyers_legal_employers.authcheckdam.pdf.

Young, Kathryne M. *How to Be Sort of Happy in Law School.* Stanford, CA: Stanford University Press, 2018.

Notes

1. Posted by Instagram account, *187fitness* (June 21, 2018).

2. Definition provided by Google, citing Oxford Dictionaries.

3. https://www.merriam-webster.com/dictionary/fear.

4. http://www.dictionary.com/browse/fear.

5. https://en.wikipedia.org/wiki/Fear.

6. https://www.merriam-webster.com/dictionary/fear.

7. Author/artist unknown.

8. Steven Pressfield, *The War of Art* (New York: Black Irish Entertainment LLC, 2002), 39.

9. Heidi K. Brown, "Turning the Fear of Lawyering into the Power of Advocacy," http://www.abajournal.com/magazine/article/fear_of_lawyering (January 2018). Some language in this paragraph and the next few paragraphs is excerpted or paraphrased from the *ABA Journal* article.

10. Brandon Webb, *Mastering Fear: A Navy SEAL's Guide* (New York: Portfolio/Penguin, 2018), 84.

11. Ibid.

12. Abigail A. Patthoff, "This Is Your Brain on Law School: The Impact of Fear-Based Narratives on Law Students," *Utah Law Review* (2015): 391, 396.

13. Catherine Gage O'Grady, "A Behavioral Approach to Lawyer Mistake and Apology," *New England Law Review* 51 (2017): 7, 12 (differentiating among mistakes due to absence of knowledge, error of judgment, etc.).

14. This is based on actual events.

15. Mihaly Csikszentmihalyi, *Flow: The Psychology of Optimal Experience* (New York: Harper Perennial, 1990), 4.

16. http://www.brainchannels.com/thinker/mihaly.html.

17. Csikszentmihalyi, 4.

18. Ibid., 3.

19. Erika Hilliard, *Living Fully with Shyness and Social Anxiety* (Philadelphia: Da Capo Press, 2005).

20. Ibid., 60.

21. Ibid., 64.

22. National Task Force on Lawyer Well-Being, "The Path to Lawyer Well-Being: Practical Recommendations for Positive Change," August 14, 2017. https:// www.americanbar.org/content/dam/aba/images/abanews/ThePathToLawyer WellBeingReportRevFINAL.pdf.

23. Ibid., 10.

24. Ibid., 13.

25. Ibid.

26. Karl A. Menninger, *The Human Mind* (1953).

27. Patthoff, 402.

28. Ibid. (internal footnotes omitted)

29. Kevin Davis, "Lawyers Shackled by Fear, Fear Not," *ABA Journal* 101, 11 (2015): 36, 40.

30. Dorothy Evensen, "To Group or Not to Group: Students' Perceptions of Collaborative Learning Activities in Law School," *Southern Illinois University Law Journal* 28 (Winter 2004): 343, 346.

31. Ibid., 383.

32. Ibid.

33. Ibid.

34. Ibid., 384.

35. https://www.ted.com/talks/amy_cuddy_your_body_language_shapes_who_ you_are.

36. Richard Friedling, "The First Trial: Beyond Mere Survival to Victory," *Association of Trial Lawyers of America 2003 Annual Convention CLE Materials* (2003): 759.

37. Ibid.

38. Ibid. (emphasis in original)

39. Patthoff, 391.

40. Ibid., 396.

41. Ibid., 392.

42. Ibid., 396.

43. Ibid., 418.

44. Ibid., 392–393.

45. Ibid., 393.

46. Ibid., 424.

47. Heidi K. Brown, "Breaking Bad Briefs," *The Journal of the Legal Profession* 41 (Spring 2017): 259; "Converting Benchslaps to Backslaps: Instilling Professional Accountability in New Legal Writers by Teaching and Reinforcing Context," *Journal of Legal Communication and Rhetoric* 11 (Fall 2014): 109.

48. National Task Force on Lawyer Well-Being, 10.

49. Ibid., 36.

50. Ibid., 38.

51. Phil Nuernberger, "From Gunfighter to Samurai: Bringing Life Quality to the Practice of Law," *New York State Bar Journal* 66 (February 1994): 6.

52. Joshua Rosenberg, "Interpersonal Dynamics: Helping Lawyers Learn the Skills, and the Importance [of] Human Relationships in the Practice of Law," *University of Miami Law Review* 58 (July 2004): 1225, 1228.

53. Ibid., 1227.

54. Ibid.

55. William A. Trine, "The Five Essential Ingredients of Success in the Courtroom," *Association of Trial Lawyers of America 2003 Annual Convention CLE Materials* (2003): 1165.

56. Davis, 38.

57. Ibid.

58. Randall Kiser, "The Emotionally Attentive Lawyer: Balancing the Rule of Law with the Realities of Human Behavior," *Nevada Law Journal* 15 (Spring 2015): 442, 443, quoting Professor Melissa Nelken.

59. National Task Force on Lawyer Well-Being, 12.

60. Stephen Ellman, Robert D. Dinerstein, Isabelle R. Gunning, Katherine R. Kruse, and Ann C. Shalleck, *Lawyers and Clients: Critical Issues in Interviewing and Counseling* (St. Paul, MN: Thomson Reuters, 2009).

61. Ibid., 36.

62. John Lande, "Tips for Lawyers Who Want to Get Good Results for Clients and Make Money," *Wyoming Lawyer* 38 (October 2015): 48.

63. Meredith Schnug, "KU's Pro Bono Program: Doing Good," *Journal of the Kansas Bar Association* 86 (October 2017): 35.

64. Morrison Torrey, "You Call That Education?" *Wisconsin Women's Law Journal* 19 (Spring 2004): 93, 108.

65. Lande, "Tips for Lawyers," 48.

66. Ellman et al., 36.

67. Ibid. "Hindering categories" include fear, "finances and reputation" related to a case, and "difference and connection" issues. Ibid., 36–37.

68. Ibid., 36. (emphasis added)

69. Ibid., 37.

70. Trine, 1165.

71. Kaci Bishop, "Framing Failure in the Legal Classroom: Techniques for Encouraging Growth and Resilience," *Arkansas Law Review* 70, 4 (January 2018): 959, 961.

72. Ibid., 965.

73. Meera Lee Patel, *My Friend Fear: Finding Magic in the Unknown* (New York: Tarcher-Perigee, 2018).

74. Ibid., 136.

75. Twyla Tharp, *The Creative Habit: Learn It and Use It for Life* (New York: Simon & Schuster, 2003), 133.

76. Steven Pressfield, *Do the Work* (The Domino Project, 2011), 15.

77. Ibid., 4.

78. Ibid., 44.

79. John Lande, "Escaping from Lawyers' Prison of Fear," *University of Missouri–Kansas City Law Review* 82 (Winter 2014): 485, 491.

80. Ibid., 492.

81. David Grand and Alan Goldberg, *This is Your Brain on Sports: Beating Blocks, Slumps and Performance Anxiety for Good!* (Indianapolis, IN: Dog Ear Publishing, 2011), 8, 35, 37.

82. Barbara Glesner Fines and Cathy Madsen, "Caring Too Little, Caring Too Much: Competence and the Family Law Attorney," *University of Missouri–Kansas City Law Review* 75 (Summer 2007): 965, 988. (internal citations omitted)

83. Ibid. (internal citations omitted)

84. Davis, 39.

85. Ibid., 40.

86. Lande, "Tips for Lawyers," 48–49.

87. Nuernberger, 6.

88. Ibid.

89. H. K. Brown, "Turning the Fear of Lawyering into the Power of Advocacy."

90. Vivia Chen, "Why We Can All Identify with Gabe MacConaill," https://thecareerist.typepad.com/thecareerist/2018/11/why-the-sidley-partner-suicide-resonates-with-all-of-us.html (November 19, 2018).

91. R. Hal Ritter Jr. and Patricia A. Wilson, "The Fine Art of Listening," *Michigan Bar Journal* 81 (January 2002): 36, 39. ("Often fear is related to a threat of injury or loss.")

92. Steven Keeva, "What Clients Want," *ABA Journal* 87 (June 2001): 48, 51, quoting prominent mediator Arnie Herz.

93. Ritter and Wilson, 39.

94. Gerald M. Welt, "Tips for Building Lawyer/Client Relationships: The First Impression," *Nevada Lawyer* 11 (January 2003).

95. Myron Kove and James M. Kosakow, *Revocable Trusts*, 5th ed. (St. Paul, MN: Thomson Reuters), Chapter 9.1, September 2016 update.

96. Henry Dahut, "A Focus on Clients," *Oregon State Bar Bulletin* 65 (April 2005): 35.

97. Ibid.

98. Ibid., 35–36.

99. Larry M. Elkin, "Some Lawyer Ads Can Scare You to Death," *Palisades Hudson Financial Group, LLC*, Blog (August 16, 2017).

100. Ibid.

101. Philip M. Genty, "Clients Don't Take Sabbaticals: The Indispensable In-House Clinic and the Teaching of Empathy," *Clinical Law Review* 7 (Fall 2000): 273, 275–276.

102. Ibid., 276.

103. Marla Lyn Mitchell-Cichon, "What Mom Would Have Wanted: Lessons Learned from an Elder Law Clinic about Achieving Clients' Estate-Planning Goals," *Elder Law Journal* 10 (2002): 289, 311.

104. Ellman et al., 46.

105. Ibid.

106. Ibid.

107. J. Mark Weiss, "Developing a Collaborative Family Law Practice: Leading Lawyers on Exploring Collaborative Law, Integrating It into a Practice, and Implementing Marketing Strategies," 2011 WL 959536 (Thomson Reuters/Aspatore 2011): *7.

108. Ibid., *2.

109. G. Nicholas Herman and Jean M. Cary, *A Practical Approach to Client Interviewing, Counseling, and Decision-Making: For Clinical Programs and Practical Skills Courses* (San Francisco: Matthew Bender, 2009), 32.

110. Roy M. Sobelson, "Lawyers, Clients and Assurances of Confidentiality: Lawyers Talking without Speaking, Clients Hearing without Listening," *Georgetown Journal of Legal Ethics* 1 (Spring 1988): 703, 712.

111. Stefan H. Krieger and Richard K. Neumann Jr., *Essential Lawyering Skills*, 4th ed. (New York: Wolters Kluwer, 2011), 112.

112. Ibid.

113. Sara E. Gold, "Trauma: What Lurks beneath the Surface," *Clinical Law Review* 24 (Spring 2018): 201, 209, citing Bessel Van Der Kolk, *The Body Keeps the Score* (Hay House, 2014), 2–3.

114. Herman and Cary, 32.

115. Linda F. Smith, "Medical Paradigms for Counseling: Giving Clients Bad News," *Clinical Law Review* 4 (Spring 1998): 391, 415.

116. Ritter and Wilson, 39.

117. Dahut, 35.

118. Sobelson, 703.

119. Weiss, *2.

120. Ibid.

121. Laurie Shanks, "Whose Story Is It, Anyway? Guiding Students to Client-Centered Interviewing through Storytelling," *Clinical Law Review* 14 (Spring 2008): 509, 513.

122. Kyle A. Lansberry and J. Robert Turnipseed, "Deposition Preparation and Defense for the Young Lawyer," *American Journal of Trial Advocacy* 24 (Fall 2000): 357, 360.

123. Ibid., 359.

124. Sarah Katz and Deeya Haldar, "The Pedagogy of Trauma-Informed Lawyering," *Clinical Law Review* 22 (Spring 2016): 359, 383.

125. Lisa Blue and Robert B. Hirschhorn, "Getting Your Client Emotionally Ready," *Blue's Guide to Jury Selection* 1 (West Academic and Association of Trial Lawyers of America, 2004), 12:6.

126. Smith, 423.

127. Serena Stier, "Reframing Legal Skills: Relational Lawyering," *Journal of Legal Education* 42 (June 1992): 303, 304.

128. Ibid., 306, quoting Charles W. Wolfram, *Modern Legal Ethics* (St. Paul, MN: West Academic, 1986), 688.

129. Stier, 309, quoting Wolfram, 691.

130. Stier, 315.

131. Shanks, 509.

132. Stephanie Sogg and Wilton S. Sogg, "Coping with Adversity: Your Clients' and Your Own," *Practical Lawyer* 46, 6 (September 2000): 25, 27.

133. Ritter and Wilson, 36.

134. Kiser, "The Emotionally Attentive Lawyer," 444, quoting Professor Melissa Nelken.

135. Fines and Madsen, 982, quoting a phrase coined by Professor Thomas L. Shaffer in the first edition of Thomas L. Shaffer and James R. Elkins, *Legal Interviewing and Counseling in a Nutshell*, 4th ed. (St. Paul, MN: West Academic, 2005), 9.

136. Fines and Madsen, 982.

137. Marjorie A. Silver, "Love, Hate, and Other Emotional Interference in the Lawyer/Client Relationship," *Clinical Law Review* 6 (Fall 1999): 259, 275.

138. Sobelson, 744.

139. Christopher T. Powell Jr., review of "How to Navigate through Federal Prison and Gain an Early Release," by Lisa Barrett with Jamila T. Davis, *Champion* 39 (September/October 2015): 62.

140. Bourree Lam, "A Therapist Who Preps White-Collar Criminals for Prison Time," https://www.theatlantic.com/business/archive/2016/08/therapist-white-collar-criminals/495308/ (August 10, 2016).

141. Ibid.

142. Ibid.

143. Email from attorney Katherine Bajuk to the author, August 9, 2018, 11:04 a.m.

144. Ibid.

145. Ibid.

146. Ibid.

147. Ibid.

148. Ibid.

149. Ibid.

150. Ibid.

151. Ibid.

152. Ibid.

153. Leslye E. Orloff, Deeana Jang, and Catherine F. Klein, "With No Place to Turn: Improving Legal Advocacy for Battered Immigrant Women," *Family Law Quarterly* 29 (Summer 1995): 313, 315.

154. Ibid., 320.

155. Ibid., 317.

156. Scott Wiener and George Gascón, "Now Immigrants Are Being Harassed on the Witness Stand in California Courtrooms," https://www.sacbee.com/opinion/california-forum/article210594384.html (May 10, 2018). *See also* Cora Engelbrecht, "Fewer Immigrants Are Reporting Domestic Abuse. Police Blame Fear of Deportation," https://www.nytimes.com/2018/06/03/us/immigrants-houston-domestic-violence.html (June 3, 2018).

157. https://www.liftonline.org/about/who-we-are/mission-and-history.

158. Phone call between attorney Devi Patel and the author, September 11, 2018.

159. Ibid.

160. Ibid.

161. Ibid.

162. Ibid.

163. Ibid.

164. Ibid.

165. Harriet Newman Cohen, *The Divorce Book for Men and Women: A Step-by-Step Guide to Gaining Your Freedom without Losing Everything Else* (New York: Avon Publishers, 1994).

166. Email from attorney Harriet Newman Cohen to the author, July 29, 2018, 8:16 p.m.

167. Getchel Lubke, "Shining a Light on The Divorce Fear," https://www.marriage.com/advice/divorce/shining-a-light-on-the-divorce-fear (February 13, 2017).

168. Karen Finn, "Dealing with Divorce and the Fears That Are Keeping You Stuck," https://drkarenfinn.com/divorce-blog/healing-after-divorce/339-dealing-with-divorce-and-the-fears-that-are-keeping-you-stuck (May 12, 2016).

169. Ibid.

170. Quoted in Fines and Madsen, 968.

171. Ibid.

172. Ibid., 972.

173. Ibid., 968.

174. Dahut, 37.

175. Maria Mkrtchyan, "How to Fight Your Fears during a Custody Battle," http://www.sheknows.com/community/parenting/how-fight-your-fears-during-custody-battle.

176. Burch, Coulston & Shepard, LLP, "Taking the Fear out of a Child Custody Dispute," Newport Beach, CA. https://www.ocdivorce.net/blog/2016/march/taking-the-fear-out-of-a-child-custody-dispute/ (March 17, 2016).

177. Ibid.

178. Weiss, *14.

179. Ibid.

180. Fines and Madsen, 969.

181. Ibid., 979, quoting Gary Skoloff and Robert J. Levy, "Custody Doctrines and Custody Practice: A Divorce Practitioner's View," *Family Law Quarterly* 36 (2002): 79, 98.

182. Morris L. Jensby, Michelle S. Putvin, and Mark A. Basurto, "Doctors, Lawyers, and 'The Talk,' The Emotional Impact of Being a Defendant," *DRI for the Defense* 59, 5 (May 2017): 84.

183. Ibid.

184. Ibid.

185. Ibid.

186. Ibid.

187. Ibid.

188. Phone call between attorney William E. Alsnauer Jr. and the author, July 17, 2018.

189. Ibid.

190. Ibid.

191. Christopher W. Martin, "The Science of the Apology: Insurance Claims and Litigation," *Journal of Texas Insurance Law* 13 (Winter 2015–2016): 40, 41.

192. Ibid.

193. Ibid.

194. Ibid.

195. Email from Professor Todd Haugh to the author, July 16, 2018, 3:17 p.m.

196. Ibid.

197. Phone call between Professor Todd Haugh and the author, September 29, 2018.

198. Ibid.

199. Ibid.

200. Ibid.

201. Email from attorney Stefanie L. DeMario-Germershausen to the author, August 8, 2018, 5:30 p.m.

202. Ibid.

203. Ibid.

204. Phone call between DeMario-Germershausen and the author, July 17, 2018.

205. Email from DeMario-Germershausen to the author, August 8, 2018, 5:30 p.m.

206. Mitchell-Cichon, 310.

207. Ibid., 302.

208. Ibid., 310.

209. https://www.duanemorris.com/attorneys/michaeldgrohman.html.

210. Phone call between attorney Michael Grohman and the author, August 6, 2018.

211. Ibid.

212. Phone call between attorney Deirdre Lok and the author, September 10, 2018.

213. Ibid.

214. Ibid.

215. Phone call between attorney Michelle Walker and the author, July 17, 2018.

216. National Task Force on Lawyer Well-Being, 29.

217. Michael Hatfield, "Fear, Legal Indeterminacy, and the American Lawyering Culture," *Lewis & Clark Law Review* 10 (Fall 2006): 511, 525.

218. Ibid., 525, n. 58.

219. Ibid.

220. Jeffrey B. Kahan, "It Is No Mistake to Admit a Mistake," *Los Angeles Lawyer* 23 (March 2000).

221. *Pescia v. Auburn Ford-Lincoln Mercury, Inc.*, 177 F.R.D. 509, 511 (M.D. Ala. 1997).

222. R. Jeffrey Neer, "What to Do When Mistakes Happen," *Los Angeles Lawyer* 29 (April 2006). ("Mistakes will undoubtedly happen in the practice of law.")

223. Julie A. Oseid and Stephen D. Easton, "'And Bad Mistakes? I've Made a Few': Sharing Mistakes to Mentor New Lawyers," *Albany Law Review* (2014): 502.

224. Ibid., 509.

225. Dolores Dorsainvil, Douglas R. Richmond, and John C. Bonnie, "My Bad: Creating a Culture of Owning Up to Lawyer Missteps and Resisting the Temptation to Bury Professional Error," *Annual Conference of the Litigation Section of the American Bar Association*, New Orleans, April 16, 2015: 2, 8, citing *Idaho State Bar v. Clark*, 283 P.3d 96, 104 (Idaho 2012) and Benjamin P. Cooper, "The Lawyer's Duty to Inform His Client of His Own Malpractice," *Baylor Law Review* 61 (Winter 2009): 174, 195. ("All professionals—even lawyers (or maybe especially lawyers)—make mistakes sometimes.")

226. Glenn M. Grossman, "What I Tell Law Students," *Maryland Bar Journal* 47 (April 2014): 61.

227. Gaston Kroub, "Beyond Biglaw: The Dean's 4-Step Formula for Dealing with Mistakes," www.abovethelaw.com (February 24, 2015). *See also* Kalia Petmecky, "Mistakes: Five Things to Do When You Make One," www.thinkandquestionbiglaw.com (March 12, 2015). ("Mistakes are inevitable at all stages of a lawyer's career. Nobody likes making mistakes; but we all make them.")

228. Ryan J. Works, "Five Practical Tips to Live by as a Young Lawyer," *Nevada Lawyer* (May 2011): 44.

229. Rachel Weiner, "This Prosecutor's Cut-and-Paste Mistake Revealed Case Against Wikileaks Founder," https://www.washingtonpost.com/local/public-safety/this-prosecutors-cut-and-paste-mistake-revealed-a-case-against-wikileaks-founder/2018/11/16/9a118702-e9b0-11e8-a939-9469f1166f9d_story.html?utm_term=.e3b05100c818 (November 16, 2018).

230. Ann Macaulay, "Lessons Learned: Lawyers' Biggest Career Mistakes and Successes," *The Canadian Bar Association* (July 3, 2007).

231. John Hyde, "Young Lawyers Should Not Live in Fear of Admitting Mistakes," *The Law Society Gazette* (January 6, 2017).

232. Ibid.

233. Benjamin Sells, *The Soul of the Law* (Chicago: ABA Publishing, 2014).

234. Ibid., 30.

235. Ibid., 114.

236. Ibid., 30–31.

237. Ibid., 31. (emphasis in original)

238. Ibid., 3. (emphasis in original)

239. Randall Kiser, *Soft Skills for the Effective Lawyer* (Cambridge, UK: Cambridge University Press, 2017), 55.

240. Ibid.

241. Ibid.

242. Ibid., 70.

243. Ibid., 178.

244. Ibid., citing Amy C. Edmondson.

245. Ibid., 178–179, citing Amy C. Edmondson.

246. Charles Duhigg, "What Google Learned from Its Quest to Build the Perfect Team," *New York Times Magazine* (February 25, 2016), https://www.nytimes.com/2016/02/28/magazine/what-google-learned-from-its-quest-to-build-the-perfect-team.html.

247. Kiser, *Soft Skills*, at 179, citing Duhigg, *New York Times Magazine*.

248. Kroub.

249. Ibid.

250. Ibid.

251. Ibid.

252. Grossman, 61.

253. Petmecky.

254. Works, 44.

255. http://iaals.du.edu/sites/default/files/reports/foundations_for_practice_whole_lawyer_character_quotient.pdf.

256. Ibid. "Working with a Consortium of law schools and a network of leaders from both law schools and the legal profession, Educating Tomorrow's Lawyers develops solutions to support effective models of legal education."

257. Ibid.

258. Ibid., 1.

259. Ibid.

260. Ibid., 2.

261. Ibid., 22.

262. Ibid.

263. Ibid., 3.

264. Ibid.

265. Ibid., 5.

266. Ibid., 28. (emphasis added)

267. Ibid., 14 (82.2% and 75.2% of respondents in the Professional Development criterion).

268. Ibid., 16.

269. Ibid.

270. Ibid., 26.

271. Ibid., 11.

272. Ibid., 37.

273. Paul Tough, *How Children Succeed: Grit, Curiosity, and the Hidden Power of Character* (New York: Houghton Mifflin Harcourt, 2012).

274. Ibid., 21.

275. Ibid., 48.

276. Ibid., 59. *See ibid.*, 196. ("[T]he character strengths that matter so much to young people's success are not innate; they don't appear in us magically as a result of good luck or good genes. And they are not simply a choice. They are rooted in brain chemistry, and they are molded, in measurable and predictable ways, by the environment in which children grow up.")

277. Thomas Lickona, *Educating for Character* (New York: Bantam Books, 1992), 67–70.

278. Tough, 76–77.

279. Ibid., 85.

280. Ibid., 121.

281. O'Grady, 29. ("The psychological difficulties that accompany mistake acknowledgment include avoiding embarrassment, humiliation, shame, hurt, anger, and the *fear* of unpleasant ramifications, including job loss.") (emphasis added)

282. *Attorney Griev. Comm'n v. Paul*, 31 A.3d 512 (Md. Ct. App. 2011).

283. Ibid., 516.

284. Ibid., 521. (emphasis added) *See also Elcock v. Henderson*, 947 F.2d 1004 (2d Cir. 1991). (Analyzing a claim of a Sixth Amendment violation by considering whether an attorney's representation of a defendant "was of poor quality and that that poor quality was caused by [the lawyer's] fear of potential disciplinary or other proceedings against him as a result of the delay.")

285. 31 A.3d at 528 (Adkins, J., Battaglia, J., Barbera, J., dissenting).

286. *In re* Pimsler, 286 A.D.2d 82 (N.Y. App. Div. 2001).

287. Ibid., 84. (emphasis added)

288. Ibid.

289. *In re* Fickler, 362 P.3d 1102 (Kan. 2015).

290. Ibid., 1107.

291. Ibid. (emphasis added)

292. Ibid., 1108.

293. *In re* Watt, 701 A.2d 1011 (R.I. 1997).

294. Ibid., 1012.

295. Ibid., 1013.

296. *In re* Hanlon, 110 P.3d 937 (Alaska 2005).

297. Ibid., 945. (emphasis added)

298. Ibid., 947.

299. *See also In re* Gieszl, No. 03-1278, 2005 WL 6317753, at * 4, *8 (Ariz. Disc. Comm'n Oct. 21, 2005). (A lawyer missed a statute of limitations deadline and attempted to cover up her mistake by preparing fraudulent settlement documents; the court acknowledged that she did so to protect "herself from humiliation and out of fear of losing her job." The court found this to be a selfish motive and suspended her bar license for one year.)

300. Dorsainvil et al., 22.

301. *In re* Disciplinary Proceeding Against Stansfield, 187 P.3d 254 (Wash. 2008).

302. Ibid., 264. *See also In re* Kitchings, 857 A.2d 1059, 1060 (D.C. Ct. App. 2004) (acknowledging a lawyer's "recognition (though belated) of his mistakes" in a disciplinary matter).

303. *Iowa Sup. Ct. Attorney Disciplinary Board*, 871 N.W.2d 109, 122 (Iowa 2015).

304. Ibid.

305. *In re* Haugabrook, 606 S.E.2d 257 (Ga. 2004).

306. Ibid., 258.

307. *In re* Inquiry Concerning Judge Fuller, 478 S.E.2d 641 (N.C. 1996).

308. Ibid., 643.

309. *People v. Miller*, 744 P.2d 489 (Col. 1987).

310. Ibid., 490.

311. *Sheridan's Case*, 813 A.2d 449 (N.H. 2002).

312. Ibid., 454.

313. O'Grady, 7.

314. Ibid., 8.

315. Ibid., 17.

316. Ibid., 10, 30 (discussing how "the hierarchical structure of many legal workplaces may unwittingly serve to discourage mistake acknowledgment or learning from mistake"; "firm leaders often view error as 'indicative of incompetence.'")

317. Ibid., 17.

318. Ibid., 18.

319. http://law.pace.edu/sites/default/files/academics/Pace_Law_School_Learning_Outcomes.pdf. (emphasis added)

320. O'Grady, 38.

321. Ibid., 44.

322. Craig Freudenrich, and Robynne Boyd, "How Your Brain Works," https://science.howstuffworks.com/life/inside-the-mind/human-brain/brain7.htm.

323. https://www.thoughtco.com/limbic-system-anatomy-373200.

324. https://www.britannica.com/science/amygdala.

325. https://youwillbearwitness.com/2018/03/01/ptsd-and-the-five-senses.

326. Patthoff, 391–392. (internal citations omitted)

327. Ibid. (internal citations omitted)

328. Andrea Ayres, "The Science of Fear and How to Overcome It," https://crew.co/blog/fear/.

329. Gary Mack and David Casstevens, *Mind Gym: An Athlete's Guide to Inner Excellence* (New York: McGraw-Hill, 2001), 31.

330. T. Scott Bledsoe and Janice J. Baskin, "Recognizing Student Fear: The Elephant in the Classroom," *College Teaching* 62 (2014): 35.

331. Ayres.

332. Kristen Ulmer, *The Art of Fear: Why Conquering Fear Won't Work and What to Do Instead* (New York: Harper Wave, 2017), 4–5.

333. Joseph Troncale, "Your Lizard Brain: The Limbic System and Brain Functioning," https://www.psychologytoday.com/intl/blog/where-addiction-meets-your-brain/201404/your-lizard-brain (April 22, 2014).

334. Weiss, *6.

335. Max Miller, http://bigthink.com/going-mental/how-the-brain-fears.

336. Scott P. Edwards, "The Amygdala: The Body's Alarm Circuit," http://www.dana.org/Publications/Brainwork/Details.aspx?id=43615 (May 2005).

337. Ibid.

338. Ulmer, 5.

339. Kaylene C. Williams, "Fear Appeal Theory," *Research in Business and Economics Journal* 5 (February 2012): 2. *See also* Sharon Begley, "The Roots of Fear," http://www.newsweek.com/roots-fear-94379 (December 15, 2007). ("The brain is therefore wired to flinch first and ask questions later.")

340. Weiss, *6.

341. Ibid.

342. Ibid.

343. Mary Pritchard, "How to Stop Fear in Its Tracks," https://www.huffingtonpost.com/mary-pritchard/overcome-fear_b_1739111.html (October 6, 2012); Russ Harris, *The Confidence Gap: A Guide to Overcoming Fear and Self-Doubt* (Boulder, CO: Trumpeter, 2011), 35.

344. Ibid.

345. Ibid., 184.

346. Williams, 2. *See also* Begley. ("The evolutionary primacy of the brain's fear circuitry makes it more powerful than the brain's reasoning faculties.")

347. Dan Gardner, *The Science of Fear: How the Culture of Fear Manipulates Your Brain* (New York: Penguin Group, 2009), 49.

348. http://www.naturalanxietysolutions.com/articles/understanding_anxiety/amygdala_anxiety.html.

349. Bledsoe and Baskin, "Recognizing Student Fear," 35.

350. Ibid.

351. Ibid.

352. Katz and Haldar, 366.

353. Ibid. (internal citations omitted)

354. Ibid. (internal citations omitted)

355. Grand and Goldberg, 8.

356. Ibid.

357. Ibid., 9. (emphasis in original)

358. https://www.americanbar.org/groups/lawyer_assistance/new_colap/resources.html.

359. Pritchard.

360. Patel, 55.

361. Ibid., 74.

362. Pritchard.

363. http://psychology.iresearchnet.com/social-psychology/social-psychology-theories/stress-appraisal-theory.

364. Ibid.

365. Monica M. Matthieu and André Ivanoff, *Using Stress, Appraisal, and Coping Theories in Clinical Practice: Assessments of Coping Strategies after Disasters*, https://pdfs.semanticscholar.org/2598/6971389db115b2a24259362ba61bdb6b5070.pdf (New York: Oxford University Press, 2006), 342.

366. Brian Lakey and Sheldon Cohen, Social Support Theory and Measurement, Chapter 2 *Social Support Measurement and Intervention*, Sheldon Cohen, Lynn Underwood, and Benjamin Gottlieb, eds. (New York: Oxford University Press, 2000), 34.

367. Pritchard.

368. Ibid.

369. Ibid.

370. Ibid.

371. Ibid.

372. Gay Hendricks, *The Big Leap* (New York: HarperOne, 2009), 17.

373. Pritchard.

374. https://drivemag.com/news/lebron-james-is-fearless-in-intel-s-autonomous-car-ad. (emphasis added)

375. https://www.ispot.tv/ad/dkXw/mercedes-amg-fearless-is-fuel.

376. https://member.carefirst.com/members/news/media-news/2015/carefirst-launches-live-fearless-ad-campaign.page.

377. Harris, 37.

378. Ibid., 164.

379. Kiser, *The Emotionally Attentive Lawyer,* 442.

380. Ibid., 450.

381. Ibid. (emphasis added)

382. Harris, 38.

383. Mark Bassingthwaighte, "Fear of the Public Eye Can Be Disastrous," *West Virginia Lawyer* 2005 (January/February): 17.

384. Gardner, 6.

385. Harold S. Kushner, *Conquering Fear* (New York: Anchor Books 2009), 9 (citing Gavin de Becker, *The Gift of Fear: And Other Survival Signals That Protect Us from Violence* (New York: Dell, 1998)).

386. Ulmer, xiii.

387. Friedling, 759.

388. Ibid.

389. Posted on Instagram account, *spoon_city* (July 13, 2018).

390. Harris, 119.

391. Ibid., 223.

392. Ibid., 168.

393. Ibid., 180.

394. Nuernberger, 6.

395. Ibid., 8.

396. Friedling, 759.

397. Ibid. (emphasis added)

398. Rebecca Bright, "Tackling Classroom Fears," National Education Association, http://www.nea.org/tools/48480.htm. (September 30, 2011).

399. Leah Levy, "How Stress Affects the Brain during Learning," *Edudemic,* October 13, 2014.

400. Ibid.

401. Ibid.

402. Bledsoe and Baskin, "Recognizing Student Fear," 35.

403. Bob Sullo, *The Motivated Student: Unlocking the Enthusiasm for Learning* (Alexandria, VA: Association for Supervision and Curriculum Development, 2009), 5.

404. Ibid.

405. Ibid.

406. Ibid., 11.

407. Bishop, 961.

408. T. Scott Bledsoe and Janice Baskin, "Strategies for Addressing Student Fear in the Classroom," www.facultyfocus.com, April 27, 2015.

409. Ibid.

410. Bledsoe and Baskin, "Recognizing Student Fear," 33.

411. Bledsoe and Baskin, "Strategies."

412. Bledsoe and Baskin, "Recognizing Student Fear," 32.

413. Ibid., 33 (citing LeDoux 1996; Cassady 2004).

414. Ibid., 35.

415. Ibid., 33.

416. Robert A. Creo, "Managing Fear and Anxiety," *Pennsylvania Lawyer* 38 (March-April 2016): 58.

417. Grand and Goldberg, 10.

418. Ibid.

419. Patel, 91.

420. Pressfield, *The War of Art.*

421. Ibid., 87.

422. Ibid., 143.

423. Susan Jeffers, *Feel the Fear . . . and Do It Anyway* (New York: Ballantine Books, 2007), 155.

424. Ibid., 162.

425. Ritter and Wilson, 38.

426. Ibid., 39.

427. Ibid., 38–39.

428. Bill Bornstein, "Medical Mistakes: Human Error or System Failure?" *Momentum*, http://www.whsc.emory.edu/_pubs/momentum/2000fall/onpoint.html (Fall 2000).

429. Melissa A. Fischer, Kathleen M. Mazor, Joann Baril, Eric Alper, Deborah DeMarco, and Michele Pugnaire, "Learning from Mistakes: Factors That Influence How Students and Residents Learn from Medical Errors," *Journal of General Internal Medicine* (May 2006): 419, 420.

430. Ibid.

431. Joshua M. Liao, "A Young Doctor's Fear of Raising Questions Causes a Mistake," *Washington Post* (March 24, 2014).

432. Ibid.

433. Ibid. (discussing a real-life medical mistake that occurred after a third-year medical student was afraid to ask an intimidating resident for guidance: "It was my first encounter with the danger that can occur when team members feel they cannot speak up"; Allen Marshall, "What a New Doctor Learned about Medical Mistakes from Her Mom's Death," https://www.propublica.org/article/what-a-new-doctor-learned-about-medical-mistakes-from-her-moms-death (January 9, 2013). ("We need to build a culture of patient safety. That means removing the stigma from patient safety and error reporting so we can collect data about errors and learn how we can fix things. That's better than not knowing the scope of the problem because people are afraid to talk about it.")

434. Anonymous, "Doctors Must Admit Mistakes: Educators; But Medical School Instructors Admit Physicians Are Reluctant to Disclose Any Error for Fear It Will Harm or Destroy Their Career," *The Times-Transcript*, Moncton, New Brunswick (April 2002).

435. Ibid.

436. Ibid.

437. NPR/TED Staff, "Mistakes in Medicine: Dr. Brian Goldman Answers Your Questions," https://www.npr.org/2014/08/21/341958526/mistakes-in-medicine-dr-brian-goldman-answers-your-questions (August 21, 2014).

438. Karen M. Scott, Patrina H. Y. Caldwell, Elizabeth H. Barnes, and Jenny Barrett, "'Teaching by Humiliation' and Mistreatment of Medical Students in Clinical Rotations: A Pilot Study," https://www.mja.com.au/system/files/issues/203_04/10.5694mja15.00189.pdf (August 17, 2015).

439. Ibid.

440. Bornstein.

441. Ibid. Dr. Bornstein compares this culture of safety to Disney's "stopping the ride" policy. "When a question of safety arises, any employee [of a Walt Disney theme park] can stop a ride without fear of criticism."

442. Staff writer, "Pennsylvania Doctor Says Medical Schools Must Teach Future Doctor How to Make Mistakes," http://www.newsindiatimes.com/pennsylvania-doctor-says-medical-schools-must-teach-future-doctor-how-to-make-mistakes (January 11, 2017).

443. Ibid.

444. NPR/TED Staff.

445. Ibid.

446. Gregory Dolin and Natalie Ram, "One Model of Collaborative Learning for Medical and Law Students at the University of Baltimore and Johns Hopkins University," *AMA Journal of Ethics* 18, 3 (March 2016): 237.

447. Ibid.

448. Ibid.

449. Fischer et al., 422.

450. Marshall.

451. William Berman, "When Will They Ever Learn? Learning and Teaching from Mistakes in the Clinical Context," *Clinical Law Review* 13 (Fall 2006): 115, 117 ("There is a significant push in the field of medicine to address physicians' mistakes in a forthright manner and to teach new physicians to own up to and learn from their mistakes.")

452. Katherine Mangan, "At Medical Schools' Simulation Centers, New Doctors Can Learn without Fear," *Chronicle of Higher Education,* https://www.chronicle.com/article/Letting-New-Doctors-Learn/133353 (August 6, 2012).

453. Mitzi Baker, "How VR Is Revolutionizing the Way Future Doctors Are Learning about Our Bodies," https://www.ucsf.edu/news/2017/09/408301/how-vr-revolutionizing-way-future-doctors-are-learning-about-our-bodies (September 18, 2017).

454. Ibid.

455. Dinah Wisenberg Brin, "The Best Response to Medical Errors? Transparency," *Association of American Medical Colleges News,* https://news.aamc.org/patient-care/article/best-response-medical-errors-transparency/ (January 16, 2018).

456. Ibid.

457. Kim Krisberg, "Integrating Patient Safety Lessons into Residency Training," *Association of American Medical Colleges News,* https://news.aamc.org/medical-education/article/patient-safety-residency-training/ (September 27, 2016); Matt Wood, "A Room of Horrors to Get Medical Trainees Ready for Real Patients," https://sciencelife.uchospitals.edu/2015/06/30/a-room-of-horrors-to-get-medical-trainees-ready-for-real-patients/ (June 30, 2015). *See also* "First Joint Patient Safety Course Brings Medical and Nursing Students Together," http://admissions.med.miami.edu/md-programs/general-md/curriculum/patient-safety-week (discussing University of Miami's Miller School of Medicine's medical error/patient safety course involving a simulation "Room of Horrors.")

458. Kim Krisberg, "New Focus in Medical Education on Learning to Recognize Causes of Diagnostic Errors," *Association of American Medical Colleges News,* https://news.aamc.org/medical-education/article/new-focus-recognize-causes-diagnostic-errors/ (October 25, 2016). *See also* http://medicine.buffalo.edu/news_and_events.host.html/content/shared/smbs/news/2011/08/medical-errors-Brennan-Taylor-052.detail.html (August 31, 2011). (Discussing an innovative training program at the University of Buffalo Jacobs School of Medicine and Biomedical Sciences that addresses medical errors head-on.)

459. http://www.omed.pitt.edu/curriculum-committee/learning-objectives.php.

460. Krisberg, "Integrating Patient Safety Lessons into Residency Training."

461. Ibid.

462. At the time Dr. Trowbridge wrote the article from which he is cited here, he was director of faculty development and associate director of medical student programs in the Department of Medicine at Maine Medical Center in Portland, as well as an assistant professor of medicine at the University of Vermont College of Medicine.

463. Robert L. Trowbridge, "Twelve Tips for Teaching Avoidance of Diagnostic Errors," *Medical Teacher* (2008): 496, 499.

464. Mark Pijl Zieber and Beverley Williams, "The Experience of Nursing Students Who Make Mistakes in Clinical," *International Journal of Nursing Education Scholarship* 12 (2015): 1–9.

465. Ibid. (internal citations omitted)

466. Ibid., 2.

467. Ibid., 7.

468. Ibid.

469. Ibid., 8.

470. Ibid., 1. (emphasis added)

471. Ibid.

472. Ibid., 8.

473. Carey M. Noland, "Baccalaureate Nursing Students' Accounts of Medical Mistakes Occurring in the Clinical Setting: Implications for Curricula," *Journal of Nursing Education*, 53, 3, Suppl. (2014): S35.

474. Ibid., S36.

475. Ibid.

476. Ibid., S37.

477. Ibid.

478. Kraig L. Schell, "Improving Pharmacy Practice by Learning from Errors," http://www.angelo.edu/faculty/kschell/downloads/Schell_errlearn.pdf (2006).

479. Ibid., 3.

480. Ibid., 4.

481. Ibid.

482. Ibid.

483. Ibid., 8.

484. Ibid.

485. Ibid., 12.

486. Patel, 22.

487. Monica Guzman, "Fear of Screwing Up," *Columbia Journalism Review*, https://www.cjr.org/first_person/fear_of_screwing_up.php (April 22, 2015).

488. Ibid.

489. Ibid.

490. Ibid.

491. Ibid.

492. Bob Moser, "Fear Itself," *Columbia Journalism Review* (Winter 2018).

493. Ibid.

494. Ibid.

495. Ibid.

496. Ben Du Plessis, "Great Journalism Takes Great Courage," http://thekjr.kings journalism.com/great-journalism-takes-great-courage/ (November 8, 2013).

497. Ibid.

498. Ibid.

499. Ibid.

500. Ibid.

501. Ibid.

502. Aidan White, "Fear in the News: The Difference between Self-censorship and Ethical Journalism," *Ethical Journalism Network*, https://ethicaljournalismnetwork.org/fear-in-the-news-the-difference-between-self-censorship-and-ethical-journalism (May 2, 2014).

503. Ibid.

504. Ibid.

505. Ibid.

506. Email from Professor Lisa Taylor to the author, June 2, 2018, 12:24 p.m.

507. Melanie Faizer, "How to Bring Mindfulness into a Journalism Curriculum," *MediaShift* (October 2, 2017).

508. Ibid.

509. Ibid.

510. https://www.ryerson.ca/media/releases/2017/04/How-to-succeed-nurturing/.

511. Email from Dr. Diana Brecher to the author, June 8, 2018, 10:19 a.m.

512. https://dartcenter.org/.

513. https://dartcenter.org/programs/training.

514. Charlotte Sector, "Intense Training Prepares Journalists for War," https://abcnews.go.com/International/story?id=1557505 (January 30, 2006).

515. David Socha, Valentin Razmov, and Elizabeth Davis, "Teaching Reflective Skills in an Engineering Course," *Proceedings of the 2003 American Society for Engineering Education Annual Conference & Exposition* (2003).

516. Robert Reinhold, "M.I.T. Giving a Course on Failure as a Dominating Theme in Society," *New York Times* (December 1, 1973).

517. Ibid.

518. Ibid.

519. Socha et al., 1.

520. Ibid., 3.

521. Ibid.

522. Ibid., 10. The students also wrote reflection pieces and took the Myers-Briggs Personality Type Indicator. *See ibid.*, 10, 13.

523. https://www.coursehero.com/file/11517432/EGR-120-Syllabus-H-Petroski/#/!

524. Henry Petroski, *Success through Failure* (Princeton, NJ: Princeton University Press, 2006), from the author's book description.

525. Bjorn Carey, "Learning from Mistakes: Stanford Engineering Course Builds Students' Confidence by Encouraging Them to Fail," https://engineering.stanford .edu/magazine/article/learning-mistakes-stanford-engineering-course-builds-students-confidence (January 6, 2014).

526. Ibid.

527. Ibid.

528. David Bayles and Ted Orland, *Art & Fear: Observations on the Perils (and Rewards) of Artmaking* (Santa Cruz, CA: The Image Continuum, 1993), 89–90.

529. James Hayton and Gabriella Cacciotti, "How Fear Helps (and Hurts) Entrepreneurs," https://hbr.org/2018/04/how-fear-helps-and-hurts-entrepreneurs (April 3, 2018).

530. Ibid.

531. Ibid.

532. Ibid.

533. Ibid.

534. Ibid.

535. Ibid.

536. Ibid.

537. http://www.imaginenation.com.au/approach-innovation/team/team-member-janet-sernack/; https://www.imaginenation.com.au/challenging-the-innovation-education-paradigm/.

538. http://www.imaginenation.com.au/innovation-blog/what-does-it-mean-to-cul tivate-a-fail-fast-organizational-culture/ (November 7, 2017). (emphasis added)

539. Ibid.

540. Ibid.

541. Ibid.

542. Ibid. (citing Edwin Catmull with Amy Wallace, *Creativity, Inc.: Overcoming the Unseen Forces That Stand in the Way of True Inspiration* (New York: Random House, 2014), 123).

543. Ibid.

544. Ion Valis, "Learning from Mistakes: Obsessing about Success Can Prevent Learning from Mistakes," https://www.london.edu/faculty-and-research/lbsr/learning-from-mistakes (April 1, 2016).

545. Catmull, 109.

546. Ibid.

547. Ibid.

548. Ibid., 108.

549. Robert V. Sicina, *Learn from Failure: The Key to Successful Decision Making* (Author-House, 2017).

550. https://www.american.edu/provost/registrar/schedule/course-descriptions.cfm?subj=IBUS&crs=303.

551. Sicina, Syllabus for *Learn from Failure: The Key to Successful Decision Making.*

552. Ibid.

553. Ibid.

554. Ibid.

555. Sicina, *Learn from Failure,* 128.

556. Patel, 156.

557. http://www.thedrum.com/news/2018/01/22/bbc-sport-showcases-animated-fearless-athletes-video-prime-the-winter-olympics.

558. https://gatorade.newsmarket.com/news-announcements/star-athletes-show-how-to-make-defeat-your-fuel/s/45e0e0a7-21a0-4a96-86ef-dfb1c182fe7d. (emphasis added)

559. George Mumford, *The Mindful Athlete: Secrets to Pure Performance* (Berkeley, CA: Parallax Press, 2015).

560. Ibid., 76.

561. Ibid., 105.

562. Ibid., 106.

563. Ibid., 165.

564. Ibid.

565. Ibid.

566. Ibid., 165–166.

567. Ibid., 166.

568. Ibid.
569. Ibid.
570. Ibid.
571. Ibid.
572. Ibid., 167.
573. Ibid., 167–168.
574. Ibid., 178.
575. Ibid., 190.
576. Ibid., 201. (emphasis in original)
577. Ibid., 207.
578. Ibid., 209.
579. Ibid., 103.
580. Ibid., 209–210.
581. Grand and Goldberg, 8.
582. Ibid., 9.
583. Ibid., 12.
584. Ibid., 27.
585. Webb, 124.
586. Bob Rotella, *How Champions Think: In Sports and In Life* (New York: Simon & Schuster Paperbacks, 2015).
587. Ibid., 13.
588. Ibid., 15.
589. Ibid.
590. Mack and Casstevens, 24.
591. Rotella, 92.
592. Ibid.
593. Ibid.
594. Ibid.
595. Ibid., 137.
596. Ibid.
597. Ibid., 138.
598. Ibid., 140.
599. Ibid., 142.
600. Ibid., 143.
601. Ibid., 142.

602. Ibid., 141.
603. Tharp, 18.
604. Ibid., 15.
605. Tara Parker-Pope, "How to Manage Stress like an Olympic Biathlete," *New York Times* (February 21, 2018).
606. Ibid.
607. Ibid.
608. Ibid.
609. Ibid.
610. Mack and Casstevens, 166.
611. Grand and Goldberg, 140.
612. Mack and Casstevens, 166.
613. Ibid.
614. Rotella, 25.
615. Mumford, 211.
616. Mack and Casstevens, 22.
617. Ibid., 167.
618. Josh Waitzkin, *The Art of Learning: An Inner Journey to Optimal Performance* (New York: Free Press, 2007), 142.
619. Rotella, 169.
620. Ibid., 170.
621. Ibid.
622. Ibid., 173.
623. John F. Eliot, Motivation: The Need to Achieve, Chapter 1 in *The Sport Psych Handbook: A Complete Guide to Today's Best Mental Training Techniques*, Shane Murphy, ed. (Champaign, IL: Human Kinetics, 2005), 10.
624. Ibid.
625. Rotella, 179.
626. Ibid., 169.
627. Grand and Goldberg, 8, 35, 37.
628. Ibid., 10.
629. Ibid.
630. Ibid., 66.
631. Ibid., 110.
632. Ibid., 141.
633. Ibid.

634. Ibid., 146.

635. Ibid., 141.

636. Ibid., 147.

637. Ibid., 147–148.

638. Ibid., 171.

639. Ibid.

640. Ibid., Chapter 10. This chapter provides tips for "get[ting] yourself unstuck." For deeper work in this area, athletes can seek professional guidance.

641. Ibid., 187.

642. Ibid., 146–148.

643. https://www.merriam-webster.com/dictionary/fortitude.

644. Tharp, 15.

645. Ulmer, 70.

646. Ibid., 22.

647. Mack and Casstevens, 157.

648. Paraphrased lyrics from "Iris (Hold Me Close)," U2 © Universal Music Publishing Group 2014.

649. https://www.merriam-webster.com/dictionary/humility.

650. https://en.oxforddictionaries.com/definition/humility.

651. Janeen Kerper, "Creative Problem Solving vs. the Case Method: A Marvelous Adventure in which Winnie-the-Pooh Meets Mrs. Palsgraf," *California Western Law Review* 34 (1998): 351, 366 cited in H. K. Brown, "Breaking Bad Briefs," 259, 291.

652. William A. Bablitch, "Reflections on the Art and Craft of Judging," *Judges' Journal* 42, 4 (2003): 7:8, also cited in H. K. Brown, "Breaking Bad Briefs," 259, 291–292.

653. Christopher L. Kukk, *The Compassionate Achiever: How Helping Others Fuels Success* (New York: Harper One, 2017), 70.

654. Ibid.

655. Ibid.

656. Ibid., 71.

657. Ibid., 72.

658. Ibid., 86.

659. Anthony Niedwiecki, "Teaching for Lifelong Learning: Improving the Metacognitive Skills of Law Students through More Effective Formative Assessment Techniques," *Capital University Law Review* 40 (2012): 149, 156–57. (emphasis added)

660. Angela Duckworth, *Grit* (New York: Scribner, 2015), 146.

661. Ibid.

662. Ibid.

663. Ibid.

664. Ulmer, xi.

665. Mack and Casstevens, 127.

666. Ulmer, xiii.

667. Ibid., xv.

668. Ibid.

669. Harris, 24.

670. Ibid., 46. (emphasis in original)

671. Ibid., 76.

672. Ibid., 81.

673. Ibid.

674. Ibid., 82.

675. Ibid., 177.

676. Ibid., 173.

677. Ibid.

678. Ibid., 81.

679. Ibid., 83.

680. Ibid., 87.

681. Ibid., 170.

682. Ibid., 184.

683. Ulmer, 144.

684. Ibid.

685. Ibid., 78.

686. Ibid., 160.

687. Ibid., 203.

688. Ibid.

689. Ibid.

690. Ibid., 214.

691. Ibid., 210.

692. Ibid., 212.

693. Ibid., 226.

694. Ibid., 256.

695. Duckworth, 56.

696. Jerome M. Organ, David B. Jaffe, and Katherine M. Bender, "Helping Law Students Get the Help They Need: An Analysis of Data Regarding Law Students' Reluctance to Seek Help and Policy Recommendations for a Variety of Stakeholders," *The Bar Examiner* 84, 4 (December 2015): 13–14.

697. Brené Brown, *Daring Greatly* (New York: Penguin Random House, 2012), 33.

698. Ibid., 2.

699. Ibid., 37. (emphasis in original)

700. Ibid., 2.

701. Ibid., 34.

702. Ulmer, 56.

703. Ivy Naistadt, *Speak without Fear* (New York: HarperCollins, 2004), 62.

704. Grand and Goldberg, 146.

705. https://www.thefreedictionary.com/shame.

706. B. Brown, 68.

707. Ibid., 69. (emphasis in original)

708. Ibid., 64.

709. Ibid., 188.

710. Ibid., 225.

711. Ibid.

712. Ibid., 61.

713. Ibid., 74.

714. Julia Cameron, *The Artist's Way: A Spiritual Path to Higher Creativity* (New York: Jeremy P. Tarcher/Putnam, 1992, 2002), 10–18.

715. Hilliard, 64.

716. Ibid., 62.

717. Ulmer, 47.

718. Ibid., 48.

719. Ibid., 51.

720. Allanah Walker, "The Actors Prepare: A Backstage Look at Pre-Show Rituals," https://www.banffcentre.ca/articles/actors-prepare-backstage-look-pre-show-rituals (April 4, 2016).

721. Neesha Arter, "Tony Award Tastemakers: What's Your Pre-Show Ritual?" http://observer.com/2015/06/tastemakers-whats-your-pre-show-ritual/ (June 3, 2015).

722. Rudie Obias, "The Pre-Show Rituals of 11 Famous Musicians," http://mentalfloss.com/article/74238/pre-show-rituals-11-famous-musicians (January 24, 2016).

723. Ellen Weinstein, *Recipes for Good Luck: The Superstitions, Rituals, and Practices of Extraordinary People* (San Francisco: Chronicle Books, 2018), 30.

724. Elisa Bray, "Before the Gig – A Chant in Latin," https://www.independent.co.uk/hei-fi/entertainment/before-the-gig-a-chant-in-latin-8105355.html (September 5, 2012).

725. The Real Health podcast with Karl Henry, https://soundcloud.com/realhealth-podcast/on-the-road-with-adam-clayton (Summer 2018).

726. Ibid.

727. Ibid.

728. Jim Taylor, "Sports: Why the World's Best Athletes Use Routines," https://www.psychologytoday.com/us/blog/the-power-prime/201207/sports-why-the-worlds-best-athletes-use-routines (July 16, 2012).

729. Chris Haynes, "Steph Curry's Pregame Show Is Anything but Routine," http://www.espn.com/nba/story/_/id/22215844/steph-curry-pregame-show-anything-routine (January 27, 2018).

730. Ibid.

731. Ibid.

732. https://www.ted.com/talks/amy_cuddy_your_body_language_shapes_who_you_are.

733. Hendricks, 18.

734. https://www.ted.com/talks/amy_cuddy_your_body_language_shapes_who_you_are.

735. B. Brown, 54.

736. Ulmer, 213.

737. Ibid.

738. Ibid., 224.

739. Ibid., 228.

740. B. Brown, 160.

741. Ibid., 80 ("sharing our experience with someone who has earned the right to hear it").

742. Ibid., 105.

743. Ibid., 171.

744. Webb, 120.

745. Tough.

746. Ibid., 48.

747. Ibid., 59. *See ibid.* at 196 ("The character strengths that matter so much to young people's success are not innate; they don't appear in us magically as a result of good luck or good genes. And they are not simply a choice. They are rooted in brain chemistry, and they are molded, in measurable and predictable ways, by the environment in which children grow up.")

748. Lickona, 67–70.

749. Tough, 85.

750. The ABA has offered CLE programs with panels of "expert loss prevention lawyers, carrier representatives, and professional responsibility counsel." *See* "Mistakes: Coping Ethically and Wisely with the Inevitable." Offered at CLECenter.com.

751. Amy Gallo, "You've Made a Mistake. Now What?" *Harvard Business Review* (April 28, 2010).

752. Rotella, 179.

753. Kukk, 70.

754. Anthony Bourdain, *No Reservations.* https://www.cnn.com/interactive/2018/06/bourdain-in-his-words/.

755. Webb, 12.

756. O'Grady, 17.

757. Bishop, 966.

758. www.mbtionline.com.

759. http://vark-learn.com/the-vark-questionnaire.

760. http://www.danielgoleman.info/ei-assessments.

761. https://www.16personalities.com.

762. https://www.lawfit.com.

763. https://www.gallupstrengthscenter.com/home/en-us.

764. Patricia Snyder, "Super Women Lawyers: A Study of Character Strengths," *Arizona Summit Law Review* 8 (Spring 2015): 261, 267. A link to the test, which is described as "the only free, scientific survey on character strengths," can be found here: http://www.viacharacter.org/www/.

765. Snyder, 266.

766. Ibid., 309, Appendix A. The character strengths associated with the other five virtues are Wisdom and Knowledge (Creativity, Curiosity, Open-mindedness, Love of Learning, Perspective), Humanity (Love, Kindness, Social Integrity), Justice (Citizenship, Fairness, Leadership), Temperance (Forgiveness and Mercy, Humility/Modesty, Prudence, Self-Regulation), and Transcendence (Appreciation for Beauty and Excellence, Gratitude, Hope, Humor, and Spirituality). Ibid.

767. Ibid., 315, Appendix D, citing Christopher Peterson and Martin E. P. Seligman, *Character Strengths and Virtues: A Handbook and Classification* (New York: Oxford University Press, 2004).

768. Ibid., 315, Appendix D.

769. Ibid., 283.

770. Ibid.

771. Ibid., 286.

772. Jessica Bennett, "On Campus, Failure Is on the Syllabus," *New York Times*, https://www.nytimes.com/2017/06/24/fashion/fear-of-failure.html (June 24, 2017).

773. Ibid.

774. Katerina P. Lewinbuk, *Connecting Ethics & Practice: A Lawyer's Guide to Professional Responsibility* (New York: Wolters Kluwer, 2017), 387.

775. B. Brown, 12.

776. Catmull, 111.

777. Rosenberg, 1234.

778. Ibid., 1259.

779. Ibid., 1260.

780. Patthoff, 396.

781. Barry Boyce, *Why Our Brain Thrives on Mistakes*, https://www.mindful.org/brain-thrives-mistakes (May 3, 2017).

782. Ibid.

783. Tharp, 212.

784. Ibid.

785. Doug Lemov, *Culture of Error,* http://teachlikeachampion.com/cultureoferror, 2.

786. Ibid.

787. Ibid., 3.

788. Ibid., 5.

789. Ibid.

790. Ibid., 7.

791. Bishop, 987.

792. Ibid., 988.

793. Ibid., 990.

794. Ibid.

795. Ibid., 993.

796. Ibid., 995.

797. Ibid., 996.

798. Ibid., 997.

799. Ibid., 998–999.

800. Ibid., 1000.

801. Ibid., 1001.

802. Ibid., 1003.

803. Williams.

804. Ibid.

805. Leah Wortham, Alexander Scherr, Nancy Maurer, and Susan L. Brooks, *Learning from Practice: A Text for Experiential Legal Education*, 3rd ed. (St. Paul, MN: West Academic Publishing, 2016).

806. Ibid., 93.

807. Ibid., 208.

808. Ibid., 223.

809. Ibid., 361.

810. Ibid., 366.

811. Ibid., 686.

812. Marjorie A. Silver, *Transforming Justice, Lawyers, and the Practice of Law* (Durham, NC: Carolina Academic Press, 2017).

813. Ibid., Chapter 9, 284, Marjorie A. Silver, *Healing Classrooms.*

814. Ibid., 330.

815. Ibid., Chapter 8, 247, Rhonda V. Magee, *Teaching Law to Transform: Mindfulness-Based Learning Communities as Incubators of Social Justice through Law.*

816. Ibid., Chapter 11, 355, n. 55, Jeanne Anselmo and Victor Goode, *Contemplative Practice for Social Justice Lawyering: From the Cushion to the Very Heart of the Struggle.*

817. Ibid., Chapter 6, 175, Pamela J. P. Denison, *Collaborative Practices.*

818. Ibid., Chapter 4, 152, Sylvia Clute, *Creating a Parallel Model of Justice: Unitive, Not Punitive.*

819. Ibid., Chapter 10, 312, Susan L. Brooks, *Creating a Beloved Community by Teaching Relational Lawyering.*

820. Ibid., 327.

821. Berman, 118.

822. Ibid., 127.

823. Ibid.

824. Ibid.

825. Ibid., 132.

826. Ibid., 132–133.

827. Ibid., 128. *See also* Kahan (discussing the appropriate path for "righting a legal wrong": admit, apologize, rectify.)

828. For example, Peterson and Seligman; Lickona; or the Values in Action Inventory of Strengths assessment, http://www.viacharacter.org/www.

829. For an interesting article describing "a project on teaching dispute resolution skills to law students conducted in the virtual world, Second Life," *see* Andrea Seielstad, "Enhancing the Teaching of Lawyering Skills and Perspectives through

Virtual World Engagement," *University of Massachusetts Law Review* 7 (2012): 40, 94. ("Students with certain disabilities, language accent, or other cultural characteristics, social phobias or feelings of alienation in the broader law school environment may find it easier to participate in classroom exercises and discussion in a virtual world environment.") Regarding fear, the author states, "Somehow common fears and barriers that often exist in real life are minimized in Second Life, at least in most cases. There is a frontier spirit, excitement, and enthusiasm that motivate people to share widely and freely in very significant and tangible ways." Ibid., 100. Further, the Maryland Volunteer Lawyers Service (MVLS), a provider of low-cost and pro bono legal services, acknowledged the discomfort that many new attorneys experience about going to court. See Annalies Winny, "State Goes High-Tech to Recruit Pro Bono Attorneys," http://www.abajournal .com/magazine/article/virtual_training_lawyers_maryland_pro_bono (August 2017). MVLS teamed up with the Young Lawyers Section of the Maryland State Bar Association and developed "a virtual reality training series that . . . demystifies the courtroom experience and entices newer, or courtroom-shy, attorneys to sign up" to volunteer. Ibid. The training videos are available on YouTube and can be downloaded on smartphones. Ibid.

830. Mark Bassingthwaighte, "The Defining Moment of a Malpractice Claim," https:// blog.alpsnet.com/the-defining-moment-of-a-malpractice-claim (April 4, 2018).

831. Ibid.

832. Mark Bassingthwaighte, "Malpractice and Fear of the Public Eye," https://blog .alpsnet.com/malpractice-and-fear-of-the-public-eye (November 9, 2012).

833. Ulmer, 213.

834. Ibid., 224.

835. Amy Florian, "Nine Steps for Calming Client Fears," *Journal of Financial Planning* (November 2009): 42.

836. Ibid.

837. Ibid.

838. Ibid., 43.

839. Kukk, 2.

840. Ibid., 92. (emphasis added)

841. Ibid., 2.

842. Ibid., 18.

843. Ibid., 23.

844. Ibid., 29.

845. Ibid., 39.

846. Ibid., 42.

847. Kiser, *Soft Skills*, 3.

848. Rotella, 235.

849. Chief Justice Robert R. Thomas, "Acknowledging Our Vulnerabilities," *Judges' Journal* 47, 2 (Spring 2008): 32, responding to the American Bar Association's "bold recognition of the issues surrounding the impaired lawyer."

850. Judith Rush and Pat Burns, "Our Ethical Responsibility to Help Ourselves and Our Colleagues," *Bench & Bar of Minnesota* 73 (March 2016): 12.

851. Ibid., 13.

852. Sells, xx.

853. Ibid., xxi.

854. Ibid., 11.

855. Ibid., 14. (emphasis in original)

856. Ibid., 13.

857. Ibid., 14.

858. Kukk, 3.

859. Ibid., 4.

860. Ibid.

861. Dana Ardi, *The Fall of the Alphas: The New Beta Way to Connect, Collaborate, Influence— and Lead* (New York: St. Martin's Press, 2013), 1.

862. Ibid., 16.

863. Ibid., 26.

864. Ibid., 140.

865. Ibid., 137.

866. www.mbtionline.com.

867. http://vark-learn.com/the-vark-questionnaire.

868. http://www.danielgoleman.info/ei-assessments.

869. https://www.16personalities.com.

870. https://www.gallupstrengthscenter.com/home/en-us.

871. Snyder, 266.

872. Ibid., 261. A link to the test, which is described as "the only free, scientific survey on character strengths," can be found here: http://www.viacharacter.org/www/.

873. Ibid., 283.

874. Berman, 128. *See also* Kahan (discussing the appropriate path for "righting a legal wrong": admit, apologize, rectify). *See also* "ABA issues new guidance on what a lawyer should do when a mistake is made," https://www.americanbar .org/news/abanews/aba-news-archives/2018/04/aba_issues_new_guida.html (April 17, 2018).

875. Ulmer, 213.

876. Ibid., 224.

877. Florian, 42.

878. Ibid.

879. Ibid.

880. Ibid., 43.

881. Kukk, 2.

882. Ibid., 92. (emphasis added)

883. Ibid., 23.

884. Ibid., 29.

885. Ibid., 39.

886. Ibid, 42.

887. Catmull, 111.

888. Ibid., 123.

889. Jeffrey Lipshaw, "What's Going On? The Psychoanalysis Metaphor for Educating Lawyer-Counselors," *Connecticut Law Review* 45 (May 2013): 1355, 1371.

890. Fines and Madsen, 965.

891. Sobelson, 704.

892. Sogg and Sogg, 28.

893. Weiss, *7.

894. Sobelson, 704.

895. Susie Salmon, "The Legal Word: Listen Like a Lawyer," *Arizona Attorney* 53 (November 2016): 12.

896. Mitchell-Cichon, 310.

897. Ritter and Wilson, 39.

898. Florian, 43.

899. Ibid.

900. Ibid.

901. Ibid.

902. Ibid.

903. Ibid.

904. Ibid.

905. Ibid.

906. Ibid.

907. Ibid.

908. https://listenlikealawyer.com/about.

909. Ritter and Wilson, 39.

910. Herman and Cary, 32.

911. Krieger and Neumann, 112.

912. Sogg and Sogg, 30.

913. Genty, 277.

914. Fines and Madsen, 980, quoting from Marsha Kline Pruett and Tamara D. Jackson, "The Lawyer's Role during the Divorce Process: Perceptions of Parents, Their Young Children, and Their Attorneys," *Family Law Quarterly* 33 (1999): 283, 294–295.

915. Jensby et al., 84.

916. Ibid.

917. Anthony Bourdain, *Medium Raw: A Bloody Valentine to the World of Food and the People Who Cook* (New York: Ecco, 2011), 255.

918. Ritter and Wilson, 39.

919. Genty, 277.

920. Ibid.

921. Orloff et al., 316.

922. Blue and Hirschhorn, 12:6.

923. Lansberry and Turnipseed, 358.

924. Ibid., 359–360.

925. Ibid., 360.

926. Ibid.

927. Robert Aron, "Your Office Image: Helping the Client Prepare for the Trauma of Trial," *Trial Communication Skills*, 2nd ed. (Eagan, MN: Thomson Reuters, December 2016 Update), Section 29:13.

928. Gold, 234 (internal citation omitted).

929. Katz and Haldar, 359 (article abstract).

930. Keeva, 52.

931. Ibid., 51.

932. Edward D. Shapiro, "Fresh Perspectives: The Practice of Holistic Lawyering," *CBA Record* 16 (February/March 2002): 38–39.

933. Ibid.

Index

Page numbers followed by f indicate figures.

A

ABA Journal, 6, 22, 28, 29, 33, 199, 265
Adrenaline, 75
Alpha leaders, 246
American Bar Association Commission
    on Lawyer Assistance, xxxvii,
    76–77
Amygdala, 71, 72–78, 72f, 156–160, 163,
    192, 221, 258
Amygdala hijack, 75
Anxiety
    internal and outward manifestations
        of, 10–11
    references in syllabus language,
        227–228
Ardi, Dana, 246, 247
Aristotle, 161
Attorney-client privileged
    communications, xxix, 34–35,
    206, 238, 252
Attorney-client relationships, 25, 259,
    266, 269
Authentic imperfection, 172

B

Bankruptcy settings, client fears in,
    52–53
Bar exam, 15
Baskin, Janice J., 76, 88–89
Bassingthwaighte, Mark, 239–240
"Behavioral Approach to Lawyer Mistake
    and Apology, A" (O'Grady),
    67–68, 273
Bench slaps, 18
Beta leaders, 246
Bishop, Kaci, 26, 88, 224, 231, 236, 270

Bledsoe, T. Scott, 76, 88–89
Blushology, 182–183
Bodies, untangling fear from, 183–188
Bono, 122–123, 159, 263
Bourdain, Anthony, 215, 216–217, 263
Brain, 71–79
    amygdala, 71, 72–78, 72f, 156–160,
        163, 192, 221, 258
    cerebral cortex, 71, 72
    frontal lobe, 71
    gray matter, 71
    gustatory cortex, 72
    hippocampus, 71, 76
    hypothalamus, 72, 72f
    limbic system, 71–72, 74
    neocortex, 72, 73
    occipital lobe, 71
    olfactory cortex, 72
    parietal lobe, 71, 72, 72f
    prefrontal cortex, 63, 72–76
    temporal lobe, 71, 72, 72f
    thalamus, 72, 72f, 73, 74
Brief Strengths Test, 225, 247
Bright, Rebecca, 87
Brown, Brené, 166, 173–174, 197,
    198–199, 226
Business education and training,
    fear and mistake-making in,
    113–115

C

Cameron, Julia, 175
Casstevens, David, 73–74, 125–126,
    155, 162
Catmull, Ed, 114–115, 226, 254
Cerebral cortex, 71, 72

From the American Bar Association

AMERICAN BAR ASSOCIATION
ABA Publishing

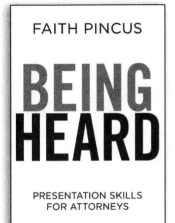

FAITH PINCUS

BEING HEARD

PRESENTATION SKILLS
FOR ATTORNEYS

Being Heard
Presentation Skills for Attorneys
by Faith Pincus

Building a Better
Law Practice
Become a Better Lawyer
in Five Minutes a Day
by Jeremy W. Richter

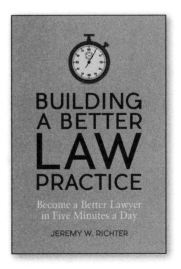

BUILDING
A BETTER
LAW
PRACTICE

Become a Better Lawyer
in Five Minutes a Day

JEREMY W. RICHTER

To order 🌐 visit **www.ShopABA.org**
or call 📞 **(800) 285-2221.**

From the American Bar Association

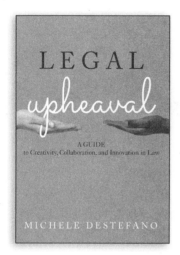

Legal Upheaval
A Guide to Creativity, Collaboration, and Innovation in Law
by Michele DeStefano

The Introverted Lawyer
A Seven-Step Journey Toward Authentically Empowered Advocacy
by Heidi K. Brown

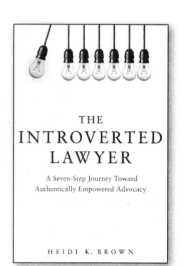

To order 🌐 visit **www.ShopABA.org**
or call 📞 **(800) 285-2221.**